Lecture Notes in Economics and Mathematical Systems 524

Springer
Berlin
Heidelberg
New York
Hong Kong
London
Milan
Paris
Tokyo

Markus Frölich

Programme Evaluation
and Treatment Choice

Springer

Author

Dr. Markus Frölich
University of St. Gallen
SIAW
Dufourstrasse 48
9000 St. Gallen
Switzerland

Library of Congress Cataloging-in-Publication Data

Frölich, Markus.
    Programme evaluation and treatment choice / Markus Frölich.
        p. cm. -- (Lecture notes in economics and mathematical systems, ISSN 0075-8442 ; 524)
    Includes bibliographical references.
    ISBN 3540443282 (softcover : alk. paper)
        1. Economic policy--Evaluation. I. Title. II. Series.

    HD75.9 .F76 2003
    338.9--dc21

                                                                    2002191205

ISSN 0075-8450
ISBN 3-540-44328-2 Springer-Verlag Berlin Heidelberg New York

Springer-Verlag Berlin Heidelberg New York
a member of BertelsmannSpringer Science+Business Media GmbH

http://www.springer.de

© Springer-Verlag Berlin Heidelberg 2003
Printed in Germany

Typesetting: Camera ready by author
Cover design: *Erich Kirchner*, Heidelberg

Printed on acid-free paper   SPIN: 10894671   55/3142/du   5 4 3 2 1 0

Preface

I am particularly grateful for invaluable discussions, suggestions and comments to Alex Keel, Michael Lechner and Jeff Smith. I also would like to thank Dragana Djurdjevic, Martin Eichler, Yuanhua Feng, Bernd Fitzenberger, Michael Gerfin, Bo Honoré, Hidehiko Ichimura, Joachim Inkmann, Francois Laisney, Christof Luchsinger, Blaise Melly, Ruth Miquel, Eva Poen, Winfried Pohlmeier, Patrick Puhani, Heidi Steiger, Conny Wunsch and Ken Zavala. Financial support by the Swiss National Science Foundation, project NSF 4043-058311 is gratefully acknowledged. Last but not least, I am indebted to my wife for her incessant support, attention and encouragement.

St. Gallen, October 2002   *Markus Frölich*

Table of Contents

1   **Introduction** 1

2   **Programme Evaluation and Treatment Choice – An Overview** 7
     2.1   Introduction in Programme Evaluation 7
         2.1.1   Potential Outcomes 7
         2.1.2   Stable-Unit-Treatment-Value Assumption 8
         2.1.3   Average Treatment Effects and Selection Bias 10
         2.1.4   Identification of Average Treatment Effects 12
         2.1.5   Estimation of Mean Counterfactual Outcomes 29
     2.2   Optimal Treatment Choice 43
         2.2.1   Definition of Optimal Treatment 44
         2.2.2   Profiling and Targeting of Programmes in Practice 47
         2.2.3   Estimating the Optimal Treatment 49
     2.3   Nonparametric Regression 50
         2.3.1   Nearest Neighbours and Local Polynomial Regression 51
         2.3.2   Properties of Local Polynomial Regression 54

3   **Nonparametric Covariate Adjustment in Finite Samples** 61
     3.1   Potential Efficiency Gains of Local Polynomial Matching 62
         3.1.1   Simulation Results at the Optimal Bandwidth Value 64
         3.1.2   Sensitivity to the Bandwidth Value 67
     3.2   Approximation to the MSE and Bandwidth Choice 69
         3.2.1   Bandwidth Choice 69
         3.2.2   MSE Approximation of Local Polynomial Matching 70
         3.2.3   Approximation Accuracy in Finite Samples 72
     3.3   Data-driven Bandwidth Choice by Cross-Validation 74
     3.4   Matching with Unknown Propensity Score 76

4   **Semiparametric Estimation of Optimal Treatment Choices** 81
     4.1   Estimation of Conditional Expected Potential Outcomes 81
         4.1.1   Semiparametric GMM Estimator 86
         4.1.2   Monte Carlo Simulation 87
     4.2   Optimal Choice and Swedish Rehabilitation Programmes 94

5   **Conclusions** 103

A   Appendix 107

B   Appendix 111

C   Appendix 115
    C.1   MSE-Approximation for Local Polynomial Matching 115
    C.2   Additional Tables to Chapter 3 120

D   Appendix 135
    D.1   Simulated Mean Squared Error for Sample Size 40 135
    D.2   Simulated Mean Squared Error for Sample Size 200 139
    D.3   Simulated Mean Squared Error for Sample Size 1000 143
    D.4   MSE Approximation: Kernel Matching, Sample Size 200 147
    D.5   MSE Approximation: Kernel Matching, Sample Size 1000 151
    D.6   MSE Approximation: Local Linear, Sample Size 200 155
    D.7   MSE Approximation: Local Linear, Sample Size 1000 159

E   Appendix 163
    E.1   Asymptotic Properties of the GMM Estimator.................. 163
    E.2   Power of the J-tests - Additional Monte Carlo Results 175
    E.3   Additional Tables to Swedish Rehabilitation Programmes 176

References 185

1 Introduction

Policy evaluation and programme choice are important tools for informed decision-making, for example with respect to active labour market programmes, welfare-to-work programmes, vocational training programmes, entrepreneurship promotion schemes, educational programmes, tuition subsidies, sickness rehabilitation programmes or disease prevention programmes. Both, policy evaluation and programme choice, are not ends in themselves but indispensable steps towards the efficient allocation of resources and towards the improvement of existing policies. Whereas the evaluation of programmes and policies is mainly concerned with an overall assessment of impact, benefits and costs, programme choice is directed towards achieving the optimal allocation of individuals to the programmes. Together they form a unified whole: For an ex-post assessment of policy impact and allocation efficiency and for deriving recommendations for how programmes should be modified and for which individuals should participate in which programmes. To take full account of their potential, policy evaluation and programme choice should be incorporated into an integrated system of resources planning and participant allocation, which would assist in assigning individuals to their optimal programmes (Statistically Assisted Programme Selection, SAPS).

Programme evaluation attempts to assess how far a programme/policy has achieved its intended aims. More precisely, it strives to measure the consequences that have ensued as a result of the programme by comparing the outcomes with and without the programme. Consider an active labour market programme, such as a vocational training programme for unemployed persons. The principal aim of the programme is to improve the employability of the participants so that they quickly become re-employed and earn higher wages. Additional aims are cost-effectiveness and the avoidance of adverse effects on the non-participants. To assess how far the primary aim has been fulfilled, it would be necessary to compare the employment situation of the participants after the programme with the employment status they would have had, if they had not participated in the programme. A naive comparison of their employment status before and after the programme is not informative since some of the participants would have found employment even without the programme. A comparison of the re-employment rates of the participants and of the non-participants is futile, too, unless the participants were chosen randomly. Because programme participation is often the result of deliberate decisions, the individuals who decided or were assigned to participate form a selected group, such that a direct comparison of their outcomes with those of the non-participants would lead to selection bias. Instead, a variety of statistical corrections are necessary to compare only like persons and to identify the average treatment effect, which is the difference between the expected outcome in the case of participation and the expected outcome in the case of non-participation. Whereas earlier evaluation studies often employed parametric selection models, these are increasingly replaced by nonparametric methods that avoid strong functional form assumptions and are, thus, more robust to misspecification. The applicability of these methods depends on the available data and on the specific details of the programme, particularly on the way how programme participation decisions were made.

Whereas most of the literature on programme evaluation has focused on the evaluation of a single programme (see, for example, the surveys by Angrist and Krueger 1999, Heckman, LaLonde, and Smith 1999) many social policies consist of a variety of different programmes (or treatments, according to the terminology of the evaluation literature). Active labour market policies, for example, usually comprehend job-search assistance, vocational training programmes, public employment programmes, wage subsidies etc. Evaluating such a diverse policy requires the identification and estimation of many different treatment effects, which makes the analysis more complex. Hence proper evaluations of policies with multiple programmes have only been carried out recently.

Treatment choice approaches policy evaluation from a different perspective. It is primarily concerned with the question of which of the available treatments a particular individual should receive. For example, a physician has to choose between different drug treatments for his patients. Similarly, a case worker in the unemployment office can choose among different active labour market programmes to assist an unemployed person. To solve the decision problem, both have to forecast ex-ante the likely consequences of each treatment or programme. On the basis of these predicted potential outcomes, the optimal programme for a particular person can be derived. This approach recognizes that people may be heterogeneous and respond differently to certain treatments. In particular, there might not be a single programme that serves all individuals best. Rather, the optimal programme choice may differ from individual to individual, and it is important that careful choices are made on an individual basis.

Under certain circumstances, self-selection by individuals would lead to optimal programme choices and, thus, to an optimal allocation of individuals to programmes. One essential requirement[1] is that individual programme choices do not cause any externalities. This is often not the case if multiple goals are pursued and different parties are involved. For example, active labour market policies are devised to improve the re-employment chances of the participants and, at the same time, to minimize programme costs. Since the direct programme costs are usually financed by public funds, this cost component would be neglected in the decision-making if individuals autonomously chose their programmes, leading to suboptimal choices (at least from the viewpoint of the policy administrator and the

---

[1] Besides the requirement of rational expectations and absence of credit constraints.

financial backers). One way to avoid gross overspending could be to narrow the spectrum of programmes offered e.g. by excluding very expensive programmes. However, the direct intervention of the programme administrator in the allocation process is often more appealing. Therefore, case workers are introduced as agents on the administrator's behalf to assign individuals to the programmes according to the policy administrator's (or society's) utility function. To derive optimal programme choices on an individual level, predictions about the expected outcomes given the individual's characteristics are needed, see Manski (2000a, b, 2001). These estimated potential outcomes are compared for the different programmes under consideration and weighted according to the importance of the different policy goals. This will lead to individualized optimal-programme recommendations. Such statistical treatment-selection rules are used in Canada and the USA to assign unemployed persons directly to active labour market programmes. Alternatively, the predicted outcomes could be provided to the case workers to improve their decision-making process.

Programme evaluation and treatment choice are usually analyzed separately in the literature. Yet these two perspectives are strongly related and are discussed jointly in this book. Central to both issues is their attempt to estimate potential outcomes based on data from past participants. Although policy evaluation also serves documentary purposes, its main aim is to assist in improving (the) policy. Average treatment effects provide a general overview of the effectiveness of particular programmes. This can be used as a basis to rank the programmes from least to most successful and to conduct cost-benefit analyses. However, the immediate policy conclusions that can be drawn from an analysis of average treatment effects are not always obvious. In particular, the question remains whether programmes with negative treatment effects should be eliminated. This depends on the degree of heterogeneity of individual treatment effects. If individuals benefit very differently from programme participation, it could be that, despite a negative average treatment effect, participation in this programme might still be highly beneficial to some individuals. As average treatment effects always represent the effect conditional on the past allocation process, they do not indicate which results might be achieved (in the future) if the individuals were allocated to the programmes in a different way. Particularly, if the elimination of a programme or the setup of a modified programme is costly, attempts to improve the allocation of participants might be more efficient for increasing the policy's effectiveness. This also avoids disrupting the structure of the existing programmes. Average treatment effects provide some general indications, but a thorough analysis of the treatment outcomes on the individual level is required. Such an analysis could be used not only to improve the allocation process in the future, but also to assess ex-post the effectiveness of the past allocation process and to estimate which policy results could have been achieved if the allocation had been optimal.

The main contributions of this book are the following:

- A discussion of programme evaluation and programme choice in the framework of multiple treatment evaluation and conflicting policy goals, including a review of nonparametric identification and the estimation of mean potential outcomes and an examination of nonparametric regression techniques.
- An investigation of the finite sample properties of various matching and re-weighting estimators and an analysis of the corresponding bandwidth selection problem. Potential and feasible precision gains relative to the standard pair-matching estimator and the sensitivity to the bandwidth value are examined through extensive Monte Carlo simulations. A second-order asymptotic approximation to the mean squared error of local polynomial matching estimators is developed and the applicability of standard cross-validation bandwidth selection is analyzed.
- The development of a semiparametric estimator of optimal treatment choices. A two step process to derive optimal programme choices is suggested. In the first step, expected potential outcomes are estimated by a semiparametric GMM estimator, which combines parametric specifications and nonparametric mean counterfactual estimates. The asymptotic properties of this estimator are derived and its finite sample properties are analyzed by Monte Carlo simulation. In the second step, the optimal treatment choice is derived by bootstrapping the distribution of the estimated potential outcomes.
- An analysis of optimal programme choices with respect to Swedish rehabilitation programmes. The potential re-employment prospects for people with long-term illnesses are estimated and their expected employment outcomes are simulated under the optimal allocation. It is found that a substantial increase in the re-employment rate from 46% to 56% could have been achievable through an improved allocation of participants to programmes.

The main results are twofold: First, the choice of an appropriate estimator for estimating the average impact of a policy can make a difference to the conclusions of an evaluation study. Conventional *matching* techniques are inefficient and may lead to concluding that a policy impact is insignificant, although a significant estimate might have been obtained, if a more precise estimator had been used. Such alternative estimators are readily available and can easily be implemented. Second, estimating optimal treatment choices on an individual level to guide the allocation of participants to the programmes, can be an important (and cost-effective) means to improve the overall effectiveness of a policy.

Chapter 2 reviews fundamental concepts in programme evaluation, treatment choice and nonparametric regression. In *Section 2.1* the concepts of potential outcomes and average treatment effects are introduced. Selection bias is discussed and various non-experimental strategies to identify treatment effects in the context of multiple treatments are presented, which include controlling-for-confounding-variables, difference-in-difference and instrumental-variable identification. The nonparametric estimation of mean counterfactual outcomes is considered in detail and generalized matching and re-weighting estimators are discussed, including an examination of propensity score matching and semiparametric efficiency bounds. *Section 2.2* examines how individuals should be allocated to programmes if outcome variables are multidimensional. The existing profiling and targeting systems are reviewed and their weaknesses are illustrated. An alternative two-step process to derive-optimal programme choices is suggested, which is based on the semiparametric estimator developed in Chapter 4. *Section 2.3* provides a brief introduction in nonparametric regression and presents basic properties used in subsequent chapters.

In *Chapter 3*, the asymptotic and finite-sample properties of various evaluation estimators are investigated. The mean squared error of kernel matching, local linear matching, Seifert&Gasser matching, re-weighting and regression-based matching are compared to the conventional pair-matching estimator when matching on an observed covariate. Since the local polynomial matching estimators require the choice of a bandwidth value, their precision gains are simulated at different values and their sensitivity to the bandwidth value is explored. As a first step towards developing a data-driven bandwidth selector, an asymptotic approximation to their mean squared error is derived and its approximation precision is evaluated. Furthermore, the applicability of cross-validation bandwidth selection is examined. The finite sample properties are also investigated when matching proceeds on an estimated variable, for example, the estimated propensity score.

In *Chapter 4*, a semiparametric GMM estimator of conditional expected potential outcomes is developed. Asymptotic normality is shown and its finite sample properties are investigated by Monte Carlo simulation. Using this estimator, heterogeneity of treatment effects and optimal treatment choices are analyzed with respect to the re-employment outcome of rehabilitation programmes for people with long-term illnesses in Sweden. Optimal treatment choices are simulated by bootstrap methods and compared to the observed allocation.

Finally, *Chapter 5* summarizes the main results, and five *appendices* contain the main proofs and additional material.

2 Programme Evaluation and Treatment Choice – An Overview

2.1 Introduction in Programme Evaluation

2.1.1 Potential Outcomes

Policy and programme evaluation in a wide sense is concerned with measuring how far a policy or a programme has achieved its intended aims. A policy is hereafter defined as a bundle of R different programmes. This includes the case of evaluating a single programme ($R = 2$, participation versus non-participation) and evaluating multiple programmes ($R > 2$). One example of policies consisting of multiple programmes are active labour market policies, which often comprise various public employment programmes, on-the-job training, retraining, classroom training, job search assistance, wage subsidies etc. Another example are rehabilitation policies for the re-integration of people with long-term illnesses, which may consist of different forms of vocational workplace training, vocational schooling, medical rehabilitation and social and psychological programmes. In the following, often the neutral term *treatment* will be used synonymously for *programme*, since the methods presented here are not restricted to the evaluation of social policies but apply similarly to, for example, the evaluation of the effectiveness of medical drugs or of different schooling choices, or of the effects of participation in the military. Since participation in a policy is often voluntary, or since full compliance in a 'mandatory' policy might not always be enforceable, the set of different treatments usually includes a 'no-programme' or 'non-participation' option. As it is assumed that all individuals are untreated before participation in the policy, i.e. that they had not participated previously in the programmes,[1] this 'non-participation' treatment is often special in the sense that it is the treatment most similar to the situation before participation in the policy. To illustrate this asymmetry, the treatment set will be indexed by $r \in \{0, .., R - 1\}$, i.e. consisting of a 'non-participation' treatment ($r = 0$) and $R - 1$ active treatments. In the case of the evaluation of a single programme the treatment set consists of $r = 0$ (non-participation) and $r = 1$ (participation).

The basic ideas and concepts of the current approaches to causal inference in programme evaluation stem from the statistical analysis of randomized experiments and potential outcomes.[2] The notion of *potential outcomes* was formalized in

---

[1] For the evaluation of sequential programmes see Lechner and Miquel (2002).

[2] For an introduction to causal reasoning see Holland (1986) and, particularly, Pearl (2000).

Neyman (1923), who considered potential yields of crop varieties on different plots of land with the plots *randomly* allocated to the crop varieties. Rubin (1974, 1977) provided a more thorough statistical framework for the concept of potential outcomes and extended it to the analysis of *observational* studies, where the units are not randomly assigned to the treatments.

Let i denote a unit (an individual, a household) which is assigned to one of R mutually exhaustive and exclusive treatments, i.e. each individual participates in exactly one of these treatments. Let

$$Y_i^0, Y_i^1, .., Y_i^{R-1}$$

denote the potential outcomes for this individual. Y_i^0 is the outcome that would be realized (after treatment) if the individual i were assigned to treatment 0. Likewise, Y_i^1 is the outcome that would be realized if the individual i were assigned to treatment 1 and so forth.[3] Ex-ante, i.e. before participation in the policy, each of these potential outcomes is latent and could be observed if the individual participated in the respective programme. Ex-post, only the outcome corresponding to the programme in which the individual eventually participated is observed. The other potential outcomes are counterfactual and unobservable by definition.

Since most policies pursue multiple and often conflicting goals, the potential outcomes can be vector-valued, $Y_i^r \in \Re^V$, to measure the results of a programme by many indicators, e.g. different economic, social, health, psychological and cost variables.

2.1.2 Stable-Unit-Treatment-Value Assumption

The definition of potential outcomes already made implicit use of the assumption of 'no interference between different units' (Cox 1958, p.19) or stable-unit-treatment-value assumption (SUTVA Rubin 1980). It is assumed that the potential outcomes $Y_i^0, Y_i^1, .., Y_i^{R-1}$ of individual i are not affected by the allocation of other individuals to the treatments. Formally, let $\mathbf{D}$ denote a treatment-allocation *vector*, which indicates for all individuals the programme in which they participate. Let $\mathbf{Y}$ denote the vector of the observed outcomes of all individuals. Define $\mathbf{Y}(\mathbf{D})$ as the potential outcome vector that would be observed if all individuals were allocated to the policy according to the allocation $\mathbf{D}$. Further let $Y_i(\mathbf{D})$ denote the i-th element of this potential outcome vector.

The stable-unit-treatment-value assumption states that for any two allocations $\mathbf{D}$ and $\mathbf{D}'$

$$Y_i(\mathbf{D}) = Y_i(\mathbf{D}') \qquad \text{if} \qquad \mathbf{D}_i = \mathbf{D}'_i,$$

where $\mathbf{D}_i$ and $\mathbf{D}'_i$ denote the i-th element of the allocations $\mathbf{D}$ and $\mathbf{D}'$, respectively. In other words, it is assumed that the observed outcome Y_i depends only on the

---

[3] Considering the potential outcomes Y_i^r as deterministic (non-random) values is only for convenience. The analysis would not change if Y_i^r were random variables.

treatment to which individual i is assigned and not on the allocation of other individuals.

This assumption might be invalidated if individuals interact, either directly or through markets. For example, if active labour market programmes change the relative supply of skilled and unskilled labour, all individuals may be affected by the resulting changes in the wage structure. In addition, programmes which affect the labour cost structure, e.g. through wage subsidies, may lead to displacement effects, where unsubsidized workers are laid off and are replaced by subsidized programme participants. Individuals might further be affected by the taxes raised for financing the policy. The magnitude of such market and general equilibrium effects often depends on the scale of the policy, i.e. on the number of participants in the programmes. Departures from SUTVA are likely to be small if only a few individuals participate in the policy, and they usually become larger with increasing numbers of participants. This is the motivation of studies attempting to estimate the general equilibrium effects in the evaluation of active labour market policies by an augmented matching function approach, such as Blanchard and Diamond (1989, 1990) or Puhani (1999). In these studies, observed variations in the scale of the policy over time or geographic location are exploited to estimate the influence of the scale of the policy on the number of unemployed persons who become re-employed. Although these studies provide important insights, their interpretation is often difficult. Apart from using arbitrary parametric specifications, they often do not rest on an explicit causal framework. In many cases, the variations in the policy scale over time are not exogenous, but influenced by the outcomes of the policy in previous periods, which makes it difficult to define a causal effect. Furthermore, disentangling the general equilibrium effects of policies with multiple programmes could be a demanding task.

A different form of interference between individuals can arise due to supply constraints. For example, if the number of programme slots of a certain programme is limited, the availability of the programme for a particular individual depends on how many participants have already been allocated to this programme. Such interaction does not directly affect the potential outcomes and, thus, does not invalidate the microeconometric evaluation approaches discussed subsequently. However, it restricts the set of feasible allocations **D** and could become relevant with respect to the implementation of optimal allocations, which are discussed in Section 2.2 and Chapter 4. Supply constraints are often (at least partly) under the control of the programme administration and could be moderated if necessary.

Henceforth, the validity of SUTVA is assumed. Such an approach is warranted if the policy under consideration is rather small in size, if market effects are unlikely, or if the counterfactual world against which the policy is evaluated is such that similar distortions through market and general equilibrium effects would persist, e.g. if the only feasible policy options are to marginally increase or decrease the scale of the policy.

2.1.3 Average Treatment Effects and Selection Bias

The difference between the potential outcome Y_i^r and the potential outcome Y_i^s can be interpreted as the gain or loss that individual i would realize if he participated in programme r relative to what he would realize if he participated in programme s. Thus the difference $Y_i^r - Y_i^s$ is the causal effect of participating in programme r *and not* participating in programme s. In the binary treatment case (i.e. the evaluation of a single programme), the difference $Y_i^1 - Y_i^0$ represents the difference between participating and not participating. Such individual treatment effects (Rubin 1974) can never be ascertained since only one of the potential outcomes $Y_i^0, Y_i^1, .., Y_i^{R-1}$ can be observed ex-post: $Y_i^{D_i}$ where $D_i \in \{0, .., R - 1\}$ indicates the programme in which individual i actually participated. Therefore programme evaluation seeks to learn about the properties of the potential outcomes in the population. Since only one of the potential outcomes can be observed for each individual, the joint distribution of the potential outcomes $Y^0, .., Y^{R-1}$ is not identified and, consequently, at most the properties of their marginal distributions can be uncovered. A parameter of interest is the *average treatment effect* (ATE)

$$E[Y^r - Y^s], \tag{2.1}$$

which is the difference between the outcome expected after participation in programme r and the outcome expected after participation in programme s for a person randomly drawn from the population. Analogously, the *average treatment effect on the treated* (ATET)

$$E[Y^r - Y^s | D = r] \tag{2.2}$$

is the expected outcome difference for a person randomly drawn from the subpopulation of participants in programme r. Lechner (2001a) defined a further parameter $E[Y^r - Y^s | D \in \{r, s\}]$ which is a weighted combination of the two average treatment effects on the treated $E[Y^r - Y^s | D = r]$ and $E[Y^r - Y^s | D = s]$. The most interesting parameter depends on the specific policy context. For example, in the binary treatment case with voluntary participation it may be more informative to know how the programme affected those who participated in it, than how it might have affected those who could have participated but decided not to. In this case, the average treatment effect on the treated $E[Y^1 - Y^0 | D = 1]$ would be more interesting than the average effect on the non-participants $E[Y^1 - Y^0 | D = 0]$. A further discussion about these evaluation parameters and their appropriateness in different circumstances is found in Heckman, LaLonde, and Smith (1999).

To identify average treatment effects from a sample of past programme participants and non-participants, additional assumptions are required. Let $\{(X_i, D_i, Y_i)\}_{i=1}^n$ be a sample of previous participants, where $Y_i = Y_i^{D_i}$ is the observed outcome and X_i are other individual characteristics. Since Y^r is only observed for the participants in programme r, the data identifies $E[Y^r | D = r]$ and $E[Y^r | X, D = r]$ for all r but not $E[Y^r]$ or $E[Y^r | D = s]$. Generally the potential outcomes are different in the various subpopulations

$$E\left[Y^{r}|D=r\right] \neq E\left[Y^{r}|D=s\right] \neq E\left[Y^{r}\right].$$

Consequently, estimating the average treatment effect on the treated (2.2) by the difference in the subpopulation means $E[Y^{r}|D=r]$ and $E[Y^{s}|D=s]$ would give a biased estimate since

$$E\left[Y^{r}|D=r\right] - E\left[Y^{s}|D=s\right] = E\left[Y^{r} - Y^{s}|D=r\right] \tag{2.3}$$
$$+ \left\{ E\left[Y^{s}|D=r\right] - E\left[Y^{s}|D=s\right]\right\}.$$

The second last term in (2.3) is the proper average treatment effect on the treated (2.2), whereas the last term in (2.3) is the *selection bias* (Heckman and Robb 1985, Manski 1993). Selection bias arises because the participants in programme r and the participants in programme s are deliberately selected groups that would have different outcomes, even if they were placed into the same programme. In making their programme participation decisions, individuals conjecture about their potential outcomes and base their choice on these guesses. In addition, unobserved character traits, such as health, motivation, ability or work commitment, lead to selection bias if they are correlated with the programme participation decision *and* the potential outcomes (e.g. earnings, employment status). Often programme participation is not completely voluntary but a joint decision of different parties, e.g. an unemployed person and a case worker. Again selection bias arises if the programme participation decision depends either consciously or unconsciously on factors related to the potential outcomes, for example, if case workers assign unemployed persons to particular programmes on the basis of their labour market history.

Hence data alone are not sufficient to identify average treatment effects. Conceptual causal models are required, which entail identifying assumptions about the process through which the individuals were assigned to the treatments, or about stability of the outcomes over time, see Pearl (2000). The corresponding minimal identifying assumptions cannot be tested with observational data and their plausibility must be assessed through prior knowledge of institutional details, the allocation process and behavioural theory. In the next section possible evaluation strategies to identify average treatment effects are presented. Which of these identification strategies, if any, is appropriate depends on the outcome variable of interest. Since selection bias is a phenomenon caused by factors that affect *jointly* the participation decision *and* the potential outcome, selection bias might occur for some outcome variables but not for others. If the effects of a policy should be ascertained with respect to a multidimensional outcome variable (Y^{r} being a vector), the appropriate identification strategy has to be chosen for each component of Y^{r} on a case by case basis. It may be that a simple evaluation strategy can be used for some outcome components, for which selection bias seems unlikely (e.g. monetary programme costs), whereas sophisticated evaluation strategies are required for other outcome components, and finally, it may happen that for some outcome components, no effect can be identified with the available data.

2.1.4 Identification of Average Treatment Effects

Below a variety of *nonparametric identification strategies* are discussed, which all rely in one way or another on comparing the observed outcomes of one group of individuals with the observed outcomes of another group of individuals to identify average treatment effects. An exception to these comparison group approaches is the before-after estimator which estimates $E[Y^r - Y^0 | D = r]$ by comparing the observed outcomes of the participants before and after the treatment. It relies on the assumption of temporal stability (Holland 1986), i.e. that the outcome observed before participation is the same as the outcome that would be observed in the 'non-participation' treatment at a later point in time. This assumption is usually not valid if the individual's environment changes over time. For example, Ashenfelter (1978) observed that the earnings of participants in active labour market programmes often had deteriorated recently before participation in the programme. If this decline in earnings represents a transitory labor market shock, it is likely that earnings would have recovered (at least partly) even without participation. The before-after estimator, however, would ascribe all increases in earnings to the programme participation. In this case, the effect of the treatment would be overstated. Particularly, if medium and long term effects of a programme shall be estimated, temporal stability is often not valid. Besides this, the before-after comparison strategy is not very suited for the evaluation of a policy consisting of multiple programmes, since it could only be used to estimate the treatment effect on the treated relative to non-participation, but not for any comparison between the active treatments.

Randomized Experiment   The ideal solution to avoid selection bias due to systematic selection of the participants is to assign individuals randomly to the programmes, as advocated in Fisher (1935). Randomization ensures that the probability to be assigned to a certain treatment is not influenced by the potential outcomes

$$P\left(D = d | Y^0, .., Y^{R-1}\right) = P\left(D = d\right)$$

or in the notation of Dawid (1979) that the potential outcomes $Y^0, .., Y^{R-1}$ are statistically independent ($\perp\!\!\!\perp$) of the treatment indicator D

$$Y^0, .., Y^{R-1} \perp\!\!\!\perp D.$$

Random programme assignment ensures that any differences between the treatment groups are by pure chance and not systematic. Consequently, the observed outcomes Y^r among the participants in programme r have the same expected value as the potential outcomes Y^r among the participants in programme s

$$E\left[Y^r | D = r\right] = E\left[Y^r | D = s\right] = E\left[Y^r\right]$$

and selection bias is thus avoided.

Yet implementing a randomized experiment for evaluating social programmes is often not trivial. Participation in a particular policy is often voluntary such that randomization can only be implemented with respect to the individuals who applied for the programme.[4] However, these might be different from the population of interest. Particularly, if randomization covers only parts of the population, the experimental results may not be generalizable to the broader population. Even if a policy is mandatory and all individuals can be randomly assigned to the treatments, full compliance is often difficult to achieve if participants must exercise some effort during the participation and may refuse their cooperation. Heckman and Smith (1995) discuss different sources that may invalidate the experimental evaluation results. *Randomization bias* occurs if the prospect of randomized allocation alters the pool of potential participants because individuals may be reluctant to apply at all or reduce any preparatory activities such as complementary training due to the fear of being randomized-out (threat of service denial). *Substitution bias* occurs if members of the control group (the randomized-out non-participants) obtain some treatment or participate in similar programmes, e.g. training obtained from private providers. In this case, the experimental evaluation measures only the incremental value of the policy relative to the programmes available otherwise. *Drop-out bias* occurs if individuals assigned to a particular programme do not (or only partly) participate in it. Heckman and Smith (1995) also mention that randomized experiments are expensive, often face political obstacles and may distort the operation of an on-going policy.[5]

Control for Confounding Variables Even if a randomized experiment would have been feasible, it often simply has not been implemented at the onset of the policy. In this case, only observational data are available and the selection problem must be solved by other means. One approach is to mimic the idea of a randomized experiment and to form comparison groups which are as similar as possible. Accordingly this identification strategy is also called quasi-experimental. The underlying motivation can be illustrated as in Rubin (1974): If two individuals i and j are found that are identical (or very similar) in all their characteristics, then also Y_i^r and Y_j^r should be similar. If one of these individuals takes part in programme r and the other in programme s, and if many such pairs are found, then the difference in observed outcomes could be used as an estimate of the average treatment effect between programme r and s. For this estimate to be consistent, the individuals within each pair must be identical with respect to all *confounding* variables X, i.e. with respect to all variables that influenced treatment selection *and* the potential outcomes. This implies that, conditional on X, the probability of being selected to a particular programme is not affected by the potential outcomes:

$$Y^r \perp\!\!\!\perp D \,|\, X \qquad \forall r. \qquad (2.4)$$

---

[4] These can be assigned to the different programmes and to the 'non-participation' treatment (randomized-out).

[5] Even if a proper experiment is conducted, it might still occur by chance that the treatment groups differ substantially in their characteristics particularly if the sample sizes are small. Although the differences in sample means provide unbiased estimates of average treatment effects, adjusting for the differences in the covariates, as discussed in Section 2.1.5, can reduce the variance of the estimates (Rubin 1974).

This assumption is known as *selection on observables* (Barnow, Cain, and Goldberger 1981), *ignorable treatment assignment* (Rosenbaum and Rubin 1983) or as *conditional independence assumption* (Lechner 1999), and it states that, given the characteristics X, knowing the programme an individual has chosen contains no additional information about his potential outcomes. In other words, treatment selection depends on the potential outcomes only to the extent to which they can be anticipated on the basis of the exogenous characteristics X, but not on an anticipation based on unobserved characteristics.

The confounding variables often include time-varying variables as well. For example, Ashenfelter (1978) noted that the decision to participate in active labour market programmes is highly dependent on the individual's previous earnings and employment histories. Recent negative employment shocks often induce individuals to participate in training programmes. Hence the employment situation in the months before the programme starts is an important determinant of the programme participation decision and is also likely to be correlated with the potential employment outcomes. However, since usually no explicit start date can be observed for the participants in the 'non-participation' treatment, the employment situation in the months before the programme started is undefined for them. To solve this problem, Lechner (1999) suggested drawing hypothetical start dates for the 'non-participants' from the distribution of start dates among the participants.[6] Lechner (2002b) analyzed the assignment of hypothetical start dates further. Instead of drawing dates from the unconditional distribution of start dates, he also considered drawing from the distribution conditional on the confounding variables. This conditional distribution can be simulated by regressing the (logarithm of the) start dates on the covariates and fitting the mean of the conditional distribution at the covariate values of the respective non-participant. In his application both methods led to similar results.

On the other hand, X must *not* include any variables that are itself affected by the policy. These are (endogenous) variables that are caused by the policy and conditioning on such variables would block the part of the causal effect that acts through these variables (Pearl 2000). The variables that must and must not be included in X cannot be inferred from the data, nor can their completeness be tested. Knowledge of the institutional details and a conceptual causal model are required to assess which variables are relevant. Hence a priori, the selection on observables assumption (2.4) can neither be regarded as a strong or a weak condition; this depends entirely on the policy specific details, the outcome variable of interest and the available data.[7] However the validity of this assumption should

---

[6] And to delete the 'non-participant' observations for which the assigned start date implies an inconsistency. For example, if unemployment is a basic eligibility condition for participation in an active labour market programme, individuals with an assigned start date *after* the termination of their unemployment spell are discarded (because participation could not have been possible at that date).

[7] The control-for-confounding-variables evaluation strategy is widely applied in the evaluation of active labour market programmes, see for instance Heckman, Ichimura, and Todd

be carefully assessed, since leaving out relevant covariates can change the estimation results considerably and lead to wrong conclusions as, for example, demonstrated in Lechner (2002b).

Generally speaking, identification by the conditional independence assumption (2.4) is easier to achieve the more bureaucratic, rule-based and deterministic the programme selection process is[8] and the more parties are involved that (truthfully) report their judgements about the individual's characteristics and behaviour (e.g. case worker's and physician's judgements in Frölich, Heshmati, and Lechner (2000a)). For example, in his analysis of the effects of voluntary participation in the military on civilian earnings, Angrist (1998) takes advantage of the fact that the military is known to screen applicants to the armed forces on the basis of particular characteristics, primarily on the basis of age, schooling and test scores. Hence these characteristics are the principal factors guiding the acceptance decision, and it appears reasonable to assume that among applicants with the same observed characteristics, those who finally enter the military and those who do not are not systematically different. A similar reasoning applies to the effects of schooling, if it is known that applicants to a school or university are screened on the basis of certain characteristics, but that conditional on these characteristics selection is on a first-come/first-serve basis.

On the other hand, if individuals decide largely autonomously, and if no details about their personal traits are available (e.g. in form of truthful self-assessments), validity of the conditional independence assumption is much harder to establish. In this case, longitudinal data containing, for example, past employment and earnings histories can help to proxy typical, though unobserved traits of the individual (e.g. ability, discipline, work commitment, health status). Such a very informative longitudinal dataset is used, for example, in Gerfin and Lechner (2002) for the evaluation of active labour market policies in Switzerland.

If the conditional independence assumption (2.4) is valid, the potential outcomes conditional on X are identified because

$$E[Y^r|X, D = r] = E[Y^r|X, D = s] = E[Y^r|X].$$

The average treatment effect (2.1) and the average treatment effect on the treated (2.2) can be obtained by weighting these outcomes by the distribution of X in the respective population. By the law of iterated expectations, the average treatment effect is identified as

---

(1997) and Dehejia and Wahba (1999) for the USA, Lechner (1999) for Eastern Germany, Gerfin and Lechner (2002) for Switzerland, Brodaty, Crepon, and Fougere (2001) for France, Larsson (2000) for Sweden and Jalan and Ravallion (2002) for Argentina.

[8] Provided a random element exists that guarantees that each individual could be assigned to each of the programmes (with non-zero probability). This is the common support condition discussed below.

$$E[Y^r - Y^s] = E[Y^r] - E[Y^s] \tag{2.5}$$
$$= E[E[Y^r|X]] - E[E[Y^s|X]]$$
$$= \int (E[Y^r|X = x, D = r] - E[Y^s|X = x, D = s]) \cdot f_X(x)dx,$$

where $f_X(x)$ is the density of X in the population. Since $E[Y^r|X, D = r]$ and $E[Y^s|X, D = s]$ can be estimated from observed data, the average treatment effect can be obtained by estimating the expected outcome conditional on X in both treatment groups and weighting them accordingly by the distribution of X in the full population.

Analogously, the average treatment effect on the treated is identified as

$$E[Y^r - Y^s|D = r] = E[Y^r|D = r] - E[E[Y^s|X, D = r]|D = r] \tag{2.6}$$
$$= E[Y^r|D = r] - \int E[Y^s|X = x, D = s] \cdot f_{X|D=r}(x)dx,$$

where $f_{X|D=r}(x)$ denotes the density of X among the participants in programme r. The former term is identified by the sample mean outcome of the participants in programme r, and the latter term can be estimated by adjusting the average outcomes in treatment group s for the distribution of X among the participants in r.

The requirement of a *common support* has been neglected in the discussion so far. Although the conditional independence assumption (2.4) identifies the conditional potential outcomes $E[Y^r|X = x]$ through observations on participants in programme r, this identification holds only for all x for which there is a positive probability that participants in programme r are observed with characteristics x. Let

$$S^r = \{x : f_{X|D=r}(x) > 0\} \tag{2.7}$$

denote the support of X among the participants in programme r, which can also be expressed as

$$S^r = \{x : p^r(x) > 0\},$$

where $p^r(x) = P(D = r|X = x)$ is the probability that an individual with characteristics x participates in programme r.[9] For any $x \notin S^r$ the expected outcome $E[Y^r|X = x, D = r]$ is not identified, since it is impossible to observe any participant in programme r with characteristics x. Let S denote the support of X in the population, i.e. $S = \{x : f_X(x) > 0\}$, which is the union of all treatment group supports: $S = \cup S^r$. The average treatment effect on the treated $E[Y^r - Y^s|D = r]$ is only identified, if $S^r \subseteq S^s$, i.e. if any x with positive mass among the participants in treatment r belongs also to the support of the treatment subpopulation s. Identification of the average potential outcome $E[Y^r]$ requires even that $S^r = S$, i.e. that each individual has also a positive probability of being observed in programme r. Analogously, the identification of the average

---

[9] The definition $S^r = \{x : p^r(x) > 0\}$ means $S^r = \{x : p^r(x) > 0$ and $p^r(x)$ is defined$\}$ and, thus, excludes all x where the density $f_X(x)$ in the population is zero.

treatment effect $E[Y^r - Y^s]$ requires $S^r = S^s = S$. In the case of randomized experiments these conditions are automatically satisfied (for the population on which randomization took place) since each individual has a positive probability of being randomized into any of the available programmes. With observational studies, however, this is often not the case. For example, in active labour market programmes being unemployed is usually a central condition for eligibility. Thus employed persons cannot be participants as they are not eligible and, hence, no counterfactual outcome is defined for them. In these cases, it might be adequate to concentrate on the part of the population for which the effect can be identified and to redefine the average treatment effect (2.1) as

$$\underset{S^r \cap S^s}{E} [Y^r - Y^s] = \underset{X|X \in (S^r \cap S^s)}{E} E[Y^r - Y^s|X]$$

and the average treatment effect on the treated (2.2) as

$$\underset{S^r \cap S^s}{E} [Y^r - Y^s|D = r],$$

where $E_{S^r \cap S^s}$ refers to the expected outcome with respect to the common support, i.e. with respect to the part of the population which has characteristics X belonging to the supports S^r and S^s. If most of the population mass belongs to the common support, these re-defined treatment effects are likely to be close to the treatment effects for the full population. Furthermore, if the potential outcomes are bounded random variables, the intervals in which the average outcomes $E[Y^r]$ and $E[Y^s]$ lie can be bounded, which directly implies bounds on the average treatment effect $E[Y^r - Y^s]$. For a further discussion about bounding the effects when $S^r \neq S^s$ see Lechner (2001b). For the remainder of this chapter, conditioning on the common support is usually kept implicit to ease notation.[10]

A way to 'verify' the validity of the conditional independence assumption (2.4), known as the 'pre-programme test', is based on observed outcomes before treatment participation (Heckman and Robb 1985). To distinguish pre- and post-treatment outcomes, the notation has to be extended to take explicit account of time. Redefine $Y_t^0, .., Y_t^{R-1}$ as the potential outcomes at a time t after the assignment to treatment. Let $Y_\tau^0, .., Y_\tau^{R-1}$ be the potential outcomes at a time τ *before* the assignment to treatment and $Y_\tau = Y_\tau^D$ the observed outcome. Suppose that the outcomes before the assignment to the treatment are not affected by the subsequent treatment, i.e. that the outcome before treatment is the same regardless of the programme in which the individual eventually participates:

$$Y_\tau^0 = Y_\tau^1 = ... = Y_\tau^{R-1}. \tag{2.8}$$

---

[10] If all pair-wise treatment effects $E[Y^r - Y^s]$ $\forall r, s$ are of interest, Lechner (2002b) suggests to define the effects with respect to the *joint common support* $\bar{S} = \overset{R-1}{\underset{r=0}{\cap}} S^r$ such that all effects are defined for the same subpopulation and can easier be compared with each other.

Hence the observed outcome before treatment $Y_\tau = Y_\tau^D$ is no longer contingent on the treatment.

Validity of the conditional independence assumption (2.4) in period t means that all confounding variables are included in X such that, conditional on X, any differences between the treatment groups are unsystematic or at least not related to the potential outcomes $Y_t^0, .., Y_t^{R-1}$. If the 'non-participation' outcome Y_t^0 is strongly related over time, it is likely that the confounding factors consist of the same variables in time t and in τ. This would imply that, conditional on X, also the outcomes observed *before* treatment are not systematically different between the treatment groups

$$E[Y_\tau|X, D = r] = E[Y_\tau|X, D = s] = E[Y_\tau|X]. \tag{2.9}$$

On the other hand, if the conditional independence assumption is invalid, there are confounding factors, which are not included in X, that influence programme selection as well as the potential outcomes and cause selection bias: $E[Y_t^r|X, D = r] \neq E[Y_t^r|X, D = s]$. Again, if the 'non-participation' outcome Y_t^0 is strongly related over time, it is likely that these factors would also generate systematic differences between the treatment groups in earlier time periods:

$$E[Y_\tau|X, D = r] \neq E[Y_\tau|X, D = s] \neq E[Y_\tau|X].$$

Large differences in the pre-programme outcomes between the treatment groups would thus cast doubts on the validity of the conditional independence assumption (2.4) and a formal test statistic can be derived as in Heckman and Robb (1985). Yet, it is not a proper test of the conditional independence assumption since its justification requires additional untestable assumptions about the relationship between pre- and post-treatment outcomes.

Furthermore, the application of the pre-programme test requires to find a time period τ where Y_τ is neither a confounding variable itself nor a variable already causally influenced by the programme. The former condition is routinely violated if previous Y_τ influence the participation decision D. For example, the past employment situation is often a strong determinant of participation in active labour market programmes. Hence Y_τ itself is a confounding variable and as such must be included in X as a conditioning variable.

The latter condition is violated if anticipation of programme participation changes the individual's behaviour even before the programme starts. For example, if an unemployed person gets informed that he is assigned to a particular labour market programme, he might immediately adjust his job-search intensity or any complementary training activities. This implies that the potential outcomes differ even before the beginning of the programme:

$$Y_\tau^0 \neq Y_\tau^1 \neq ... \neq Y_\tau^{R-1}. \tag{2.10}$$

Accordingly the observed outcome $Y_\tau = Y_\tau^D$ depends on the treatment eventually received. In this case, the equality (2.9) no longer holds.

In these cases the pre-programme test cannot be applied and this discussion highlights the importance of taking account of the time structure of the outcome variable. In different periods of time τ *before* the start of the programme, the variable Y_τ can be a confounder (in which case it must be included in X), an outcome variable causally affected through programme anticipation (in which case it must *not* be included in X), or neither confounding nor causally affected (in which case the pre-programme test can be applied).

Difference in Difference - Predictable Bias Assumption In many evaluation settings it may not be feasible to observe all confounding variables. In these cases the evaluation strategy has to cope with selection on unobserved variables. Nevertheless, average treatment effects may still be identified either through an instrumental variable (see next section) or if the average selection bias can be estimated from pre-treatment outcomes. This latter approach is based on a similar motivation as the pre-programme test: If systematic differences in the pre-programme outcomes between different treatment groups occur, these differences may not only indicate that not all confounding variables have been included, but may further be useful to predict the magnitude of selection bias in the post-programme outcomes.

If X does not contain all confounding variables, adjusting for the differences in the X distributions, analogously to (2.6), will not yield a consistent estimate of the average treatment effect on the treated because

$$E\left[Y_t^r | D = r\right] - \int E\left[Y_t^s | X = x, D = s\right] \cdot f_{X|D=r}(x) dx$$

$$\neq E\left[Y_t^r | D = r\right] - \int E\left[Y_t^s | X = x, D = r\right] \cdot f_{X|D=r}(x) dx = E\left[Y_t^r - Y_t^s | D = r\right]$$

since $E[Y_t^s | X, D = r] \neq E[Y_t^s | X, D = s]$. The difference

$$\int \left(E\left[Y_t^s | X = x, D = r\right] - E\left[Y_t^s | X = x, D = s\right]\right) \cdot f_{X|D=r}(x) dx$$

is the systematic bias in the potential outcome Y_t^s in period t that still remains even after adjusting for the different distributions of X.

Pre-programme outcomes might help to estimate this systematic bias with respect to the 'non-participation' outcome Y_t^0. Therefore the following discussion centers on the identification of average treatment effects on the treated relative to non-participation: $E[Y_t^r - Y_t^0 | D = r]$.[11] Define the *average selection bias*

$$B_t = \int \left(E\left[Y_t^0 | X = x, D = r\right] - E\left[Y_t^0 | X = x, D = 0\right]\right) \cdot f_{X|D=r}(x) dx$$

as the systematic outcome difference between the group of non-participants ($D = 0$) and the group of participants ($D = r$) if both groups would participate in

---

[11] Estimates of $E[Y_t^r - Y_t^s | D = r]$ for $s \neq 0$ or of $E[Y_t^s]$ for $s \neq 0$ generally cannot be obtained with this approach, since the pre-programme outcomes are only informative about the potential 'non-participation' outcome Y_t^0.

treatment 0. If, for example in the evaluation of active labour market programmes, the individuals who decided to participate were on average more able, it is likely that their labour market outcomes would also have been better even without participation in the programme. In this case, the average selection bias B_t would be positive. If the potential outcome in the case of non-participation Y_t^0 is related over time, it is likely that these differences between the treatment groups would also persist in other time periods including periods before the start of the programme. In other words, the more able persons would also had enjoyed better labour market outcomes in periods before treatment.

If the pre-programme outcome in period τ is not causally affected by the programme, so that (2.8) holds, the 'non-participation' outcomes $Y_\tau^0 = Y_\tau$ are observed for the different treatment groups and the corresponding average selection bias in period τ

$$B_\tau = \int \left(E\left[Y_\tau | X = x, D = r\right] - E\left[Y_\tau | X = x, D = 0\right] \right) \cdot f_{X|D=r}(x) dx$$

is identified from the observed pre-programme data.

Assuming that the average selection bias is stable over time (Eichler and Lechner 2002)

$$B_t = B_\tau \tag{2.11}$$

the average treatment effect on the treated is identified as

$$E\left[Y_t^r - Y_t^0 | D = r\right]$$
$$= E\left[Y_t^r | D = r\right] - \left(\int E\left[Y_t^0 | X = x, D = 0\right] \cdot f_{X|D=r}(x) dx + B_t \right)$$
$$= \left(E\left[Y_t^r | D = r\right] - E\left[Y_\tau | D = r\right] \right)$$
$$- \int \left(E\left[Y_t^0 | X = x, D = 0\right] - E\left[Y_\tau | X = x, D = 0\right] \right) f_{X|D=r}(x) dx. \tag{2.12}$$

This resembles a difference-in-difference type estimator adjusted for the distribution of the X covariates, which is further discussed in Section 2.1.5. For an application of nonparametric difference-in-difference estimation to the evaluation of active labour market programmes in East Germany, see Eichler and Lechner (2002) or Bergemann, Fitzenberger, Schultz, and Speckesser (2000) and Bergemann, Fitzenberger, and Speckesser (2001).

The bias-stability assumption (2.11) is not strictly necessary. Instead, it suffices if B_t can be consistently estimated from the average selection biases in pre-programme periods (*predictable-bias assumption*). If (causally unaffected) pre-programme outcomes are observed for many periods, the average selection bias can be estimated in each period and any regular trends observed in $\hat{B}_\tau, \hat{B}_{\tau-1}, \hat{B}_{\tau-2},...$ may lead to better predictions of the bias B_t than simply estimating B_t by the selection bias in period τ, as the bias-stability assumption (2.11) would suggest.

Loosely speaking, the predictable-bias-assumption (with the bias-stability-assumption as a special case) is weaker than the conditional independence assumption (2.4) since it allows that $B_t \neq 0$, whereas the conditional independence assumption requires $B_t = 0$. However, both assumptions are not nested because B_t may be zero while $\hat{B}_\tau, \hat{B}_{\tau-1}, \hat{B}_{\tau-2},..$ may be unable to predict $B_t = 0$.[12] A further difference occurs if the pre-programme outcomes Y_τ are themselves confounders, i.e. influencing the treatment selection decision and the post-programme outcomes. If, in addition, all other confounding variables are observed, the independence assumption (2.4) would be valid conditional on the pre-programme outcomes *and* the other confounders. This would imply zero selection bias ($B_t = 0$) and the applicability of the control-for-confounding-variables approach. The difference-in-difference approach, on the other hand, would introduce selection bias ($B_t \neq 0$) by not conditioning on the pre-programme outcome Y_τ (i.e. not including Y_τ in X).

A weakness of the difference-in-difference approach is that it does not entail any theoretical guidelines for deciding which variables (if any at all) should be included in the conditioning set X.[13] Heckman, Ichimura, and Todd (1997), Heckman, Ichimura, Smith, and Todd (1998) and Smith and Todd (2002) consider a stronger version of the bias-stability-assumption (2.11), which requires that the bias is stable not only on average but for any possible value of X

$$E\left[Y_t^0 - Y_\tau | X, D = r\right] = E\left[Y_t^0 - Y_\tau | X, D = 0\right]. \qquad (2.13)$$

This stronger assumption demands that all variables that affect the increase (growth) in the non-participation outcome over time ($Y_t^0 - Y_\tau$) and the selection to treatment 0 or r are included in X. Although this stronger assumption does not help to identify the average treatment effect on the treated, it may be useful in the search to identify the relevant conditioning variables X: because if (2.13) is true then also (2.11) holds.

Instrumental Variables Identification An alternative strategy to handle selection on the basis of unobserved characteristics exploits the identifying power of an instrumental variable, which is a variable that influences the probability to participate in a particular treatment but has no effect on the potential outcomes. It affects the observed outcome only indirectly through the participation decision. Causal effects can be identified through a variation in this instrumental variable since the effect of this variation is entirely channeled via the programme selection. Causal inference through instrumental variables has been analyzed by Imbens and Angrist (1994), Angrist, Imbens, and Rubin (1996), Heckman and Vytlacil (1999) and Imbens (2001), among others. As this identification strategy is not much further examined in this book, only its basic ideas are outlined and illustrated for the binary treatment case ($R = 2$) with a binary instrumental variable $Z \in \{0, 1\}$.

---

[12] For instance, if $B_t = 0$ and $B_\tau \neq 0$ and, erroneously, bias stability (2.11) is assumed.

[13] Although the guideline for the control-for-confounding-variables approach is rather vague, it still gives some indication which variables are relevant and which are not.

The extension to situations where the instrumental variable itself is endogenous is considered in Frölich (2001b).

A fundamental result of instrumental variables identification is that average treatment effects can only be identified with respect to the subpopulation that could be induced to change programme status by a variation in the instrumental variable (Imbens and Angrist 1994). For subpopulations that would participate in the same treatment regardless of a hypothetical exogenous change in the value of Z, their counterfactual outcomes are not identified. This is similar to the common support restriction discussed above. Hence an average treatment effect for the full population could only be identified if all individuals change programme status with a variation in Z. Otherwise, only a *local average treatment effect* (LATE) for the subpopulation responsive to Z is identified (Imbens and Angrist 1994).

Define $D_{i,Z_i=0}$ as the programme participation status $D \in \{0,1\}$ that would be observed for individual i if Z_i were set exogenously to the value 0. Define $D_{i,Z_i=1}$ analogously as the participation status that would be observed if Z_i were set to 1. Hence $D_{i,Z_i=0}$ and $D_{i,Z_i=1}$ are *potential* participation indicators, and let D_{i,Z_i} denote the *observed* value of D_i for individual i, i.e. the participation decision corresponding to the realized value Z_i. According to the potential participation behaviour, the population of all individuals can be partitioned into 4 subpopulations: Individuals for whom $D_{i,Z_i=0} = D_{i,Z_i=1} = 1$ always participate in the programme regardless of the value of the instrumental variable. On the other hand, individuals with $D_{i,Z_i=0} = D_{i,Z_i=1} = 0$ never participate. Individuals for whom $D_{i,Z_i=0} = 0$ and $D_{i,Z_i=1} = 1$ participate in the programme only if the instrument takes the value 1 and do not participate otherwise. These individuals 'comply' with their instrument assignment and are denoted compliers. Finally, individuals with $D_{i,Z_i=0} = 1$ and $D_{i,Z_i=1} = 0$ participate only if the instrument takes the value 0 and are called defiers. Thus each individual can be classified either as an always-participant, a never-participant, a complier or a defier. Let τ_i denote the participation-type of individual i:

$$
\begin{array}{l|l}
\multicolumn{2}{c}{\text{Definition of types}} \\
\hline
\tau_i = a \;\text{if } D_{i,Z_i=0} = 1 \text{ and } D_{i,Z_i=1} = 1 & \text{Always-participant} \\
\tau_i = n \;\text{if } D_{i,Z_i=0} = 0 \text{ and } D_{i,Z_i=1} = 0 & \text{Never-participant} \\
\tau_i = c \;\text{if } D_{i,Z_i=0} = 0 \text{ and } D_{i,Z_i=1} = 1 & \text{Complier} \\
\tau_i = d \;\text{if } D_{i,Z_i=0} = 1 \text{ and } D_{i,Z_i=1} = 0 & \text{Defier.}
\end{array}
\tag{2.14}
$$

Since the individuals of type always-participant and of type never-participant cannot be induced to change treatment state through a variation in the instrumental variable, the impact of D on Y can at most be ascertained for the subpopulation of compliers and defiers. To analyze identification of local average treatment effects by instrumental variables, the potential outcomes framework needs to be extended: Define $Y_{i,Z_i}^{D_i=0}$ and $Y_{i,Z_i}^{D_i=1}$ as the *potential* outcomes for individual i, where $Y_{i,Z_i}^{D_i=0}$ is the outcome that would be observed for individual i if D_i were set to 0, and $Y_{i,Z_i}^{D_i=1}$ is the outcome that would be observed if individual i were assigned to the programme. Define $Y_{i,Z_i=0}^{D_i}$ and $Y_{i,Z_i=1}^{D_i}$ as the outcomes that would be observed if the instrument Z_i were set to 0 or 1, respectively. Similarly, $Y_{i,Z_i=0}^{D_i=0}$, $Y_{i,Z_i=0}^{D_i=1}$, $Y_{i,Z_i=1}^{D_i=0}$, $Y_{i,Z_i=1}^{D_i=1}$ are the outcomes that could be observed if the instrument Z_i *and* the participation indicator D_i were set exogenously. The conceptual difference between the potential outcomes $Y_{i,Z_i=0}^{D_i=0}$, $Y_{i,Z_i=0}^{D_i=1}$, $Y_{i,Z_i=1}^{D_i=0}$, $Y_{i,Z_i=1}^{D_i=1}$ and the potential outcomes $Y_{i,Z_i=0}^{D_i}$, $Y_{i,Z_i=1}^{D_i}$ is that in the former case Z and D are fixed by external intervention, whereas in the latter case only Z is set exogenously and D_i is determined by the participation behaviour of individual i. In other words, the former outcomes isolate the direct effect of the instrument Z on Y, while the latter embed the direct effect and the indirect effect of Z on Y via the treatment participation D. Finally, $Y_i = Y_{i,Z_i}^{D_i}$ is the observed outcome where Z_i and D_i are the realized values for individual i.

With these definitions the expected value of the outcome variable Y can be written as the expected value of Y in the four subpopulations defined by (2.14) weighted by the relative size of these subpopulations:

$$\begin{aligned}
E[Y] = {} & E\left[Y_i | \tau_i = a\right] \cdot P\left(\tau_i = a\right) \qquad\qquad (2.15)\\
& + E\left[Y_i | \tau_i = n\right] \cdot P\left(\tau_i = n\right) \\
& + E\left[Y_i | \tau_i = c\right] \cdot P\left(\tau_i = c\right) \\
& + E\left[Y_i | \tau_i = d\right] \cdot P\left(\tau_i = d\right).
\end{aligned}$$

Analogously, the conditional expectation of Y given the instrument can be written as:

$$\begin{aligned}
E[Y|Z=0] = {} & E\left[Y_{i,Z_i}^{D_i} | Z_i = 0, \tau_i = a\right] \cdot P\left(\tau_i = a | Z_i = 0\right) \\
& + E\left[Y_{i,Z_i}^{D_i} | Z_i = 0, \tau_i = n\right] \cdot P\left(\tau_i = n | Z_i = 0\right) \\
& + E\left[Y_{i,Z_i}^{D_i} | Z_i = 0, \tau_i = c\right] \cdot P\left(\tau_i = c | Z_i = 0\right) \\
& + E\left[Y_{i,Z_i}^{D_i} | Z_i = 0, \tau_i = d\right] \cdot P\left(\tau_i = d | Z_i = 0\right) \\
= {} & E\left[Y_{i,Z_i=0}^{D_i=1} | Z_i = 0, \tau_i = a\right] \cdot P\left(\tau_i = a | Z_i = 0\right) \\
& + E\left[Y_{i,Z_i=0}^{D_i=0} | Z_i = 0, \tau_i = n\right] \cdot P\left(\tau_i = n | Z_i = 0\right) \\
& + E\left[Y_{i,Z_i=0}^{D_i=0} | Z_i = 0, \tau_i = c\right] \cdot P\left(\tau_i = c | Z_i = 0\right) \\
& + E\left[Y_{i,Z_i=0}^{D_i=1} | Z_i = 0, \tau_i = d\right] \cdot P\left(\tau_i = d | Z_i = 0\right)
\end{aligned}$$

and

$$\begin{aligned}
E[Y|Z=1] = {} & E\left[Y_{i,Z_i=1}^{D_i=1} | Z_i = 1, \tau_i = a\right] \cdot P\left(\tau_i = a | Z_i = 1\right) \\
& + E\left[Y_{i,Z_i=1}^{D_i=0} | Z_i = 1, \tau_i = n\right] \cdot P\left(\tau_i = n | Z_i = 1\right) \\
& + E\left[Y_{i,Z_i=1}^{D_i=1} | Z_i = 1, \tau_i = c\right] \cdot P\left(\tau_i = c | Z_i = 1\right) \\
& + E\left[Y_{i,Z_i=1}^{D_i=0} | Z_i = 1, \tau_i = d\right] \cdot P\left(\tau_i = d | Z_i = 1\right).
\end{aligned}$$

Suppose

[Assumption 1: Unconfounded participation type] that the relative size of the subpopulations always-participants, never-participants, compliers and defiers is independent of the instrument:

$$P\left(\tau_i = t | Z_i = 0\right) = P\left(\tau_i = t | Z_i = 1\right) \qquad \text{for } t \in \{a, n, c, d\}. \qquad (2.16)$$

Suppose further

[Assumption 2: Mean exclusion restriction] that the potential outcomes are mean independent of the instrumental variable Z in each subpopulation

$$E\left[Y_{i,Z_i}^{D_i=0} | Z_i = 0, \tau_i = t\right] = E\left[Y_{i,Z_i}^{D_i=0} | Z_i = 1, \tau_i = t\right] \quad \text{for } t \in \{n, c, d\} (2.17)$$

$$E\left[Y_{i,Z_i}^{D_i=1} | Z_i = 0, \tau_i = t\right] = E\left[Y_{i,Z_i}^{D_i=1} | Z_i = 1, \tau_i = t\right] \quad \text{for } t \in \{a, c, d\}.$$

With this exclusion restriction the expected value of Y given Z is independent of Z in the always- and in the never-participant subpopulation. Hence when taking the difference $E[Y|Z = 1] - E[Y|Z = 0]$ the respective terms for the always- and for the never-participants cancel:

$$E\left[Y|Z = 1\right] - E\left[Y|Z = 0\right]$$
$$= \left(E\left[Y_{i,Z_i=1}^{D_i=1} | Z_i = 1, \tau_i = c\right] - E\left[Y_{i,Z_i=0}^{D_i=0} | Z_i = 0, \tau_i = c\right]\right) \cdot P\left(\tau_i = c\right)$$
$$+ \left(E\left[Y_{i,Z_i=1}^{D_i=0} | Z_i = 1, \tau_i = d\right] - E\left[Y_{i,Z_i=0}^{D_i=1} | Z_i = 0, \tau_i = d\right]\right) \cdot P\left(\tau_i = d\right)$$

and with the mean exclusion restriction for the compliers and the defiers:

$$= \left(E\left[Y_{i,Z_i}^{D_i=1} - Y_{i,Z_i}^{D_i=0} | \tau_i = c\right]\right) \cdot P\left(\tau_i = c\right)$$
$$- \left(E\left[Y_{i,Z_i}^{D_i=1} - Y_{i,Z_i}^{D_i=0} | \tau_i = d\right]\right) \cdot P\left(\tau_i = d\right). \qquad (2.18)$$

The difference $E\left[Y|Z = 1\right] - E\left[Y|Z = 0\right]$ thus represents the difference between the average treatment effect on the compliers (who switch into treatment as a reaction on a change in the instrument from 0 to 1) and the average treatment effect on the defiers (who switch out of treatment). An estimate of (2.18) is not very informative since, for example, an estimate of zero could be the result of a treatment without effect as well as the result of a treatment with a large impact but offsetting flows of compliers and defiers. Hence the exclusion restriction (2.17) is not sufficient to isolate a meaningful treatment effect. However, as (2.18) indicates, a treatment effect could be identified if either no compliers $P\left(\tau_i = c\right) = 0$ or no defiers $P\left(\tau_i = d\right) = 0$ existed. If an instrumental variable is found that affects *all* individuals in the 'same direction', e.g. that either induces individuals to switch into participation or leaves their participation status unchanged, but does not induce any individual to switch out of treatment, the average treatment effect on the responsive subpopulation is identified.

[Assumption 3: Monotonicity] Suppose that the subpopulation of defiers has relative size zero

$$P\left(\tau = d\right) = 0, \tag{2.19}$$

or in other words, that $D_{i,Z_i=1} \geq D_{i,Z_i=0}$ for all i. Suppose further
[Assumption 4: Existence of compliers] that the instrumental variable does have an impact on treatment choice, i.e. that the subpopulation of compliers exists

$$P\left(\tau = c\right) > 0. \tag{2.20}$$

With these additional assumptions, the expression (2.18) can be written as

$$E\left[Y_{i,Z_i}^{D_i=1} - Y_{i,Z_i}^{D_i=0} \mid \tau_i = c\right] = \frac{E\left[Y|Z = 1\right] - E\left[Y|Z = 0\right]}{P\left(\tau = c\right)},$$

where $E\left[Y_{i,Z_i}^{D_i=1} - Y_{i,Z_i}^{D_i=0} \mid \tau_i = c\right]$ is the average treatment effect in the subpopulation of compliers.

Noting further that $P(D = 1|Z = 0) = P\left(\tau = a\right) + P\left(\tau = d\right)$ and $P(D = 1|Z = 1) = P\left(\tau = a\right) + P\left(\tau = c\right)$, it follows with (2.19) that the relative size of the subpopulation of compliers is identified as

$$P\left(\tau = c\right) = P\left(D = 1|Z = 1\right) - P\left(D = 1|Z = 0\right).$$

Hence the average treatment effect on the compliers is identified as

$$E\left[Y_{i,Z_i}^{D_i=1} - Y_{i,Z_i}^{D_i=0} \mid \tau_i = c\right] = \frac{E\left[Y|Z = 1\right] - E\left[Y|Z = 0\right]}{E\left[D|Z = 1\right] - E\left[D|Z = 0\right]}. \tag{2.21}$$

This is the average treatment effect on those individuals who are induced to switch into the programme due to the instrumental variable. Since the subpopulation of compliers is not identified, it often may be difficult to interpret this treatment effect. As the complier subpopulation is defined through the instrumental variable, any local average treatment effect is directly tied to its instrumental variable and cannot be interpreted on its own. For example, if the instrumental variable Z represents the size of a programme (e.g. the number of available slots), the local average treatment effect would represent the impact of the programme if it were extended from size z_0 to size z_1 on the subpopulation which would participate only in the enlarged programme.

A central condition for the identification of the local average treatment effect (2.21) is the mean exclusion restriction (2.17). This mean exclusion restriction combines two conceptually distinct assumptions, which can be seen by rewriting (2.17) for the potential outcome $Y_{i,Z}^{D_i=1}$ as

$$E\left[Y_{i,Z_i=0}^{D_i=1}|Z_i = 0, \tau_i = t\right] = E\left[Y_{i,Z_i=1}^{D_i=1}|Z_i = 0, \tau_i = t\right]$$

$$= E\left[Y_{i,Z_i=1}^{D_i=1}|Z_i = 1, \tau_i = t\right] \tag{2.22}$$

for $t \in \{a, c, d\}$. The first equality sign corresponds to an exclusion assumption on the *individual level*. It is assumed that the potential outcome $Y_i^{D_i=1}$ for individual i is unaffected by an exogenous change in Z_i. It rules out any direct systematic impact of Z on the potential outcomes on an individual level (and this assumption is satisfied for instance if $Y_{i,Z_i=0}^{D_i=1} = Y_{i,Z_i=1}^{D_i=1}$). The second equality sign in (2.22) represents an unconfoundedness assumption on the *population level*. It assumes that the potential outcome $Y_{i,Z_i=1}^{D_i=1}$ is identically distributed in the subpopulation of individuals for whom the instrument Z_i takes the value 0 and in the subpopulation of individuals with $Z_i = 1$. This assumption rules out selection effects on the population level. Hence the second part of the mean exclusion restriction (2.22) refers to the composition of individuals for whom $Z = 1$ or $Z = 0$ is observed, whereas the first part refers to how the instrument affects the outcome Y of a particular individual.

The second part of the mean exclusion assumption (2.22) is trivially satisfied if the instrument Z is randomly assigned. Nevertheless randomization of Z does not guarantee that the exclusion assumption holds on the individual level. On the other hand, if Z is chosen by the individual itself, unconfoundedness of Z (on the population level) is unlikely to hold. For example, Card (1995) uses college proximity as an instrument for estimating the returns to schooling. Living closer to a college is likely to induce some children to obtain more college education. Although it appears reasonable that distance to the nearest college by itself does not affect the subsequent potential labour market outcomes of the child (first part of (2.22)), it might be that the families who decide to reside nearer or farther to a college are rather different. In this case the instrumental variable is subject to self-selection and the mean exclusion assumption (2.17) is unlikely to be satisfied.

In situations where the instrumental variable is not randomly assigned, the instrument Z might also be confounded with the potential participation indicators $D_{i,Z_i=0}$ and $D_{i,Z_i=1}$, thus invalidating the unconfounded participation-type assumption (2.16). E.g. the composition of always-participants, never-participants and compliers might be different among families who decide to reside close to a college than among those who live distant to a college. To identify an average treatment effect when the instrument Z itself is confounded with the potential participation indicators $D_{i,Z_i=0}$, $D_{i,Z_i=1}$ or with the potential outcomes $Y_{i,Z_i}^{D_i=0}$, $Y_{i,Z_i}^{D_i=1}$, it is necessary to consider extended versions of Assumptions 1 and 2 where the unconfounded-participation type and mean exclusion assumptions are required to hold only conditional on all confounding variables X. These extensions are examined, for example, in Frölich (2001b).[14]

Identification of treatment effects on the basis of Assumptions 1 to 4 has been applied, for example, in Hearst, Newman, and Hulley (1986) and Angrist (1990) to estimate the effects of participating in the Vietnam war on mortality and civilian earnings, respectively. A suited instrumental variable was provided through the U.S. conscription policy during the years of the Vietnam war, which conscripted

---

[14] The confounding variables X are all variables that affect Z *and* $D_{i,Z_i=0}$, $D_{i,Z_i=1}$ or Z and $Y_{i,Z_i}^{D_i=0}$, $Y_{i,Z_i}^{D_i=1}$.

individuals on the basis of randomly drawn birth dates. Imbens and van der Klaauw (1995) used variations in the compulsory conscription policy in the Netherlands during World War II to estimate the effect of veteran status on earnings. Angrist and Krueger (1991) estimated the returns to schooling using the quarter of birth as an instrumental variable for educational attainment. According to U.S. compulsory school attendance laws, compulsory education ends when the pupil reaches a certain age, and thus, the month in which termination of the compulsory education is reached depends on the birth date. Since the school year starts for all pupils in summer/autumn, the minimum education varies with the birth date, which can be exploited to estimate the impact of an additional year of schooling on earnings. For a survey of other 'natural' or 'quasi' experiments see Meyer (1995).

Regression-Discontinuity Design A particular type of instrumental variable identification is exploited in the regression-discontinuity design. This approach uses discontinuities in the programme selection process to identify a causal effect. Suppose a (continuous) variable Z influences an outcome variable Y and also another variable D, which itself affects the outcome variable Y. Hence, Z has a direct impact on Y as well as an indirect impact on Y via D. This latter impact represents the causal effect of D on Y, which can be identified if the direct and the indirect impacts of Z on Y can be told apart. In the case that the direct impact of Z on Y is known to be smooth but the relationship between Z and D is discontinuous, any discontinuities (jumps) in the observed relationship between Z and Y at locations where the relation Z to D is discontinuous can be attributed to the indirect impact of Z on Y via D.

This idea has been utilized by Thistlethwaite and Campbell (1960) to estimate the effect of receiving a National Merit Award on subsequent career aspirations. Since the Award is only granted if a test score Z exceeds a certain threshold z_0, the treatment status D (Award granted: $D = 1$, not granted: $D = 0$) depends in a discontinuous way on the test score Z. Let Y^1 and Y^0 denote the corresponding potential outcomes. Certainly the test score Z influences not only D but also affects the potential outcomes directly. Hence Z is not a proper instrumental variable, since the exclusion restriction is not satisfied. Nevertheless, in a small neighbourhood around the discontinuity at z_0, the direct impact of Z on the potential outcomes is likely to vary only a little with Z. Hence *locally* the instrumental variable assumptions (exclusion restriction, monotonicity) are satisfied, and the difference between the mean outcome for individuals just above the threshold z_0 and the mean outcome for individuals just below the threshold represents the causal effect $E[Y^1 - Y^0|Z = z_0]$. Again, this is a kind of local average treatment effect since it is identified only for the subpopulation of individuals with test score equal to z_0.

In the above example programme participation status $D = 1(Z > z_0)$ is a deterministic function of Z, which is also called a *sharp design* (Trochim 1984) since *all* individuals change programme participation status exactly at z_0. This requires a strictly rule-based programme selection process (such as age limits or other eligibility criteria). For example, Hahn, Todd, and van der Klaauw (1999) analyze the effect of antidiscrimination laws on the employment of minority workers by exploiting the fact that only firms with more than 15 employees are subject to these antidis-crimination laws.

Often, however, the participation decision is not completely determined by Z, even in a rule-based selection process. Case workers may have some discretion about whom they offer a programme, or they may base their decision also on criteria that are unobserved to the econometrician. Additionally, individuals offered a programme may decline participation. In this *fuzzy design* not all individuals would change programme participation status from $D = 0$ to $D = 1$ if Z were increased from $z_0 - \varepsilon$ to $z_0 + \varepsilon$. Rather, the relation between Z and D may be discontinuous at z_0 only on average. In the fuzzy design the *expected* value of D given Z (which is the probability of treatment receipt) is supposed to be discontinuous at z_0:

$$\lim_{\varepsilon \to 0} E\left[D|Z = z_0 + \varepsilon\right] \neq \lim_{\varepsilon \to 0} E\left[D|Z = z_0 - \varepsilon\right]. \tag{2.23}$$

For example, van der Klaauw (2002) analyses the effect of financial aid offers to college applicants on their probability of subsequent enrollment. College applicants are ranked according to their test score achievements into a small number of categories. The amount of financial aid offered depends largely on this classification. Yet, the financial aid officer also takes other characteristics into account, which are not observed by the econometrician. Hence the treatment assignment is not a deterministic function of the test score Z, but the conditional expectation function $E[D|Z]$ displays jumps because of the test-score rule.[15]

Hahn, Todd, and van der Klaauw (2001) analyze nonparametric identification in the case of a fuzzy regression-discontinuity design, where $D \in \{0, 1\}$ is a random function of Z but $E[D|Z]$ is discontinuous at z_0.[16] Since Z may also influence the potential outcomes directly, the treatment effect is not identified without further assumptions. Supposing that the direct influence of Z on the potential outcomes is continuous, the potential outcomes change little when Z is varied within a small neighbourhood. Under a localized version of the unconfounded-participation-type assumption, the exclusion restriction and the monotonicity assumption (discussed in the previous section on instrumental variables identification), they show that the average treatment effect on the *local compliers* is identified as

$$\lim_{\varepsilon \to 0} E\left[Y^1 - Y^0 \,|D\,(Z = z_0 + \varepsilon) = 1, D\,(Z = z_0 - \varepsilon) = 0\right]$$

$$= \frac{\lim_{\varepsilon \to 0} E\left[Y|Z = z_0 + \varepsilon\right] - \lim_{\varepsilon \to 0} E\left[Y|Z = z_0 - \varepsilon\right]}{\lim_{\varepsilon \to 0} E\left[D|Z = z_0 + \varepsilon\right] - \lim_{\varepsilon \to 0} E\left[D|Z = z_0 - \varepsilon\right]}. \tag{2.24}$$

---

[15] Further applications of the regression-discontinuity approach include the effects of unem-ployment benefits on recidivism rates of prisoners (Berk and Rauma 1983), the effects of classroom size on students' test scores (Angrist and Lavy 1999), or parents' willingness to pay for higher quality schooling for their children (Black 1999), among others.

[16] Obviously, this includes the sharp design as a special case.

The *local compliers* is the group of individuals whose Z value lies in a small neighbourhood of z_0 and whose treatment status D would change from 0 to 1 if Z were changed exogenously from $z_0 - \varepsilon$ to $z_0 + \varepsilon$. As a special case, in the sharp design all individuals are locally compliers and change their treatment status at z_0. Thus the denominator of (2.24) would be 1.

The regression-discontinuity approach permits identification of a treatment effect under weak conditions. In particular a type of instrumental variable assumption needs to hold only *locally*. On the other hand, the average treatment effect is identified only for the local compliers. And due to its local nature of identification, no $\sqrt{n}$-consistent estimator can exist for estimating it.

Bounds In evaluation settings where none of the above outlined identification strategies is feasible, it might still be possible to estimate intervals wherein the average treatment effects lie. Such bounds on the treatment effects have been derived by Manski (1989, 1990, 1997) in a series of papers. Consider the simplest case where no further information is available except that the outcome variables Y^r and Y^s have bounded support: $Y^r \in [\underline{Y}, \bar{Y}]$, $Y^s \in [\underline{Y}, \bar{Y}]$. With these bounds on the support of Y^r, the expected outcome of Y^r is bounded to lie in the interval

$$E[Y^r] = E[Y^r|D = r] \cdot P_{D=r} + E[Y^r|D \neq r] \cdot P_{D\neq r}$$
$$\in \left[E[Y^r|D = r] P_{D=r} + P_{D\neq r}\underline{Y} , E[Y^r|D = r] P_{D=r} + P_{D\neq r}\bar{Y} \right],$$

where $P_{D=r} = P(D = r)$ is shorthand notation for the size of the subpopulation participating in programme r. The width of this interval decreases with $P(D = r)$ since the expected outcome is only identified in this subpopulation. Using an analogous argument for $E[Y^s]$, the average treatment effect $E[Y^r - Y^s]$ can be bounded to lie in the interval

$$E[Y^r - Y^s] \in [\, E[Y^r|D = r] P_{D=r} - E[Y^s|D = s] P_{D=s} + P_{D\neq r}\underline{Y} - P_{D\neq s}\bar{Y},$$
$$E[Y^r|D = r] P_{D=r} - E[Y^s|D = s] P_{D=s} + P_{D\neq r}\bar{Y} - P_{D\neq s}\underline{Y} \,].$$

The width of this interval is

$$(\bar{Y}\text{-}\underline{Y}) \left(P(D \neq r) + P(D \neq s) \right)$$
$$= (\bar{Y}\text{-}\underline{Y}) \left(2 - P(D = r) - P(D = s) \right)$$

and narrows for larger probabilities to participate in programme r or s. However, even in the binary treatment case, where $P(D = r) + P(D = s) = 1$, the interval width is $(\bar{Y}\text{-}\underline{Y})$ and a zero treatment effect cannot be ruled out. Hence without further assumptions, such as monotonous instrumental variables as in Manski (1997) or Manski and Pepper (2000), these bounds on the treatment effects provide only limited information.

2.1.5 Estimation of Mean Counterfactual Outcomes

After a proper identification strategy has been established, the treatment effects of interest can be estimated. Although identification is the fundamental and crucial task in programme evaluation, the choice of an appropriate estimator can still make a difference. Keeping in mind that collection of informative and reliable data on participants and non-participants is often costly and time-consuming, an estimator should be chosen which uses the available information in an efficient way. This seems to be particularly important in programme evaluation where the interpretation and the consequences of evaluation studies often hinge on whether a programme effect is estimated as statistically significant or not. Even in the case where two estimators generate the same point estimates, the interpretation of these estimates depends on their variability, such that the estimate according to the more precise estimator is more likely to be statistically significant. Since insignificant programme effects are often interpreted as 'no effect', the choice of the estimator affects ceteris paribus the odds of the evaluation study's conclusions.

An important element in the estimation of programme effects is the conditional expected potential outcome Y^s weighted by the distribution of X among the participants in programme r

$$(EY)_{s|r} = \int E[Y^s|X = x, D = s] \cdot f_{X|D=r}(x)dx. \tag{2.25}$$

Under the control-for-confounding-variables approach, the term (2.25) equals the average counterfactual outcome for the participants in programme r:

$$E[Y^s|D = r]$$

since

$$E[Y^s|D = r] = E[E[Y^s|X, D = s]|D = r].$$

The expression (2.25) represents the adjustment of the expected potential outcome Y^s for the distribution of the confounding variables among the participants in programme r. The estimation of (2.25) is the decisive part for the estimation of average treatment effects on the treated $E[Y^r - Y^s|D = r]$ since $E[Y^r|D = r]$ can be estimated simply by the sample mean of the participants in programme r.

The estimation of objects like (2.25) is also central to the estimation of average treatment effects $E[Y^r] - E[Y^s]$ and average treatment outcomes $E[Y^s]$ because $E[Y^s]$ can be written as

$$E[Y^s] = E[Y^s|D = s] \cdot P(D = s) + E[Y^s|D \neq s] \cdot P(D \neq s),$$

where $E[Y^s|D = s]$, $P(D = s)$ and $P(D \neq s)$ can be estimated by sample means. The estimation of the average counterfactual outcome

$$E[Y^s|D \neq s] = E[E[Y^s|X, D = s]|D \neq s] \tag{2.26}$$

$$= \int E[Y^s|X = x, D = s] \cdot f_{X|D \neq s}(x)dx$$

proceeds by weighting the conditional expectation function $E[Y^s|X]$ by the density $f_{X|D \neq s}$, i.e. by the density of X among the population not participating in programme s. This is analogous to (2.25) with $f_{X|D=r}$ replaced by the density function

$f_{X|D\neq s}$. Such estimates of average counterfactual outcomes (2.26) are also key elements in the semiparametric treatment choice estimator developed in Chapter 4.

In addition, also the difference-in-difference or predictable-bias approach, discussed above, relies on weighting conditional expectation functions by density functions of other subpopulations to estimate the selection bias in different periods. In particular, estimates of $\int E\left[Y_t^0|X = x, D = 0\right] f_{X|D=r}(x)dx$ and $\int E\left[Y_\tau|X = x, D = 0\right] f_{X|D=r}(x)dx$ are required in (2.12). Thus the estimation of objects like (2.25) forms a crucial building block for many programme evaluation estimators. In the remainder of this chapter, various nonparametric estimators of (2.25) and their asymptotic properties are discussed. In Chapter 3 the finite-sample properties of these *covariate-distribution adjustment* estimators are investigated and recommendations for their use developed.

The general framework for nonparametric covariate-distribution adjustment can be characterized as follows: Data on an outcome variable Y^s and covariates X are sampled randomly from a 'source' population (e.g. the participants in programme s). In addition, a second sample, drawn from a 'target' population (e.g. the participants in programme r), is available, which contains only information on the covariates X but not on their potential outcome variable Y^s. Denote the observations sampled from the source population by $\{(Y_{si}, X_{si})\}_{i=1}^{n_s}$, with $f_s(x)$ the density of X_{si}. Denote the sample drawn from the target population by $\{X_{rj}\}_{j=1}^{n_r}$, with density function f_r. Suppose further that the support of X in the target population is a subset of the support of X in the source population, to ensure that the conditional expectation function in the source population is identified at every X_{rj}.[17] This is a shorthand notation for the sample of participants in programme s: $\{(Y_{si}, X_{si})\}_{i=1}^{n_s} \equiv \{(Y_i^s, X_i)|D_i = s\}_{i=1}^n$ and the sample of participants in programme r: $\{X_{rj}\}_{j=1}^{n_r} \equiv \{X_i|D_i = r\}_{i=1}^n$, where $f_s \equiv f_{X|D=s}$ and $f_r \equiv f_{X|D=r}$ and n_s and n_r are the number of observed participants in programme s and programme r, respectively. (For the estimation of average counterfactual outcomes (2.26) the target population needs to be redefined correspondingly such that the target sample $\{X_{rj}\}_{j=1}^{n_r}$ represents all observations that participated in any programme except s.) Nonparametric covariate-distribution adjustment proceeds by weighting the conditional expectation function $E[Y^s|X]$ in the source population by the density f_r in the target population.

Generalized Matching Estimators A class of estimators of (2.25) is obtained by replacing the target distribution f_r by its empirical distribution function in the target sample and estimating nonparametrically the conditional expectation function $m_s(x) = E[Y^s|X = x, D = s]$ from the source sample. This yields the *generalized matching estimator*

$$\frac{1}{n_r}\sum_{j=1}^{n_r}\hat{m}_s\left(X_{rj}\right), \tag{2.27}$$

---

[17] Estimation of the common support is discussed in Heckman, Ichimura, and Todd (1998), Lechner (2002b) and in Chapter 4.

where $\hat{m}_s(x)$ is an estimate of $m_s(x)$. This estimator adjusts the conditional expected outcome for the distribution of X in the target population by evaluating and averaging $m_s(x)$ only at the values X_{rj} that are observed in the target sample. A variety of estimators to estimate $m_s(X_{rj})$ from the source sample $\{Y_{si}, X_{si}\}_{i=1}^{n_s}$ have been suggested:

A simple and common method to implement the estimator (2.27) is based on *pair-matching* (Rubin 1974). Pair-matching proceeds by finding for each observation of the target sample an observation of the source sample with identical (or very similar) covariates X. These 'matched' source sample observations mirror the covariate distribution of the target sample and their average outcome provides an estimate of (2.25). In other words, pair-matching estimates $\hat{m}_s(X_{rj})$ by the observed outcome Y_{si} of that source sample observation i which is most similar in its covariates X_{si} to X_{rj}. Building on this idea, alternative estimators estimate $\hat{m}_s(X_{rj})$ by a weighted mean of the observed outcomes of those source sample observations that are similar to X_{rj}, and accordingly (2.27) is called a generalized matching estimator.

Whereas pair-matching assigns zero weights to all observations except the closest observation to X_{rj}, parametric regression-based matching estimators use all observations of the source sample regardless of their similarity to X_{rj}. In particular, least squares regression estimates $\hat{m}_s(x)$ as $x'\hat{\beta}$ with $\hat{\beta} = (\mathbf{X}_s'\mathbf{X}_s)^{-1}(\mathbf{X}_s'\mathbf{Y}_s)$, where $\mathbf{X}_s$ is the matrix of all X_{si}' and $\mathbf{Y}_s$ is the column vector containing all Y_{si}. Hence the imputed value at X_{rj} is $\hat{m}_s(X_{rj}) = X_{rj}'\hat{\beta}$ and the *least squares matching* estimator of (2.25) is

$$\bar{X}_r'(\mathbf{X}_s'\mathbf{X}_s)^{-1}(\mathbf{X}_s'\mathbf{Y}_s), \tag{2.28}$$

where $\bar{X}_r = \frac{1}{n_r}\sum X_{rj}$ is the average of the covariates in the target sample.

In between these two extremes, pair-matching and least squares matching, exist a variety of nonparametric estimators of $m_s(X_{rj})$, which take account only of the source sample observations that lie in a neighbourhood of X_{rj} and downweight observations according to their dissimilarity to X_{rj}. These include k-nearest neighbours and local polynomial regression, which lead to the *k-NN matching* and the *local polynomial matching* estimator, respectively. Consistency of the matching estimator requires consistent estimation of $m_s(x)$, which in turn requires that the local neighbourhood of X_{rj} shrinks with increasing sample size. Hence the least squares matching estimator is in general inconsistent, whereas pair-matching and k-NN matching and local polynomial matching with an appropriately chosen bandwidth value are consistent (see Section 2.3). Thus in principle, implementation of the generalized matching estimator is straightforward by choosing a consistent nonparametric regression estimator and averaging the imputed values $\hat{m}_s(X_{rj})$ for the target observations.

In practice, however, nonparametric covariate-distribution adjustment often needs to be performed with respect to a high-dimensional X vector. For example, in the control-for-confounding-variables approach, X includes all variables that affect the participation decision and the potential outcome. Nonparametric estimation of the regression function $m_s(x) = E[Y^s|X = x, D = s]$ becomes then rather difficult since the convergence rate of nonparametric regression estimators decreases with the number of (continuous) covariates (Stone 1980). Pair-matching, for example, would require to find for each target sample observation a source sample observation which is identical (or very similar) in all characteristics. To circumvent this dimensionality problem, similarity between observations is often measured through a multivariate distance metric, which maps the mismatch in the characteristics onto the real line. One such metric is the Mahalanobis distance $\langle \cdot, \cdot \rangle_M$, which weights the distance in the covariates by the inverse of their variance matrix

$$\langle X_{si}, X_{rj} \rangle_M = (X_{si} - X_{rj})' \left[\widehat{Var}(X) \right]^{-1} (X_{si} - X_{rj}),$$

where $\widehat{Var}(X)$ is an estimate of the variance of X in the source or the target population or a weighted average of these. Pair-matching on the Mahalanobis distance proceeds by finding for each target sample observation X_{rj} the source sample observation with the smallest distance $\langle X_{si}, X_{rj} \rangle_M$.

The Propensity Score However the choice of a distance metric (such as the Mahalanobis distance) to reduce the dimensionality is rather ad-hoc. Besides the fact that a different distance metric might have produced rather different results, it is not even guaranteed that the estimate is consistent. Nevertheless, a distance metric based on the balancing score property of the propensity score has favourable theoretical properties. For the case of binary treatment evaluation ($R = 2$), Rosenbaum and Rubin (1983) showed that conditional independence (2.4) of programme selection and potential outcomes given X also implies independence conditional on the (one-dimensional) probability to participate in the programme given X, which they called the *propensity score*. Imbens (2000) and Lechner (2001a) generalized this result to the evaluation of multiple treatments ($R > 2$), where the appropriate propensity score is the probability to participate in treatment s for an individual who participates either in treatment r or s and has characteristics X.

Suppose that the potential outcome Y^s conditional on X is identically distributed in source and target population

$$Y^s \perp\!\!\!\perp D \,|\, X, D \in \{r, s\}, \tag{2.29}$$

which is a slightly weaker version of the conditional independence assumption (2.4). Define the (one-dimensional) propensity score $p^{s|rs}(x)$ as the probability of belonging to the target population instead of belonging to the source population

$$p^{s|rs}(x) = P(D = s | X = x, D \in \{r, s\}) = \frac{p^s(x)}{p^r(x) + p^s(x)}, \tag{2.30}$$

where $p^r(x) = P(D = r|X = x)$ and $p^s(x) = P(D = s|X = x)$. Then, as shown by Lechner (2001a), conditional independence on X implies conditional independence on the propensity score $p^{s|rs}$

$$\Longrightarrow Y^s \perp\!\!\!\perp D \,|p^{s|rs}(X), D \in \{r, s\}. \tag{2.31}$$

Proof. The proof is adopted from Lechner (2001a). Since conditional independence in (2.31) is required only with respect to the subpopulations r and s, the participation indicator $D \in \{r, s\}$ is binary and all that needs to be shown is that

$$P\left(D = s \,|Y^s, p^{s|rs}(X), D \in \{r, s\}\right) = P\left(D = s \,|p^{s|rs}(X), D \in \{r, s\}\right).$$

By the law of total probability and using (2.29):

$$P\left(D = s|Y^s, p^{s|rs}(X), D \in \{r, s\}\right)$$
$$= E\left[P\left(D = s|Y^s, X, D \in \{r, s\}\right) \,|Y^s, p^{s|rs}(X), D \in \{r, s\}\right]$$
$$= E\left[p^{s|rs}(X) \,|Y^s, p^{s|rs}(X), D \in \{r, s\}\right]$$
$$= p^{s|rs}(X)$$
$$= E\left[p^{s|rs}(X) \,|p^{s|rs}(X), D \in \{r, s\}\right]$$
$$= E\left[P\left(D = s|X, D \in \{r, s\}\right) \,|p^{s|rs}(X), D \in \{r, s\}\right]$$
$$= P\left(D = s|p^{s|rs}(X), D \in \{r, s\}\right).$$

The intuition behind (2.31) is that the propensity score balances the distribution of X in the source and the target population. In other words, conditional on $p^{s|rs}$ the distribution of X is identical in the source and the target population[18]

$$X \perp\!\!\!\perp D \,|p^{s|rs}(X), D \in \{r, s\}.$$

Although an observation of the source sample and an observation of the target sample with the same propensity score value $p^{s|rs}$ do not necessarily have the same X value (thus preventing the application of (2.29)), the probability that X equals a particular value is the same for both observations and the conditional independence assumption (2.29) can be invoked separately at every possible X value.

The validity of (2.31) implies that the counterfactual outcome $E\left[Y^s|D = r\right]$ can be estimated consistently by solely adjusting the distribution of the propensity score $p^{s|rs}$:

$$E[Y^s|D = r] = E\left[E\left[Y^s|p^{s|rs}(X), D = s\right]|D = r\right] \tag{2.32}$$
$$= \int E\left[Y^s|p^{s|rs}, D = s\right] \cdot f_{p^{s|rs}|D=r}(p^{s|rs}) \cdot dp^{s|rs},$$

where $f_{p^{s|rs}|D=r}$ is the distribution of the propensity score in the target population. Hence matching on the one-dimensional propensity score $p^{s|rs}$ instead on X

---

[18] This is a mechanical result because $D \in \{r, s\}$ is binary and thus $P(D = s|X, p^{s|rs}(X), D \in \{r, s\}) = p^{s|rs}(X)$.

gives a consistent estimator of the counterfactual mean (2.25). For example, if pair-matching is used, it suffices to find pairs of participants and non-participants that have the same propensity score. They no longer need to be identical on all X covariates.

An analogous relationship holds for the estimation of the counterfactual mean $E[Y^s|D \neq s]$ (2.26) where the target population consists of all subpopulations which do not participate in programme s. The appropriate propensity score is $p^s(x)$ since $P(D = s|X = x) + P(D \neq s|X = x)$ add up to one in (2.30), and consequently a propensity score matching estimator based on p^s

$$E[Y^s|D \neq s] = E[E[Y^s|p^s(X), D = s]|D \neq s]$$
$$= \int E[Y^s|p^s, D = s] \cdot f_{p^s|D \neq s}(p^s) \cdot dp^s$$

is consistent.

Remarkably, propensity score matching can even be used for estimating (2.25) in situations where the conditional independence assumption is not valid. The equality of propensity score matching and matching on X

$$\int E[Y^s|X = x, D = s] \cdot f_{X|D=r}(x)dx$$
$$= \int E\left[Y^s|p^{s|rs}, D = s\right] \cdot f_{p^{s|rs}|D=r}(p^{s|rs}) \cdot dp^{s|rs} \quad (2.33)$$

is a mechanical result of the balancing property of the propensity score and independent of any properties of the potential outcomes. This equivalence has not been recognized in the evaluation literature and is proven in Appendix A. As a consequence, propensity score matching can also be used in the difference-in-difference or predictable-bias evaluation approach, which is often pursued when the conditional independence assumption appears to be controversial. Hence $E[E[Y_t^0 - Y_\tau|X, D = 0]|D = r]$ in (2.12) can be estimated by propensity score matching as

$$E\left[E\left[Y_t^0 - Y_\tau|X, D = 0\right]|D = r\right]$$
$$= E\left[E\left[Y_t^0 - Y_\tau|p^{0|r0}(X), D = 0\right]|D = r\right]$$
$$= \int E\left[Y_t^0|p^{0|r0}(X), D = 0\right] \cdot f_{p^{0|r0}|D=r}(p^{0|r0}) \cdot dp^{0|r0}$$
$$- \int E\left[Y_\tau|p^{0|r0}(X), D = 0\right] \cdot f_{p^{0|r0}|D=r}(p^{0|r0}) \cdot dp^{0|r0},$$

where $p^{0|r0}$ is the appropriate propensity score. Notice that panel data is not required since the covariate adjustment can proceed separately for Y_t^0 and Y_τ.

Propensity score matching circumvents the dimensionality problem since the nonparametric regression needs to be performed only with respect to the one-dimensional propensity score and thus avoids the so-called 'curse of dimensionality'. For this reason, propensity score matching has been used in many applied evaluation studies, e.g. Brodaty, Crepon, and Fougere (2001), Dehejia and Wahba (1999), Frölich, Heshmati, and Lechner (2000a), Gerfin and Lechner (2002), Heckman, Ichimura, and Todd (1997), Heckman, Ichimura, Smith, and Todd (1998), Jalan and Ravallion (2002), Larsson (2000), Lechner (1999), Puhani (1999) etc. However, in most cases the propensity scores themselves are unknown and need to be estimated consistently. Parametric estimation of the propensity scores for the evaluation of multiple treatments is discussed in Lechner (2002a), who compares binary probit models, multinomial logit models and simulated multinomial probit models. Semiparametric estimation of the propensity score is analyzed in Todd (1999). Propensity score matching proceeds then with respect to the estimated propensity score.

Although matching on the propensity score balances the distribution of X in source and target sample and thus provides a consistent estimate of the counterfactual mean (2.25), it may not be the most precise estimator in finite samples, as the components of X might affect the propensity score $p^{s|rs}(x)$ and the conditional expectation function $m_s(x) = E[Y^s|X = x, D = s]$ to different degrees. Some covariates may affect strongly the conditional expectation $m_s(x)$ but have only little weight among the determinants of the participation probability $p^{s|rs}(x)$, whereas other covariates may be important determinants of $p^{s|rs}(x)$ but have little impact on $m_s(x)$. In this case, observations with a similar propensity score value are also likely to be similar with respect to the latter covariates, but may not be so with respect to the former covariates, since their influence on $p^{s|rs}$ is small. Hence observations with identical propensity score values may be very dissimilar with respect to the main determinants of $m_s(x)$. However, as the main purpose of matching is to balance particularly the covariates that are highly influential on the potential outcome, conditioning on the propensity score may not be the most efficient method in finite samples. To achieve a balancing of the relevant variables in finite samples, matching on the principal covariates determining $m_s(x)$ or on the propensity score and a subset of covariates might be more appropriate. The latter refers to the *augmented propensity score* approach, where matching proceeds on a vector $(p^{s|rs}, \tilde{X})$ consisting of the propensity score $p^{s|rs}$ and a subset of covariates $\tilde{X}$, which are important determinants of $m_s(x)$ but might be 'under-represented' in $p^{s|rs}$. For example, in the evaluation of active labour market programmes, it might occur that programme assignment decisions are largely driven by the employment offices' case workers whereas subsequent labour market programmes depend mainly on individual characteristics. The use of the augmented propensity score has already been suggested by Rosenbaum and Rubin (1983) in their analysis of balancing scores that are 'finer' than the propensity score. All the above discussed balancing properties hold as well with the augmented propensity score, as can easily be seen by repeating the proof. The augmented propensity score has, for example, been used in Lechner (1999), with respect to time-varying and time-invariant covariates, and in Lechner (2002a), where he compares propensity score matching on $p^{s|rs}(x)$ to matching on $(p^s(x), p^r(x))$.[19]

The Re-weighting Estimator An alternative estimation strategy to adjust for the differences in the covariate composition among source and target population relies on weighting the observed outcomes by the density ratio of X, which is considered in Horvitz and Thompson (1952), Imbens (2000), Hirano, Imbens, and Ridder (2000) and Ichimura and Linton (2001). Since observations (Y^s, X) at X locations where the density $f_s(x)$ in the source population is large are relatively over-represented and observations where $f_s(x)$ is small are relatively under-represented, a weighted average of Y^s should downweight the former observations and upweight the latter observations by the ratio f_r/f_s of the density of X in the target and the source population. Rewriting the object of interest (2.25) as

$$\int E\left[Y^s|X = x, D = s\right] \cdot f_r(x)dx = \int E\left[Y^s|X = x, D = s\right] \cdot \frac{f_r(x)}{f_s(x)} f_s(x)dx$$

$$= E\left[Y^s \frac{f_r(X)}{f_s(X)} \,|D = s\right]$$

suggests the *re-weighting estimator*

$$\frac{1}{n_s}\sum_{i=1}^{n_s} Y_{si} \cdot \frac{\hat{f}_r(X_{si})}{\hat{f}_s(X_{si})} \tag{2.34}$$

as an alternative estimator of (2.25), where the covariate densities f_s and f_r can be estimated from the source and the target sample, respectively. By multiplying the observations Y^s of the source sample with the density ratio f_r/f_s the estimator rectifies the relative over/under-representation of source sample observations at large/small values of f_s.

The re-weighting estimator can also be written in terms of the propensity score by noting that the propensity score ratio equals the density ratio times the size ratio of the subpopulations:[20]

$$\frac{p^{s|rs}(X)}{1 - p^{s|rs}(X)} = \frac{f_s(X)}{f_r(X)} \frac{P(D = s)}{P(D = r)}. \tag{2.35}$$

The relative size of the source population to the target population, $P(D = s)/P(D = r)$, can be consistently estimated by n_s/n_r if sampling from the source

---

[19] Conditioning on $(p^s(x), p^r(x))$ is 'finer' than conditioning on $p^{s|rs}(x)$, since $p^{s|rs} = p^s/(p^s + p^r)$.

[20] Proof: By Bayes' theorem $P(D = r|X) = f_{X|D=r}(X)P(D = r)/f_X(X)$. Hence $p^{s|rs}(x) = \frac{p^s(x)}{p^r(x)+p^s(x)} = \frac{f_{X|D=s}(X)P(D=s)}{f_{X|D=r}(X)P(D=r)+f_{X|D=s}(X)P(D=s)}$ and $\frac{p^{s|rs}(x)}{1-p^{s|rs}(x)} = \frac{f_{X|D=s}(X)P(D=s)}{f_{X|D=r}(X)P(D=r)}$.

and the target population was done with the same probability. Accordingly (2.25) can also be expressed as

$$\int E\left[Y^s | X = x, D = s\right] \cdot f_r(x) dx = E\left[Y^s \cdot \frac{1 - p^{s|rs}(X)}{p^{s|rs}(X)} \frac{P(D = s)}{P(D = r)} | D = s\right],$$

and estimated as

$$\frac{1}{n_s} \sum_{i=1}^{n_s} Y_{si} \cdot \frac{1 - p^{s|rs}(X_{si})}{p^{s|rs}(X_{si})} \frac{n_s}{n_r} = \frac{1}{n_r} \sum_{i=1}^{n_s} Y_{si} \cdot \frac{1 - p^{s|rs}(X_{si})}{p^{s|rs}(X_{si})}. \qquad (2.36)$$

Again the conditional independence assumption (2.4) is not needed to justify using the propensity score for consistent estimation of (2.25).[21]

Asymptotic Properties of Treatment Effect Estimators   The asymptotic properties of the generalized matching estimator and the re-weighting estimator have been studied in the binary treatment framework ($R = 2$) by Hahn (1998), Heckman, Ichimura, and Todd (1998), Hirano, Imbens, and Ridder (2000), Ichimura and Linton (2001) and Abadie and Imbens (2001) under the conditional independence assumption (2.4). Hahn (1998) derived the $\sqrt{n}$-semiparametric variance bounds for nonparametric estimation of the average treatment effect and the average treatment effect on the treated. Adopted to the multiple treatment framework, the variance bound for estimating the expected potential outcome $E[Y^s]$ is

$$\frac{1}{n} \int \left(\frac{\sigma_s^2(x)}{p^s(x)} + (E[Y^s|X = x] - E[Y^s])^2 \right) f_X(x) dx$$

$$= \frac{1}{n} \left(\int \frac{\sigma_s^2(x)}{P^s} \frac{f_X^2(x)}{f_s^2(x)} f_s(x) dx + \int (E[Y^s|X = x] - E[Y^s])^2 f_X(x) dx \right)$$

$$= \frac{1}{n} \left(\frac{1}{P^s} \mathop{E}_{f_s(x)} \left[\sigma_s^2(x) \frac{f_X^2(x)}{f_s^2(x)} \right] + \mathop{Var}_{f(x)} E[Y^s|X] \right),$$

and for estimating the average treatment effect $E[Y^r - Y^s]$ is

$$\frac{1}{n} \int \left(\frac{\sigma_r^2(x)}{p^r(x)} + \frac{\sigma_s^2(x)}{p^s(x)} + (E[Y^r - Y^s|X = x] - E[Y^r - Y^s])^2 \right) f_X(x) dx$$

$$(2.37)$$

$$= \frac{1}{n} \left(\frac{1}{P^s} \mathop{E}_{f_s(x)} \left[\sigma_s^2(X) \frac{f_X^2(X)}{f_s^2(X)} \right] + \frac{1}{P^r} \mathop{E}_{f_r(x)} \left[\sigma_r^2(X) \frac{f_X^2(X)}{f_r^2(X)} \right] + \mathop{Var}_{f(x)} E[Y^r - Y^s|X] \right)$$

---

[21] Notice that in the literature the re-weighting estimator (2.36) is usually expressed by using $p^{r|rs}$ instead of $p^{s|rs}$, i.e. as $n_r^{-1} \sum Y_{si} \cdot p^{r|rs}(X_{si}) / (1 - p^{r|rs}(X_{si}))$ which equals $n_1^{-1} \sum Y_i (1 - D_i) p(X_i) / (1 - p(X_i))$ in the binary treatment case, e.g. in Imbens (2000).

where $P^s = P(D = s)$ and $\sigma_s^2(x) = Var(Y^s|X = x)$.

For estimating the mean counterfactual outcome $E[Y^s|D = r]$ and the average treatment effect on the treated $E[Y^r - Y^s|D = r]$ only the observations on the participants in programme r and programme s are used. The observations on the participants in the other programmes are not informative, neither for the estimation of $E[Y^s|X = x, D = s]$ nor for the estimation of the distribution of X in the subpopulation of participants in programme r (Programme-r-subpopulation). Hence observations with $D \notin \{r, s\}$ are irrelevant. (See also the discussion below on the value of the propensity score.) Consequently, the normalizing factor for the asymptotic variance is $\frac{1}{n_r + n_s}$ instead of $\frac{1}{n}$.

The variance bound for estimating the mean counterfactual outcome $E[Y^s|D = r]$ is

$$\frac{1}{n_r + n_s} \int \left(\frac{\sigma_s^2(x) p^{r|rs^2}(x)}{P^{r|rs^2} p^{s|rs}(x)} + \frac{p^{r|rs}(x)}{P^{r|rs^2}} \left(E[Y^s|X = x] - E[Y^s|D = r]\right)^2 \right) f_{rs}(x) dx \tag{2.38}$$

$$= \frac{1}{n_r + n_s} \left(\int \frac{\sigma_s^2(x)}{P^{s|rs}} \frac{f_r^2(x)}{f_s(x)} dx + \int \frac{f_r(x)}{P^{r|rs}} \left(E[Y^s|X = x] - E[Y^s|D = r]\right)^2 dx \right)$$

$$= \frac{1}{n_r + n_s} \frac{1}{P^{r|rs}} \left(\frac{P^r}{P^s} \underset{f_s(x)}{E} \left[\sigma_s^2(X) \frac{f_r^2(X)}{f_s^2(X)} \right] + \underset{f_r(x)}{Var} E[Y^s|X] \right)$$

where $P^{r|rs} = P(D = r|D \in \{r, s\})$ and $f_{rs}(x)$ is the density of X in the union of the programme-r- and programme-s-subpopulations with $f_{rs}(x) = f_r(x)P^{r|rs} + f_s(x)P^{s|rs}$ and $p^{r|rs}(x) = f_r(x)P^{r|rs}/f_{rs}(x)$.[22] The variance bound of the average treatment effect on the treated $E[Y^r - Y^s|D = r]$ is

$$\frac{1}{n_r + n_s} \int \left(\begin{array}{c} \frac{\sigma_r^2(x) p^{r|rs}(x)}{P^{r|rs^2}} + \frac{\sigma_s^2(x) p^{r|rs^2}(x)}{P^{r|rs^2} p^{s|rs}(x)} \\ + \frac{p^{r|rs}(x)}{P^{r|rs^2}} \left(E[Y^r - Y^s|X = x] - E[Y^r - Y^s|D = r]\right)^2 \end{array} \right) f_{rs}(x) dx \tag{2.39}$$

$$= \frac{1}{n_r + n_s} \frac{1}{P^{r|rs}} \left(\underset{f_r(x)}{E} \left[\sigma_r^2(X) \right] + \frac{P^r}{P^s} \underset{f_s(x)}{E} \left[\sigma_s^2(X) \frac{f_r^2(X)}{f_s^2(X)} \right] + \underset{f_r(x)}{Var} E[Y^r - Y^s|X] \right).$$

A remarkable result of Hahn (1998) is that a projection on the propensity score (i.e. matching on the propensity score) does not change the variance bound and that knowledge of the true propensity score is not informative for estimating average treatment effects. The variance bound (2.37) is the same regardless of whether the propensity score is known. Hence asymptotically the propensity score does not

---

[22] Because $\frac{f_r(x)P^{r|rs}}{f_{rs}(x)} = \frac{f_r(x)P(D=r)/(P(D=r)+P(D=s))}{f_r(x)P^{r|rs}+f_s(x)P^{s|rs}} = \frac{f_r(x)P(D=r)}{f_r(x)P(D=r)+f_s(x)P(D=s)} =$
$\frac{f_r(x)P(D=r)}{f_r(x)P(D=r)+f_s(x)P(D=s)} = \frac{p^r(x)}{p^r(x)+p^s(x)} = p^{r|rs}(x)$.

lead to any reduction in dimensionality. However, the variance bound (2.39) of the average treatment effect on the treated changes when the true propensity score is known. Hahn (1998) attributes this to the 'dimension reduction' property of the propensity score. In my opinion this interpretation is highly misleading. I rather argue that the only value of knowing the true propensity score is that the observed X values of individuals who participated in other programmes than r can be used to improve the estimation of the density $f_{X|D=r}(x)$ among the programme-r-participants.

If the propensity score would indeed contribute to reducing the dimensionality of the estimation problem, it should also help to estimate potential outcomes $E[Y^s]$ and average treatment effects $E[Y^r - Y^s]$ more precisely. On the other hand, the propensity score provides information about the ratio of the density in the source and the target population and thus allows source observations to identify the density of X in the target population and vice versa. Consider the binary treatment case with $r = 1$ (treated participants) and $s = 0$ (non-participants). The (Y, X) observations of the treated sample are informative for estimating $E[Y^1|X]$, whereas the (Y, X) observations of the non-participant sample are informative for estimating $E[Y^0|X]$. Since the joint distribution of Y^1, Y^0 is not identified, the observations of the treated sample cannot assist in estimating $E[Y^0|X]$ and vice versa. The X observations of both samples are useful for estimating the distribution function of X in the population. With this information the average treatment effect can be estimated by weighting the estimates of $E[Y^1|X]$ and $E[Y^0|X]$ by the distribution of X in the population. Knowledge of the propensity score is of no use. Now consider the estimation of the average treatment effect on the treated $E[Y^1 - Y^0|D = 1]$ or of the counterfactual outcome $E[Y^0|D = 1]$. Again the (Y, X) observations of both samples identify the conditional expectation functions separately. These conditional expectation functions are weighted by the distribution of X among the treated, which can be estimated by the empirical distribution function of X in the treated sample. The non-participant observations are not informative for estimating the distribution of X among the treated. However, if the relationship between the distribution of X among the treated and the distribution of X among the non-participants were known, the X observations of the non-participants would be useful for estimating the distribution of X among the treated. Since the propensity score ratio equals the density ratio times the size ratio of the subpopulations (2.35), and since the relative size of the treated subpopulation $P(D = 1)$ can be estimated precisely, both the treated and the non-participant observations can be used to estimate $f_{X|D=1}$ if the propensity score is known. Consider a simple example: In the case of random assignment with $p^1(x) = 0.5$ for all x, the distribution of X is the same among the treated and the non-participants, and using only the treated observations to estimate $f_{X|D=1}$ would neglect half of the informative observations. With knowledge of the propensity score the counterfactual outcome $E[Y^0|D = 1]$ is identified as

$$E\left[Y^0|D=1\right] = \int E\left[Y^0|X=x, D=0\right]\cdot f_{X|D=1}(x)dx \qquad (2.40)$$

$$= \frac{1}{P\left(D=1\right)}\int E\left[Y^0|X=x, D=0\right]p^1(x)\cdot f_X(x)dx$$

and could be estimated by the empirical moment estimator

$$\frac{\displaystyle\sum_{D_i\in\{0,1\}} \hat{m}_0\left(X_i\right)p^1\left(X_i\right)}{\displaystyle\sum_{D_i\in\{0,1\}} p^1\left(X_i\right)},$$

which uses the X observations of both the treated *and* the non-participants. This estimator is suggested by Hahn (1998, Proposition 7) and achieves the variance bound for known propensity score.

The value of knowing the propensity score for estimating the distribution function $f_{X|D=1}$ becomes even more obvious when rewriting (2.40) as

$$E\left[Y^0|D=1\right] = \int E\left[Y^0|X=x, D=0\right]\cdot f_{X|D=1}(x)dx$$

$$= \frac{P\left(D=0\right)}{P\left(D=1\right)}\int E\left[Y^0|X=x, D=0\right]\frac{p^1(x)}{1-p^1(x)}\cdot f_{X|D=0}(x)dx,$$

if $p^1(x)\neq 1\ \forall x$. This suggests the empirical moment estimator

$$\frac{\displaystyle\sum_{D_i=0} \hat{m}_0\left(X_i\right)\frac{p^1(X_i)}{1-p^1(X_i)}}{\displaystyle\sum_{D_i=0} \frac{p^1(X_i)}{1-p^1(X_i)}},$$

which uses *only* non-participant observations ($D_i = 0$) to estimate the counterfactual outcome for the treated. Hence with knowledge of the propensity score the counterfactual outcome $E[Y^0|D = 1]$ *for the treated* could be estimated nonparametrically even without a single treated observation!

In the case of multiple treatment evaluation there are a variety of propensity scores. Knowledge of $p^{r|rs}$ would allow using the X observations of the s sample to improve the precision of estimating the distribution of X in the r subpopulation. Knowledge of $p^{r|rt}$ would allow using the X observations of a t sample for estimating $f_{X|D=r}(x)$. Knowledge of p^r would allow using all X observations to improve upon the estimation of $f_{X|D=r}(x)$. Hence, in the multiple treatment setting, the variance bound for the average treatment effect on the treated depends on which and how many propensity scores are known.

Besides deriving the efficiency bounds, Hahn (1998) further gives general conditions under which a generalized matching estimator based on a particular nonparametric series regression estimator attains both variance bounds (2.37) and (2.39).

Abadie and Imbens (2001) analyze the asymptotic efficiency of κ-nearest-neighbours matching estimators in estimating average treatment effects when κ is fixed, i.e. when the number of neighbours is fixed and does not grow with increasing sample size.[23] This includes the standard pair-matching estimator ($\kappa = 1$). They consider matching with respect to the X variables and show that 1) these estimators do not attain the variance bound (2.37) and, hence, are inefficient. 2) The bias term of the estimator is of order $O(n^{-2/c})$ where c is the number of continuous covariates. Consequently, if the number of continuous covariates is 4, the estimator is asymptotically biased. If the number of continuous covariates is even larger, the estimator does no longer converge at rate $\sqrt{n}$. 3) The bias term can be removed through re-centering. However, since re-centering leaves the variance term unchanged, the modified estimator is still inefficient.

Heckman, Ichimura, and Todd (1998) analyze local polynomial matching for the estimation of average treatment effects on the treated. They prove $\sqrt{n}$-consistency and asymptotic normality when matching with respect to X, with respect to the known propensity score or with respect to the estimated propensity score. The asymptotic distribution consists of a bias term and a variance term. The variance term equals (2.39) when matching with respect to X. When matching with respect to the known propensity score the variance term corresponds to (2.39) with X replaced by the propensity score and the density functions $f.(x)$ replaced by density functions with respect to the propensity score. Heckman, Ichimura, and Todd (1998) show that this variance term can be either larger or smaller than the variance when matching on X and conclude that neither matching on X nor matching on the propensity score necessarily dominates the other. (However, they ignore in their discussion the different bias terms.) This ambiguity holds also when the propensity score is estimated since the variance contribution due to estimating the propensity score may be small. This variance contribution of estimated-propensity-score matching is derived for a propensity score estimated parametrically or nonparametrically by local polynomial regression with a suitably chosen bandwidth value.

Hirano, Imbens, and Ridder (2000) analyzed the efficiency of the re-weighting estimator for estimating average treatment effects and average treatment effects on the treated. They show that re-weighting using a propensity score estimated by a particular series estimator attains the variance bounds (2.37) and (2.39).

Ichimura and Linton (2001) derived higher-order expansions for the re-weighting estimator. Including second-order terms in the analysis is relevant since the first-order approximations do not depend on the smoothing or bandwidth parameters used in the nonparametric first step, such that optimal bandwidth choice cannot be discussed with first-order asymptotics. (This is also found in the analysis of the generalized matching estimator in Section 3.) They consider estimation of the propensity score by local linear regression methods and show that the optimal bandwidth is of order $O(n^{-1/3})$ and $O(n^{-2/5})$ for a bias corrected version.

---

[23] Consistent estimation of $E[Y^r|X, D = r]$ would require $\kappa \to \infty$ as $n \to \infty$.

The analysis of the asymptotic properties of the evaluation estimators implied no firm recommendations on which estimator to use in practice. Generalized matching estimators as well as re-weighting estimators with estimated propensity scores can be efficient. Yet their small-sample properties have not been subject to extensive investigation and the previous asymptotic considerations may be of limited use to choose an adequate estimator. Although, from an asymptotic perspective, matching on the propensity score implies no reduction in dimensionality and there are no reasons why matching should not proceed with respect to X, propensity score matching can often be quite useful since "in practice inference for average treatment effects is often less sensitive to misspecification of the propensity score than to specifications of the conditional expectation of the potential outcomes" (Imbens 2000).[24] In Chapter 3 the finite sample properties of generalized matching estimators including pair-matching, least squares matching and various local polynomial matching estimators and the re-weighting estimators are examined. In addition, the bandwidth selection problem is investigated. In spite of the undecided conclusions resulting from the asymptotic considerations, it appears that some rather stable recommendations can be drawn for the choice of evaluation estimators in finite samples.

2.2 Optimal Treatment Choice

While the previous section focused on the estimation of average treatment effects as the basis for an overall assessment of a policy, e.g. in form of a cost-benefit analysis, this chapter discusses evaluation from the perspective of how individuals should be allocated to the available programmes to increase overall performance. Since the effectiveness of a policy depends not only on the treatments themselves but also on the allocation of the participants to these treatments (including the 'non-participation treatment'), improving the process of participant-to-programme selection might lead to substantial improvements in overall effectiveness. How easily these gains could be realized, however, depends on the heterogeneity of the individual treatment effects. If the treatment effects are identical for all individuals, the *optimal treatment* is the same for each individual and all individuals should participate in the programme with the highest expected potential outcome.[25] Yet if treatment response is heterogeneous, optimal treatment choices are likely to differ between individuals and the policy's effectiveness depends on the allocation of individuals to the programmes. A particular programme may be beneficial to some individuals but harmful to others. A negative average treatment effect is

---

[24] However, in specific situations, for instance if the outcome variable is bounded, nonparametric regression on X might work better than is widely thought, see Frölich (2001a).

[25] If general equilibrium effects influence the potential outcomes or if supply constraints limit the number of participants in certain programmes, it might be superior to allocate the individuals to a variety of programmes. However, which individuals are allocated to which programmes would be irrelevant.

not necessarily indicative of a deficient programme, but might be the result of an ineffective participant-to-programme selection. The estimation of average treatment effects for the full population and various subpopulations may be of little use to actually guide the selection of individuals to the programmes and to develop constructive advice for policy improvement. In addition a detailed analysis of individual effect heterogeneity is required.

However, most evaluation studies do not attempt to investigate heterogeneous response among individuals beyond broad subgroup analyses, where average effects are estimated separately for men/women or different age groups (Manski 2000b, 2001). For example, in Friedlander, Greenberg, and Robins's (1997) survey of the evaluation of social programmes, treatment effects are considered separately for women and men, different age groups and race, but no further disaggregation is considered. Nevertheless those studies that examine heterogeneous response usually find supporting evidence: Heckman, Smith, and Clements (1997) tested and rejected the constant treatment effect assumption for the Job-Training-Partnership-Act programme (JTPA, USA).[26] While beneficial to many participants, this programme seems to be harmful to other participants. Also Black, Smith, Berger, and Noel (1999), Gerfin and Lechner (2002) and Manski (2000b), among others, detected effect heterogeneity.

2.2.1 Definition of Optimal Treatment

To take full account of individual effect heterogeneity, optimal programme choice must be examined on an individual basis. If programme selection were fully de-centralized and all individuals self-selected into the programmes on the basis of rational expectations, an optimal allocation would emerge quite automatically. This is the basis of many economic models including the Roy (1951) model. Roy analyzed the determinants of union status and in his model individuals forecast their potential earnings in unionized and non-unionized sectors and select into the more opportune jobs. In many situations, however, the assumption that individuals form rational expectations about their potential outcomes appears rather strong. Furthermore, programme decisions are often also influenced by the case worker in charge, administrative directives or supply constraints.

Yet even if each individual knew his potential outcomes and could decide freely among the available programmes, an optimal allocation would only result if all benefits and costs would accrue to and be borne by the individuals themselves. Social policies, however, usually include a transfer component, e.g. in the form of publicly subsidized treatments. For example, active labour market programmes are commonly provided free of charge to the participants. Hence the outcome variable is at least two-dimensional, consisting of benefit and cost components. Furthermore the cost components contain as well direct costs of the programme as opportunity

---

[26] They simulated the joint probability distributions that are consistent with the observed marginal distributions of Y^0 and Y^1, attached equal probability to these distributions and tested the common effect assumption $Var[Y^1 - Y^0] = 0$.

costs, such as the time spent participating in the programme. The individuals and the policy administration value these costs differently according to who is bearing the cost. In addition, the case workers acting as agents of the policy administrator may interact in the programme selection decision and may follow to some extent their own preferences and interests. Thus there is often little reason to assume that the observed participant-programme allocation is indeed optimal and intervening to improve the selection process may be worthwhile.

Consider first the case of a one-dimensional outcome variable, i.e. containing only one benefit component but no cost component. Manski (2000a, b, 2001) examined optimal treatment choice from a normative perspective by analyzing how a benevolent central planner would allocate individuals to treatments. The planner would seek to allocate individuals to the treatments such that social welfare would be maximized. Since the planner can discriminate between individuals only on the basis of observable characteristics X, the programme allocation will be a mapping from X to the available treatments $\{0, .., R-1\}$. Manski shows that if the planner aims to maximize utilitarian welfare, the optimal treatment choice is assigning each individual to that programme that promises the largest expected potential outcome *conditional* on the individual's observed characteristics.[27] Since the conditional expected potential outcomes $E[Y^r|X]$ are unknown, the allocation rule must be based on estimates of $E[Y^r|X]$, which results in a statistical treatment selection rule. (For an earlier reference on statistical treatment rules see Wald (1950)).

To analyze optimality of particular statistical treatment rules, Manski (2000b) compares two polar rules: The unconditional and the conditional success rule. The unconditional success rule neglects covariate information and assigns all individuals to the treatment with the highest estimated average outcome $E[Y^r]$. The conditional success rule differentiates among individuals according to their covariates and assigns them to the treatment with highest conditional potential outcome $E[Y^r|X]$. Since in finite samples the conditional outcomes are less precisely estimated than the unconditional means, the conditional success rule entails the risk that due to large estimation error individuals might be allocated worse than if they had all been assigned to the same programme. However, Manski shows that even at quite small sample sizes the conditional success rule is superior to the unconditional rule if the outcome variable Y is bounded, and he suggests to use covariate information to its full extent.

Dehejia (2002) analyzed the individual's treatment choice problem in the binary treatment framework ($R = 2$) from a different perspective. In a Bayesian approach he modelled parametrically the uncertainty in the decision-making situation and looked for first-order stochastic dominance relationships between participation and non-participation, using the data of the GAIN experiment (Greater Avenues for Independence, USA). His approach, however, seems to be more difficult to extend to the multiple treatment case ($R > 2$) and to multidimensional outcome variables.

---

[27] In the case of supply constraints the situation becomes more complex. This is not further considered here, and it is assumed that the availability of a treatment does not depend on how many other individuals are allocated to this treatment.

Multidimensional outcome variables are relevant since most policies are envisaged to pursue multiple, usually conflicting goals, e.g. high benefit at low costs. In addition, similar outcomes may be valued differently. For example, re-employment on the basis of a permanent contract may be higher valued than re-employment on the basis of a fixed-term contract (Brodaty, Crepon, and Fougere 2001). To account for multiple goals the potential outcomes may be vectors $Y^r \in \Re^V$ consisting each of V different components, which may include besides economic and monetary indicators also health, social and psychological indicators. Let $u(\cdot) : \Re^V \mapsto \Re$ be a known utility function that maps the outcome space onto the real line. This utility function weights these different outcome components (including programme costs) according to the relative importance attached to the different policy goals (by the central planner).

To maximize the overall effectiveness of the policy, each individual should be allocated to that programme that yields the largest utility.[28] Since the idiosyncratic potential outcomes cannot be inferred for any particular individual, the statistical treatment rule should be based on the observed individual characteristics $X \in \Re^k$. Accordingly, to maximize the expected goals-weighted-utility, each individual with characteristics X_i should be allocated to his optimal programme $r^*(X_i)$ where

$$r^*(x) = \underset{r \in \{0,..,R-1\}}{\arg\max}\ E\left[u\left(Y^r\right)|X = x\right]. \tag{2.41}$$

This equals

$$r^*(x) = \underset{r \in \{0,..,R-1\}}{\arg\max}\ u\left(E[Y^r|X = x]\right), \tag{2.42}$$

if u is a linear utility function weighting the different policy goals. Hence the estimated optimal programme $\hat{r}^*(x)$ is the programme with the highest estimated, goals-weighted conditional potential outcome. The estimation of the potential outcomes $E[Y^r|X = x]$ proceeds separately for each $r \in \{0,..,R-1\}$, because the joint distribution of the potential outcome vectors $Y^0, .., Y^{R-1}$ is not identified.[29]

The estimation of the conditional expected potential outcomes $E[Y^r|X]$ for each individual is central for the derivation of individual optimal programme recommendations. These could be estimated from observations on past programme participants, provided that the relationship between the potential outcomes Y^r and X is still valid for future participants, i.e. that it did not change over time in a different way for different individuals. If experimental data were available the (nonparametric) estimation of $E[Y^r|X]$ would be straightforward. However, if former programme participants were not randomly assigned to the programmes,

---

[28] Implementing such an optimal allocation, i.e. enforcing compliance when policy goals and individuals' goals conflict, is another matter and not discussed here.

[29] In case the utility function is unknown except for the signs of its partial derivatives, optimal treatment choices cannot be inferred for all individuals. However, it may still be possible to derive for some x dominance relationships between programmes, for instance, by pairwise comparisons between programmes or for a subset of the outcome components.

selection bias has to be taken into account. To avoid selection bias Manski (1997) derives bounds on the individual treatment effects under weak assumptions such as monotonicity or concavity and shows that these bounds may in some cases be sufficiently informative to establish dominance relationships between certain treatments for a particular person. Nevertheless, in the case of multidimensional outcome variables, and with a variety of programmes to choose from (if $R > 2$), it is unlikely that informative bounds can be derived for many individuals.

As an alternative, $E[Y^r|X]$ could be identified by the conditional independence assumption (2.4) which, however, requires more informative data. In particular, all variables that affected the participation decision of the former participants and their potential outcomes must be included in X. This conditional independence assumption is also the basis of the existing statistical assignment systems.

2.2.2 Profiling and Targeting of Programmes in Practice

Statistically assisted programme assignment systems have been introduced in Australia, Canada, Netherlands and the USA to allocate unemployed persons to active labour market programmes such as job search assistance, training and employment programmes[30] and to assign welfare recipients to welfare-to-work programmes (Eberts 2002). These systems can broadly be categorized into targeting systems and profiling systems.

Targeting systems attempt to estimate treatment effects on an individual basis and assign each individual to the programme with the largest estimated treatment effect. The existing targeting systems, the Service and Outcome Measurement System (SOMS) in Canada and the Frontline Decision Support System (FDSS) in the USA, are rather simple, parametric models based on a single regression with a large number of variables and interaction terms. Although the application of fully parametric single regression techniques conceals the framework of potential outcomes, the approach is based on the identification of conditional expected potential outcomes by the conditional independence assumption as discussed in the previous section.

Profiling, on the other hand, is not based on a counterfactual analysis. Instead of estimating the individual potential outcomes for all available treatments, only the potential outcome for the 'non-participation' treatment is estimated. This estimated outcome is called a profiling score (or risk index) which indicates the 'urgency' for treatment, and the individuals with highest profiling scores receive the most intensive (expensive) programmes. In the context of active labour market programmes, profiling is often performed with respect to the probability of becoming long-term unemployed. The unemployed persons with longest expected unemployment durations are assigned with high priority to the more intensive labour market programmes. This already illustrates the difference between profiling and targeting. Whereas targeting would be based on estimates

---

[30] See OECD (1998), Colpitts (1999), de Koning (1999), DOL (1999), Black, Smith, Berger, and Noel (1999) and Eberts and O'Leary (1999).

of the expected unemployment duration in the case of non-participation *and* in the case of participation in the various programmes, profiling assigns individuals according to the expected unemployment duration in the case of non-participation only. Profiling is based on the claim that individuals with higher long-term unemployment risk are those who benefit most from more intensive programmes.

Hence profiling is an indirect method for selecting optimal treatments and rests on the assumption of a strong positive correlation between the profiling score and the individual treatment effects. Provided that such a close relationship between the profiling score and the treatment effects exists, profiling might be a convenient way to allocate participants if estimation of the profiling score is more precise than estimation of the potential outcomes. However, it is often rather unlikely that the treatment effect grows monotonously with the profiling score. For example, Black, Smith, Berger, and Noel (1999) and Berger, Black, and Smith (2001) find, in their analysis of the worker profiling system in the USA, that individuals in the middle ranges of the profiling score benefitted most from treatment. The treatment effect even became negative for unemployed persons with high long-term unemployment risk. Profiling is likely to perform even worse if a variety of different and heterogenous programmes ($R > 2$) is available and/or if a multidimensional outcome variable has to be taken into account. In the latter case it is unclear how these different outcome components, e.g. unemployment duration and programme costs, could be aggregated into a single profiling score in a consistent manner without considering counterfactual unemployment outcomes.

Profiling is also often justified on the basis of *equity* considerations (Fraser 1999). For example, with respect to profiling the potential long-term unemployed, it is argued that these persons are worst off and deserve qualified labour market programmes to improve their situation. However, this argument is contradictory if treatment effects are negative, i.e. indicating that participation is harmful to the participant.[31] In addition, Berger, Black, and Smith (2001) dispute in a search theoretic model the basic premise of the argument that potential long-term unemployment and individual welfare are negatively correlated.

Hence the profiling approach is fundamentally flawed, and the existing models are often rather ad-hoc and rely on parametric specifications with few explanatory variables. For example, the profiling system of Pennsylvania relies on only 8 explanatory variables to predict long term unemployment risk[32] and does not even contain race, age and gender, as prohibited by law (O'Leary, Decker, and Wandner 1998). As a consequence, the ability of these profiling systems to predict unemployment durations is often very weak (Berger, Black, and Smith 2001).

The targeting systems on the other hand are more promising. However, the existing systems (SOMS, FDSS) have a number of shortcomings. First, they are based on fully parametric models and may not be robust to misspecifications

---

[31] This is not unusual with active labour market programmes, see e.g. Bloom, Orr, Bell, Cave, Doolittle, Lin, and Bos (1997), Fay (1996), Gerfin and Lechner (2002), Lechner (2000) or Puhani (1999).

[32] More precisely, the probability of exhausting the maximum unemployment benefit period.

of the functional forms. Second, they do not provide the user (case worker) with the estimates of the potential outcomes and hide the estimation uncertainty accompanying these estimates. In particular, the statistical uncertainty associated with choosing the maximum among estimated outcomes is not properly reflected in their single-regression approaches. To overcome these weaknesses a semiparametric estimator of the conditional expected potential outcomes is developed in Chapter 4, and treatment choice with estimated outcomes is discussed below.

2.2.3 Estimating the Optimal Treatment

The first step to estimating optimal programme choices is the estimation of the conditional expected potential outcomes $E[Y^r|X]$. With identification guaranteed by the conditional independence assumption, $E[Y^r|X]$ can be estimated from a sample of former participants without selection bias. However, since the conditional independence assumption requires the inclusion of all confounding variables, X may be rather high-dimensional, making nonparametric estimation of $E[Y^r|X]$ difficult (see Section 2.3). Alternatively, a fully parametric approach specifies the functional form of the regression function $E[Y^r|X]$ up to a finite number of coefficients and is thus more precise in estimating $E[Y^r|X]$, provided the specified form is correct. But, if the functional form is misspecified, parametric regression is inconsistent. To avoid this dimensionality problem, the evaluation literature focused on the estimation of average outcomes $E[Y^r]$ or of expected outcomes conditional on the propensity score $E[Y^r|p^r]$, which can be estimated nonparametrically as discussed in Section 2.1 and Chapter 3. These nonparametric estimates of $E[Y^r]$ or $E[Y^r|p^r]$ provide some information that can be used to improve and robustify the estimation of the conditional expected potential outcomes $E[Y^r|X]$. Since the former can be estimated without relying on parametric assumptions, a semiparametric GMM estimator[33] that combines these nonparametric estimates with a parametric specification of the conditional regression function $E[Y^r|X]$ is developed in Chapter 4. This introduction of nonparametric estimates can help to robustify the estimates of $E[Y^r|X]$ in the case of misspecification of the functional form.

In the second step, after the conditional expected potential outcomes $\hat{Y}^r(x) = \hat{E}[Y^r|X = x]$ have been estimated for a particular individual with characteristics x, the optimal treatment-choice recommendation is derived. Obviously, according to (2.42) the estimated optimal programme is

$$\hat{r}^*(x) = \underset{r \in \{0,..,R-1\}}{\arg\max} \ u\left(\hat{Y}^r(x)\right).$$

However, this procedure does not take account of the estimation variability associated with the estimates $\hat{Y}^r(x)$. In practice, it would be of interest to know

---

[33] General method of moments estimator (Hansen 1982).

how strong the evidence is that a certain programme is the optimal one, since very noisy estimates of the conditional outcomes might pretend treatment choice heterogeneity even if there is a common optimal treatment. To assess such a situation, multiple-comparisons-with-the-best (MCB) techniques have been developed (Hsu 1996, Horrace and Schmidt 2000), which provide an ordering of significantly different programmes and test the hypothesis that programme r^* is the best treatment at a confidence level α, i.e. that

$$P \left(\underset{r \in \{0,..,R-1\}}{\arg \max} \; u \left(\hat{Y}^r(x) \right) = r^* \right) \geq 1 - \alpha. \tag{2.43}$$

However MCB methods are usually designed for consistent, parametric estimators and thus incorporate only variance but not bias. Furthermore, with more complex estimators the variance component is usually estimated on the basis of asymptotic approximations, which may be less precise in finite samples. As an alternative, I propose simulating the joint distribution of $\hat{Y}^0(x), \hat{Y}^1(x), .., \hat{Y}^{R-1}(x)$ by the bootstrap to approximate, for a particular individual, the probability that a certain programme is preferable to all others. If the number of programmes R is large, it might often occur that no programme dominates all others with high probability, but that a semi-ordering into best, intermediate and worst programmes is possible. The subset of best programmes jointly dominates all other programmes with high probability, but among these best programmes, no statistically significant ordering is possible. On the other hand, α should also be adjusted to the number of programmes.

Based on these estimates a statistical system could be implemented that assists in selecting adequate programmes for future participants. The eventual programme choice could be combined with other considerations (e.g. waiting time for treatment), particularly if the evidence that one programme is superior to all others is weak. Providing the case workers also with the estimated conditional potential outcomes and their confidence intervals leaves them with more information and discretion than the statistical systems reviewed in the previous section.

2.3 Nonparametric Regression

The basis of the generalized matching estimators (2.27) discussed in Section 2.1 is the nonparametric estimation of $m(x) = E[Y^s|X = x]$ from a sample of observations $\{(Y_{si}, X_{si})\}_{i=1}^{n_s}$. Matching estimators on the basis of the propensity score $p^{s|rs}(x)$ seek to estimate $m(\rho) = E[Y^s|p^{s|rs} = \rho]$ from the sample $\{(Y_{si}, p^{s|rs}(X_{si}))\}_{i=1}^{n_s}$ or from $\{(Y_{si}, \hat{p}^{s|rs}(X_{si}))\}_{i=1}^{n_s}$, where $\hat{p}^{s|rs}(x)$ is an estimate of the propensity score. These estimates are evaluated at the $\{X_{rj}\}_{j=1}^{n_r}$ locations of the target sample, and their average (2.27) gives an estimate of the counterfactual mean (2.25).

2.3.1 Nearest Neighbours and Local Polynomial Regression

The simplest nonparametric regression estimator of $m(x) = E[Y^s | X = x]$ is first-nearest-neighbour regression. (The following discussion holds analogously for the estimation of $m(\rho) = E[Y^s | p^{s|rs} = \rho]$.) First-nearest-neighbour regression estimates $m(x)$ by the value Y_{si} of the observation i that is closest to x in terms of its X_{si} values:

$$\hat{m}(x) = Y_{si} \qquad \text{where } i = \arg\min_l \|X_{sl} - x\|.$$

If X is multidimensional, closeness is measured by a distance metric, e.g. Mahalanobis distance. In the evaluation literature this estimator is often called *pair-matching* with replacement because the iterative computation of the estimator (2.27) proceeds by finding for each observation X_{rj} of the target sample the closest X_{si} observation of the source sample. In other words, this estimator matches to each target observation the closest source observation and estimates the counterfactual mean (2.25) by the average outcome of the 'matched' source observations.

In the evaluation literature a variety of modifications to the pair-matching estimator have been developed. Pair-matching without replacement (or first-nearest-*remaining*-neighbour regression) withdraws the observation (Y_{si}, X_{si}) after it has been matched to a target observation, so that it is no longer available as a match to other target sample observations. Thus it restricts the frequency a source sample observation can be used as a match to at most once. Due to this procedure the estimate depends on the sequence of the target sample observations and is, thus, not invariant to the ordering of the data. Because pair-matching without replacement uses each source sample observation at most once, usually it has smaller variance but larger bias than conventional pair-matching with replacement. However, pair-matching without replacement is only possible if $n_s \geq n_r$, i.e. if the source sample consists of more observations than the target sample. It is likely to perform very poorly if $n_s \approx n_r$ since in this case the matching process would be forced to choose almost all source observations regardless of their X_{si} values and, thus, would not be able to balance the covariate distributions. Hence pair-matching without replacement usually is not applicable for the evaluation of multiple treatments since source and target sample can be of similar size and, furthermore, are used interchangeably, for example to estimate the treatment effects $E[Y^r - Y^s | D = r]$ and $E[Y^r - Y^s | D = s]$.

Cochran and Rubin (1973) suggested *caliper matching* as a pair-matching variant that tries to avert very distant matches. It proceeds like first-nearest neighbour regression but considers the estimate of $m(x)$ as undefined if no neighbour is found within a pre-specified distance C:

$$\hat{m}(x) = Y_{si} \qquad \text{if } \|X_{si} - x\| \leq C \qquad \text{where } i = \arg\min_l \|X_{sl} - x\|$$

$$\text{and undefined otherwise,}$$

where C is the caliper width. With caliper matching the estimator (2.27) is modified to

$$\frac{\sum_{j=1}^{n_r} \hat{m}\left(X_{rj}\right) \cdot 1\left(\hat{m}\left(X_{rj}\right) \text{ is defined}\right)}{\sum_{j=1}^{n_r} 1\left(\hat{m}\left(X_{rj}\right) \text{ is defined}\right)}.$$

See also Gu and Rosenbaum (1993) for a comparison of these pair-matching variants.

An extension of first-nearest-neighbour regression is κ-nearest neighbour regression which estimates $m(x)$ by the average outcome of the κ closest neighbours

$$\hat{m}(x) = \frac{1}{\kappa} \sum_{l \in I_\kappa(x)} Y_{sl}$$

where $I_\kappa(x)$ is a set containing the indices of the κ observations of $\{X_{si}\}_{i=1}^{n_s}$ that are closest to x. The variance of the κ-NN estimator $\hat{m}(x)$ decreases with the number of neighbours. On the other hand, its bias increases with κ since more distant observations are included to estimate $m(x)$. Consistency of the estimator $\hat{m}(x)$ requires that bias and variance converge to zero with growing sample size, which in turn requires that $\kappa \to \infty$ at an appropriate rate. Hence κ-NN regression with fixed κ (e.g. $\kappa = 1$) does not lead to a consistent estimate of $E[Y^s|X]$. Furthermore, matching estimators (2.27) based on κ-NN regression with κ fixed are inefficient for estimating the counterfactual mean, see Abadie and Imbens (2001) and the discussion in Section 2.1.5.[34] Hence κ should be chosen by data-driven methods that ensure that κ grows without bound as the sample size increases.

Kernel based regression methods are an alternative to κ-NN regression and much research has been devoted to them.[35] The basic difference between κ-NN and kernel based techniques is that the latter estimates $m(x)$ by smoothing the data in a fixed (i.e. deterministic) neighbourhood of x whereas the former smooths the data in a neighbourhood of stochastic size. For example, 10-NN regression estimates $m(x)$ by the average outcome of Y of all observations in a neighbourhood of x where the size of the neighbourhood is determined such that it contains exactly 10 observations of the sample $\{X_{si}\}_{i=1}^{n_s}$. Hence the size of the neighbourhood depends on x and the sample $\{X_{si}\}_{i=1}^{n_s}$. Kernel based regression methods use all observations within a neighbourhood of size pre-specified by the researcher. Furthermore, kernel based regression methods downweight observations according to their distance to x such that observations that are farther apart have less influence on the estimate.[36]

---

[34] An argument often made in favour of pair-matching is that pairing can reduce data collection costs by selecting suitable control observations (non-participants) that shall be interviewed in the follow-up data collection period. This argument may be reasonable with respect to data collection but is improper with respect to the choice of evaluation estimator once the data have been collected.

[35] Other widespread nonparametric regression techniques include splines, wavelets and series regression, see Eubank (1988), Härdle (1991) or Pagan and Ullah (1999).

[36] Such a weighting function can be incorporated into the κ-NN estimation framework, too. Ultimately also the neighbourhood of kernel based methods depends on the sample

Local polynomial regression is a class of kernel-based nonparametric regression estimators which includes the Nadaraya (1965)-Watson (1964) kernel regression estimator, local linear regression (Fan 1992), local quadratic regression and so forth. The following introduction focuses mainly on one-dimensional nonparametric regression as it is applied in the subsequent chapters. One-dimensional regression is relevant for programme evaluation if matching is on a one-dimensional X variable or on a distance metric as for example the propensity score. For discussions on local polynomial regression in the multidimensional context see Ruppert and Wand (1994), Fan and Gijbels (1996) and Fan, Gasser, Gijbels, Brockmann, and Engel (1997).

The local polynomial regression estimate $\hat{m}(x)$ is a weighted least squares estimate where observations (Y_{si}, X_{si}) receive weights that decrease to zero with increasing distance to x. A polynomial of order p is fitted locally to the data in the neighbourhood of x, and $m(x)$ is estimated by the coefficient $\hat{\beta}_0$ of the coefficient vector $(\hat{\beta}_0, .., \hat{\beta}_p)'$ that solves

$$\min_{\beta_0,..,\beta_p} \sum_i \left(Y_{si} - \sum_{q=0}^{p} \beta_q \left(X_{si} - x \right)^q \right)^2 K \left(\frac{X_{si} - x}{h} \right), \qquad (2.44)$$

where p is the polynomial order, $K(\cdot)$ a symmetric weight function with $\int K(u)du = 1$, $\int uK(u)du = 0$, $\int u^2 K(u)du < \infty$ and h a bandwidth parameter. When using a kernel K with bounded support, all observations that lie outside the neighbourhood spanned by h receive zero weights. In the following chapters the compactly supported Epanechnikov kernel $K(u) = \frac{3}{4}(1 - u^2) \, 1_{[-1,1]}(u)$ is always used. The solution $\hat{m}(x)$ can be written explicitly as

$$\hat{m}(x) = e_1' \cdot \begin{pmatrix} Q_0(x) & Q_1(x) & \cdots & Q_p(x) \\ Q_1(x) & Q_2(x) & \cdots & Q_{p+1}(x) \\ \vdots & \vdots & \ddots & \vdots \\ Q_p(x) & Q_{p+1}(x) & \cdots & Q_{2p}(x) \end{pmatrix}^{-1} \cdot \begin{pmatrix} T_0(x) \\ T_1(x) \\ \vdots \\ T_p(x) \end{pmatrix},$$

where $e_1' = (1,0,0,..)$, $Q_l(x) = \sum K \left(\frac{X_{si}-x}{h} \right) \left(X_{si} - x \right)^l$ and $T_l(x) = \sum K \left(\frac{X_{si}-x}{h} \right) \left(X_{si} - x \right)^l Y_{si}$ (Fan, Gasser, Gijbels, Brockmann, and Engel 1997).

According to the polynomial order the local polynomial estimator is also called Nadaraya-Watson kernel ($p = 0$), local linear ($p = 1$), local quadratic ($p = 2$) or local cubic ($p = 3$) regression. Polynomials of order higher than three are rarely used in practice, except for estimating local bias in data-driven bandwidth selectors. Nadaraya-Watson kernel and local linear regression are most common in econometrics. Local polynomial regression of order two or three is more suited

---

$\{X_{si}\}_{i=1}^{n_s}$ when using data-driven bandwidth selection methods and it depends furthermore on x if local bandwidth values $h(x)$ are used. If in addition the number of neighbours $\kappa(x)$ is chosen by data-driven methods and separately for each x, both methods are largely equivalent.

than kernel or local linear regression for modelling peaks and oscillating regression curves in larger samples, but it often proves unstable in small samples since more data points in each smoothing interval are required (Loader 1999). The expressions of $\hat{m}(x)$ up to polynomial order three are

$$\hat{m}_{p=0}(x) = \frac{T_0(x)}{Q_0(x)} = \frac{\sum Y_{si} K\left(\frac{X_{si}-x}{h}\right)}{\sum K\left(\frac{X_{si}-x}{h}\right)} \tag{2.45}$$

$$\hat{m}_{p=1}(x) = \frac{Q_2 T_0 - Q_1 T_1}{Q_2 S_0 - Q_1^2}$$

$$\hat{m}_{p=2}(x) = \frac{(Q_2 Q_4 - Q_3^2)T_0 + (Q_2 Q_3 - Q_1 Q_4)T_1 + (Q_1 Q_3 - Q_2^2)T_2}{Q_0 Q_2 Q_4 + 2Q_1 Q_2 Q_3 - Q_2^3 - Q_0 Q_3^2 - Q_1^2 Q_4}$$

$$\hat{m}_{p=3}(x) = \frac{A_0 T_0 + A_1 T_1 + A_2 T_2 + A_3 T_3}{A_0 Q_0 + A_1 Q_1 + A_2 Q_2 + A_3 Q_3},$$

where $A_0 = Q_2 Q_4 Q_6 + 2Q_3 Q_4 Q_5 - Q_4^3 - Q_2 Q_5^2 - Q_3^2 Q_6$, $A_1 = Q_3 Q_4^2 + Q_1 Q_5^2 + Q_2 Q_3 Q_6 - Q_1 Q_4 Q_6 - Q_2 Q_4 Q_5 - Q_3^2 Q_5$, $A_2 = Q_1 Q_3 Q_6 + Q_2 Q_4^2 + Q_2 Q_3 Q_5 - Q_3^2 Q_4 - Q_1 Q_4 Q_5 - Q_2^2 Q_6$, $A_3 = Q_3^3 + Q_1 Q_4^2 + Q_2^2 Q_5 - Q_1 Q_3 Q_5 - 2Q_2 Q_3 Q_4$. Inserting the expressions (2.45) in (2.27) gives a *local polynomial matching* estimator.

2.3.2 Properties of Local Polynomial Regression

Asymptotic Properties Stone (1980, 1982) showed that the optimal rate of convergence for nonparametric estimation of a $\bar{p}$ times continuously differentiable function $m(x)$, $x \in \Re^k$ is in L_2-norm

$$n_s^{-\frac{\bar{p}}{2\bar{p}+k}}$$

and in sup-Norm (i.e. uniform convergence)

$$\left(\frac{n_s}{\ln n_s}\right)^{-\frac{\bar{p}}{2\bar{p}+k}}.$$

Hence the rate of convergence decreases with k, the dimension of X. This is known as the curse of dimensionality and implies that nonparametric regression becomes more difficult for higher-dimensional X.[37] On the other hand, the optimal rate of convergence increases with the number of continuous derivatives of $m(x)$, and for $\bar{p}$ very large it is close to the parametric rate. Stone (1980, 1982) showed further that a local polynomial regression estimator of order $\bar{p} - 1$ attains the optimal rate of convergence. Below some properties of local polynomial regression are presented for X one-dimensional ($k = 1$).

---

[37] To avoid the curse of dimensionality in the estimation of the conditional expected potential outcomes a semiparametric estimator is developed in Chapter 4.

Fan (1992, 1993) analyzed the local linear estimator ($p = 1$) and showed that the local bias and the local variance of the Nadaraya-Watson ($p = 0$) and the local linear estimator are of the same order if x is estimated at interior points:

	$p = 0$	$p = 1$	
Bias	$h^2 \frac{\mu_2}{\mu_0} \left(\frac{m'(x) f'_s(x)}{f_s(x)} + \frac{m''(x)}{2} \right)$	$h^2 \frac{\mu_2}{\mu_0} \frac{m''(x)}{2}$	(2.46)
Variance	$\frac{1}{n_s h} \frac{\bar{\mu}_0}{\mu_0^2} \frac{\sigma^2(x)}{f_s(x)}$	$\frac{1}{n_s h} \frac{\bar{\mu}_0}{\mu_0^2} \frac{\sigma^2(x)}{f_s(x)}$,	

where $\mu_l = \int u^l K(u)\, du$ and $\bar{\mu}_l = \int u^l K^2(u)\, du$. Fan also showed that the bias of the local linear estimator is of the same order at boundary points as in the interior, whereas the bias of the Nadaraya-Watson estimator is of order $O(h)$ when estimated at values x at the boundaries of its support. Fan (1993) demonstrated that the local linear estimator attains full asymptotic efficiency in a minimax sense among all linear smoothers and has high efficiency among all smoothers, see also Fan, Gasser, Gijbels, Brockmann, and Engel (1997)

Ruppert and Wand (1994) extended these results to polynomials of arbitrary order and provided formula for the local bias and the local variance which are valid as well in the interior as for boundary points. These results are provided for the Nadaraya-Watson and the local linear estimator in Corollary 1 in Appendix B. Corollary 1 implies that the local bias is of the same order in the interior and at the boundary for odd-order polynomials whereas it is of lower order in the interior for even-order polynomials:

	$p = 0$	$p = 1$	$p = 2$	$p = 3$
Bias in interior	$O\left(h^2\right)$	$O\left(h^2\right)$	$O\left(h^4\right)$	$O\left(h^4\right)$
Bias at boundary	$O\left(h^1\right)$	$O\left(h^2\right)$	$O\left(h^3\right)$	$O\left(h^4\right)$
Variance	$O\left(\frac{1}{n_s h}\right)$	$O\left(\frac{1}{n_s h}\right)$	$O\left(\frac{1}{n_s h}\right)$	$O\left(\frac{1}{n_s h}\right)$.

To achieve the fastest rate of convergence with respect to mean squared error the bandwidth h should be chosen to balance squared bias and variance, which leads to the convergence rates:

Convergence rate	$p = 0$	$p = 1$	$p = 2$	$p = 3$
in the interior	$n_s^{-\frac{2}{5}}$	$n_s^{-\frac{2}{5}}$	$n_s^{-\frac{4}{9}}$	$n_s^{-\frac{4}{9}}$
at the boundary	$n_s^{-\frac{1}{3}}$	$n_s^{-\frac{2}{5}}$	$n_s^{-\frac{3}{7}}$	$n_s^{-\frac{4}{9}}$

In most applications of propensity score matching the propensity score is unknown such that the above results are not directly applicable. Heckman, Ichimura, and Todd (1998) analyzed local polynomial regression when the propensity score as well as the support S^r of X in the source population are estimated. They showed first that the local polynomial regression estimator $\hat{m}(x)$ can be written in an asymptotically linear form with trimming

$$(\hat{m}(x) - m(x))\, 1(x \in \hat{S}^r) = \frac{1}{n_s} \sum_i \psi(Y_{si}, X_{si}; x) + \hat{b}(x) + \hat{R}(x), \qquad (2.47)$$

with the properties:

a) $E[\psi(Y_{si}, X_{si}; X)|X = x] = 0$

b) $\underset{n_s \to \infty}{plim} \; n_s^{-\frac{1}{2}} \sum_i \hat{b}(X_{si}) < \infty$

c) $n_s^{-\frac{1}{2}} \sum_i \hat{R}(X_i) = o_p(1)$.

$\hat{S}^r$ is an estimator of the support of X in the source population. ψ is a mean-zero influence function which determines the local variance of the estimate. ψ may depend on the sample size, for example through a bandwidth value that decreases with sample size. The term $b(x)$ represents the local bias and $R(x)$ is a remainder term of lower order.

This representation of the local polynomial regression estimator is used in Chapter 3 to derive the mean squared error of the matching estimator and in Chapter 4 to derive the asymptotic distribution of the semiparametric estimator of the conditional expected potential outcomes. For X one-dimensional and m twice continuously differentiable, the local influence functions are identical at interior points for the local constant and the local linear estimator:

$$\psi(Y_{si}, X_{si}, x) = (Y_{si} - m(X_{si})) \cdot \frac{K\left(\frac{X_{si}-x}{h}\right)}{hf_s(x)}, \qquad (2.48)$$

as derived in Fan (1992), Ruppert and Wand (1994) and Heckman, Ichimura, and Todd (1998).

Heckman, Ichimura, and Todd (1998) showed furthermore that nonparametric regression on the propensity score $p^{s|rs}(x)$ is asymptotically linear with trimming, even if the propensity score itself is estimated, provided it is estimated parametrically or nonparametrically by local polynomial regression. Sufficient conditions and the resulting influence functions are given in the Corollaries 2 and 3 in Appendix B. The linear asymptotic representation with trimming is used in Chapter 3 to analyze the mean squared error of matching estimators and in Chapter 4 to derive the asymptotic properties of the semiparametric estimator of the conditional expected potential outcomes.

Finite Sample Properties Despite its favourable asymptotic properties, local linear regression with a global bandwidth value often leads to a very rugged curve in regions of sparse data (Seifert and Gasser 1996). Since the denominator in (2.45) can be very small, or even zero if a compact kernel is used, the local linear estimator has infinite unconditional variance and unbounded conditional variance (Seifert and Gasser 1996).[38] They also showed that the probability for the occurrence of sparse regions is substantial if the X_{si} observations are randomly spaced. The gravity of this behaviour becomes apparent from their simulation results, which reveal that the mean integrated squared error (MISE) of the local linear estimator explodes at bandwidth values that are only slightly below the asymptotically optimal bandwidth. A simple but inefficient solution consists in

---

[38] At least 4 observations in each smoothing interval are required for finite unconditional variance, but even then the conditional variance is still unbounded.

deliberate over-smoothing. Another strategy, based on the idea of ridge regression, suggests to add a small amount to the denominator in (2.45) to avoid near-zero or zero denominators. Fan (1992) proposed adding the term n^{-2} to the denominator and the local linear estimator is implemented as such in the subsequent Monte Carlo simulations. Yet, further adjustments are necessary for reliable small sample behaviour. Seifert and Gasser (1996, 2000) proposed two modifications of the estimator. To improve numerical stability the regression line in (2.44) is centered at $\bar{x}$ instead at x, where $\bar{x}$ refers to the middle of the data in the smoothing window:

$$\min_{a,b} \sum_i (Y_{si} - a - b(X_{si} - \bar{x}))^2 K\left(\frac{X_{si} - x}{h}\right) \quad \text{with } \bar{x} = \frac{\sum X_{si} K\left(\frac{X_{si} - x}{h}\right)}{\sum K\left(\frac{X_{si} - x}{h}\right)}.$$

$m(x)$ is estimated as $\hat{m}(x) = \hat{a} + \hat{b}(x - \bar{x})$, which is equal to $\hat{m}(x) = \frac{\tilde{T}_0}{\tilde{Q}_0} + \frac{\tilde{T}_1}{\tilde{Q}_2}(x - \bar{x})$ where $\tilde{Q}_l(x) = \sum K\left(\frac{X_{si} - x}{h}\right)(X_{si} - \bar{x})^l$ and $\tilde{T}_l(x) = \sum K\left(\frac{X_{si} - x}{h}\right)(X_{si} - \bar{x})^l Y_{si}$. Their second modification consists in adding a ridge parameter R to $\tilde{Q}_2$ to avoid zero and almost zero denominators:

$$\hat{m}_{SG}(x) = \frac{\tilde{T}_0}{\tilde{Q}_0} + \frac{\tilde{T}_1(x - \bar{x})}{\tilde{Q}_2 + R}, \qquad (2.49)$$

where R is chosen by the improved 'rule-of-thumb' of Seifert and Gasser (2000)

$$R = \frac{5}{16h} \cdot |x - \bar{x}|$$

for the Epanechnikov kernel. Since the ridging term converges to zero, the Seifert&Gasser (SG) local linear variant is asymptotically equivalent to local linear regression.

Other possible solutions to avoiding zero or near-zero denominators, which are not further pursued here, include (a) non-compact kernels, (b) locally adaptive bandwidths and (c) artificial observations and design transformations. a) Kernels with unbounded support, e.g. Gaussian weights, have also been considered in Seifert and Gasser (1996, 2000) and behaved more stable than the standard local linear estimator, but less promising than the ridging estimator with compact kernel (2.49). Moreover, a compact kernel is computationally advantageous and the Epanechnikov kernel is optimal for local polynomial regression at interior points and performs also very well for boundary points, independently of the polynomial degree p (Fan, Gasser, Gijbels, Brockmann, and Engel 1997). b) Locally increasing the bandwidth value in regions of sparse data can overcome the instability of the local linear estimator, as advocated for example in Fan and Gijbels (1995), Fan, Hall, Martin, and Patil (1996), Schucany (1995) or Ruppert (1997). However, in small samples, estimates of the local bandwidths can be highly variable (Fan, Hall, Martin, and Patil 1996). c) Hall and Turlach (1997) proposed placing artificial design points in regions where data are sparse by linearly interpolating between available observations. Hall, Park, and Turlach (1998) suggested transforming irregular spaced observations into a regularly spaced design, estimating the regression curve by local polynomial regression and re-transforming the design back into the irregularly spaced design. These proposals were examined in some preliminary simulations and proved less fruitful for the estimation of (2.27).

The behaviour of all nonparametric regression estimators depends on the proper choice of a bandwidth value. Asymptotic rates of convergence are of little guidance for choosing the bandwidth for a particular dataset. A versatile approach to bandwidth selection is cross-validation (Stone 1974). Cross-validation is based on the principle of maximizing the out-of-sample predictive performance. If a quadratic loss function is used to assess the estimation of $m(x)$ at a particular point x, a bandwidth value h should be selected to minimize $E[(\hat{m}(x; h) - m(x))^2]$. If a single bandwidth value is used to estimate the function $m(x)$ at all points x, the (global) bandwidth should be chosen to minimize the mean integrated squared error $\text{MISE}(h) = E \int (\hat{m}(x; h) - m(x))^2 dx$. Since $m(x)$ is unknown, a computable approximation to minimizing mean integrated squared error is minimizing average squared error

$$\arg\min_{h} \frac{1}{n_s} \sum_{i} (Y_{si} - \hat{m}(X_{si}; h))^2. \tag{2.50}$$

However, minimizing average squared error leads to the selection of too small bandwidth values. For example, if a compact kernel is used and h is very small, the local neighbourhood of X_{si} would contain only the observation (Y_{si}, X_{si}). As the estimate $\hat{m}(X_{si})$ is a weighted average of the Y observations in the neighbourhood, the estimate of $m(X_{si})$ would be Y_{si}. Hence (2.50) would be minimized by a bandwidth value h close to zero. To avoid underestimating the optimal bandwidth, the observation (Y_{si}, X_{si}) should be excluded from the sample when estimating $m(X_{si})$. The corresponding estimate $\hat{m}_{-i}(X_{si})$ is called the leave-one-out estimate and represents the out-of-sample prediction from the sample $\{(Y_{sl}, X_{sl})\}_{l \neq i}$ at X_{si}. The resulting cross validation function is defined as

$$CV(h; n_s) = \sum_{i} (Y_{si} - \hat{m}_{-i}(X_{si}; h))^2, \tag{2.51}$$

and h is chosen to minimize (2.51). For properties of cross validation bandwidth selection see Härdle and Marron (1987).

Instead of out-of-sample-prediction validation, the average squared error criterion (2.50) could be modified to correct the downward bias by 'penalizing' very small bandwidth values. These are similar in spirit to the 'in-sample' model selection criteria in parametric regression, which seek to account for the degrees of freedom by penalizing models with a large number of coefficients. A variety of penalized cross-validation criteria for bandwidth selection have been proposed including Akaike's (1970) information criterion, Shibata's (1981) model selector and Rice's (1984) bandwidth selector:

$$CV_A(h; n_s) = \exp\left(\frac{2}{n_s h}\right) \cdot \sum (Y_{si} - \hat{m}(X_{si}; h))^2 \qquad (2.52)$$

$$CV_S(h; n_s) = \left(1 + \frac{2}{n_s h}\right) \cdot \sum (Y_{si} - \hat{m}(X_{si}; h))^2$$

$$CV_R(h; n_s) = \left(1 - \frac{2}{n_s h}\right)^{-1} \cdot \sum (Y_{si} - \hat{m}(X_{si}; h))^2,$$

see also Pagan and Ullah (1999).

As an alternative to cross validation, a variety of plug-in bandwidth selectors have been developed e.g. Fan and Gijbels (1995), Fan, Hall, Martin, and Patil (1996), Ruppert, Sheather, and Wand (1995), Ruppert (1997) and Schucany (1995). Plug-in bandwidth selectors proceed by estimating bias and variance at one or a at variety of pilot bandwidth values and choose a bandwidth to balance squared bias and variance. For a lucid discussion of plug-in and cross validation bandwidth-selection see Loader (1999).

All these bandwidth selectors are designed to estimate the optimal bandwidth for the estimation of $m(x)$. In programme evaluation, however, the estimates $\hat{m}(x)$ are only intermediate products for the generalized matching estimator (2.27). Consequently, the bandwidth choice problem for the estimator (2.27) may be rather different than for the estimation of $m(x)$, and the presented bandwidth selectors may be inconsistent when applied to the generalized matching estimator. This is further considered in the next chapter.

3 Nonparametric Covariate Adjustment in Finite Samples

In this chapter the finite-sample properties of various estimators of the covariate-adjusted mean (2.25) are investigated. Estimates of (2.25) are essential ingredients for policy evaluation under the control-for-confounding-variables and under the difference-in-difference identification approaches (discussed in Section 2.1.4). Hence precise estimation of covariate-adjusted means is of importance, particularly if average treatment effects are analyzed for smaller subpopulations.[1] In addition, estimation of covariate-adjusted means is also central for deriving individually optimal treatment choices in Chapter 4.

Since little is known about the respective benefits and weaknesses of nonparametric estimators of (2.25), this chapter analyzes their behaviour in finite-samples. The estimators compared are pair-matching (with replacement), least squares regression matching, kernel matching, local linear matching, Seifert&Gasser matching and the re-weighting estimator (2.34) or (2.36), respectively. With the exception of re-weighting, all estimators are generalized matching estimators (2.27) with different (nonparametric) estimators of $m(x) = E[Y^s | X = x, D = s]$. Pair-matching estimates $m(X_{rj})$ by using first-nearest neighbour regression. Since it is the most commonly used matching estimator, pair-matching is considered as the benchmark henceforth. Least squares matching (2.28) is a fully parametric estimator without local adaptation of the regression slope to the neighbourhood of X_{rj}. Whereas pair-matching is the most localized estimator, relying on only one observation in the neighbourhood, least squares matching corresponds to local linear matching with a bandwidth value of infinity. Between these two extremes are the local polynomial regression estimators situated: Kernel matching, local linear matching and Seifert&Gasser (SG) matching.[2]

First, the *potential* precision gains of the local polynomial matching estimators vis-à-vis pair-matching are assessed via Monte Carlo simulation. Potential precision gains refer to the difference between the mean squared error of pair-matching and the MSE of the local polynomial matching estimator at its optimal bandwidth, i.e. at the bandwidth value where it attains the minimal MSE.

---

[1] Or if the available dataset is very small.

[2] Some simulations were also carried out with local quadratic and local cubic matching and with a local linear variant of Hall, Park, and Turlach (1998). These estimators, however, did not perform well in small samples.

These simulations demonstrate the order of magnitude of the precision gains that could be achieved if the optimal bandwidth value were known or could be estimated by a perfect data-driven bandwidth selector. Also, the mean squared error of the least squares matching and the re-weighting estimator, which both do not require choosing a bandwidth parameter, are simulated. The mean squared errors of all estimators are compared to the variance bound (2.38).

Whereas least squares matching and re-weighting perform rather poorly, the potential precision gains of local polynomial matching turn out to be considerable. Yet to reap these precision gains, a suited data-driven bandwidth selector is required. To assess the bandwidth-choice problem for the local polynomial matching estimator, second-order asymptotic approximations to the MSE are developed and the similitude of approximated and simulated MSE in small samples is judged. (Second-order approximations are required since the first-order approximation does not depend on the bandwidth parameter.) Since these asymptotic approximations turn out as not very reliable for choosing the optimal bandwidth value in small samples, the performance of conventional cross-validation bandwidth selection is finally examined.

Whereas these analyses so far are based on matching on a one-dimensional, known variable, e.g. matching on a distance metric (Mahalanobis distance) or an index function (e.g. the known propensity score), Section 3.4 examines matching on an estimated propensity score. A general finding is that SG matching with a bandwidth value chosen by cross-validation leads to a reduction in mean squared error of about 25% relative to pair-matching when matching is on an observed covariate and to a reduction of about 40% when matching proceeds on an estimated propensity score. In the latter case, this means that pair-matching requires almost 70% more observations to achieve the same precision as SG matching. Whereas kernel matching is also usually superior to pair-matching, the performance of local linear matching is more ambiguous.

3.1 Potential Efficiency Gains of Local Polynomial Matching

As point of departure for the analysis of the behaviour of covariate-distribution adjustment estimators in finite samples, the mean squared error of matching and re-weighting estimators is examined when the covariate X, to be adjusted for, is one-dimensional and observed. X could be a single variable, an index of variables, a distance metric (e.g. Mahalanobis) or the known propensity score. (If covariate adjustment needs to be carried out with respect to multiple covariates, propensity score matching could be performed. Matching on an estimated propensity score is considered in Section 3.4.) In a variety of Monte Carlo designs the mean squared error is simulated for each estimator[3] and compared with the MSE of pair-matching. The MSE of the three local polynomial matching estimators (Kernel, local linear, SG) is simulated at many different bandwidth values. This

---

[3] The re-weigthing estimator (2.34) is computed using the true densities f_s, f_r.

allows an assessment of the potential (i.e. maximum) precision gains of local polynomial matching vis-a-vis pair-matching and of their sensitivity to the bandwidth value. Only if these precision gains are 'robust' over an extensive region of bandwidth values, a data-driven bandwidth selector might stand a chance to select a proper bandwidth value to realize these efficiency gains.

The notation and setup are as in Section 2.1.5: Data $\{(Y_{si}, X_{si})\}_{i=1}^{n_s}$ are sampled randomly from a source population, and a second sample $\{X_{rj}\}_{j=1}^{n_r}$ is drawn from a target population. $f_s(x)$ denotes the density of X in the source population and $f_r(x)$ the density of X in the target population. $m(x)$ denotes the conditional expectation $E[Y^s | X = x, D = s]$ in the source population. From these two samples the covariate-adjusted mean outcome (2.25)

$$\int m(x) f_r(x) dx$$

shall be estimated.

The Monte Carlo designs consist of 6 combinations for the densities f_s and f_r, eight different regression curves $m(x)$, and different sample sizes n_s, n_r. The X covariates are drawn in different combinations from the three truncated normal distributions (N_1, N_2, N_3) displayed in Figure 3.1. For example, the density-combination $f_s = N_1$ and $f_r = N_2$ denotes that the X covariate of the source population is drawn from N_1 and that of the target population from N_2. In all combinations the covariate has always the same support $[0, 1]$ in the source and in the target population, and hence, there is no need for trimming as it has been suggested by Heckman, Ichimura, and Todd (1998) for situations where the supports need to be estimated. Nevertheless, the overlapping probability mass varies and is smaller for the combinations N_1-N_3 and N_3-N_1 than for the others, such that precision should be lower for these two combinations.

The Y observations are sampled from one of the eight regression curves depicted in Figure 3.2 disturbed by an additive mean-zero, uniform error term with standard deviation 0.1 (see also Tables C.1 and C.2 in Appendix C). The regression curves are chosen to comprehend different properties, such as linear, monotonous and non-monotonous functions and different degrees of smoothness. The dots in Figure 3.2 represent illustrative sample observations to demonstrate the signal-to-noise ratio. Figure 3.3 shows an exemplary sample, drawn from the density combination N_3-N_1 and regression curve m_4.

For each of these 48 settings the mean squared error of the estimators is simulated through repeated drawings. In each replication the conditional expectation function $E[Y|X]$ is estimated from the source sample and evaluated at the covariate values of the target sample, conditional on a given bandwidth value h. The mean squared error of the local polynomial matching estimators is simulated at 50 different bandwidth values h. ($h = 0.02, 0.04, .., 1.00$ for sample size $n_s = 40$, $h = 0.01, 0.02, .., 0.50$ for $n_s = 200$, and $h = 0.0075, .., 0.375$ for $n_s = 1000$). In addition, the asymptotic variance bound (2.38) is computed.

Fig. 3.1. Design densities N_1, N_2, N_3 of the matching covariate X

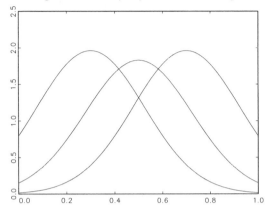

Note: Density distributions from which source and target sample are drawn. The density functions are from left to right $N_1(u) = 1.100 \exp\left(-(u-0.3)^2/\left(2\sigma_x^2\right)\right) \cdot 1_{[0,1]}(u)/\sqrt{2\pi\sigma_x^2}$, $N_2(u) = 1.026 \exp\left(-(u-0.5)^2/\left(2\sigma_x^2\right)\right) \cdot 1_{[0,1]}(u)/\sqrt{2\pi\sigma_x^2}$ *and* $N_3(u) = 1.100 \exp\left(-(u-0.7)^2/\left(2\sigma_x^2\right)\right) \cdot 1_{[0,1]}(u)/\sqrt{2\pi\sigma_x^2}$ *with* $\sigma_x^2 = 0.05$.

Fig. 3.2. Regression curves $m(x)$

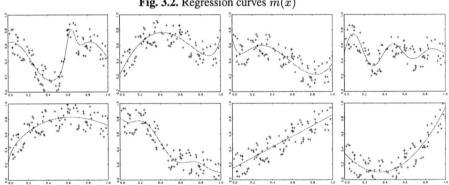

Note: Regression curves m_1 *to* m_4 *from left to right in the upper panel, regression curves* m_5 *to* m_8 *in the lower panel.*

3.1.1 Simulation Results at the Optimal Bandwidth Value

Tables C.3 to C.7 in Appendix C provide the simulation results for pair-matching, least-squares matching, kernel, local linear and Seifert&Gasser (SG) matching and for the re-weighting estimator. The results for kernel, local linear and SG matching are each given at their simulated *optimal* bandwidth value, which is the value corresponding to the smallest MSE. These results show the potential precision gains of local polynomial matching that could be achieved if the optimal bandwidth value were known or chosen by a perfect bandwidth selector. The

Fig. 3.3. Exemplary draw from density combination $N_3 - N_1$ and m_4

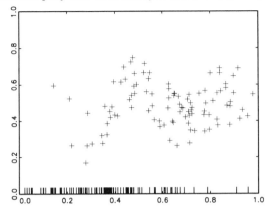

Note: The source population is represented by + symbols and combines draws from density N_3 and outcomes $Y = m_4(X) + u$ where u is a mean-zero uniform error term with standard deviation 0.1 and $m_4(\cdot)$ is the upper right regression curve in Figure 3.2. The target population is represented by draws from density N_1 and marked along the X-axis. Their outcomes are unobserved.

first three tables contain the results for symmetric sample sizes $n_s = n_r = 40$, $n_s = n_r = 200$, and $n_s = n_r = 1000$, respectively. Table C.6 contains the results when the sample drawn from the source population is much larger than the target sample ($n_s = 200, n_r = 40$). This corresponds to the usual situation in treatment evaluation, where the number of control observations is much larger than the number of treated individuals. Finally, Table C.7 considers the opposite case where only $n_s = 40$ control observations are available, which are matched to $n_r = 200$ treated observations.

The first two columns in each table indicate the simulation design (regression curve and density combination). Columns 3 and 4 contain the simulated mean squared error and the variance of the pair-matching estimator (multiplied by 10^3). Column 5 provides the MSE of least squares matching. In columns 6 to 17, the results for the local polynomial matching estimators at their simulated optimal bandwidth are given. The columns labelled h^{opt} indicate this optimal bandwidth value where the estimator's MSE is minimized. These optimal bandwidth values display a considerable variation among regression curves and density combinations. The columns MSE and Var contain the absolute values of the mean squared error and variance at this optimal bandwidth. Columns 6, 10, and 14 give the MSE relative to the MSE of pair-matching (in%). A value of 70% thus indicates that MSE is reduced by 30% vis-à-vis pair-matching. In column 18 the mean squared error of the re-weighting estimator is given. Finally, the last column provides the asymptotic variance bound (2.38) computed for the various simulation designs. The last two rows of each table summarize the results by the mean and the median of the column entries averaged over all 48 simulation designs. For example, the MSE of pair-matching is on average $2.48 \cdot 10^{-3}$ with median $1.91 \cdot 10^{-3}$ for sample sizes $n_s = n_r = 40$ (Table C.3).

Some general patterns emerge from these tables. For the two more difficult density combinations $N_1 - N_3$ and $N_3 - N_1$, where more mass of the target population lies in regions where source observations are sparse, mean squared error is often more than twice as high than for the other density combinations. For most simulation designs least squares matching and the re-weighting estimator perform much worse than pair-matching and local polynomial matching. Only for the regression curve m_7 does least squares matching provide good results because the true regression curve is linear.[4] On the other hand, local polynomial matching performs in most settings better than pair-matching. SG matching is usually the most precise, followed by kernel matching, and finally by local linear matching.

For symmetric sample sizes ($n_s = n_r = 40$, 200, or 1000) the mean squared error of all estimators, except for the inconsistent least squares matching estimator, decreases at a rate $\frac{1}{n}$ and the relative efficiency of local polynomial matching and pair-matching remains remarkably constant, independent of sample size. On average, kernel matching reduces MSE by about 30%, local linear matching by about 22% and SG matching by about 33%, relative to pair-matching.[5] With respect to the median, these efficiency gains are even larger. If any trend is discernible, it seems to indicate that local polynomial matching becomes more efficient relative to pair-matching with growing sample size.[6] Furthermore, the relative efficiency between SG matching and local linear matching remains constant, indicating that the variance problems of conventional local linear regression, as discussed in the previous section, are not restricted to very small samples but are also present in fairly large samples (of size 1000).

In terms of variance and bias, pair-matching and local linear matching are almost unbiased with their variance contributing on average more than 97% to their MSE, except for sample size 40 where the variance contribution to the MSE is on average 92% for pair-matching and 95% for local linear matching. Small-sample bias is more pronounced for kernel and SG matching. About 14% of the mean squared error of SG matching stems from squared bias for sample size 40 and 9% for sample size 200. For kernel matching the squared bias proportion is even 19% (13%) for samples of size 40 (200). In absolute numbers, kernel matching has smallest variance, while pair-matching followed by local linear matching exhibit the largest variances. Furthermore, the variances of pair-matching and local linear matching are generally higher than the variance approximation according to the

---

[4] Whereas the re-weighting estimator is generally unbiased, squared bias contributes a significant portion to the MSE of least squares matching.

[5] Average efficiency gains are measured by the average relative MSE and not by the average absolute MSE, since the latter would over-weight designs with large MSE and under-weight designs with small MSE.

[6] The simulations for sample size 1000 are based on less replications, and thus, are less precise.

variance bound (2.38), given in the last column of the Tables C.3 to C.7. On the other hand, the variances of kernel and SG matching are frequently lower than the variance bound. This might be explained by the larger local bias of kernel and SG matching, since Seifert&Gasser local linear regression reduces local variance at the cost of local bias, and kernel regression often exhibits large bias in regions of high curvature and at the boundary. It is unclear how to interpret these findings in light of the trade-off between asymptotic bias and asymptotic variance, but it might indicate that kernel and SG matching achieve the efficiency bound at the optimal bandwidth value.

The simulation results for non-symmetric sample sizes are presented in Tables C.6 and C.7. If the source sample is larger than the target sample, as it is often the case in treatment evaluation, all estimators improve their relative efficiency against pair-matching. Table C.6 corresponds to a situation where the control observations outnumber the treated observations by five to one ($n_s = 200$, $n_r = 40$). The MSE of kernel matching is on average about 40% lower than the MSE of pair-matching, while it is reduced by 35% with local linear matching and by about half with SG matching. Still though, the relative ordering of the estimators remains unchanged, as it is also the case in the reverse situation of a small source sample and a larger target sample ($n_s = 40$, $n_r = 200$, Table C.7). In this case, the efficiency gains vis-à-vis pair-matching are only about 20%, 16% and 25% for kernel, local linear and SG matching, respectively. Pair-matching is relatively less worse in these circumstances, because the number of treated observations is much larger than the number of control observations. Hence pair-matching is forced to use the control observations many times. In other words, pair-matching already incorporates weighting the control observations, but is restricted to using integer weights. Such a situation occurs in treatment evaluation when the counterfactual outcome for the non-treated needs to be estimated, as it is necessary for the estimation of the average treatment effect or the average effect on the untreated, or in the evaluation of multiple treatments where source and target populations interchange (Lechner 2002a).

3.1.2 Sensitivity to the Bandwidth Value

The previous analyses indicated that local polynomial matching, at its optimal bandwidth h^{opt}, is more precise than pair-matching. On the other hand, this (simulated) optimal bandwidth h^{opt} does vary considerably among regression curves and among density combinations as can be seen from Tables C.3 to C.7. This might either imply that the optimal bandwidth depends crucially on the distribution of outcome and covariates in the source and the target population or that MSE(h) is nearly flat in extended regions around the minimum so that variations in the simulated optimal bandwidth would be spurious. Since the optimal bandwidth is usually unknown in practice, sensitivity to bandwidth choice is a crucial concern. To assess robustness to bandwidth choice, it is revealing to look at the entire MSE-bandwidth graph as depicted in Figure 3.4 for regression curve m_3 and sample size $n_s = n_r = 200$. (The graphs for the other regression curves are found in Appendix D.)

In Figure 3.4 the MSE of pair-matching appears as a horizontal line, since it does not depend on the bandwidth. The MSE of kernel matching (short-dashed), local linear matching (long-dashed) and SG matching (solid) are plotted for bandwidth values h from 0.01 to 0.50. The upper left picture corresponds to the density combination $N_1 - N_2$, the upper middle picture to density combination $N_1 - N_3$, the upper right picture to $N_2 - N_1$, and so forth. Thus the two pictures in the middle correspond to the more difficult estimation settings where the two densities overlap less than in the four other settings (cf. Figure 3.1).

Fig. 3.4. Simulated MSE for regression curve m_3 (sample size $n_0 = n_1 = 200$)

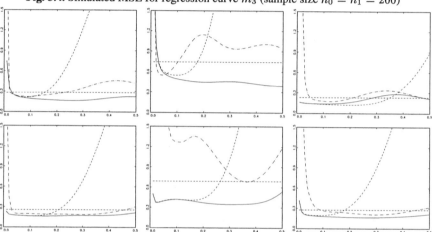

Abscissa: Bandwidth h from 0.01 to 0.50, Ordinate: MSE*1000; Pair-matching (horizontal line), kernel matching (short-dashed), local linear matching (long-dashed) and Seifert&Gasser matching (solid). Density combinations $N_1 - N_2$, $N_1 - N_3$, $N_2 - N_1$ from top left to top right picture, density combinations $N_2 - N_3$, $N_3 - N_1$, $N_3 - N_2$ from bottom left to bottom right picture. (See Figure 3.1.)

Some general patterns emerge from the graphs in Figure 3.4 (and in Appendix D). The problems of local linear matching with small bandwidths become obvious as its mean squared error becomes very large for bandwidth values approaching zero. Although local linear matching often performs better than pair-matching for some bandwidth values, it usually does so only in rather narrow bandwidth regions. Furthermore, the MSE-graph of local linear matching often has local minima in the more difficult density combinations ($N_1 - N_3$, $N_3 - N_1$), even at large sample sizes. This corresponds to the trade-off between choosing a small bandwidth value to estimate $m(x)$ with low bias in regions of dense data and choosing a large bandwidth to estimate $m(x)$ with less variability in regions of sparse data. It might be difficult for a data-driven bandwidth selector to distinguish between these minima to find the global minimum.

For kernel and SG matching, the results appear more favourable. Frequently kernel matching outperforms pair-matching in bandwidth regions from about $h = 0.05$ to 0.15. However, at larger bandwidths its MSE increases steeply. SG matching appears much less sensitive to bandwidth choice and its MSE explodes less often at very small or large bandwidth values. Commonly its MSE is quite flat and lies below the MSE of pair-matching in bandwidth regions from $h = 0.03$ to 0.25.

Another way to assess robustness is to look at the average MSE in a region around the optimal bandwidth. Considering a neighbourhood of span 0.2 around h^{opt}, i.e. if h were drawn randomly from the interval $[h^{opt} - 0.1, h^{opt} + 0.1]$, the average efficiency gain of kernel matching relative to pair-matching is still 8% (median 16%) and for SG matching 25% (median 34%) for sample size 200. In contrast, local linear matching would lead on average to a 71% *higher* MSE than pair-matching (median increase -2%). These figures are similar for samples of size 40 when allowing for a neighbourhood of span 0.4 around h^{opt} and for sample size 1000 with neighbourhood-span 0.15. For the sample size combination ($n_s = 40$, $n_r = 200$) the robustness of SG matching to bandwidth choice becomes even more apparent. If the bandwidth is randomly selected from the interval $h^{opt} \pm 0.2$, the MSE of SG matching is on average still 13% (median 26%) lower than the MSE of pair-matching, whereas kernel matching on average would have a 12% (median increase 6%) larger MSE, and the MSE of local linear matching would be about $2\frac{1}{2}$ times the MSE of pair-matching (median increase 15%).

Summing up these results, local polynomial matching appears superior to least squares matching, to re-weighting and also to pair-matching, but it should be taken into account that the different local polynomial matching estimators vary in their potential efficiency gains and robustness to bandwidth choice.

3.2 Approximation to the MSE and Bandwidth Choice

3.2.1 Bandwidth Choice

The previous simulation results demonstrated that in most cases substantial efficiency gains vis-à-vis pair-matching could be achieved by local polynomial matching. Particularly, SG matching and to a lesser extent also kernel matching turned out to be quite insensitive to the bandwidth value, whereas this is not the case for local linear matching. To realize these precision gains a suitable data-driven bandwidth selector is required. The performance of data-driven bandwidth selectors for nonparametric regression is often assessed by the mean integrated squared error criterion $\text{MISE}(h) = E \int (\hat{m}(x; h) - m(x))^2 dx$, as discussed in Section 2.3. Yet, since estimation of $m(x)$ is only an intermediate step for the generalized matching estimator (2.27), it is not obvious whether minimizing MISE is a sensible criterion. The MISE criterion would take account only of the source sample and neglect the location of the target population. Yet precise estimation of $m(x)$ in regions where the target population is concentrated is more important than in regions where the source population is located. Furthermore, by averaging over the imputed values $\hat{m}(X_{rj})$ the general matching estimator adds another smoothing step, which might change its sensitivity to the bandwidth value. To gain insight into the bandwidth selection problem for the generalized matching estimator (2.27), an approximation to the mean squared error of local polynomial matching is derived, which might be used as a first step towards a data-driven bandwidth selector.

3.2.2 MSE Approximation of Local Polynomial Matching

In the derivation of the MSE approximation, I draw on the results of Heckman, Ichimura, and Todd (1998) about asymptotically linear representations of local polynomial regression. To abstract from the estimation of the common support, I assume henceforth that the support of X in the target population is contained in the support of X in the source population: $S^r \subseteq S^s$. This condition is satisfied in all the settings considered in this chapter with $S^r = S^s = [0, 1]$, see Figure 3.1. Using (2.47) and (2.48) of Section 2.3, the local polynomial regression estimator $\hat{m}(x)$ of $m(x) = E[Y^s | X = x, D = s]$ can be written in the form

$$\hat{m}(x) - m(x) = \frac{1}{n_s} \sum_i \psi(Y_{si}, X_{si}; x) + b(x) + R(x),$$

with mean-zero influence function ψ, local bias $b(x)$ and a remainder term $R(x)$. The local influence function ψ for an interior point x is

$$\psi(Y_{si}, X_{si}, x) = (Y_{si} - m(X_{si})) \cdot \frac{K\left(\frac{X_{si} - x}{h}\right)}{h f_s(x)}$$

for Nadaraya-Watson kernel regression ($p = 0$) and for local linear regression ($p = 1$). Inserting these expressions in (2.27) yields an asymptotic representation of the *local polynomial matching* estimator

$$\frac{1}{n_r} \sum_{j=1}^{n_r} \hat{m}(X_{rj})$$

$$= \frac{1}{n_r} \sum_{j=1}^{n_r} \left(m(X_{rj}) + b(X_{rj}) + R(X_{rj}) + \frac{1}{n_s} \sum_{i=1}^{n_s} \psi(Y_{si}, X_{si}; X_{rj}) \right). \quad (3.1)$$

In Appendix C an approximation to the mean squared error of local polynomial matching is derived on the basis of this asymptotically linear representation (3.1). The approximate MSE is

$$MSE \approx \left(\int b(x) f_r(x) dx \right)^2 \qquad (3.2)$$

$$+ \frac{1}{n_r} \int (m(x) + b(x) - \theta)^2 f_r(x) dx$$

$$+ \frac{1}{n_s} \int \sigma_s^2(x) \frac{f_r^2(x)}{f_s(x)} dx + \frac{\bar{\mu}_0}{n_r n_s h \mu_0^2} \int \frac{\sigma_s^2(x)}{f_s(x)} f_r(x) dx,$$

where $\theta = \int (m(x) + b(x)) f_r(x)\, dx$, $\sigma_s^2(x) = Var[Y^s | X = x]$ and $\bar{\mu}_0 = \int K(u)^2\, du$. The first term of (3.2) is the squared bias contribution to the MSE, while the second, third and fourth terms represent the variance of local polynomial matching. The second term stems from the variation of $m(x)$ and $b(x)$ along x. The third term represents the covariances and the fourth term the variances of ψ. If only the terms of highest order are considered in the MSE approximation (3.2), the bias of local polynomial matching is

$$\underset{f_r(x)}{E} [b(X)] \tag{3.3}$$

and its variance simplifies to

$$\frac{1}{n_r}\frac{1}{f_r(x)} Var\, E[Y^s | X, D = s] + \frac{1}{n_s}\frac{1}{f_s(x)} E \left[\sigma_s^2(X) \frac{f_r^2(X)}{f_s^2(X)} \right]. \tag{3.4}$$

These highest order terms correspond to the results of Heckman, Ichimura, and Todd (1998, p. 277ff), and the variance expression equals the variance bound (2.38). However, these first-order asymptotic results are useless for analyzing the bandwidth choice problem since the variance term (3.4) does not depend on the bandwidth value h. (This would suggest deliberate undersmoothing to make the average bias term (3.3) small.) Hence for examining bandwidth choice, second-order asymptotic expressions like (3.2) must be considered. To assess the accuracy of this MSE approximation in finite samples and analyze sensitivity to bandwidth choice, the approximation (3.2) can be computed for different regression curves $m(x)$, densities f_s, f_r and values of h, n_s, n_r and compared to the simulated MSE of the previous section. For the calculation of (3.2) the local bias $b(x)$ is given by (2.46).

However, the expressions for the local influence function (2.48) and the local bias (2.46) are valid only at interior points and need to be modified for points at the boundary. Since much of the density mass of the target population might be located in the boundary region of the source population, taking account of boundary regions might be important. Therefore, the MSE approximation given in Appendix C (together with the local bias and variance expressions of Corollary 1 instead of the simpler expressions (2.46)) incorporates boundary effects as well. This refined approximation, based on (C.5), (B.1) and (B.2), is henceforth referred to as *two-terms approximation*, whereas the approximation (3.2) together with the (interior) bias expressions (2.46) is referred to as *first-term approximation*.

The approximations to the MSE are quite different from the mean integrated squared error criterion

$$MISE = \int \left(b^2(x) + Var\,[\hat{m}(x)] \right) dx \tag{3.5}$$

$$= \int b^2(x)\, dx + \frac{\bar{\mu}_0}{n_s h \mu_0^2} \int \frac{\sigma^2(x)}{f_s(x)}\, dx.$$

This indicates that conventional bandwidth selectors might not be consistent for local polynomial matching.

3.2.3 Approximation Accuracy in Finite Samples

To assess the reliability of these approximations and their usefulness for the development of a bandwidth selector, the MSE approximations are compared to the simulated MSE of Section 3.1 for each regression curve and density combination. *Two-terms* (C.5) and *first-term approximation* (3.2) are both calculated to assess accuracy loss when using the simpler first-term approximation, which is valid only for interior points. The approximations are computed for kernel and for local linear matching using the same bandwidth grid as in Section 3.1. In Figure 3.5 the results are plotted for kernel matching and regression curve m_3, together with its simulated MSE and the MISE approximation (3.5). The MISE approximation visualizes how the bandwidth dependence of local polynomial matching differs from standard nonparametric curve estimation. (The graphs for the other regression curves are found in Appendix D.)

Fig. 3.5. Approximations to the MSE for Kernel matching (curve m_3, sample size 200)

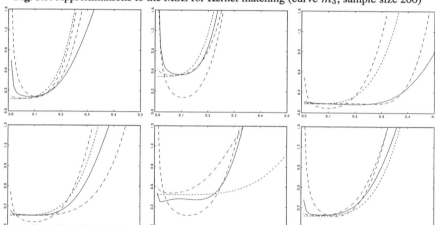

Abscissa: Bandwidth h, Ordinate: MSE*1000, MISE*100. Simulated MSE (solid), two-terms approximation to MSE (dotted-dashed), first-term approximation to MSE (short-dashed) and approximation to MISE (long-dashed). Density combinations $N_1 - N_2$, $N_1 - N_3$, $N_2 - N_1$ from top left to top right picture, density combinations $N_2 - N_3$, $N_3 - N_1$, $N_3 - N_2$ from bottom left to bottom right picture. (See Figure 3.1.)

As in Figure 3.4, the graph in the upper left of Figure 3.5 refers to the density combination $N_1 - N_2$, the upper middle to $N_1 - N_3$ and so forth. The solid curve repeats the simulated MSE of Figure 3.4. The first-term (short-dashed), the two-terms (dotted-dashed) and the MISE (long-dashed) approximations are displayed for the bandwidth values $h = 0.01$ to 0.50. The simulated and the approximated MSE are directly comparable since both are scaled by 10^3, whereas the MISE approximation is scaled by 10^2 to fit into the same graph and, thus, only its shape and the location of its minimum can be interpreted. Since the MISE approximation does not take into account the location of the target population, its graph is identical for the density combinations $N_1 - N_2$ and $N_1 - N_3$ as well as for $N_2 - N_1$ and $N_2 - N_3$ and for $N_3 - N_1$ and $N_3 - N_2$. (In other words, its graph changes only in every second picture.)

As a first impression, the MSE approximations are quite close to the simulated MSE in relatively large bandwidth regions, particularly for sample sizes 1000. The MSE approximations respond to the location of the target population and resemble the simulated MSE in level and shape, with the two-term approximation usually being somewhat more precise. However, both approximations are often rather flat for bandwidth values below 0.10, and particularly the first-term approximation does not rise steeply for small bandwidth values (despite increasing local variance), as the last term in (3.2) is divided by $n_r \cdot n_s$. (In the MISE approximation (3.5) the integrated variance is divided only by n_s). For h converging to zero, eventually the last term in (3.2) would dominate and also the first-term approximation would converge to infinity (for fixed sample size). However, this effect seems to take place only for extremely small bandwidth values, and in the graphs the MSE approximation rather appears to level off to the variance bound (2.38) (compare to the last column of Tables C.4 and C.5). The two-term approximation is often quite flat for bandwidths smaller than 0.10, too, and does not increase very much at small bandwidth values. By contrast, the simulated MSE sometimes explodes for small bandwidth values, particularly in the more difficult density combinations $N_1 - N_3$ and $N_3 - N_1$.

Thus the MSE approximations would tend to *undersmooth* in the sense that they risk choosing very low bandwidth values at which the true mean squared error might be very large. Undersmoothing might even be a greater risk if, as usual, the elements of the MSE approximations are not known and need to be estimated. The steep increase of the MSE approximations at large bandwidth values, which always sets in at lower bandwidth values than for the simulated MSE, would prevent choosing a bandwidth too large. But the nearly flat MSE approximation at lower bandwidth values would complicate the bandwidth choice and might often result in choosing bandwidth values too small. Because of this limited sensitivity to low bandwidth values, these MSE approximations appear not to be suited as a basis for data-driven bandwidth selection.

On the other hand, the MISE approximation displays more curvature around its minimum and increases steeply at small and large bandwidth values. Although neither its shape nor its level resemble the MSE, the *simulated* MSE at the MISE-minimizing bandwidth value is often not much higher than at its optimal bandwidth value. Moreover, no obvious pattern of over- or undersmoothing can be detected, suggesting that a conventional bandwidth selector might still be a useful starting point for kernel matching.

For local linear matching, the MSE approximations, particularly the two-term approximation, are often very different from the simulated MSE. (Results are found in Appendix D.) The simulated MSE frequently has local minima, while the MSE approximations are always globally convex. Moreover, the MSE approximations would often suggest a rather small bandwidth value, whereas the minimum of the simulated MSE is often at very large bandwidths. Similarly, the MISE approximation would often fail in picking a suited bandwidth value, too. Hence bandwidth selection seems to be difficult for local linear matching.

3.3 Data-driven Bandwidth Choice by Cross-Validation

As the approximations to the MSE of local polynomial matching seem not to be suited for bandwidth selection in finite samples, and since kernel and SG matching appeared to be quite robust to bandwidth choice in the previous sections, a conventional MISE-targeting bandwidth selector, although not asymptotically optimal, might still lead to satisfactory bandwidth choices.

The performance of leave-one-out cross validation and of the penalized cross validation bandwidth selectors of Akaike, Rice and Shibata (2.52) were compared. Only the results for the Akaike selector are reported here, which performed slightly better than the others. The Akaike penalized cross-validation selector chooses the bandwidth h that minimizes the criterion

$$CV_A(h; n_s) = \exp\left(\frac{2}{n_s h}\right) \cdot \sum_{i=1}^{n_s} (Y_{si} - \hat{m}(X_{si}; h))^2. \tag{3.6}$$

With this data-driven bandwidth selector, the previous simulation study is repeated. For all regression curves and density combinations, source and target samples are drawn, the CV-minimizing bandwidth is determined from the source sample (using the same bandwidth grid as before), and the local polynomial matching estimator is computed with this bandwidth. This is repeated 5'000 to 10'000 times. (For sample size 1000 only 100 replications.) Tables C.8 to C.12 summarize these results for kernel matching, local linear matching and SG matching. For each estimator the first column provides the relative MSE compared to pair-matching, the second column indicates which fraction (in %) of the MSE is due to variance and the third column provides the relative MSE compared to the MSE at its optimal bandwidth h^{opt} (see Tables C.3 to C.7). The fourth column gives the mean of the bandwidths selected by cross-validation and the fifth column provides their standard deviation.

Comparing the results to pair-matching, on average kernel and SG matching are always preferable to pair-matching. On the other hand, local linear matching performs usually worse than pair-matching, except when the source sample is much larger than the target sample ($n_s = 200$, $n_r = 40$). A notable exception is the linear regression curve m_7, where local linear matching achieves substantial reductions in MSE by choosing large bandwidth values. SG matching has in all sample size configurations the lowest MSE. For symmetric sample sizes ($n_s = n_r$) its average efficiency gains vis-à-vis pair-matching increase from about 19% (median 25%) for sample size 40 to about 26% (median 33%) for sample size 1000. Kernel and local linear matching improve their relative position to pair-matching with growing sample size, too. These improvements, however, are much less pronounced for kernel matching, which reduces MSE vis-à-vis pair-matching by 13% in samples of size 40 and 17% for sample size 1000. Local linear matching performs significantly worse than pair-matching in small samples and seems to break even only at sample size 1000. With non-symmetric sample sizes, all local polynomial estimators become by another 10%-points more precise if the source sample is much larger than the target sample ($n_s = 200$, $n_r = 40$, i.e. more control than treated individuals), and the MSE of SG matching is then about 35% below that of pair-matching. On the other hand, if the source sample is smaller than the target sample, and thus the number of control observations is small ($n_s = 40$, $n_r = 200$), pair-matching becomes relatively more efficient as it uses the few control observations repeatedly, and only SG matching still realizes significant reductions in MSE of about 10% vis-à-vis pair-matching.

In addition to these average gains in precision, SG matching hardly performs worse than pair-matching. For sample sizes 40 and 200, its MSE is only in 2 of the 48 simulation designs more than 30% larger than the MSE of pair-matching, only once for sample size 1000, never in the sample size combination $200 - 40$, and 5 times in the sample size combination $40 - 200$. For kernel matching these frequencies are more than twice as large, and they are even worse for local linear matching. Local linear matching performs even for sample sizes 1000 and in the favourable sample size combination $n_s = 200$, $n_r = 40$ in more than 8 out of 48 simulation designs by more than 30% worse than pair-matching. This again demonstrates the robustness of the SG estimator to design choice.

These results show that reductions in MSE vis-a-vis pair-matching are feasible by using cross-validation bandwidth selection. It remains to assess how efficient cross-validation bandwidth selection is. The columns labelled MSE^o in Tables C.8 to C.12 measure the efficiency loss to the optimal bandwidth by comparing the MSE of matching with cross-validation-bandwidth-selection with the MSE at its optimal bandwidth h^{opt}, given in Tables C.3 to C.7.[7] For all three local polynomial estimators, this efficiency ratio improves markedly when the sample size increases from 40 to 200, but does not improve further when the sample size is increased to 1000. On average, the MSE of kernel matching with cross-validation bandwidth selection is about 47% larger than at its optimal bandwidth in small samples (n_s or $n_r = 40$, Tables C.8, C.11, C.12) and about 32% larger in samples of size 200 or 1000 (Tables C.9, C.10). The corresponding figures for local linear matching are 56% and 33%, respectively. In contrast, the efficiency loss for SG matching is only about 25% in small samples and 12% in medium and large samples.

Very large efficiency losses often occur for kernel and local linear matching with the more difficult density combinations $N_1 - N_3$ and $N_3 - N_1$, usually together with a bandwidth choice below the optimal bandwidth value. In general, the bandwidths chosen by cross-validation are on average smaller than the optimal

---

[7] Note that, apart from simulation error, even efficiency *gains* could occur, since the data-driven bandwidth selector chooses the bandwidth value conditional on a given dataset, whereas the simulated optimal bandwidths are unconditional.

bandwidths of Tables C.3 to C.7 for kernel and local linear matching in all sample size combinations, while no such clear pattern can be detected for SG matching. However, this does not imply that simply selecting larger bandwidth values would generally have been preferable for kernel or local linear matching. Hence the development of better bandwidth selectors might be worthwhile for the kernel and local linear matching estimators, but the scope for improvement seems to be limited for SG matching.

3.4 Matching with Unknown Propensity Score

The results so far demonstrated the superiority of SG and kernel matching to pair-matching in finite-samples, when matching proceeds on a univariate and observed covariate X, e.g. a single characteristic, an index of characteristics, a distance metric, or a known propensity score. In this section estimation of the counterfactual mean is analyzed when the covariate itself is not observed but estimated. Matching proceeds then on the estimated propensity score, where the propensity score

$$p^{s|rs}(x) = P(D = s | X = x, D \in \{r, s\}),\qquad(3.7)$$

is the probability of belonging to the source population conditional on either belonging to the source or the target population and given characteristics $X = x$. For implementing propensity score matching, first an estimate of $p^{s|rs}(x)$ needs to be obtained for all observations $\{(Y_{si}, X_{si})\}_{i=1}^{n_s}$ and $\{X_{rj}\}_{j=1}^{n_r}$. With $p^{s|rs}$ estimated, the corresponding generalized propensity-score-matching estimator of (2.25) is

$$\frac{1}{n_r} \sum_{j=1}^{n_r} \hat{m}(\hat{p}_{rj}^{s|rs}),$$

where $\hat{p}_{rj}^{s|rs} = \hat{p}^{s|rs}(X_{rj})$ and $m(\rho) = E[Y^s | p^{s|rs} = \rho, D = s]$, as discussed in Section 2.1. The re-weighting estimator (2.36) becomes

$$\frac{1}{n_r} \sum_{i=1}^{n_s} Y_{si} \cdot \frac{1 - \hat{p}_{si}^{s|rs}}{\hat{p}_{si}^{s|rs}}.\qquad(3.8)$$

Since the term $(1 - \hat{p}_{si}^{s|rs})/\hat{p}_{si}^{s|rs}$ can become arbitrarily large for estimated propensity score values close to zero, some form of trimming is necessary to obtain stable estimates. Eight different trimming rules have been implemented: Either capping the ratio $(1 - \hat{p}_{si}^{s|rs})/\hat{p}_{si}^{s|rs}$ at 100, 50, 20, 10 or 5, respectively, or trimming (deleting) the 1,2 or 5% observations with the largest ratio.

Pair-matching, the re-weighting estimator, and kernel, local linear and SG matching with Akaike penalized cross-validation bandwidth selection (bandwidth grid $h = 0.01, 0.02, ..., 0.80$) are evaluated for a variety of simulation designs with propensity scores estimated by probit. Samples of size $n_s + n_r = 200$, 500, or 2000, respectively, with 3 observed characteristics X_1, X_2, X_3 are drawn and the observations are split into the source and the target sample by the selection rule

$$D_i = r \quad \text{if} \quad \alpha + X_i'\beta + \varepsilon_i \geq 0$$
$$= s \quad \text{otherwise,}$$

with ε_i a normal random error term. X_1 is a $\chi^2_{(1)}$ random variable, X_2 is uniformly$_{[0,1]}$ distributed and X_3 is either binary or normally distributed. The ratio n_s/n_r of control to treated observations is random and about one, see Table C.13. The propensity score $p^{s|rs}(X_{1i}, X_{2i}, X_{3i})$ is estimated for each observation by probit. Six different selection rules (see Table C.13) and six different outcome regression curves with additive normal error (see Table C.14) are analyzed. The simulations are based on 5'000 to 20'000 replications (only 200 replications for sample size 2000), and the results for all 36 designs are given in Tables C.15 to C.17. Columns one and two indicate selection rule and regression curve, and columns three and four contain the mean squared error of pair-matching and the fraction (in %) that is due to its variance. The columns labelled MSE^r give the relative MSE (relative to pair-matching, in %), and the columns labelled %Var indicate the fraction of the MSE that is contributed by the variance. Finally, the columns denoted by h contain the mean of the selected bandwidth values.

Across Tables C.15 to C.17 the local polynomial matching estimators are usually substantially superior to pair-matching. The relative efficiency of kernel and SG matching vis-à-vis pair-matching seems to decrease slightly with growing sample size, from reductions in MSE of 32% (42%) at sample size 200 to 24% (35%) at sample size 2000 for kernel matching (SG matching). On the other hand, the efficiency gains of local linear matching are stable at about 21%. Although kernel matching has on average a lower mean squared error than local linear matching, it seems to be less robust to selection rule and regression curve, since it performs worse than pair-matching in about 7-9 out of the 36 designs. With local linear matching this occurs only in 3-4 designs. The MSE of SG matching is never larger than that of pair-matching for sample size 200, only once for sample size 500, and twice for sample size 2000.

Concerning variance and bias, the results are similar to those obtained in Section 3.1. Pair-matching and local linear matching are nearly unbiased, whereas about 25% of the MSE of kernel matching and about 20% of the MSE of SG matching are due to squared bias. Setting this in relation to their average MSE indicates again that reducing local variance at the cost of incurring bias could be beneficial.

For detecting systematic under- or oversmoothing of the cross-validation bandwidth selector, the local polynomial matching estimators are also evaluated at 0.7, 0.8, 0.9, 1.1, 1.2 and 1.3 times the bandwidth selected by cross-validation. For kernel matching, smaller bandwidths would have been preferable on average, whereas local linear matching would have been slightly better off with larger bandwidths. Again, SG matching is hardly affected by changes in the bandwidth value.

Interpreting the results of the re-weighting estimator is less straightforward. Re-weighting without trimming is unbiased but has a very large mean squared error, and its relative efficiency to the other estimators *worsens* drastically with increasing sample size. At sample size 200, its MSE is on average about twice the MSE of pair-matching and in median it is slightly below that of pair-matching. At sample size 2000, its MSE is on average about 10 times the MSE of pair-matching and, in addition, the median relative MSE has risen to 150%. Because of these results, the re-weighting estimator has also been implemented with eight different trimming rules. These trimming rules are arbitrary and the results presented in the last two columns of Tables C.15 to C.17 correspond to the trimming rule for which average MSE turned out to be lowest. In this sense it is the simulated 'optimal' trimming rule in the spirit of the analysis of Section 3.1. The results for the other trimming rules lie somewhere in-between these and those without trimming. At sample size $n_s + n_r = 200$ the 'optimal' trimming rule was capping the multiplier $(1 - \hat{p}_{si}^{s|rs})/\hat{p}_{si}^{s|rs}$ at 10. In other words, modifying the estimator (3.8) to

$$\frac{1}{n_r}\sum_{i=1}^{n_s}Y_{si} \cdot \min\left\{C, \frac{1 - \hat{p}_{si}^{s|rs}}{\hat{p}_{si}^{s|rs}}\right\},$$

where $C = 10$ is the capping level. For sample size 500, the propensity score ratio was capped at $C = 20$ and for sample size 2000 at $C = 50$. Trimming observations, i.e. deleting observations with very large $\hat{p}_i/(1 - \hat{p}_i)$ ratios, instead of capping, was less successful.

A first observation is that trimming introduced finite-sample bias, with squared bias contributing to about 15% of MSE. With 'optimal' trimming the re-weighting estimator performs better than pair-matching and better than local linear matching in samples of size 200 and 500. However, its relative efficiency vis-à-vis all matching estimators worsens steadily with increasing sample size, in spite of its advantageous 'optimal' trimming rule flexibility. At sample size 2000, it is already inferior to local linear matching. At all sample sizes, it is clearly inferior to SG matching.

These results for matching on the estimated propensity score confirm the findings of Sections 3.1 and 3.3. SG matching with cross validation bandwidth-selection yields substantial precision gains vis-a-vis the conventional pair-matching estimator. To a lesser extent also kernel matching is superior to pair-matching. Local linear matching, on the other hand, is the least precise among the three compared local polynomial matching estimators. This relative ordering is remarkably stable for different sample sizes. The re-weighting estimator is sensitive to the trimming level and is inferior to local polynomial matching (particularly in larger samples). Without trimming re-weighting fails completely, and further use of the re-weighting estimator requires the development of an estimator of the optimal trimming level.

The MSE of SG matching is on average about 25% smaller than the MSE of pair-matching when matching on an observed covariate. On the other hand, when matching on an estimated propensity score, the reduction in MSE is about 40%. (The corresponding values for kernel matching are 15% and 30%, respectively.)

The reason for this difference is that pair-matching becomes less precise (relative to all other estimators) when matching proceeds on estimated covariates, because it compares each target sample observation with only *one* source sample observation. Although the observations within each matched pair are supposed to have identical characteristics, they might indeed be rather different if the covariates are imprecisely estimated. Hence matching each target sample observation to many source sample observations (as in local polynomial matching) reduces not only the susceptibility of the estimate with respect to the variability in the outcome Y but also with respect to the variance of the estimated covariates.

A reduction in MSE of about 40% means that pair-matching needs almost 70% more observations to achieve the same precision as SG matching. If the source sample is larger than the target sample ($n_s > n_r$), which is often the case in binary treatment evaluation with a large control sample, the precision gains of local polynomial matching vis-a-vis pair-matching are even larger.[8]

---

[8] Although SG matching seems to lead to substantial reductions in mean squared error, conducting inference with SG matching has not been analyzed so far. In practice, one is not only interested in the point-estimate of the covariate-adjusted mean but also in an estimate of the estimator's variability. This requires estimating the estimator's bias and variance. Whereas the variance could often be estimated by resampling techniques, an estimation of the bias might be more difficult. From this perspective, a matching estimator that undersmooths (such as pair-matching) has the advantage that its bias is of lower order and thus vanishes asymptotically (though not in finite samples), at the expense of a larger mean squared error.

4 Semiparametric Estimation of Optimal Treatment Choices

In this chapter semiparametric estimation of the conditional expected potential outcomes $E[Y^r|X]$ is considered, which are the central ingredients to the derivation of optimal treatment choices, as discussed in Section 2.2. The previous chapter has shown that nonparametric regression, particularly SG matching, is suited for estimating average treatment effects in small samples or for small subpopulations. However the task of estimating treatment effects on an individual level is even more demanding, since the characteristics vector X usually must contain many covariates to identify the outcomes $E[Y^r|X]$ by the conditional independence assumption (2.4). Fully nonparametric estimation of $E[Y^r|X]$ might then be very imprecise. As an alternative, a semiparametric approach is developed in this chapter, which combines nonparametric SG matching on a subpopulation level with parametric specifications.

The asymptotic properties of the proposed GMM estimator are derived. The applicability of the GMM statistic for testing whether the parametric regression function is correctly specified is examined. Finally, optimal choices among Swedish rehabilitation programmes for people with long-term illnesses are derived and compared to the observed participant-programme allocation. The outcomes that could have been achieved had all individuals been allocated to programmes according to the statistical model are predicted and the potential for policy improvement through better participant allocation is assessed.

4.1 Estimation of Conditional Expected Potential Outcomes

Estimating the conditional expected potential outcomes $E[Y^r|X]$ from a sample of former participants (including non-participants) requires a handling of the selection problem if former programme participants had not been allocated randomly to the treatments. Selection bias can be avoided by including in X all variables that affected the programme selection decision of the former participants as well as their potential outcomes, which implies conditional independence (2.4) and gives

$$E[Y^r|X] = E[Y^r|X, D = r] = E[Y^r|X, D \neq r].$$

Hence the conditional outcome $E[Y^r|X = x]$ is identified from a sample $\{(X_i, D_i, Y_i)\}_{i=1}^n$ drawn from a formerly treated population. However, $E[Y^r|X = x]$ is identified only for all $x \in S^r$, where $S^r =$

$\{x : f_{X|D=r}(x) > 0\} = \{x : p^r(x) > 0\}$ is the support (2.7) of X among the former participants in programme r, because no observations can be available at any $x \notin S^r$. Accordingly $E[Y^r|X = x]$ could be estimated nonparametrically for all $x \in S^r$.

Validity of the conditional independence assumption (2.4), however, often requires the inclusion of rather many variables in X, rendering nonparametric estimation difficult. Alternatively, parametric regression is often suggested to estimate conditional expectation functions and proceeds by specifying the conditional expectation function $E[Y^r|X]$ to belong to a certain class of (vector-valued) functions $\varphi^r(x; \theta^r)$, for example linear functions, with unknown coefficient vector θ^r of dimension k. If the expectation function indeed were correctly specified, there would exist a true coefficient vector θ_0^r such that for all x

$$E[Y^r|X = x] = \varphi^r(x; \theta_0^r) \qquad \forall x. \qquad (4.1)$$

The coefficients θ^r would then be estimated by parametric regression (e.g. by Maximum Likelihood or GMM) from the observed outcomes Y_i of the former participants in programme r (i.e. with $D_i = r$). Nevertheless, in most evaluation settings the true functional form of the expected potential outcomes is unknown and $E[Y^r|X = x]$ is likely to be misspecified by $\varphi^r(x; \cdot)$. In this case, the estimated conditional outcome $\hat{E}[Y^r|X = x] = \varphi^r(x; \hat{\theta}^r)$, where $\hat{\theta}^r$ are the estimated coefficients, is inconsistent for almost all x.

This tension between parametric and nonparametric regression motivates the development of a semiparametric estimator that incorporates both elements to obtain more reliable estimates of $E[Y^r|X]$ in the case of misspecification. The underlying idea is based on the observation that parametric estimation of $E[Y^r|X]$ takes into account only the observations $\{(X_i, Y_i)|D_i = r\}$ of former participants in programme r but ignores completely the observations $\{X_i|D_i \neq r\}$ of the participants in other programmes. Hence the parametric estimator is centered at the distribution of X among the programme-r-participants and not at the distribution in the population. Thus as parametric regression seeks to minimize mean squared error with respect to the population of programme-r-participants, the estimates of $E[Y^r|X = x]$ may be severely biased particularly in regions with a low density of $f_{X|D=r}(x)$, because such regions have little weight in the estimator's loss function. However, if the former participants have not been randomly assigned to the programmes, the density distribution $f_{X|D=r}$ among the former programme-r-participants does usually not coincide with the density f_X in the population. Indeed, if the participants in programme r are rather different from the participants in other programmes, biased estimates of $E[Y^r|X = x]$ are particularly worrying in regions where $f_{X|D=r}(x)$ is small but $f_X(x)$ large. Accordingly, the parametric estimates of the average potential outcome $E[Y^r]$ and the average counterfactual outcome $E[Y^r|D \neq r]$ usually will be inconsistent. On the other hand, consistent nonparametric estimators of $E[Y^r]$ and $E[Y^r|D \neq r]$ are readily available (as discussed in the previous chapters). Incorporating these consistent estimates into the parametric estimator forces the centering of its average bias at the population distribution f_X instead of at $f_{X|D=r}$. This should improve the estimate of $E[Y^r|X = x]$ in regions where $f_X/f_{X|D=r}$ is large, which is illustrated in Figure 4.1.

Fig. 4.1. Parametric and semiparametric estimation

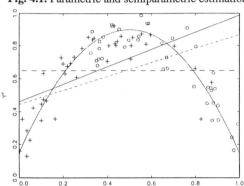

Note: True mean function $E[Y^r|X]$ is parabolic with population mean 0.65 (dashed horizontal line), but is parametrically specified as linear. Observations (Y_i^r, X_i) of the participants in programme r are represented by + signs. Observations (X_j) of the non-participants are depicted by o signs. (The counterfactual outcome Y_j^r of the non-participants is unobserved and only shown for illustration.) Estimated regression lines: OLS (solid) and semiparametric GMM (short-dashed).

In Figure 4.1, Y^r and X are both one-dimensional and the true mean function $E[Y^r|X]$ is parabolic. The mean function is parametrically (mis)-specified as linear. The + and o signs represent observations on programme-r-participants and participants in other programmes, respectively. For the participants (+) the outcomes (Y_i^r, X_i) are observed and the mass of the density $f_{X|D=r}$ lies mostly between 0 and 0.6. For the non-participants (o) only X_j is observed while their counterfactual outcome Y_j^r is unobservable and shown only for illustration. The density $f_{X|D\neq r}$ of the non-participants is concentrated between 0.4 and 1. Estimating $E[Y^r|X]$ by least squares regression gives the solid regression line. Expectably the least squares regression fits a line between the participant observations (+) but ignores the non-participants (o) completely. This leads to a very large bias for $x > 0.8$. However, if it were known that the true mean $E[Y^r]$ in the full population is 0.65 (dashed horizontal line), which could be estimated nonparametrically by taking account of the X_j observations of the non-participants, this additional information should be incorporated into the estimator. The corresponding semiparametric estimator, as described in the next section, yields the short-dashed regression line with $E[E[Y^r|X]] = 0.65$. This regression line is a worse fit than the previous parametric regression line with respect to the participants (+). However it is much less biased for $x > 0.7$, where a substantial mass of the population not participating in programme r lies.

Hence to avoid large and systematic biases in the estimated expected potential outcomes in regions with low density among the participants but high density among the non-participants, I propose to complement a parametric specification of the conditional expectation function with nonparametric estimates of average counterfactual outcomes. As discussed in the previous chapters, average counterfactual outcomes $E[Y^r|D \neq r]$ can be estimated nonparametrically using

$$E_{S^r} [Y^r|D \neq r] = E_{S^r} [E [Y^r|X, D = r] |D \neq r] \qquad (4.2)$$

or exploiting the balancing property of the propensity score

$$= E_{S_r} [E[Y^r|p^r(X), D = r] |D \neq r],$$

where $p^r(x) = P(D = r|X = x)$ is the propensity score. The definition of the average counterfactual outcome is restricted to the support S^r since $E[Y^r|X, D = r]$ is not identified outside it (see the discussion above and in Section 2.1.4). A propensity score matching estimator of (4.2) is

$$\widehat{E_{S_r}}[Y^r|D \neq r] = \frac{\sum \hat{m}^r (\hat{p}_i^r) \cdot 1(D_i \neq r) \cdot 1 (\hat{p}_i^r > 0)}{\sum 1(D_i \neq r) \cdot 1 (\hat{p}_i^r > 0)}, \qquad (4.3)$$

where $\hat{p}_i^r = \hat{p}^r(X_i)$ is a preliminary estimator of the participation probability and $\hat{m}^r(p)$ for $p > 0$ is a nonparametric regression estimate of $m^r(p) = E[Y^r|p^r(X) = p]$, which is obtained from the observations on the programme-r-participants $\{(X_i, Y_i)|D_i = r\}$. The expression $1(\hat{p}_i^r > 0)$ represents the support condition that $f_{X|D=r}(X_i)$ is bounded away from zero. As a general convention all operations with respect to Y^r are defined as *element-wise* if Y^r is a vector, i.e. a multidimensional outcome variable.

The analogous estimator of the average counterfactual outcome using the parametric model would be

$$\widehat{E_{S_r}}[Y^r|D \neq r] = \frac{\sum \varphi^r (X_i, \hat{\theta}^r) \cdot 1(D_i \neq r) \cdot 1 (\hat{p}_i^r > 0)}{\sum 1(D_i \neq r) \cdot 1 (\hat{p}_i^r > 0)}, \qquad (4.4)$$

which would be consistent if the parametric model were correctly specified. (4.4) is the mean of the *out-of-sample prediction* from the sample of participants in programme r to the population of non-participants. Similarly (4.3) represents the out-of-sample-prediction mean according to the nonparametric estimator. If the parametric model were correct, (4.4) and (4.3) would converge to the same limit. Otherwise, a large difference between (4.4) and (4.3) can indicate a misspecification of the parametric regression plane, and the inclusion of the nonparametric estimates can reduce the bias of the estimated regression curve $\hat{E}[Y^r|X]$. My proposal is to include the difference between (4.4) and (4.3)

$$\frac{\sum (\varphi^r (X_i, \theta^r) - \hat{m}^r (\hat{p}_i^r)) \cdot 1(D_i \neq r) \cdot 1 (\hat{p}_i^r > 0)}{\sum 1(D_i \neq r) \cdot 1 (\hat{p}_i^r > 0)} \qquad (4.5)$$

into the loss function of the estimator to ensure that the out-of-sample prediction mean according to the parametric model does not deviate too much from the nonparametric out-of-sample prediction mean.

These considerations hold analogously for any subpopulation defined on the X characteristics. Let $\Lambda(x)$ be a $L \times 1$ vector-valued indicator function defining L different subpopulations. For example, the 3 populations: *all*, *men*, *age 40 to 50 years* would be defined by

$$\Lambda(x) = \begin{pmatrix} 1 \\ 1(x_{\text{gender}} = \text{male}) \\ 1(x_{\text{age}} \in [40, 50]) \end{pmatrix}, \tag{4.6}$$

where x_{gender} and x_{age} refer to the respective elements of the characteristics vector. Analogous to (4.5), θ^r should be chosen in a way to keep the out-of-sample prediction differences between parametric model and nonparametric estimates

$$\frac{\sum \left(\Lambda(X_i) \otimes \varphi^r(X_i, \theta^r) - \hat{\mathbf{m}}_{VL}^r(\hat{p}_i^r) \right) \cdot 1(D_i \neq r) \cdot 1(\hat{p}_i^r > 0)}{\sum 1(D_i \neq r) \cdot 1(\hat{p}_i^r > 0)} \tag{4.7}$$

small in all subpopulations. In (4.7) $\otimes$ is the Kronecker product operator. $\hat{\mathbf{m}}_{VL}^r(\cdot)$ is the $VL \times 1$ column vector of all stacked nonparametric estimates of $E[Y^r|p^r]$ for all populations, *multiplied* with the population indicator function. In other words, the first V elements of $\hat{\mathbf{m}}_{VL}^r$ represent the estimates for all V outcome components for subpopulation 1, the following V elements correspond to subpopulation 2 and so forth. More precisely, let $\hat{m}_{vl}^r(p)$ for $p > 0$ be an estimator of the expectation $E[Y_v^r|p^r(X) = p, \Lambda_l(X) = 1]$, i.e. the expectation of the v-th variable of the potential outcome vector Y^r conditional on the participation probability p^r in the l-th subpopulation defined by $\Lambda_l(X)$. Let $\hat{m}_l^r(\cdot) = (\hat{m}_{1l}^r(\cdot), .., \hat{m}_{vl}^r(\cdot), .., \hat{m}_{Vl}^r(\cdot))'$ be the element-wise defined estimator of the potential outcome vector Y^r in the population l, i.e. of $E[Y^r|p^r(X) = p, \Lambda_l(X) = 1]$. Stacking these estimators for the L subpopulations and multiplying element-wise with the population indicator function Λ gives

$$\hat{\mathbf{m}}_{VL}^r(\hat{p}^r(X_i)) =$$
$$(\hat{m}_1^{r\prime}(\hat{p}^r(X_i)) \cdot \Lambda_1(X_i), ..., \hat{m}_l^{r\prime}(\hat{p}^r(X_i)) \cdot \Lambda_l(X_i), ...,$$
$$\hat{m}_L^{r\prime}(\hat{p}^r(X_i)) \cdot \Lambda_L(X_i))'. \tag{4.8}$$

Including additional subpopulations in (4.7) anchors the parametric model more closely at the nonparametric estimates and, thus, controls deviations more finely. On the other hand, if smaller subpopulations are included, their nonparametric estimates will be less precise and their additional value as anchor for the parametric model would be limited. However, the optimal number and size of populations included depends itself on the degree of heterogenous response.

4.1.1 Semiparametric GMM Estimator

For coalescing the parametric and nonparametric elements, the GMM framework seems ideally suited. The parametric specification (4.1) implies $E[A^r(X) \cdot (Y^r - \varphi^r(X, \theta_0^r))] = 0$ if the parametric specification φ^r is correct, where $A^r(X)$ is an instrument matrix. Choosing A^r to be a $k \times V$ matrix would lead to a just-identified parametric GMM estimator, since θ_0^r contains k coefficients. To align the parametric and the nonparametric out-of-sample predictions, the k moments emanating from the parametric model can be augmented by a second set of VL moments according to the distance vector (4.7). If the parametric specification is correct, both the parametric and the nonparametric estimator of the average counterfactual outcome $E_{S_r}[Y^r | D \neq r]$ are consistent and the difference (4.7) converges to zero. This leads to the moment vector

$$g_n^r(\theta^r, \hat{\mathbf{m}}_{VL}^r, \hat{p}^r)$$
$$= \frac{1}{n} \sum_i \left(\begin{array}{c} A^r(X_i) \cdot (Y_i - \varphi^r(X_i, \theta^r)) \cdot 1(D_i = r) \\ (\Lambda(X_i) \otimes \varphi^r(X_i, \theta^r) - \hat{\mathbf{m}}_{VL}^r(\hat{p}_i^r)) \cdot 1(D_i \neq r) \cdot 1(\hat{p}_i^r > 0) \end{array} \right) \quad (4.9)$$

of length $k + VL$. The first k moments are evaluated for the observations with $D_i = r$, since Y^r can be observed only for the participants. The lower part of the moment vector contains the out-of-sample predictions for the non-participants.[1] The coefficients θ^r are estimated by GMM as the solution to

$$\hat{\theta}_n^r = \arg\min_{\theta^r} g_n^{r\prime} W^r g_n^r, \quad (4.10)$$

where W^r is a positive semidefinite matrix that attaches different weights to the moments. Assigning zero weights to the VL nonparametric moments would lead to the fully parametric estimator.

If the parametric specification is correct and the nonparametric estimator $\hat{m}^r(\hat{p}^r)$ of $E[Y^r | p^r]$ is asymptotically linear with trimming (see Section 2.3), the coefficient estimates $\hat{\theta}^r$ are consistent and $\sqrt{n}$-asymptotically normal with approximate variance

$$\frac{1}{n}(G^{r\prime}W^r G^r)^{-1} G^{r\prime}W^r E[J^r J^{r\prime}] W^r G^r (G^{r\prime}W^r G^r)^{-1}, \quad (4.11)$$

---

[1] Obviously, the second set of moments could further be augmented by including the mean out-of-sample prediction differences separately for the participants in programme 0, programme 1 and so forth, instead of aggregating all non-participants via $1(D_i \neq r)$. In this case, however, some of the moments might rely only on a very small number of effective observations if the number of participants is unevenly distributed among the available programmes. For instance, in the application to Swedish rehabilitation programmes, presented below, the largest participant group consists of about 3500 observations whereas the smallest contains only 360 observations. Hence it seems more flexible to consider the group of non-participants $D_i \neq r$ as a whole and generate instead additional moment conditions by defining further subpopulations $\Lambda(X_i)$ on basis of the X characteristics to ensure that the subpopulations are not too small.

where $G^r = E\left[\frac{\partial g_n^r(\theta_0^r, \hat{m}_{VL}^r, \hat{p}^r)}{\partial \theta'}\right]$ is the expected gradient and

$$J^r = g^r(Y, D, X, \theta_0^r, \mathbf{m}_{VL}^r) - \begin{pmatrix} \mathbf{0}_k \\ E[\Psi_{11,p}^r(Y, D, X; X_2)1(D_2 \neq r)|Y, D, X] \\ \vdots \\ E[\Psi_{VL,p}^r(Y, D, X; X_2)1(D_2 \neq r)|Y, D, X] \end{pmatrix}$$

$$- \begin{pmatrix} \mathbf{0}_k \\ \lambda_{1,r}^{-1} \cdot E[\Psi_{11,m}^r(Y, D, X; X_2)1(D_2 \neq r)|Y, D, X] \\ \vdots \\ \lambda_{L,r}^{-1} \cdot E[\Psi_{VL,m}^r(Y, D, X; X_2)1(D_2 \neq r)|Y, D, X] \end{pmatrix},$$

where the expectation is taken with respect to X_2 and D_2, and $\lambda_{l,r} = \lim_{n \to \infty} \frac{n_{l,r}}{n}$ with $n_{l,r}$ the number of participants in treatment r belonging to subpopulation l. $\mathbf{0}_k$ is a column vector of zeros of length k. The terms $\Psi_{vl,p}^r$ and $\Psi_{vl,m}^r$ are influence functions which take account of the variance due to the preliminary estimation of p^r and m^r, respectively. Proofs and expressions for $\Psi_{vl,p}^r, \Psi_{vl,m}^r$ are given in Appendix E.

Furthermore, the statistic $n \cdot g_n^{r'} \hat{\Omega}^r g_n^r$, with $\hat{\Omega}^r$ being a consistent estimate of $[EJ^r J^{r'}]^{-1}$, is asymptotically χ^2 distributed with degrees of freedom equal to the number of overidentifying restrictions VL

$$n \cdot g_n^{r'} \hat{\Omega}^r g_n^r \xrightarrow{d} \chi_{(VL)}^2, \tag{4.12}$$

provided the asymptotic bias is reduced to a smaller order by undersmoothing. Hence the J-test of overidentifying restrictions (Hansen 1982) can be used to test whether the parametric specification is correct.

On the other hand, if the parametric specification (4.1) is incorrect, the GMM estimator tries to fit the parametric plane among the participants and at the same time intends to minimize the discrepancy between the parametric and the nonparametric out-of-sample prediction mean. In this situation the nonparametric estimates should help to avoid systematically large biases in the estimated regression curve $\hat{E}[Y^r|X]$. A general proof of this property, however, seems difficult. Although it is obvious that attaching positive weight to the semiparametric moments in (4.10) leads asymptotically to a smaller average bias among the non-participants, this relationship is unclear in finite samples and also with respect to average squared bias or average squared error. Therefore the properties of the GMM estimator in finite samples are examined by Monte Carlo simulation.

4.1.2 Monte Carlo Simulation

In a small Monte Carlo experiment, the precision in estimating conditional expected potential outcomes $E[Y^1|X = x]$ is compared for three estimators: The fully parametric estimator, the GMM estimator with identity weighting matrix and the GMM estimator with $\hat{\Omega}^1$ weighting matrix. (In the following the superscript 1 is suppressed to ease notation.) The parametric estimator corresponds to the solution of (4.10) with a weighting matrix W that attaches zero weights to the VL nonparametric moments. The first GMM estimator employs an identity matrix for W. The second GMM estimator uses the first GMM estimates to estimate the inverse of the covariance matrix of the moment vector by $\hat{\Omega} = [\hat{E}JJ']^{-1}$, which is then employed as the weighting matrix in (4.10). In a (correctly specified) parametric setup the second GMM estimator would represent the efficient GMM estimator (Hansen 1982). However, in the case of misspecification the second GMM estimator is not necessarily superior to the first GMM estimator, since the 'efficient' weighting by $[EJJ']^{-1}$ takes only notice of variance but not of the bias of the parametric specification. This leads to a weighting matrix $\hat{\Omega}$ which assigns most of the weight to the k parametric moments and little to the nonparametric moments, because the variance of the nonparametric estimates is much higher compared to the parametric moments. Accordingly the GMM estimator with the weighting matrix $\hat{\Omega}$ is governed by the parametric moments and its coefficient estimates are usually more similar to those of the fully parametric estimator. However, the uncertainty which stems from not knowing the true form of the conditional expectation function is not incorporated in these weights. Such considerations of robustness to misspecification are neglected in the weighting matrix $\hat{\Omega}$. Thus in the case of serious misspecification the second GMM estimator might pay too little attention to the nonparametric estimates.

The simulations proceed by repeatedly drawing samples $\{(X_i, D_i, D_i Y_i^1)\}_{i=1}^n$, estimating the coefficients θ and computing (out-of-sample) mean squared prediction error (MSE) by comparing the estimated potential outcome $\hat{E}[Y^1|X = x]$ with the true conditional expected outcome for 10^5 different values of x (drawn from the same population as the sample). $D_i \in \{0, 1\}$ is binary, and the potential outcome Y_i^1 is one-dimensional ($V=1$) and is observed only if $D_i = 1$. Restricting D_i to be binary is without loss of generality, since the GMM estimator (4.9) distinguishes only between observations with $D_i = r$ and $D_i \neq r$.

The parametric estimator computes θ by least squares. The first GMM estimator uses the least squares estimates as starting values and retains these if optimization of the GMM function (4.10) fails. With these GMM estimates, the asymptotic covariance matrix $E[JJ']$ of the moment vector g_i is calculated and the second GMM estimator is computed with the inverse of this covariance matrix as weighting matrix. As preliminary estimates, the participation probabilities $\hat{p}_i$ are estimated by Probit and the regression curves $m(p) = E[Y|p(X) = p]$ by Seifert and Gasser (1996, 2000) local linear regression for the various subpopulations as discussed in Chapter 3. The support condition is implemented for the GMM estimators by trimming all observations with estimated participation probability $\hat{p}_i$ below the smallest value of $\hat{p}_i$ among the participants ($D_i = 1$).

The X characteristics consist of 3 explanatory variables (X_{i1}, X_{i2}, X_{i3}) drawn from the (non-symmetric) $\chi^2_{(2)}, \chi^2_{(3)}, \chi^2_{(4)}$ distribution and divided by 2,3,4, respectively, to standardize their mean.[2] The observations X_i are assigned to the treatment and control group according to the selection rule $D_i = 1(X_{i1} + X_{i2} + X_{i3} + \varepsilon_i > 4.5)$ with ε standard normally distributed. About 46% of the population are assigned to the treatment group ($D=1$).

The Y_i data are generated according to one of three different Y-models with ξ a standard normal error term:

$$\text{Y-model 1 } Y_i = X_{i1}^2 + X_{i2}^2 + X_{i3}^2 + \xi_i$$
$$\text{Y-model 2 } Y_i = \sqrt{X_{i1} - 0.5} + 2\sqrt{X_{i2} - 0.5} - \sqrt{X_{i3} - 0.5} + \xi_i$$
$$\text{Y-model 3 } Y_i = X_{i1}X_{i2} + X_{i1}X_{i3} + X_{i2}X_{i3} + \xi_i.$$

Four different specifications for the parametric component $\varphi(x, \theta)$ are examined, which are all linear models and vary in their regressor-set included:

Specification	No. regressors	Regressors
φ_0	$k = 4$	$const, X_{i1}, X_{i2}, X_{i3}$
φ_1	$k = 4$	$const, X_{i1}^2, X_{i2}^2, X_{i3}^2$
φ_2	$k = 4$	$const, \sqrt{X_{i1} - 0.5}, \sqrt{X_{i2} - 0.5}, \sqrt{X_{i3} - 0.5}$
φ_3	$k = 7$	$const, X_{i1}, X_{i2}, X_{i3}, X_{i1}X_{i2}, X_{i1}X_{i3}, X_{i2}X_{i3}.$

Hence the specification φ_0 is incorrect for all Y-models, φ_1 is correct only for Y-model 1, φ_2 is correct only for Y-model 2 and φ_3 is correct only for Y-model 3.

The GMM estimators are examined for various numbers of subpopulations L included. The GMM estimator with one nonparametric moment ($L=1$) includes the difference between the parametric and the nonparametric average counterfactual outcome in the entire population. The GMM estimator with four nonparametric moments ($L=4$) includes additionally the moments for the three subpopulations defined by $X_1 < 1.5$, $X_2 < 1.5$, and $X_3 < 1.5$, respectively. The estimator with $L=7$ nonparametric moments adds the three subpopulations: $\{X_1 < 1.5 \wedge X_2 < 1.5\}$, $\{X_1 < 1.5 \wedge X_3 < 1.5\}$ and $\{X_2 < 1.5 \wedge X_3 < 1.5\}$. The estimator with $L=10$ nonparametric moments further includes the subpopulations defined by $X_1 < 1$, $X_2 < 1$, and $X_3 < 1$, respectively. Finally, the estimator with $L=14$ moments appends the subpopulations $X_1 > 2$, $X_2 > 2$, $X_3 > 2$, and $\{X_1 < 1.5 \wedge X_2 < 1.5 \wedge X_3 < 1.5\}$. Whereas the first four populations are large and cover each at least 60% of the population, the subsequent subpopulations become smaller (populations five to seven cover each about 37% and subpopulations eight to ten each about 30% of the population) and the last four populations each cover only about 20% of the population. Thus not only does the number of overidentifying moment restrictions grow with increasing L, but also the precision of the estimated nonparametric averages decreases since the additional populations are smaller and render nonparametric estimation more difficult. Hence in this setup it is to be expected that the GMM estimators with a large number of moments should be less precise.

The expected outcomes vary considerably among these subpopulations. Whereas in Y-model 1 the expected potential outcome EY^1 in the population is

---

[2] A value of 0.5 is added such that their minimum value is 0.5 (and mean 1.5).

Table 4.1. Mean squared error with incorrect parametric specifications for Y model 1

Y-model 1			n=500					n=2000			
	φ_0		φ_2		φ_3		φ_0		φ_2		φ_3
L=0	9.75		22.14		13.23		9.53		21.21		13.12
L=1	7.08	7.52	17.63	17.21	8.62	8.70	6.58	7.24	17.05	16.76	7.55	8.03
L=4	7.27	7.74	17.27	17.35	8.44	9.23	6.69	7.26	16.75	17.22	7.41	8.26
L=7	7.38	7.91	17.24	17.45	8.46	9.35	6.77	7.34	16.73	17.27	7.45	8.37
L=10	7.48	8.14	17.21	18.15	8.58	9.90	6.82	7.39	16.71	17.88	7.51	8.75
L=14	7.49	8.22	17.20	18.08	8.50	9.52	6.84	7.63	16.72	17.81	7.52	8.42

Note: MSE for various parametric specifications ($\varphi_0, \varphi_2, \varphi_3$) for the fully parametric estimator (L=0), and for the first GMM estimator (left column) and the second GMM estimator (right column) for different numbers of nonparametric moments (L=1,4,7,10,14). The total number of moments is $L+k$ where $k=4$ in specifications $\varphi_0, \varphi_1, \varphi_2$ and $k=7$ in φ_3. The true data generating process corresponds to Y-model 1. 1000 replications.

13.1 for the participants and 5.3 for the non-participants, the outcome difference between participants and non-participants can be as large as 8.2 (for the populations ten and eleven) and as small as 0.8 (for population fourteen). Similar heterogeneity occurs for Y-model 2 and 3. For example, in Y-model 2 the expected outcome for the participants is usually larger than for the non-participants, but this relationship is reversed in subpopulation five. In Y-model 2 the expected outcomes for participants and non-participants are 2.2 and 1.5, respectively, and in Y-model 3 these figures are 9.6 and 4.3.

In Table 4.1 the mean squared error of the fully parametric and both GMM estimators is given for the (incorrect) specifications $\varphi_0, \varphi_2, \varphi_3$, respectively, when the Y_i observations are generated by Y-model 1. The left part of the table provides the results for sample size 500, the right part for sample size 2000. The row $L=0$ contains the MSE of the parametric estimator (with no nonparametric moment conditions). The results for the GMM estimators are given for various number of moments ($L=1,4,7,10,14$), with the MSE of the first GMM estimator in the left column and the MSE of the second GMM estimator in the right column. It is seen that the GMM estimators always have lower MSE than the fully parametric estimator, and that the first GMM estimator generally performs somewhat better than the second. The MSE of the second GMM estimator usually increases with the number of moments included, whereas the first GMM estimator is less susceptible to the number of moments. Regarding sample size, the MSE of the parametric estimator decreases only a little when the sample size is quadrupled, while the GMM estimators become relatively more precise. Generally, the relative reductions in MSE vis-a-vis the parametric estimator are between 20-36% for the first GMM estimator and 16-34% for the second GMM estimator at sample size 500, and 20-44% (16-39%) at sample size 2000.

The results according to Y-model 2 are given in Table 4.2. For sample size 2000 the results are similar to those of Table 4.1. The GMM estimators are generally

Table 4.2. Mean squared error with incorrect parametric specifications for Ymodel 2

Y-model 2							n=500					n=2000	
	φ_0		φ_1		φ_3		φ_0		φ_1		φ_3		
L=0	9.72		36.90		12.30		8.27		35.50		9.92		
L=1	10.33	9.40	32.68	33.92	11.56	11.14	7.77	8.05	30.05	31.92	8.38	9.15
L=4	10.24	10.09	33.15	34.58	13.28	11.44	7.53	7.81	30.46	31.89	8.09	8.26
L=7	10.74	10.23	33.49	34.88	17.42	11.63	7.55	7.90	30.62	31.90	8.97	8.33
L=10	10.97	10.38	33.60	35.09	20.89	11.82	7.47	7.94	30.79	32.09	10.35	8.24
L=14	11.09	10.30	33.73	35.19	20.51	11.93	7.50	7.90	30.84	32.00	10.26	8.23

Note: See note below Table 4.1. All figures multiplied by 100. True data generating process is Y-model 2.

Table 4.3. Mean squared error with incorrect parametric specifications for Ymodel 3

Y-model 3							n=500					n=2000	
	φ_0		φ_1		φ_2		φ_0		φ_1		φ_2		
L=0	2.45		4.49		6.39		2.39		4.32		6.25		
L=1	1.65	1.74	4.20	4.26	3.05	3.20	1.54	1.64	3.96	4.19	2.93	3.07
L=4	1.75	1.84	4.20	4.27	3.14	3.26	1.59	1.63	3.99	4.27	2.96	3.05
L=7	1.82	2.01	4.20	4.33	3.24	3.39	1.64	1.76	3.98	4.26	3.02	3.13
L=10	1.84	2.06	4.20	4.40	3.28	3.52	1.65	1.79	4.00	4.32	3.04	3.23
L=14	1.86	2.08	4.20	4.42	3.30	3.52	1.67	1.79	4.00	4.39	3.06	3.23

Note: See note below Table 4.1. True data generating process is Y-model 3.

more precise than the parametric estimator, with the first GMM estimator usually being preferable to the second. However, in specification φ_3 the first GMM estimator becomes slightly inferior to the parametric estimator when the number of nonparametric population moments L exceeds the number of X regressors, which is $k = 7$ for specification φ_3. For sample size 500 the results are mixed. Whereas the first GMM estimator is clearly the best with specification φ_1, it is usually somewhat worse with specification φ_0. In specification φ_3 the first GMM estimator worsens considerably with growing sample size and the dominant estimator is the second GMM estimator. However, the first GMM estimator's large MSE in specification φ_3 when the number of moments is large reduces by half when the sample size is increased to 2000, whereas the MSE decreases only slightly for the other two estimators. At sample size 2000 the precision gains of the GMM estimators relative to the parametric estimator are between -3 to 19% for the first and 3 to 17% for the second GMM estimator.

The results for Y-model 3 in Table 4.3 indicate a clear superiority of the GMM estimators for all specifications φ_0, φ_1 and φ_2, with the first GMM estimator dominating in all cases. The mean squared error of the GMM estimators is usually much lower than the MSE of the parametric estimator and the efficiency gains are in some cases larger than 50%, particularly when only few nonparametric population moments are included. The best results are usually obtained with $L \leq k$, i.e. less (or equal) overidentifying moments than regressors.

Taken together, these results suggest that the inclusion of nonparametric population moments can increase the precision in estimating conditional expected potential outcomes substantially (even reduce MSE up to half) when the true form of the expected potential outcomes is unknown.

In Table 4.4 the properties of the GMM estimator in the case of correct specification of the parametric model are examined, i.e. Y-model 1 with specification φ_1, Y-model 2 with φ_2 and Y-model 3 with φ_3. In the upper part the MSE for the parametric and the GMM estimators is given. It is seen that although the mean squared error of the GMM estimators is relatively much higher than that of the parametric estimator, the absolute magnitude in precision loss is negligible when compared to the absolute efficiency gains seen in Tables 4.1 to 4.3, particularly for Y-models 1 and 3. If one knew the correct specification with (near) certainty this would be of great concern. Otherwise, these efficiency losses of the GMM estimators are outweighed by the improved robustness in the case of misspecification.

Furthermore, the size of the test for overidentifying restrictions is analyzed, which tests whether the parametric model is correctly specified. Since the J-test (4.12) is known to tend to over-reject in many situations (Altonji and Segal 1996, Burnside and Eichenbaum 1996, Hall and Horowitz 1996, Imbens, Spady, and Johnson 1998), alternatively also a Lagrange Multiplier (LM) test proposed in Imbens, Spady, and Johnson (1998) is examined, which is asymptotically $\chi^2_{(VL)}$ distributed as well.[3] Imbens, Spady, and Johnson (1998) analyzed various alternative test statistics of which the LM test

$$LM = \hat{\lambda}' \left(\sum \hat{\pi}_i g_i g_i' \right) \left[\sum \hat{\pi}_i^2 g_i g_i' \right]^{-1} \left(\sum \hat{\pi}_i g_i g_i' \right) \hat{\lambda} \xrightarrow{d} \chi^2_{(VL)} \qquad (4.13)$$

performed best in their Monte Carlo simulations, where the $\hat{\pi}_i$ are estimated empirical likelihood (or exponential tilting) probabilities[4] and $\hat{\lambda}$ are estimated Lagrange multipliers. A convenient way to compute the empirical probability weights $\hat{\pi}_i$ provides the estimator of Back and Brown (1993)

$$\hat{\pi}_i = \frac{1}{n} \frac{1 - g_n \hat{\Omega} g_i}{1 - g_n \hat{\Omega} g_n},$$

which comes in a closed form solution and is semiparametrically efficient in estimating the empirical distribution function (Brown and Newey 2002). With this estimator of the empirical probabilities the Lagrange multiplier is

---

[3] Again, assuming that the asymptotic bias of $g_n^r(\hat{\theta}^r)$ is reduced to a smaller order by undersmoothing.

[4] Empirical Likelihood was introduced by Owen (1988) and Qin and Lawless (1994), empirical tilting by Imbens, Spady, and Johnson (1998). The approach used here follows Brown, Newey, and May (2001) and treats the coefficients θ as given and maximises with respect to π_i.

Table 4.4. Mean squared error and J-tests under correct specification

		n=500						n=2000				
		Y-model 1		Y-model 2		Y-model 3		Y-model 1		Y-model 2		Y-model 3
L=0		0.01		2.01*		0.03		0.00		0.52*		0.01
L=1		0.09	0.02	3.48	2.28	0.09	0.03	0.01	0.00	1.14	0.55	0.02	0.01
L=4		0.12	0.02	6.24	2.99	0.14	0.05	0.02	0.00	1.80	0.79	0.02	0.01
L=7		0.14	0.02	9.32	3.17	0.17	0.07	0.02	0.00	2.60	0.90	0.04	0.01
L=10		0.16	0.03	10.87	3.50	0.20	0.09	0.03	0.00	3.26	1.07	0.04	0.01
L=14		0.16	0.04	10.44	3.47	0.19	0.09	0.03	0.00	3.11	1.03	0.04	0.02
Tests		10%	5%	10%	5%	10%	5%	10%	5%	10%	5%	10%	5%
L=1	J_1	71.1	65.6	26.8	20.3	61.4	54.2	57.1	49.8	38.9	32.1	51.3	43.0
	LM_1	72.2	65.8	32.3	24.5	62.5	52.3	59.4	51.6	47.8	39.7	53.2	45.9
	J_2	21.3	13.3	18.3	12.0	20.5	13.4	8.5	4.2	21.2	14.6	9.4	4.6
	LM_2	1.4	0.6	21.4	14.3	7.0	3.9	0.0	0.0	19.8	13.3	1.4	0.5
L=4	J_1	78.5	72.5	71.1	64.1	82.9	77.3	51.6	46.4	73.0	66.0	57.8	49.6
	LM_1	61.6	49.9	52.2	35.7	34.0	19.2	43.0	37.9	74.7	69.1	42.3	31.5
	J_2	43.7	34.2	36.1	27.1	46.9	38.1	13.0	9.0	36.3	27.5	14.2	9.9
	LM_2	4.9	3.2	25.6	18.6	11.8	7.1	0.1	0.1	29.2	23.9	0.7	0.4
L=7	J_1	83.3	77.6	75.6	69.5	87.6	82.2	71.2	64.6	82.2	76.3	90.1	85.1
	LM_1	45.8	30.0	15.4	7.2	20.4	12.3	44.2	37.8	77.2	72.0	45.1	30.4
	J_2	52.3	41.2	33.5	24.8	50.8	41.74	43.3	32.4	40.8	31.3	58.8	47.7
	LM_2	6.7	4.9	14.4	9.3	8.0	4.0	0.3	0.2	27.0	21.6	10.1	6.4
L=10	J_1	89.7	86.1	84.8	79.7	93.4	89.9	83.5	77.1	90.5	87.1	95.2	92.3
	LM_1	45.2	31.9	11.3	5.7	21.8	15.5	41.1	35.3	79.2	73.4	35.0	23.9
	J_2	73.3	63.8	50.6	41.3	70.5	61.8	66.4	57.1	62.9	53.8	77.7	70.2
	LM_2	14.7	10.0	14.7	9.0	11.9	6.9	2.6	1.6	34.4	29.2	18.5	12.9
L=14	J_1	92.8	89.3	88.7	83.5	95.9	93.2	86.2	80.8	92.1	89.5	95.5	93.0
	LM_1	35.4	23.7	10.6	5.5	20.7	14.2	36.7	31.8	78.4	71.0	21.0	13.2
	J_2	82.8	75.3	61.9	52.8	80.3	72.8	75.2	66.3	71.8	63.6	82.6	75.5
	LM_2	13.2	8.7	15.8	9.6	10.5	6.0	3.8	2.2	37.7	30.1	12.5	8.9

*Note: *The MSE results for Y-model 2 are multiplied by 100. Correct parametric specification for Y-model 1 is φ_1, for Y-model 2 is φ_2 and for Y-model 3 is φ_3. Upper part of table provides for each model the MSE of the parametric estimator (L=0), and the MSE of the first GMM estimator (left column) and of the second GMM estimator (right column) for different numbers of nonparametric moments (L=1,4,7,10,14). Lower part of table contains the simulated size of the J and the LM tests at nominal size 10% (left column) and 5% (right column) for different numbers of nonparametric moments (L=1,4,7,10,14). J_1 and LM_1 are the J and the LM test based on the estimates of the first GMM estimator, $J_1 = J(\hat{\theta}_1)$, $LM_1 = LM(\hat{\theta}_1)$; J_2 and LM_2 are the J and the LM test based on the estimates of the second GMM estimator, $J_2 = J(\hat{\theta}_2)$, $LM_2 = LM(\hat{\theta}_2)$. 1000 replications.*

$$\hat{\lambda} = -\hat{\Omega}g_n,$$

where $\hat{\Omega} = [\hat{E}JJ']^{-1}$ is the inverse of the estimated covariance matrix of the moment vector, see also Brown, Newey, and May (2001) or Inkmann (2001, p.98 ff.). The J-test (4.12) and the LM-test (4.13) are computed for the first and for the second GMM estimator, with g_i and $\hat{\Omega}$ estimated at their respective estimates $\hat{\theta}_1$ and $\hat{\theta}_2$, and are compared to their nominal size of 5% and 10%, respectively.

The results are given in the lower part of Table 4.4 with J_1 and LM_1 referring to the tests computed at the estimates $\hat{\theta}_1$ of the first GMM estimator and J_2 and LM_2 referring to the second GMM estimator. The column titled 10% provides the rejection frequency using the 10%-critical value of the $\chi^2_{(L)}$ distribution with degrees of freedom equal to the number of subpopulations L. The column titled 5% contains the rejection frequency at the theoretical 5% level. It is seen that the J-tests strongly tend to over-reject in most cases, which may not be surprising in light of the previous findings in the literature. However, also the LM-tests depart considerably from their nominal size. Closest to its theoretical value comes the LM_2 test evaluated at the second GMM estimator with L=7 subpopulation restrictions, which still displays considerable under-rejection in Y-model 1 and over-rejection in Y-model 2. Regarding the power of these tests in the case of misspecification it can be seen that both the J and the LM tests reject at a very high frequency. Particularly, at sample size 2000 and few overidentifying moments L rejection rates are often close to 100%. (The corresponding tables can be found in Appendix E.)

These results might indicate that larger sample sizes are required for the asymptotic results to hold.[5] Another interpretation is that the asymptotic bias in $g_n^r(\hat{\theta}^r)$ has not been reduced sufficiently by undersmoothing, so that (4.12) and (4.13) converge to a non-central χ^2 distribution, thus implying that the results in Table 4.4 are based on wrong critical values.

4.2 Optimal Choice and Swedish Rehabilitation Programmes

The proposed GMM estimator is now applied to analyze optimal choices among rehabilitation programmes in Sweden. The Swedish rehabilitation policy distinguishes between vocational and non-vocational rehabilitation and is directed towards individuals with reduced work capacity due to long-term sickness (of at least one month). Non-vocational rehabilitation contains medical rehabilitation as well as social rehabilitation for individuals with alcohol, drug or psychiatric problems and intends to re-establish independence of the sick individual from medical or therapeutic assistance. Vocational rehabilitation consists of workplace training and occupation-related educational measures and aims at restoring lost working capacity and re-integration into the labour market. A data set for the

---

[5] In this case, refinements could be obtained by using bootstrap versions of these tests as discussed in Brown and Newey (2002) and Hall and Horowitz (1996).

Table 4.5. Treatment groups and their re-employment rate

	All	No Reha	Workplace	Educational	Medical
# Observations	6287	3502	1118	360	1307
Re-employment rate	46.3	48.3	52.4	28.9	40.5

Note: Share of transitions to employment at the end of sickness (in %).

evaluation of the effects of vocational rehabilitation has been collected by the Swedish National Social Insurance Board, of which 6287 cases in Western Sweden are analyzed. The data set is very informative about the selection process, containing information on medical examination, medical recommendation, case workers' recommendations, the individual's sickness history and so forth, which renders the conditional independence assumption (2.4) plausible. For details on the data set, the selection of cases and the justification of the conditional independence assumption see Frölich, Heshmati, and Lechner (2000a). The various rehabilitation programmes are classified here as in Frölich, Heshmati, and Lechner (2000b) into 4 categories: *No rehabilitation, workplace rehabilitation, educational rehabilitation* and *medical&social rehabilitation*.

In a retrospective analysis, for each of the 6287 sickness cases, it is estimated which of the 4 programme categories would have been the optimal choice. Comparing these estimates with the observed allocation allows an assessment how much the process of allocating participants to programmes could be improved. The success of rehabilitation is measured by the *employment* status (employed/non-employed) at the end of the sickness spell, where employment could be either with a new or with the current employer. This measures the success of *short-term* reintegration into the labour market, which is one of the aims of vocational rehabilitation programmes. It should be noted, however, that concentrating on a single outcome variable does not do justice to the multi-facetted goals of rehabilitation programmes, where, for example, medical and social rehabilitation aims primarily at improving health conditions than rapid labour market reintegration. In addition the durability of re-employment would be of interest. A more comprehensive analysis, however, was not possible due to the lack of follow-up data and identification concerns. In particular, conditional independence (2.4) seems not to be plausible with respect to after-treatment health status since pre-treatment health conditions are not reported as detailed as deemed necessary (Frölich, Heshmati, and Lechner 2000a). Nevertheless, labour market reintegration is still of high interest from the viewpoint of an economist.

Table 4.5 provides the number of participants in each rehabilitation group and the share of participants who engaged in employment at the end of their sickness spell. On average, 46% of all cases are employed at the end of sickness. The average employment rate is 48% for the participants in *No rehabilitation*, 52% for the participants in *workplace* rehabilitation, 29% for the participants in *educational* rehabilitation and 41% for the participants in *medical* rehabilitation.

Table 4.6. Nonparametrically estimated mean potential outcomes (in %)

	$\hat{E}\left[Y^{No}\right]$	$\hat{E}\left[Y^{Work}\right]$	$\hat{E}\left[Y^{Edu}\right]$	$\hat{E}\left[Y^{Med}\right]$
Re-employment rate	46.0	45.6	32.9	41.0

Note: Mean potential outcomes estimated by SG propensity score matching.

However, the gross success rates of Table 4.5 are not particularly informative since the participants in the different programmes are rather different in their characteristics. Therefore, Table 4.6 provides the estimated mean potential outcomes $E[Y^{No}]$, $E[Y^{Work}]$, $E[Y^{Edu}]$ and $E[Y^{Med}]$, where the different compositions of characteristics are adjusted for by SG matching. In the absence of general equilibrium effects, these estimates can be interpreted in this way: If all observations had participated in *No* or *workplace* rehabilitation, the employment rate would have been about 46%. Had all observations participated in *educational* rehabilitation, 33% would have had encountered re-employment. Finally, the re-employment rate would have been 41% if all observations had been allocated to *medical* rehabilitation. The differences between these estimates represent average treatment effects and indicate that *educational* rehabilitation fails completely in fostering re-integration in the labour market, as has also been observed in Frölich, Heshmati, and Lechner (2000b). This raises the question whether *educational* rehabilitation should be eliminated completely. Or whether there are individuals for whom *educational* rehabilitation is the optimal programme and which would lose if this option were no longer available. Of particular interest is which employment rate could have been achieved if all individuals had been allocated optimally to the programmes.

To address these questions, the optimal programme is estimated for each of the 6287 observations. With the outcome variable being binary, the expectation function is specified as a probit

$$E[Y^r | X = x] \doteq \Phi(x'\theta^r) \qquad \forall r \in \{No, Work, Edu, Med\}, \qquad (4.14)$$

where Φ is the cumulative distribution function of the standard normal distribution. The coefficients θ^r can be different for each programme $r \in \{No, Work, Edu, Med\}$. The scores of the log likelihood function $\frac{\partial \ln l(x'\theta^r)}{\partial \theta^r} = \frac{\phi(x'\theta^r)}{\Phi(x'\theta^r)(1 - \Phi(x'\theta^r))} x (y - \Phi(x'\theta^r))$ are taken as the instruments $A^r(X_i)$ in (4.9). The mean difference between the parametric and the nonparametric model for 11 (sub)populations are included in the GMM estimator (see Table E.4 in Appendix E). 38 explanatory characteristics (plus a constant) are included in X, comprising socioeconomic variables, indicators on sickness history and variables characterizing the current sickness spell. These variables were selected according to the analysis of the selection process in Frölich, Heshmati,

Table 4.7. Distribution of optimal programme choices

Best programme is	No Reha	Workplace	Educational	Medical
for so many individuals:	1865	1860	1519	1043

Note: Number of individuals for whom No rehabilitation, workplace rehabilitation, educational rehabilitation or medical rehabilitation, respectively, is the estimated optimal programme.

and Lechner (2000b), augmented by variables that are considered relevant for predicting employment prospects. See also Table E.5 in Appendix E.[6]

The participation probabilities $\hat{p}^r$ are estimated by probit, and the support restriction is implemented by discarding all observations with $\hat{p}_i^r$ below the lowest participation probability among the participants in programme r. The regression curves $m^r(p^r)$ are estimated separately for each subpopulation by SG matching, using only the observations belonging to that subpopulation. The bandwidth is chosen by cross validation. (The implied average potential outcomes for all subpopulations are given in Table E.4 in Appendix E).

With these preliminary estimates the coefficients θ^{No}, θ^{Work}, θ^{Edu}, θ^{Med} are estimated by the GMM estimator (4.10) using the identity matrix as weighting matrix, as suggested by the Monte Carlo experiment.[7] With these coefficient estimates the expected potential outcomes $\hat{Y}_i^{No}, \hat{Y}_i^{Work}, \hat{Y}_i^{Edu}, \hat{Y}_i^{Med}$ are predicted for each observation, and the optimal programme for observation i is the programme corresponding to the maximum of these four potential outcomes. Table 4.7 shows for how many individuals *No, workplace, educational* or *medical* rehabilitation, respectively, is the estimated optimal programme. It is seen that although *No* and *workplace* rehabilitation are optimal for the majority of all individuals, for 1519 observations *educational* rehabilitation would have been the optimal choice still. This could suggest that the complete elimination of *educational* rehabilitation might not be the best policy option, but rather that an improved allocation of participants might be recommendable.

In the analysis so far, the sampling variability of the estimated coefficients has been neglected. To take this into account, the distribution of $\hat{\theta}^{No}, \hat{\theta}^{Work}, \hat{\theta}^{Edu}, \hat{\theta}^{Med}$ is simulated by bootstrap. A programme r is only defined as optimal for individual i if the simulated probability that programme

---

[6] The same variables are also used for the mean potential outcomes in Table 4.6. Some variables that were included in Frölich, Heshmati, and Lechner (2000b) are left out here since they caused a singularity problem in the bootstrap simulation described below. These are: widowed, county Halland, county Göteborg (county Värmland included instead), indications of alcohol abuse, disability pension recommended by case worker, rehabilitation prevented by other factors, physician *and* case worker recommended a wait&see strategy.

[7] The J and LM tests for θ^{No} are J_1: 45.2, LM_1: 55.6, J_2: 27.1 LM_2: 30.7, for θ^{Work} are J_1: 74.0, LM_1: 60.4, J_2: 12.3 LM_2: 23.9, for θ^{Edu} are J_1: 54.0, LM_1: 30.4, J_2: 21.7 LM_2: 23.0 and for θ^{Med} are J_1: 81.4, LM_1: 52.6, J_2: 27.4 LM_2: 40.3. Notation as in Table 3.4. According to the $\chi^2_{(11)}$ critical values all specifications are incorrect.

Table 4.8. Distribution of optimal programme simulated by bootstrap

Best programme is	No Reha	Workplace	Educational	Medical	Undefined
at 1-α= 90% for	142	100	23	16	6006 individuals
at 1-α= 70% for	618	540	294	180	4655 individuals
at 1-α= 60% for	920	893	552	352	3570 individuals
at 1-α= 50% for	1302	1386	905	606	2088 individuals

Note: Number of individuals for whom the corresponding programme is the estimated optimal programme with simulated probability 1-α=0.9, 0.7, 0.6, 0.5, respectively. 350 bootstrap replications.

r corresponds to the maximum of $\hat{Y}_i^{No}, \hat{Y}_i^{Work}, \hat{Y}_i^{Edu}, \hat{Y}_i^{Med}$ exceeds a certain threshold. According to (2.43), r_i^* is the optimal programme for individual i if

$$P\left(\arg\max_r \left\{\hat{Y}_i^{r=No}, \hat{Y}_i^{r=Work}, \hat{Y}_i^{r=Edu}, \hat{Y}_i^{r=Med}\right\} = r_i^*\right) \geq 1 - \alpha,$$

where the probability measure is simulated by bootstrap replications. A threshold of 1-α=0.7 requires that in at least 70% of the bootstrap iterations, r_i^* corresponds to the maximum of the estimated potential outcomes. Table 4.8 provides the number of individuals for whom *No, workplace, educational* or *medical* rehabilitation, respectively, is optimal with at least 90, 70, or 50% simulated probability. For all other individuals the optimal programme is undefined. Table 4.8 again shows that for some individuals *educational* rehabilitation would be the optimal programme. Albeit a substantial amount of uncertainty is visible from the large number of individuals without defined optimal programme choice even at the 0.5 level, optimal treatment choice seems to vary among the individuals. *Educational* rehabilitation still seems to be the best choice for some individuals despite its weak average performance.

It is revealing to compare this simulated optimal allocation with the allocation observed. Table 4.9 cross-tabulates the number of participants in a certain programme $D_i \in \{No, Work, Edu, Med\}$ who have the same optimal programme $r_i^* \in \{No, Work, Edu, Med, indefinite\}$ at the 1-α level 70%, 60% and 50%, respectively. The row labelled 'Total' gives the total number of individuals for whom a certain programme is determined as optimal. This row corresponds to the results of Table 4.8. For example, for the 3502 individuals participating in *No rehabilitation*, an optimal programme is determined in 866 cases at the 70% level. In 399 cases this is *No rehabilitation*, in 198 cases it is *workplace* rehabilitation, in 156 cases it is *educational* rehabilitation and in 113 cases it is *medical* rehabilitation. Particularly striking are the results for *educational* rehabilitation. Of the participants in *educational* rehabilitation only a few (19 cases) would have been assigned to *educational* rehabilitation under optimal allocation, whereas most of the 294 cases for whom *educational* rehabilitation seems to be optimal actually participated in other programmes. These results are similar at the 60% and 50% level. This corroborates the finding that the participants

Table 4.9. Optimal treatment choice versus actual allocation

	r_i^* at 1-α =70%					r_i^* at 1-α =60%					r_i^* at 1-α =50%				
	N	W	E	M	i	N	W	E	M	i	N	W	E	M	i
D_i=N	399	198	156	113	2636	586	352	312	213	2039	828	603	507	351	1213
D_i=W	76	170	73	19	780	122	249	119	40	588	179	338	196	82	323
D_i=E	22	53	19	8	258	30	79	37	13	201	48	114	56	25	117
D_i=M	121	119	46	40	981	182	213	84	86	742	247	331	146	148	435
Total	618	540	294	180	4655	920	893	552	352	3570	1302	1386	905	606	2088
Δ%			61.5					64.7					67.4		

Note: Number of participants in programme $D_i \in \{No, Work, Edu, Med\}$ who have the same optimal programme $r_i^* \in \{No, Work, Edu, Med, indefinite\}$ at the level 1-α=0.7 (left), 0.6 (middle) and 0.5 (right). The column labelled i stands for indefinite optimal programme. Δ gives the fraction of misclassification in %, i.e. the number of cases for whom D_i and r_i^* do not coincide (off-diagonal elements) to the total number of cases with defined optimal programme, leaving apart the undefined cases.

in *educational* rehabilitation are not well selected. The fraction of misclassification Δ (in %) indicates how much optimal and actual classification deviate from each other. Leaving apart the cases for whom no optimal programme is defined, Δ is computed as the number of cases for which actual selection D_i and optimal choice r_i^* do not coincide (off-diagonal elements) divided by the total number of defined optimal programme choices. Table 4.9 shows that at a probability level of 0.7 more than 60% of the optimal programme choices differ from the actual allocation, indicating that substantial improvements might be possible by better programme selection. The misclassification level increases to 67% at the 0.5 level, which might be attributable to additional noise, since the optimal programme classifications are becoming less unambiguous.

Since the optimal programme choices are estimated on an individual level, it is difficult to summarize the optimal allocation in a few numbers or aggregate statistics. Nevertheless some distinguishing trends between optimal and actual allocation can be spotted in Tables 4.10 and E.5 in Appendix E. Table 4.10 provides the means of selected characteristics in the participant groups according to the actual and the optimal selection process, at 1-α level 50%. (Table E.5 in Appendix E provides this comparison for the other characteristics.) In the first four columns the means for the different treatment groups are given according to the optimal allocation. (The 2088 individuals without defined optimal treatment are not included.) The column 'All' shows the means in the full sample and the last four columns provide the average characteristics among the actual participants. A striking difference with respect to age can be seen. Whereas the distribution of the age groups 18-35, 36-45 and 46-55 years among the actual participant groups does not depart very much from the distribution in the full sample, the optimal choice seems to depend strongly on the individual's age. Whereas the young are clearly over-represented among those who are advised to participate in *medical* and, particularly, in *educational* rehabilitation, only very few among the 46-55

Table 4.10. Average characteristics in treatment groups: Optimal vs. actual allocation

Variable	r_i^* =				All	D_i =			
	N	W	E	M		N	W	E	M
Age: 18-35 years	12	20	59	52	32	31	34	37	31
Age: 46-55 years	40	62	10	30	37	41	31	32	36
Gender: male	56	36	48	44	45	45	45	46	46
Employment status: unemployed	2	27	47	2	19	20	9	32	21
Educated blue-collar worker	43	9	19	17	20	20	23	23	20
Occupation in manufacturing	51	23	23	38	32	30	38	32	32
Previous sickness days > 60 days	19	32	25	5	22	20	24	35	22
Prior participation in vocational rehabilitation	4	15	21	0	11	7	15	23	14
Medical diagnosis: Psychiatric problems	20	21	11	15	18	18	13	28	18
Medical recommendation: wait and see	79	64	19	53	55	61	40	37	56
Predicted employment probability	69.3	52.6	54.5	67.2		48.5	51.9	30.2	41.1

Note: Average characteristics multiplied by 100. The first four columns refer to the optimal allocation (r_i^*) at level 1-α=0.5. The column labelled 'All' gives the mean for the full sample, and the last four columns provide the means among the actual participants (D_i). The last row presents the average predicted potential employment probabilities in the corresponding treatment groups. See also Table E.5.

years old are best served by *educational* rehabilitation. With respect to gender it seems as if men should more often attend *No rehabilitation*, whereas women might benefit more from *workplace* rehabilitation. Regarding prior unemployment, it is noteworthy that hardly any unemployed are found among those advised to participate in *No* or in *medical* rehabilitation, but that they make up about half of those advised to *educational* rehabilitation. Educated blue collar workers are under-represented among the individuals for whom *workplace* rehabilitation appears to be optimal, whereas manufacturing workers are over-represented among those advised to *No rehabilitation*. For individuals who had been sick for more than 60 days in the last six months or who had previously participated in vocational rehabilitation, *medical* rehabilitation is hardly ever an unambiguously optimal choice. Furthermore, in the optimal allocation, individuals with psychiatric problems and individuals for whom a wait-and-see strategy has been advised, are clearly under-represented in *educational* rehabilitation relative to the actual allocation observed. Generally the differences in the characteristics are much more pronounced in the optimal than in the actual allocation, indicating that the actual selection process is not very sensitive to observable characteristics.

In the last row of Table 4.10, the individually *predicted* potential employment outcomes are averaged within the participant groups according to the optimal and the actual allocation. The predicted average employment rates in the actual participant groups correspond quite well to the observed outcomes of Table 4.5. When re-allocating the participants to the programmes in an optimal way, substantial increases in the predicted employment rates are achieved even for *educational* rehabilitation, as evidenced from Table 4.10. To summarize this analysis, it is illuminating to tentatively predict the re-employment rate that would have been achieved had all individuals participated in their optimal programme. When allocating all individuals to their optimal programme if defined at the 0.5 level, and all other individuals (for whom no optimal programme is defined) randomly (with equal probability) to any programme, the predicted average employment rate is 54.5%. If, on the other hand, the individuals without unambiguous optimal programme are allocated randomly to either *No* or to *workplace* rehabilitation, the predicted employment rate is 55.7%. Thus compared to the current selection process and to the re-employment rates that would be expected if all individuals were assigned to the same programme (see Table 4.6), an increase in the re-employment rate of about 9%-points seems to be possible through an improved participants allocation.

In like manner the question whether *educational* rehabilitation should be completely eliminated can be re-assessed. If *educational* rehabilitation were no longer available, the predicted average employment rate would be 54.9%, when individuals without unambiguous optimal programme are assigned randomly to either *No* or to *workplace* rehabilitation. Thus although *educational* rehabilitation is the optimal programme for some individuals, their second-best choice seems to be not much worse.

Similar results are also obtained for different sets of X variables and different moments specifications (see the sensitivity analysis in Appendix E). Comparing the above derived optimal allocation (with 11 population moments) with the optimal allocations that would result if 1, 6, 16 or 21, respectively, population-moments were included, it is seen that the fraction of misclassification Δ (in %) between the main specification and any of these other specifications is at most 0.1% at the $1-\alpha=0.7$ level, at most 2.4% at the 0.6 level and at most 11% at the 0.5 level (Tables E.7 to E.10). Also, compared to the parametric estimator (with 0 overidentifying moments), the number of misclassifications is low (1.1%, 4.1% and 14.1% at the 0.7, 0.6, 0.5 level, respectively, Table E.6). If the set of 11 population moments is maintained and the set of explanatory variables X is changed, the estimated optimal allocation changes more markedly. With a set of 28 or 30 variables, the resulting allocations are still very similar (Δ of about 0.5%, about 5% and about 14.5% at the 0.7, 0.6, 0.5 level, respectively, Tables E.11 and E.12). However when leaving out relevant information on sickness history, diagnosis, geographic location etc. (retaining only 24 variables), the misclassification rates increase to 15.8%, 26.4% and almost 40%, respectively (Table E.13). Hence detailed information might be necessary to obtain informed programme choices.

In light of these robust results, it seems as if educational rehabilitation could be abolished without any harm and that more care should be dedicated to participant selection and compliance.

5 Conclusions

This book has reviewed a variety of aspects of programme evaluation and treatment choice. An overview over nonparametric identification and estimation of average treatment effects has been given in the framework of multiple treatment evaluation. Different estimators of the mean counterfactual outcomes have been examined and their finite sample properties have been investigated. In addition, the optimal allocation of individuals to the programmes has been discussed and a two-step semiparametric estimation method of optimal programme choices has been developed and applied to Swedish rehabilitation programmes. The main results can be summarized in two sets of conclusions.

The first set of main conclusions regards the choice of a programme evaluation estimator for estimating average treatment effects. As a general result, kernel matching and particularly *SG matching*, a matching estimator based on a local linear ridge regression variant proposed by Seifert and Gasser (1996, 2000), seem to be most reliable in finite samples. The relative ordering of the various estimators with respect to mean squared error is remarkably stable across sample sizes and simulation schemes (known and unknown optimal bandwidth, known and unknown propensity score): *SG matching* always proved to be superior to all other estimators, followed by kernel matching. The relative ordering among pair-matching, local linear matching and re-weighting with trimming is less clear-cut. Local linear matching is susceptible to regions of sparse data and sensitive to bandwidth choice. The re-weighting estimator, considered in Hirano, Imbens, and Ridder (2000), Ichimura and Linton (2001) and Imbens (2000), is sensitive to trimming and its relative performance worsens with increasing sample size. Re-weighting without trimming, however, fails completely, and further use of the re-weighting estimator would require the development of an appropriate method for estimating the optimal trimming level.

Since the kernel, local linear and SG matching estimators require the choice of a bandwidth value, a second-order approximation to their mean squared error was developed as a first step towards a potential bandwidth selector, which however did not turn out to be very reliable for bandwidth choice in small samples. On the other hand, cross-validation, although asymptotically inefficient, is a rather successful bandwidth selector in finite samples. This holds particularly for SG matching, which is remarkably robust to bandwidth choice. Using cross-validation bandwidth selection, SG matching almost never performed worse than standard pair-matching. On average SG matching turned out to be about 25% more precise than pair-matching, when matching is on an observed covariate. When matching on an estimated propensity score, SG matching is about 40% more precise, because the variance of the pair-matching estimator is particularly affected by the variance of the estimated propensity score. In this case, pair-matching would need about 70% more observations to achieve the same precision as SG matching. These precision gains of SG matching are even larger if the number of control observations (non-participants) is larger than the number of treated observations (participants). The respective efficiency gains of kernel matching vis-à-vis pair-matching are about 15% when matching on an observed covariate, and 30% when matching on an estimated propensity score. Given the simplicity of its implementation, these simulation results strongly advocate the use of SG matching.

The second main set of conclusions regards *individual effect heterogeneity* and optimal programme choice. Here, the recognition of treatment effect heterogeneity among individuals seems important. Usually not all individuals respond in the same way to a particular treatment and the optimal treatment is not necessarily the same for all. Hence the overall effectiveness of a policy depends not only on the available programmes but also on the allocation of individuals to these programmes. Under certain conditions, decentralized self-selection by the individuals leads to an optimal allocation and thus to the maximum effectiveness which is attainable with the available programmes. In many settings, and in particular in the evaluation of social policies, these conditions are unlikely to be met. First, it may be argued whether individuals have rational expectations about their potential outcomes. But it is mainly the fact that the costs and benefits accrue to different parties which prevents an optimal allocation by self-selection. Usually only parts of the costs are borne directly by the participants, as the direct programme costs are often financed by public resources (taxes, unemployment insurance). In this case, the observed allocation and thus the effectiveness of the policy is likely to be suboptimal. If individual treatment effect heterogeneity is substantial, the scope for improvement through a better participant-programme selection can be considerable.

It has been seen that consistent estimation of the conditional expected potential outcomes $E[Y^r|X]$, for all programmes r, is important for the derivation of treatment recommendations on an individual basis. Estimating only the 'non-participation' outcome $E[Y^0|X]$, as it is done in the applied profiling systems, is of little use for an informative programme selection and may even lead to worse choices. With the approach developed in this book, expected outcomes $E[Y^r|X]$ and optimal treatment choices can be estimated semiparametrically, and the results of the Monte Carlo experiment suggest that precision gains can be achieved by incorporating the nonparametric elements. These estimates can be used for policy simulation and to assess the relevance of individual treatment effect heterogeneity.

In the application to Swedish rehabilitation programmes, it turned out that individual heterogeneity seems to be important and that an improved participant allocation could make a substantial contribution to the overall effectiveness of the policy. Whereas the average re-employment rate according to the observed allocation is 46.3%, the simulated re-employment rate according to the simulated optimal allocation is about 56%. On the other hand, if individual heterogeneity is neglected and all individuals were assigned to the programme with the largest average treatment effect in the population, the re-employment rate would have been only about 46%. Although these results are rather tentative and represent only a first step in the analysis of optimal treatment choice, they still provide some indications that the potential for policy improvement through a better participant allocation could be considerable. This could be achieved either by allocating individuals according to their estimated potential outcomes or by assisting the decision makers in their programme choice through the provision of the relevant disaggregated information.

A Appendix

In this appendix the equality (2.33) is proven. It is shown that propensity score matching leads to a consistent estimator of the covariate adjusted mean (2.25) even if the conditional independence assumption (2.4) is not valid. Hence propensity score matching can also be employed in the difference-in-difference or predictable-bias evaluation approach (see Section 2.1.4). The propensity score property is thus a mechanical result of a particular density ratio and is completely unrelated to properties of the potential outcomes.

It shall be shown that the covariate adjustment estimator (2.25)

$$\int E\left[Y^s|X = x, D = s\right] \cdot f_{X|D=r}(x)dx \qquad (A.1)$$

is equivalent to the corresponding propensity score adjustment estimator

$$\int E\left[Y^s|p^{s|rs}(X) = \rho, D = s\right] \cdot f_{p^{s|rs}|D=r}(\rho)d\rho \qquad (A.2)$$

even if the potential outcome is not conditionally independent of D.

First, some particular properties of the density of the propensity score in the source and the target population are shown, which are then used to proof the equivalence of (A.1) and (A.2). The notation is as before: $f_r(x) \equiv f_{X|D=r}(x)$ denotes the density of X in the target population ($D = r$) and $f_s(x) \equiv f_{X|D=s}(x)$ the density of X in the source population ($D = s$). Further, $f_X(x)$ is the density of X in the full population ($D \in \{0, .., R-1\}$).

The relevant propensity score is

$$p^{s|rs}(x) = P(D = s|X = x, D \in \{r, s\}) = \frac{p^s(x)}{p^r(x) + p^s(x)}.$$

The density of the propensity score in the source population is

$$f_{p^{s|rs}|D=s}(\rho) = \frac{\partial}{\partial \rho} E\left[1\left(p^{s|rs}(X) \leq \rho\right)|D = s\right]$$

$$= \int 1\left[p^{s|rs}(x) = \rho\right] \cdot f_{X|D=s}(x)dx. \qquad (A.3)$$

The density of the propensity score in the target population is

$$f_{p^{s|rs}|D=r}(\rho) = \int 1\left[p^{s|rs}(x) = \rho\right] \cdot f_{X|D=r}(x)dx. \qquad (A.4)$$

Using Bayes' theorem[1] the propensity score can be written as

$$p^{s|rs}(x) = \frac{f_{X|D=s}(x)P(D = s)}{f_{X|D=s}(x)P(D = s) + f_{X|D=r}(x)P(D = r)}$$

which gives

$$f_{X|D=r}(x) = \frac{f_{X|D=s}(x)P(D = s)\left(1 - p^{s|rs}(x)\right)}{P(D = r)p^{s|rs}(x)}$$

and inserting in (A.4) yields

$$f_{p^{s|rs}|D=r}(\rho) = \frac{P(D = s)}{P(D = r)} \int 1\left[p^{s|rs}(x) = \rho\right] \frac{1 - p^{s|rs}(x)}{p^{s|rs}(x)} f_{X|D=s}(x)dx.$$

Notice that the term in the integral is always zero unless $p^{s|rs}(x) = \rho$. Hence it follows

$$= \frac{P(D = s)}{P(D = r)} \int 1\left[p^{s|rs}(x) = \rho\right] \frac{1 - \rho}{\rho} f_{X|D=s}(x)dx$$

$$= \frac{P(D = s)}{P(D = r)} \frac{1 - \rho}{\rho} \cdot \int 1\left[p^{s|rs}(x) = \rho\right] f_{X|D=s}(x)dx.$$

Noting that the integrand equals (A.3) it follows that the density of the propensity score in the target population (A.4) can be expressed as

$$f_{p^{s|rs}|D=r}(\rho) = \frac{P(D = s)}{P(D = r)} \frac{1 - \rho}{\rho} f_{p^{s|rs}|D=s}(\rho)$$

or for $\rho > 0$ and $f_{p^{s|rs}|D=s}(\rho) > 0$ as

$$\frac{f_{p^{s|rs}|D=r}(\rho)}{f_{p^{s|rs}|D=s}(\rho)} = \frac{P(D = s)}{P(D = r)} \frac{1 - \rho}{\rho}. \qquad (A.5)$$

With this result the equivalence of (A.1) and (A.2) can be proven. The expected value conditional on the propensity score in (A.2) can be written as

---

[1] Which says $p^s(x) = f_{X|D=s}(x)P(D = s)/f_X(x)$.

$$E\left[Y^s|p^{s|rs}(X) = \rho, D = s\right]$$

$$= \frac{\int \int y \cdot 1\left[p^{s|rs}(x) = \rho\right] f_{Y^s|X,D=s}(y, x) \cdot f_{X|D=s}(x)dydx}{\int 1\left[p^{s|rs}(x) = \rho\right] f_{X|D=s}(x)dx}$$

$$= \frac{\int \left(\int y \cdot f_{Y^s|X,D=s}(y, x)dy\right) \cdot 1\left[p^{s|rs}(x) = \rho\right] f_{X|D=s}(x)dx}{f_{p^{s|rs}|D=s}(\rho)}$$

$$= \frac{\int E\left[Y^s|X = x, D = s\right] \cdot 1\left[p^{s|rs}(x) = \rho\right] f_{X|D=s}(x)dx}{f_{p^{s|rs}|D=s}(\rho)}$$

$$= \frac{\int m(x) \cdot 1\left[p^{s|rs}(x) = \rho\right] f_{X|D=s}(x)dx}{f_{p^{s|rs}|D=s}(\rho)}$$

where $m(x) = E\left[Y^s|X = x, D = s\right] = \int y \cdot f_{Y^s|X,D=s}(y, x)dy$ and (A.3) has been used.

Plugging this into (A.2) gives

$$\int \frac{\int m(x) \cdot 1\left[p^{s|rs}(x) = \rho\right] f_{X|D=s}(x)dx}{f_{p^{s|rs}|D=s}(\rho)} \cdot f_{p^{s|rs}|D=r}(\rho)d\rho$$

$$= \int \int m(x) \cdot 1\left[p^{s|rs}(x) = \rho\right] \frac{f_{p^{s|rs}|D=r}(\rho)}{f_{p^{s|rs}|D=s}(\rho)} f_{X|D=s}(x)dxd\rho.$$

Notice that the integrand is zero for all x and ρ unless $\rho = p^{s|rs}(x)$. Hence the double integral collapses to a single integral[2]

$$= \int m(x) \cdot 1\left[p^{s|rs}(x) = p^{s|rs}(x)\right] \frac{f_{p^{s|rs}|D=r}\left(p^{s|rs}(x)\right)}{f_{p^{s|rs}|D=s}\left(p^{s|rs}(x)\right)} f_{X|D=s}(x)dx$$

$$= \int m(x) \cdot \frac{P(D = s)}{P(D = r)} \frac{1 - p^{s|rs}(x)}{p^{s|rs}(x)} f_{X|D=s}(x)dx$$

by (A.5). By (2.35) this equals

$$= \int m(x) \cdot \frac{P(D = s)}{P(D = r)} \frac{f_{X|D=r}(X)}{f_{X|D=s}(X)} \frac{P(D = r)}{P(D = s)} f_{X|D=s}(x)dx$$

$$= \int E\left[Y^s|X = x, D = s\right] \cdot f_{X|D=r}(X)dx,$$

which is identical with (A.1). Hence propensity score matching can also be used for covariate-distribution adjustment in cases where the conditional independence assumption (2.4) is invalid.

---

[2] Indeed the double integral covers each x only once since it integrates for each value of ρ within the according equivalence class $\chi_\rho = \{x : p^{s|rs}(x) = \rho\}$.

B Appendix

In this appendix four corollaries with results relevant to nonparametric regression are presented. Corollary 1 provides an approximation to the local bias and the local variance of one-dimensional local polynomial regression estimators $\hat{m}(x)$, which are valid as well in the interior as at boundary points. Corollaries 2 and 3 show that nonparametric regression on the true or on the estimated propensity score is asymptotically linear with trimming. (These corollaries are reproduced from Heckman, Ichimura, and Todd (1998) in a simplified version. The original results are valid for local polynomial regression of any order.) Corollary 4 presents some results about U-statistics, which are used for deriving the properties of the semiparametric estimator of Chapter 4.

Corollary 1 (Bias and variance of local polynomial regression, Ruppert and Wand, 1994). *For X univariate with compact support $[a, b]$ and symmetric kernel function $K(\cdot)$ compact in $[-1, 1]$ the local bias is*

$$E[\hat{m}(x, h) - m(x)|X_1, .., X_n] = \left(\int_{(a-x)/h}^{(b-x)/h} u^{p+1} K^*(u; x, h) du \right) \frac{m^{(p+1)}(x)}{(p+1)!} h^{p+1}$$

$$+ \left(\int_{(a-x)/h}^{(b-x)/h} u^{p+2} K^*(u; x, h) du \right) \left(\frac{m^{(p+1)}(x)}{(p+1)!} \frac{f'(x)}{f(x)} + \frac{m^{(p+2)}(x)}{(p+2)!} \right) h^{p+2}$$

$$- \Lambda(x, h) \frac{m^{(p+1)}(x)}{(p+1)!} \frac{f'(x)}{f(x)} h^{p+2} + o_p(h^{p+2}), \quad \text{(B.1)}$$

and the local variance is

$$Var[\hat{m}(x, h)|X_1, .., X_n] = \left(\int_{(a-x)/h}^{(b-x)/h} K^{*2}(u; x, h) du \right) \frac{\sigma^2(x)}{nhf(x)} (1 + o_p(1)),$$

$$\text{(B.2)}$$

where $K^*(u; x, h)$ is the equivalence kernel. The equivalence kernels for local constant and local linear regression are

$$K^*_{p=0}(u; x, h) = \mu_0^{-1}(x, h) \cdot K(u)$$

$$K^*_{p=1}(u; x, h) = \frac{\mu_2(x, h) - u\mu_1(x, h)}{\mu_2(x, h)\mu_0(x, h) - \mu_1^2(x, h)} \cdot K(u).$$

where $\mu_q(x, h)$ represents the truncated kernel moments:

$$\mu_q(x, h) = \int\limits_{(a-x)/h}^{(b-x)/h} u^q K(u)du,$$

and the term $\Lambda(x, h)$ is

$$\Lambda_{p=0}(x, h) = \frac{\mu_1^2(x, h)}{\mu_0^2(x, h)}$$

$$\Lambda_{p=1}(x, h) = \frac{\mu_1^2\mu_2\mu_3 + \mu_0\mu_2^2\mu_3 - \mu_0\mu_1\mu_3^2 - \mu_1\mu_2^3}{(\mu_0\mu_2 - \mu_1^2)^2}$$

for local constant and local linear regression, respectively. (In the expression $\Lambda_{p=1}(x, h)$ the dependence of the kernel moments $\mu_q(x, h)$ on (x, h) is kept implicit to ease notation.)

These formulae simplify considerably at interior points, since $\mu_q(x, h) = \mu_q$, $K^*(u; x, h) = K^*(u)$ and $\mu_q = 0$ for q odd. In addition, for p even, the leading term in (B.1) is zero. Retaining only the first remaining term in the bias approximation gives the expressions (2.46) for interior points.

Corollary 2 (Asymptotic linearity of $\hat{m}^r(p^r)$, Heckman, Ichimura, and Todd, 1998). *Assuming that*

(i) sampling of (Y_j^r, X_j, D_j) is iid with finite variance of Y_j^r, and $X_j \in \Re^k$
(ii) the regression function $m^r(p^r)$ is twice continuously differentiable with second derivative Hölder continuous,
(iii) the stochastic bandwidth sequence a_{n_r} satisfies $\underset{n_r \to \infty}{plim}\ \frac{a_{n_r}}{h_{n_r}} = a_0 > 0$ for some deterministic sequence $\{h_{n_r}\}$ that satisfies $\frac{n_r h_{n_r}}{\ln n_r} \to \infty$ and $\lim n_r h^4 < \infty$,
(iv) the kernel function K is compact and symmetric, $\int K(u)du = 1$, $\int uK(u)du = 0$,
(v) $\hat{S}^r = \{x : \hat{f}_{X|D=r}(x) \geq q_0\}$ is estimated s.t. $\sup_{x \in S^r} \left| \hat{f}_{X|D=r}(x) - f_{X|D=r}(x) \right|$ converges a.s. to zero, where $S^r = \{x : f_{X|D=r}(x) \geq q_0\}$; $\hat{f}_{X|D=r}$ is a kernel density estimate with kernel moments 1 through k equal to zero, and $f_{X|D=r}$ is $k + 1$ times continuously differentiable with $(k + 1)$-th derivative Hölder continuous,
(vi) $m^r(\cdot)$ is estimated at interior points,
then the local polynomial regression estimator $\hat{m}^r(p^r(x))$ of polynomial order ≤ 1 is asymptotically linear with trimming:

$$[\hat{m}^r(p^r(x)) - m^r(p^r(x))] \cdot 1(x \in \hat{S}^r) =$$

$$n_r^{-1} \sum_j \psi_m(Y_j^r, p^r(X_j); p^r) \cdot 1(D_j = r) + \hat{b}_m(p^r) + \hat{R}_m(p^r),$$

with

a) $E[\psi_m(Y_j^r, p^r(X_j); p^r)] = 0$

b) $\underset{n_r \longrightarrow \infty}{plim} \ n_r^{-\frac{1}{2}} \sum \hat{b}_m(p^r(X_j)) < \infty$

c) $n_r^{-\frac{1}{2}} \sum \hat{R}_m(p^r(X_j)) = o_p(1).$

Corollary 3 (Asymptotic linearity of $\hat{m}^r(\hat{p}^r)$, Heckman, Ichimura, and Todd, 1998). *Suppose that*
(i) the estimator $\hat{p}^r(x)$ of the participation probability is asymptotically linear with trimming

$$(\hat{p}^r(x) - p^r(x)) \, 1(x \in \hat{S}^r) = n^{-1} \sum_j \psi_p(D_j, X_j; x) + \hat{b}_p(x) + \hat{R}_p(x),$$

(ii) $\frac{\partial \hat{m}^r(p^r)}{\partial p^r}$ and $\hat{p}^r(x)$ are uniformly consistent and converge to $\frac{\partial m^r(p^r)}{\partial p^r}$ and $p^r(x)$, respectively, with $\frac{\partial m^r(p^r)}{\partial p^r}$ continuous,

(iii) $\underset{n_r \to \infty}{plim} \ n_r^{-\frac{1}{2}} \sum_j \hat{b}_m(p^r(X_j)) 1(D_j = r) = b_m,$

(iv) $\underset{n \to \infty}{plim} \ n^{-\frac{1}{2}} \sum_j \frac{\partial m^r(p^r(X_j))}{\partial p^r} \cdot \hat{b}_p(p^r(X_j)) = b_{m_p},$

(v) $\underset{n \to \infty}{plim} \ n^{-\frac{1}{2}} \sum_j \left[\frac{\partial \hat{m}^r(\bar{p}^r(X_j))}{\partial p^r} - \frac{\partial m^r(p^r(X_j))}{\partial p^r} \right] \cdot \hat{R}_p(X_j) = 0,$

(vi) $\underset{n \to \infty}{plim} \ n^{-\frac{3}{2}} \sum_l \sum_j \left[\frac{\partial \hat{m}^r(\bar{p}^r(X_j))}{\partial p^r} - \frac{\partial m^r(p^r(X_j))}{\partial p^r} \right] \cdot \psi_p(D_l, X_l; X_j) = 0,$

where $\bar{p}^r(x)$ is defined by a Taylor expansion of $\hat{m}^r(\hat{p}^r(x))$ about $p^r(x)$:
$\hat{m}^r(\hat{p}^r(x)) = \hat{m}^r(p^r(x)) + \partial \hat{m}^r(\bar{p}^r(x))/\partial p^r \cdot (\hat{p}^r(x) - p^r(x)),$
then the estimator $\hat{m}^r(\hat{p}^r(x))$ of $m^r(p^r(x)) = E[Y^r|p^r(X) = p^r(x)]$ is also asymptotically linear with trimming:

$$[\hat{m}^r(\hat{p}^r(x)) - m^r(p^r(x))] \cdot 1(x \in \hat{S}_r) \tag{B.3}$$

$$= n_r^{-1} \sum_j \psi_m(Y_j^r, p^r(X_j); p^r) 1(D_j = r)$$

$$+ \frac{\partial m^r(p^r(x))}{\partial p^r} \cdot n^{-1} \sum_j \psi_p(D_j, X_j; x) + \hat{b}(x) + \hat{R}(x)$$

with
a) $E[\psi_m(Y_j^r, p^r(X_j); p^r)] = 0$
b) $E[\psi_p(D_j, X_j; x)] = 0$
c) $\underset{n \to \infty}{plim} \ n^{-\frac{1}{2}} \sum \hat{b}(X_j) = b_m + b_{mp} < \infty$
d) $n^{-\frac{1}{2}} \sum \hat{R}(X_j) = o_p(1).$

If the participation probability $p^r(x)$ is estimated either nonparametrically by local polynomial regression or parametrically, e.g. by maximum likelihood, the conditions (i) to (vi) are satisfied (Heckman, Ichimura, and Todd 1998). In the latter case the local bias $\hat{b}_p(x)$ is zero.

Corollary 4 (Asymptotic equivalence of V-statistic, U statistic and its projection). *Let* $H_n(x_1, x_2)$ *be a symmetric function and* $X_1, .., X_n$ *be iid random vectors. A natural estimator of* $E[H_n]$ *is the one-sample U-statistic*

$$U_n = \binom{n}{2}^{-1} \sum_{1 \leq i < j \leq n} H_n(X_i, X_j).$$

The associated von Mises statistic is

$$V_n = n^{-2} \sum_{i=1}^{n} \sum_{j=1}^{n} H_n(X_i, X_j)$$

and the projection of the U-statistic is defined as

$$\hat{U}_n = \frac{n-2}{n} E[H_n] + \frac{2}{n} \sum_{i=1}^{n} E[H_n(X_1, X_2)|X_1 = X_i].$$

If $E\|H_n\|^2 = o(n)$ *then* $n^{\frac{1}{2}}(U_n - \hat{U}_n) = o_p(1)$ *and* $n^{\frac{1}{2}}(V_n - \hat{U}_n) = o_p(1)$. *See Hoeffding (1948) and Serfling (1980). Extended by Powell, Stock, and Stoker (1989) to allow* H_n *to depend on the sample size.*

C Appendix

C.1 MSE-Approximation for Local Polynomial Matching

In this appendix the approximation to the mean squared error of the generalized matching estimator (2.27) of the covariate-adjusted mean (2.25) is derived (see Section 3.2). In the following it is supposed that X is one-dimensional with compact support $supp(X) = [a, b]$ and symmetric kernel function $K(\cdot)$, which is compact in $[-1, 1]$ and integrates to one. As shown by Heckman, Ichimura, and Todd (1998) the local polynomial regression estimator of $m(x) = E[Y|X = x]$ can be written in the asymptotically linear form

$$\hat{m}(x) - m(x) = \frac{1}{n_s} \sum \psi\left(Y_{si}, X_{si}; x\right) + b(x) + R(x),$$

with ψ a local influence function, local bias $b(x)$ and a remainder term $R(x)$.

For example, the influence function for local constant (Nadaraya-Watson) regression is

$$\psi\left(Y_{si}, X_{si}, x\right) = \left(Y_{si} - m\left(X_{si}\right)\right) \cdot \frac{K\left(\frac{X_{si}-x}{h}\right)}{E\left[K\left(\frac{X_{si}-x}{h}\right)\right]},$$

which converges to

$$\longrightarrow \left(Y_{si} - m\left(X_{si}\right)\right) \cdot \frac{K\left(\frac{X_{si}-x}{h}\right)}{hf_s(x)\mu_0(x, h)}$$

where

$$\mu_q(x, h) = \int_{(a-x)/h}^{(b-x)/h} u^q K(u) du.$$

For local polynomial regression in general, the influence function can easier be represented by using equivalence kernels as developed e.g. in Ruppert and Wand (1994). The influence function can be written as

$$\psi\left(Y_{si}, X_{si}, x\right) = \left(Y_{si} - m\left(X_{si}\right)\right) \cdot \frac{K_p^*\left(\frac{X_{si}-x}{h}, x, h\right)}{hf_s(x)}, \qquad \text{(C.1)}$$

where K_p^* is the equivalence kernel. The equivalence kernels for local constant ($p = 0$) and for local linear regression ($p = 1$) are

$$K_{p=0}^*(u; x, h) = \mu_0^{-1}(x, h) \cdot K(u)$$

$$K_{p=1}^*(u; x, h) = \frac{\mu_2(x, h) - u\mu_1(x, h)}{\mu_2(x, h)\mu_0(x, h) - \mu_1^2(x, h)} \cdot K(u).$$

These equivalence kernels capture as well the interior (i.e. all x that are at least one bandwidth apart from either boundary of the support) as the boundary region. In the interior these expressions simplify considerably, because with kernel function compact in $[-1, 1]$ the kernel moments $\mu_q(x, h) = \mu_q$ do no longer depend on x if $b - x > h$ and $x - a > h$. Furthermore, with a symmetric kernel, μ_q is zero for q odd, and $\mu_0 = 1$ for a kernel integrating to one. This gives expression (2.48) for local constant and for local linear regression when x is an interior point.

Using the general expression (C.1), the bias and the variance of the local polynomial matching estimator (3.1) is derived. The bias is

$$E\left[\frac{1}{n_r}\sum_{j=1}^{n_r}\left(m\left(X_{rj}\right) + b\left(X_{rj}\right) + R\left(X_{rj}\right) + \frac{1}{n_s}\sum_{i=1}^{n_s}\psi\left(Y_{si}, X_{si}, X_{rj}\right)\right)\right]$$

$$- \int m(x)f_r(x)dx$$

$$= E\left[m\left(X_{rj}\right) + b\left(X_{rj}\right)\right] - \int m(x)f_r(x)dx = \int b(x)f_r(x)dx.$$

The variance of (3.1) is

$$Var\left(\frac{1}{n_r}\sum_{j=1}^{n_r}\left(m\left(X_{rj}\right) + b\left(X_{rj}\right) + R\left(X_{rj}\right) + \frac{1}{n_s}\sum_{i=1}^{n_s}\psi\left(Y_{si}, X_{si}, X_{rj}\right)\right)\right)$$

$$= Var\left(\frac{1}{n_r}\sum_{j=1}^{n_r}\left(m\left(X_{rj}\right) + b\left(X_{rj}\right) + R\left(X_{rj}\right)\right)\right)$$

$$+ Var\left(\frac{1}{n_r n_s}\sum_{j=1}^{n_r}\sum_{i=1}^{n_s}\psi\left(Y_{si}, X_{si}, X_{rj}\right)\right) \quad \text{(C.2)}$$

because the covariance terms $E[(m(X_{rj}) + b(X_{rj})) \cdot \psi(Y_{sk}, X_{sk}, X_{rl})] = E[E[(m(X_{rj}) + b(X_{rj})) \cdot \psi(Y_{sk}, X_{sk}, X_{rl})]|X_{rj}, X_{rl}]$ are zero since $E[\psi(Y_{si}, X_{si}, X)|X = x] = 0$.

The first term in the variance expression captures the variance due to the variation of m and the local bias b along x. With X_{rj} iid it corresponds to

$$Var\left(\frac{1}{n_r}\sum_{j=1}^{n_r}\left(m\left(X_{rj}\right)+b\left(X_{rj}\right)+R\left(X_{rj}\right)\right)\right)$$

$$=\frac{1}{n_r}Var\left(\left(m\left(X_{rj}\right)+b\left(X_{rj}\right)+R\left(X_{rj}\right)\right)\right)$$

$$=\frac{1}{n_r}\left[\int\left(m\left(x\right)+b\left(x\right)\right)^2 f_r\left(x\right)dx-\left(\int\left(m\left(x\right)+b\left(x\right)\right)f_r\left(x\right)dx\right)^2\right],$$

where the lower-order remainder term has been dropped.

The second term in the variance expression (C.2) captures the variance stemming from the local variance of the nonparametric regression estimator. Summing up all covariance elements yields

$$Var\left(\frac{1}{n_r n_s}\sum_{j=1}^{n_r}\sum_{i=1}^{n_s}\psi\left(Y_{si},X_{si},X_{rj}\right)\right)$$

$$=\frac{1}{n_r^2 n_s^2}E\sum_{j=1}^{n_r}\sum_{i=1}^{n_s}\sum_{l=1}^{n_r}\sum_{k=1}^{n_s}\psi\left(Y_{si},X_{si},X_{rj}\right)\psi\left(Y_{sk},X_{sk},X_{rl}\right)$$

$$=\frac{1}{n_r^2 n_s^2}\cdot E\sum_{j=1}^{n_r}\sum_{i=1}^{n_s}\sum_{l=1}^{n_r}\sum_{k=1}^{n_s}\left(Y_{si}-m\left(X_{si}\right)\right)\frac{K_p^*\left(\frac{X_{si}-X_{rj}}{h},X_{rj},h\right)}{hf_s\left(X_{rj}\right)}$$

$$\cdot\left(Y_{sk}-m\left(X_{sk}\right)\right)\frac{K_p^*\left(\frac{X_{sk}-X_{rl}}{h},X_{rl},h\right)}{hf_s\left(X_{rl}\right)}$$

after inserting (C.1).

Note first that the covariances for $i\neq k$ are all zero because the terms $(Y_{si}-m(X_{si}))$ and $(Y_{sk}-m(X_{sk}))$ factor and integrate to zero conditional on X_{sk} or X_{si}. Second, the terms with $i=k$ and $j\neq l$ can be expressed as

$$\frac{1}{h^2}\int_a^b\int_a^b\int_a^b\sigma^2\left(X_{si}\right)\frac{K_p^*\left(\frac{X_{rj}-X_{si}}{h},X_{rj},h\right)}{f_s\left(X_{rj}\right)}\frac{K_p^*\left(\frac{X_{rl}-X_{si}}{h},X_{rl},h\right)}{f_s\left(X_{rl}\right)}$$

$$\cdot f_r(X_{rj})f_r(X_{rl})f_s(X_{si})dX_{rj}dX_{rl}dX_{si}$$

$$=\int_a^b\int_{\frac{a-X_{si}}{h}}^{\frac{b-X_{si}}{h}}\int_{\frac{a-X_{si}}{h}}^{\frac{b-X_{si}}{h}}\sigma^2\left(X_{si}\right)\frac{K_p^*\left(u,X_{si}+uh,h\right)}{f_s\left(X_{si}+uh\right)}\frac{K_p^*\left(v,X_{si}+uh,h\right)}{f_s\left(X_{si}+uh\right)}$$

$$\cdot f_r\left(X_{si}+uh\right)f_r\left(X_{si}+vh\right)f_s\left(X_{si}\right)du\cdot dv\cdot dX_{si}$$

with the change in variables $u = (X_{rj} - X_{si})/h$ and $v = (X_{rl} - X_{si})/h$, and $\sigma^2(X_{si}) = Var[Y_{si}|X_{si}]$. Assuming that f_r and f_s are differentiable, $f_r(X_{si} + uh)$ can be approximated by a series $f_r(X_{si}) + uhf_r'(X_{si}) + o_p(h)$, which converges to $f_r(X_{si})$ at $h = 0$, see Heckman, Ichimura, and Todd (1998, p. 279). Also the equivalent kernel $K_p^*(u, X_{si} + uh, h) \approx K_p^*(u, X_{si}, h)$ for small values of h. Notice that this latter approximation is only relevant for boundary points, since in the interior $K_p^*(u, X_{si}, h)$ does not depend on X_{si}. Thus for decreasing bandwidth values the previous expression converges to

$$
\longrightarrow \int_a^b \int_{\frac{a-X_{si}}{h}}^{\frac{b-X_{si}}{h}} \int_{\frac{a-X_{si}}{h}}^{\frac{b-X_{si}}{h}} \sigma^2(X_{si}) K_p^*(u, X_{si}, h) K_p^*(v, X_{si}, h) \cdot \frac{f_r^2(X_{si})}{f_s(X_{si})} du\, dv\, dX_{si}
$$

$$
= \int_a^b \left(\sigma^2(X_{si}) \frac{f_r^2(X_{si})}{f_s(X_{si})} \int_{\frac{a-X_{si}}{h}}^{\frac{b-X_{si}}{h}} K_p^*(u, X_{si}, h)\, du \int_{\frac{a-X_{si}}{h}}^{\frac{b-X_{si}}{h}} K_p^*(v, X_{si}, h)\, dv \right) dX_{si}
$$

$$
= \int \sigma^2(x) \frac{f_r^2(x)}{f_s(x)} dx, \tag{C.3}
$$

since for local constant regression: $\int_{\frac{a-X_{si}}{h}}^{\frac{b-X_{si}}{h}} K_p^*(u, X_{si}, h)\, du$ equals

$\mu_0^{-1}(X_{si}, h) \int_{\frac{a-X_{si}}{h}}^{\frac{b-X_{si}}{h}} K(u) du = \mu_0^{-1}(X_{si}, h)\mu_0(X_{si}, h) = 1$ and analogously

$\int_{\frac{a-X_{si}}{h}}^{\frac{b-X_{si}}{h}} \frac{(\mu_2(X_{si},h) - u\mu_1(X_{si},h)) \cdot K(u)}{\mu_2(X_{si},h)\mu_0(X_{si},h) - \mu_1^2(X_{si},h)} = \frac{\mu_2(X_{si},h)\mu_0(X_{si},h) - \mu_1(X_{si},h)\mu_1(X_{si},h)}{\mu_2(X_{si},h)\mu_0(X_{si},h) - \mu_1^2(X_{si},h)} = 1$ for local linear regression.

Finally the covariance terms with $i = k$ and $j = l$ can be expressed as

$$
\frac{1}{h^2} \int_a^b \int_a^b \sigma^2(X_{si}) \frac{K_p^*\left(\frac{X_{rj}-X_{si}}{h}, X_{rj}, h\right)^2}{f_s^2(X_{rj})} \cdot f_r(X_{rj}) f_s(X_{si}) dX_{rj} dX_{si}
$$

$$
= \frac{1}{h} \int_a^b \int_{\frac{a-X_{si}}{h}}^{\frac{b-X_{si}}{h}} \sigma^2(X_{si}) \frac{K_p^*(u, X_{si} + uh, h)^2}{f_s^2(X_{si} + uh)} \cdot f_r(X_{si} + uh) f_s(X_{si}) du\, dX_{si}
$$

with the change in variables $u = (X_{rj} - X_{si})/h$. As before, $f_r(X_{si} - uh)$ converges to $f_r(X_{si})$ and $K_p^*(u, X_{si} + uh, h) \approx K_p^*(u, X_{si}, h)$ for decreasing bandwidth values h and thus

$$\longrightarrow \frac{1}{h}\int_{a}^{b}\sigma^2\left(X_{si}\right)\frac{f_r\left(X_{si}\right)}{f_s\left(X_{si}\right)}\left(\int_{\frac{a-X_{si}}{h}}^{\frac{b-X_{si}}{h}}K_p^*\left(u,X_{si},h\right)^2 du\right)dX_{si}$$

$$= n_s\int Var[\hat{m}(x)]f_r\left(x\right)dx \tag{C.4}$$

with the local variance $Var\left[\hat{m}(x)\right]$ according to expression (B.2) in Corollary 1.

Collecting the $n_s n_r\left(n_r-1\right)$ covariance terms with $i=k$ and $j\neq l$ and the $n_s n_r$ covariance terms with $i=k$ and $j=l$ gives

$$Var\left(\frac{1}{n_r n_s}\sum_{j=1}^{n_r}\sum_{i=1}^{n_s}\psi\left(Y_{si},X_{si},X_{rj}\right)\right)$$

$$\approx \frac{1}{n_s}\int\sigma^2\left(x\right)\frac{f_r^2\left(x\right)}{f_s\left(x\right)}dx+\frac{1}{n_r}\int Var[\hat{m}(x)]f_r\left(x\right)dx.$$

Combining this with the first variance component and the bias term gives as an approximation to the MSE

$$MSE\approx\left(\int b(x)f_r(x)dx\right)^2 \tag{C.5}$$

$$+\frac{1}{n_r}\left[\int\left(m\left(x\right)+b\left(x\right)\right)^2 f_r\left(x\right)dx-\left(\int\left(m\left(x\right)+b(x)\right)f_r\left(x\right)dx\right)^2\right]$$

$$+\frac{1}{n_s}\int\sigma^2\left(x\right)\frac{f_r^2\left(x\right)}{f_s\left(x\right)}dx+\frac{1}{n_r}\int Var[\hat{m}(x)]f_r\left(x\right)dx,$$

with the expressions for local bias and local variance given by Corollary 1.

If the support of X is unbounded and all points are in the interior, i.e. $a=-\infty$, $b=\infty$, the MSE approximation simplifies to (3.2) for both the local constant and the local linear regression estimator. In this case, also the approximation to the local bias simplifies to the expression given in (2.46) when only the first leading term of the bias expression is retained.

C.2 Additional Tables to Chapter 3

Table C.1. Population regression curves m_1 to m_8

$m_1(x) = 0.4 + 0.25 \sin(8x - 5) + 0.4 \exp(-16(4x - 2.5)^2)$
$m_2(x) = 0.5 - 4(x - 0.2)^2 - 1.2 \ln(1.1 - x)$
$m_3(x) = 0.2 + 2(x - 0.9)^2 + 5(x - 0.7)^3 + 100(x - 0.6)^{10}$
$m_4(x) = 0.5 + 0.3 e^{-2x} \sin(16x)$
$m_5(x) = 0.2 + \sqrt{x} - 0.6(x - 0.1)^2$
$m_6(x) = -0.1 + 0.25(x + 0.3)^{-1} + 0.4 \exp(-24(x - 0.25)^2) + 0.1 \exp(-60(x - 0.75)^2)$
$m_7(x) = 0.15 + 0.7x$
$m_8(x) = 0.1 + 2(x - 0.35)^2$

Table C.2. Expected values of regression curves m_1 to m_8

Target population density	Expected value of regression curve							
	m_1	m_2	m_3	m_4	m_5	m_6	m_7	m_8
N_1	0.39	0.65	0.52	0.51	0.70	0.57	0.39	0.17
N_2	0.42	0.67	0.45	0.50	0.77	0.40	0.50	0.23
N_3	0.52	0.62	0.35	0.50	0.79	0.27	0.61	0.37

Note: Expected values of Y computed with respect to the density of the target population, see Figure 3.1.

Table C.3. Mean squared error at optimal bandwidth value (sample size $n_s = n_r = 40$)

	Densities	Pair-matching MSE	Pair-matching Var	OLS MSE	Kernel matching MSE^r	Kernel matching MSE	Kernel matching VAR	Kernel matching h^{opt}	Local linear matching MSE^r	Local linear matching MSE	Local linear matching VAR	Local linear matching h^{opt}	Seifert&Gasser matching MSE^r	Seifert&Gasser matching MSE	Seifert&Gasser matching VAR	Seifert&Gasser matching h^{opt}	Weighting MSE	Efficient Var
	N_1-N_2	2.51	2.50	8.90	89.7	2.25	1.94	0.14	92.4	2.31	2.29	0.20	75.1	1.88	1.85	0.24	11.13	1.71
	N_1-N_3	4.70	4.54	49.76	87.3	4.10	3.53	0.14	161.4	7.58	6.59	0.24	76.0	3.57	3.29	0.20	72.32	3.23
m_1	N_2-N_1	1.93	1.89	6.20	73.8	1.42	1.42	0.68	78.6	1.52	1.52	0.18	62.8	1.21	1.16	0.26	7.07	1.41
	N_2-N_3	1.99	1.97	2.27	73.1	1.45	1.44	0.16	71.9	1.43	1.41	0.30	59.8	1.19	1.17	0.26	9.23	1.47
	N_3-N_1	7.91	5.18	11.34	27.0	2.13	2.13	0.44	115.9	9.17	6.31	0.24	71.1	5.63	3.35	0.12	64.14	3.17
	N_3-N_2	2.64	2.38	2.80	65.7	1.73	1.73	0.16	85.8	2.27	1.85	0.18	65.1	1.72	1.68	0.18	5.25	1.71
	N_1-N_2	1.27	1.21	4.18	42.1	0.54	0.53	0.72	99.4	1.27	1.24	0.60	53.9	0.69	0.68	0.32	8.47	0.75
	N_1-N_3	3.38	3.11	29.61	81.1	2.74	0.55	1.00	89.9	3.04	3.00	0.54	82.7	2.80	1.79	0.26	58.31	2.48
m_2	N_2-N_1	1.46	1.37	3.18	72.1	1.06	0.48	1.00	88.5	1.30	1.28	0.54	67.0	0.98	0.88	0.36	5.74	0.87
	N_2-N_3	1.20	1.20	1.71	64.2	0.77	0.71	0.16	64.6	0.78	0.77	0.78	53.2	0.64	0.62	0.36	5.36	0.72
	N_3-N_1	5.32	3.39	15.59	9.5	0.50	0.50	0.74	72.3	3.85	3.39	0.24	75.0	3.99	1.81	0.30	52.65	2.63
	N_3-N_2	1.33	1.20	1.85	41.9	0.56	0.55	0.36	86.8	1.16	1.10	0.32	53.3	0.71	0.68	0.32	10.66	0.75
	N_1-N_2	1.36	1.34	1.39	87.8	1.19	0.88	0.16	69.1	0.94	0.93	0.72	67.6	0.92	0.78	0.38	2.24	0.89
	N_1-N_3	2.97	2.91	5.87	102.8	3.05	2.12	0.16	72.8	2.16	2.15	0.70	93.5	2.78	1.89	0.24	16.42	2.58
m_3	N_2-N_1	1.11	1.11	1.30	51.4	0.57	0.55	0.26	92.2	1.03	1.01	0.50	58.6	0.65	0.63	0.24	7.03	0.65
	N_2-N_3	1.27	1.26	0.86	66.6	0.84	0.78	0.18	71.1	0.90	0.89	1.00	60.4	0.76	0.71	0.26	1.45	0.81
	N_3-N_1	2.63	2.60	2.09	61.0	1.61	1.43	0.20	110.0	2.89	1.89	1.00	51.3	1.35	1.30	0.58	63.15	2.42
	N_3-N_2	1.34	1.34	0.97	74.1	0.99	0.86	0.16	75.3	1.01	0.99	1.00	64.3	0.86	0.77	0.34	9.03	0.89
	N_1-N_2	1.20	1.19	1.11	46.2	0.55	0.55	0.52	85.2	0.76	0.76	0.84	52.7	0.63	0.63	0.18	6.58	0.70
	N_1-N_3	2.73	2.59	3.62	20.2	0.55	0.55	0.76	64.6	1.76	1.75	0.86	45.6	1.25	1.24	0.44	54.62	2.32
m_4	N_2-N_1	1.50	1.48	1.18	43.3	0.65	0.48	1.00	84.9	1.27	1.17	1.00	71.2	1.07	1.02	0.14	8.03	0.81
	N_2-N_3	1.01	1.01	0.59	40.7	0.41	0.41	0.64	55.6	0.56	0.56	0.98	52.6	0.53	0.52	0.22	5.51	0.55
	N_3-N_1	5.86	4.35	2.33	10.0	0.58	0.40	1.00	40.6	2.38	2.22	1.00	34.2	2.00	1.87	0.92	76.81	2.58
	N_3-N_2	1.46	1.37	0.88	26.1	0.38	0.38	1.00	62.8	0.92	0.92	1.00	55.8	0.81	0.80	0.06	7.70	0.70
	N_1-N_2	1.11	1.10	1.99	49.0	0.54	0.51	0.26	85.2	0.95	0.95	0.60	54.9	0.61	0.59	0.22	16.19	0.66
	N_1-N_3	2.42	2.34	11.89	27.3	0.66	0.60	0.40	113.5	2.75	2.43	0.54	39.5	0.96	0.95	0.46	119.1	2.26
m_5	N_2-N_1	1.38	1.30	1.45	82.4	1.13	0.88	0.14	64.5	0.89	0.88	0.62	73.2	1.01	0.84	0.54	5.78	0.84
	N_2-N_3	0.95	0.94	1.19	33.3	0.32	0.31	0.54	65.3	0.62	0.62	0.66	48.4	0.46	0.46	0.30	12.01	0.49
	N_3-N_1	4.58	3.16	9.31	96.4	4.42	2.08	0.16	77.6	3.56	3.09	0.48	92.4	4.23	1.93	0.20	59.29	2.61
	N_3-N_2	1.20	1.08	1.24	71.7	0.86	0.60	0.18	68.1	0.82	0.81	0.60	59.0	0.71	0.58	0.40	10.17	0.66
	N_1-N_2	1.99	1.97	2.01	99.3	1.98	1.59	0.14	88.2	1.76	1.74	0.20	85.6	1.71	1.32	0.26	1.02	1.60
	N_1-N_3	3.06	2.85	4.85	106.9	3.27	2.07	0.14	73.4	2.25	2.23	0.12	63.5	1.94	1.91	0.70	7.03	2.75
m_6	N_2-N_1	1.94	1.94	1.66	87.6	1.70	1.52	0.14	84.2	1.64	1.62	1.00	81.2	1.58	1.45	0.56	14.12	1.57
	N_2-N_3	1.43	1.42	2.12	70.1	1.00	0.88	0.18	77.5	1.11	1.10	0.12	73.6	1.05	0.97	0.16	0.71	0.98
	N_3-N_1	4.90	4.42	9.44	162.1	7.94	4.26	0.14	81.5	3.99	3.94	0.62	149.6	7.33	3.97	0.20	118.4	3.33
	N_3-N_2	2.19	2.12	2.16	119.1	2.61	1.77	0.14	86.2	1.89	1.83	0.70	104.8	2.30	1.61	0.22	13.97	1.60
	N_1-N_2	1.49	1.42	0.98	92.8	1.38	0.99	0.14	65.6	0.98	0.98	1.00	63.9	0.95	0.85	1.00	13.31	1.00
	N_1-N_3	3.58	2.97	1.48	116.7	4.18	2.27	0.14	42.8	1.53	1.53	1.00	50.7	1.81	1.25	1.00	118.6	2.65
m_7	N_2-N_1	1.31	1.29	0.87	77.5	1.01	0.88	0.14	67.8	0.89	0.89	1.00	65.3	0.85	0.80	1.00	1.27	0.88
	N_2-N_3	1.34	1.32	0.86	76.6	1.03	0.90	0.14	65.6	0.88	0.88	1.00	63.5	0.85	0.80	1.00	12.84	0.88
	N_3-N_1	3.74	3.06	1.48	112.8	4.22	2.26	0.14	39.7	1.48	1.48	1.00	48.7	1.82	1.26	1.00	14.08	2.65
	N_3-N_2	1.49	1.42	0.98	94.3	1.40	0.99	0.14	65.8	0.98	0.98	1.00	63.9	0.95	0.85	1.00	2.36	1.00
	N_1-N_2	1.90	1.53	3.52	107.2	2.03	1.16	0.14	79.9	1.52	1.48	0.26	77.3	1.47	1.04	0.40	8.10	1.14
	N_1-N_3	8.80	4.93	30.97	133.0	11.71	4.49	0.14	62.4	5.49	4.50	0.48	125.3	11.03	4.02	0.20	96.62	3.47
m_8	N_2-N_1	1.14	1.11	3.35	40.0	0.46	0.46	0.46	77.6	0.89	0.88	0.16	52.0	0.59	0.59	0.28	1.39	0.65
	N_2-N_3	2.28	2.14	3.35	104.3	2.38	1.82	0.12	71.1	1.62	1.62	0.64	84.5	1.93	1.52	0.56	11.33	1.70
	N_3-N_1	3.02	2.64	32.00	35.0	1.06	1.02	0.32	76.8	2.32	1.37	0.12	41.5	1.25	1.24	0.40	12.44	2.42
	N_3-N_2	1.61	1.59	4.79	65.2	1.05	0.99	0.20	78.0	1.26	1.26	0.12	66.9	1.08	1.03	0.20	1.01	1.14
Mean		2.48	2.14	6.11	71.2	1.85	1.25	0.34	77.7	1.96	1.77	0.60	67.3	1.81	1.31	0.40	25.83	1.58
Median		1.91	1.74	2.14	72.6	1.09	0.89	0.17	76.1	1.46	1.39	0.61	63.9	1.13	1.04	0.30	10.41	1.27

Note: The first two columns indicate regression curve and density combination. The following columns provide the simulation results for the pair-matching, least squares, kernel, local linear and Seifert&Gasser matching estimator at the simulated optimal bandwidth value h^{opt}. The columns labelled MSE and Var provide the absolute values of the mean squared error and the variance of the estimator at its optimal bandwidth h^{opt} (multiplied by 1000). The columns labelled MSE^r give the mean squared error relative to the mean squared error of pair-matching. The second-last column contains the simulated MSE of the re-weighting estimator. The last column provides the approximation according to the asymptotic variance bound. Results based on 10^4 replications. Bandwidth grid = 0.02, 0.04,...,1.00.

Table C.4. Mean squared error at optimal bandwidth value (sample size $n_s = n_r = 200$)

Densities		Pair-matching MSE	Var	OLS MSE	Kernel matching MSE^r	MSE	VAR	h^{opt}	Local linear matching MSE^r	MSE	VAR	h^{opt}	Seifert&Gasser matching MSE^r	MSE	VAR	h^{opt}	Weighting MSE	Efficient Var
m_1	N₁–N₂	0.45	0.45	4.47	81.8	0.37	0.35	0.07	81.4	0.37	0.37	0.13	72.0	0.33	0.32	0.13	2.26	0.34
	N₁–N₃	0.94	0.89	37.17	67.2	0.63	0.62	0.07	124.0	1.16	1.11	0.26	60.3	0.57	0.56	0.21	14.54	0.65
	N₂–N₁	0.37	0.37	3.05	78.3	0.29	0.27	0.08	81.0	0.30	0.29	0.09	59.5	0.22	0.21	0.17	1.41	0.28
	N₂–N₃	0.39	0.39	0.71	72.7	0.28	0.28	0.12	70.8	0.27	0.27	0.35	62.8	0.24	0.24	0.21	1.85	0.29
	N₃–N₁	1.06	0.97	6.14	39.6	0.42	0.42	0.44	101.5	1.08	1.04	0.35	102.0	1.08	0.71	0.14	12.83	0.63
	N₃–N₂	0.45	0.44	0.54	71.7	0.32	0.32	0.13	75.4	0.34	0.33	0.16	72.2	0.32	0.29	0.16	1.06	0.34
m_2	N₁–N₂	0.25	0.25	2.24	65.7	0.17	0.15	0.10	87.5	0.22	0.20	0.08	58.5	0.15	0.15	0.16	1.69	0.15
	N₁–N₃	0.73	0.73	23.83	74.8	0.55	0.47	0.11	73.4	0.54	0.50	0.50	63.8	0.47	0.39	0.22	11.76	0.50
	N₂–N₁	0.27	0.27	1.76	72.9	0.20	0.18	0.07	79.5	0.22	0.21	0.07	61.0	0.17	0.16	0.22	1.15	0.17
	N₂–N₃	0.24	0.24	0.91	62.0	0.15	0.14	0.10	68.7	0.16	0.16	0.16	57.2	0.14	0.13	0.20	1.07	0.14
	N₃–N₁	1.16	0.92	12.16	98.2	1.14	0.65	0.11	69.9	0.81	0.80	0.09	95.4	1.11	0.64	0.13	10.57	0.53
	N₃–N₂	0.27	0.26	0.71	39.0	0.11	0.11	0.33	70.9	0.19	0.19	0.10	55.8	0.15	0.15	0.25	2.13	0.15
m_3	N₁–N₂	0.28	0.28	0.56	74.7	0.21	0.19	0.08	77.2	0.22	0.22	0.09	57.1	0.16	0.16	0.26	0.44	0.18
	N₁–N₃	0.74	0.73	3.89	73.4	0.54	0.48	0.10	73.2	0.54	0.54	0.04	52.7	0.39	0.38	0.50	3.29	0.52
	N₂–N₁	0.23	0.23	0.44	52.6	0.12	0.11	0.20	75.1	0.17	0.17	0.13	59.8	0.14	0.13	0.10	1.41	0.13
	N₂–N₃	0.26	0.26	0.18	63.3	0.16	0.16	0.11	72.2	0.19	0.18	0.30	62.3	0.16	0.16	0.16	0.29	0.16
	N₃–N₁	0.69	0.69	0.60	54.6	0.38	0.34	0.02	98.9	0.68	0.68	0.37	50.5	0.35	0.34	0.30	12.65	0.48
	N₃–N₂	0.28	0.28	0.19	70.3	0.19	0.18	0.08	75.7	0.21	0.21	0.30	60.1	0.17	0.16	0.26	1.81	0.18
m_4	N₁–N₂	0.24	0.24	0.37	44.7	0.11	0.11	0.49	75.6	0.18	0.18	0.14	50.1	0.12	0.12	0.16	1.32	0.14
	N₁–N₃	0.68	0.68	1.99	18.2	0.12	0.12	0.50	82.8	0.57	0.52	0.50	44.0	0.30	0.28	0.01	10.74	0.46
	N₂–N₁	0.27	0.27	0.29	61.5	0.16	0.16	0.08	66.4	0.18	0.18	0.09	60.1	0.16	0.16	0.14	1.61	0.16
	N₂–N₃	0.21	0.21	0.12	39.9	0.08	0.08	0.50	58.8	0.12	0.12	0.16	47.8	0.10	0.10	0.18	1.11	0.11
	N₃–N₁	1.16	1.08	0.69	25.1	0.29	0.15	0.50	144.2	1.67	1.47	0.13	76.9	0.89	0.71	0.07	15.44	0.52
	N₃–N₂	0.27	0.27	0.18	33.6	0.09	0.09	0.50	84.5	0.23	0.22	0.13	60.4	0.16	0.16	0.09	1.55	0.14
m_5	N₁–N₂	0.23	0.23	0.87	49.8	0.11	0.11	0.19	109.1	0.25	0.20	0.13	56.7	0.13	0.13	0.13	3.25	0.13
	N₁–N₃	0.67	0.66	9.17	21.8	0.15	0.13	0.35	67.7	0.45	0.44	0.46	41.9	0.28	0.25	0.01	23.71	0.45
	N₂–N₁	0.27	0.27	0.70	72.9	0.20	0.18	0.06	77.8	0.21	0.20	0.07	63.0	0.17	0.17	0.30	1.15	0.17
	N₂–N₃	0.19	0.19	0.56	32.2	0.06	0.06	0.50	66.6	0.13	0.12	0.14	49.6	0.10	0.10	0.17	2.45	0.10
	N₃–N₁	0.99	0.82	7.25	115.0	1.14	0.64	0.10	66.2	0.66	0.61	0.40	107.2	1.06	0.59	0.13	11.83	0.52
	N₃–N₂	0.24	0.23	0.55	75.1	0.18	0.13	0.10	75.3	0.18	0.16	0.50	56.6	0.13	0.13	0.32	2.04	0.13
m_6	N₁–N₂	0.42	0.42	0.41	90.0	0.38	0.33	0.08	81.5	0.35	0.33	0.33	79.6	0.34	0.33	0.49	0.20	0.32
	N₁–N₃	0.79	0.76	2.30	95.6	0.76	0.56	0.09	69.9	0.55	0.54	0.02	53.5	0.42	0.42	0.50	1.41	0.55
	N₂–N₁	0.40	0.40	0.43	79.4	0.32	0.31	0.07	77.5	0.31	0.31	0.28	71.8	0.29	0.29	0.37	2.84	0.31
	N₂–N₃	0.29	0.29	0.74	69.5	0.20	0.19	0.09	75.5	0.22	0.21	0.15	70.8	0.21	0.20	0.08	0.14	0.20
	N₃–N₁	0.86	0.85	6.39	129.7	1.11	0.72	0.09	145.8	1.25	1.25	0.23	105.1	0.90	0.60	0.15	23.57	0.67
	N₃–N₂	0.41	0.41	0.79	102.1	0.42	0.34	0.08	90.0	0.37	0.37	0.16	74.0	0.31	0.30	0.32	2.84	0.32
m_7	N₁–N₂	0.30	0.30	0.19	87.0	0.26	0.21	0.08	71.0	0.21	0.21	0.50	80.8	0.24	0.20	0.13	2.63	0.20
	N₁–N₃	0.79	0.76	0.28	109.0	0.86	0.56	0.10	57.2	0.45	0.45	0.50	96.7	0.76	0.51	0.13	23.68	0.53
	N₂–N₁	0.26	0.26	0.17	71.1	0.19	0.18	0.07	68.7	0.18	0.18	0.50	69.7	0.18	0.17	0.09	0.26	0.18
	N₂–N₃	0.27	0.27	0.17	69.3	0.19	0.18	0.07	68.7	0.18	0.18	0.50	68.9	0.19	0.18	0.09	2.56	0.18
	N₃–N₁	0.79	0.76	0.29	108.9	0.86	0.56	0.10	56.3	0.45	0.45	0.50	96.1	0.76	0.51	0.13	2.80	0.53
	N₃–N₂	0.31	0.30	0.19	84.8	0.26	0.21	0.09	69.2	0.21	0.21	0.50	78.1	0.24	0.20	0.13	0.47	0.20
m_8	N₁–N₂	0.34	0.32	1.91	113.9	0.39	0.26	0.09	91.4	0.31	0.31	0.15	63.1	0.22	0.21	0.31	1.61	0.23
	N₁–N₃	1.46	1.16	25.61	173.4	2.53	1.18	0.10	53.3	0.78	0.77	0.40	151.1	2.21	1.02	0.13	19.45	0.69
	N₂–N₁	0.23	0.23	1.86	39.1	0.09	0.09	0.46	73.7	0.17	0.17	0.07	55.0	0.13	0.13	0.15	0.28	0.13
	N₂–N₃	0.44	0.44	1.85	85.1	0.37	0.35	0.06	88.3	0.39	0.37	0.11	70.1	0.31	0.31	0.31	2.26	0.34
	N₃–N₁	0.79	0.74	25.88	27.4	0.22	0.21	0.29	83.2	0.66	0.66	0.40	49.8	0.39	0.32	0.01	2.50	0.48
	N₃–N₂	0.34	0.34	2.17	63.0	0.22	0.21	0.14	77.5	0.26	0.26	0.06	65.1	0.22	0.22	0.11	0.20	0.23
Mean		0.50	0.47	4.04	70.9	0.39	0.29	0.17	79.8	0.41	0.40	0.25	68.3	0.38	0.30	0.19	5.17	0.32
Median		0.36	0.35	0.72	71.4	0.24	0.21	0.10	75.4	0.29	0.28	0.16	62.5	0.24	0.22	0.16	2.09	0.25

Note: The first two columns indicate regression curve and density combination. The following columns provide the simulation results for the pair-matching, least squares, kernel, local linear and Seifert&Gasser matching estimator at the simulated optimal bandwidth value h^{opt}. The columns labelled MSE and Var provide the absolute values of the mean squared error and the variance of the estimator at its optimal bandwidth h^{opt} (multiplied by 1000). The columns labelled MSE^r give the mean squared error relative to the mean squared error of pair-matching. The second-last column contains the simulated MSE of the re-weighting estimator. The last column provides the approximation according to the asymptotic variance bound. Results based on 10^4 replications. Bandwidth grid = 0.01,0.02,...,0.50.

Table C.5. Mean squared error at optimal bandwidth value (sample size $n_s = n_r = 1000$)

	Densities	Pair-matching MSE	Pair-matching Var	OLS MSE	Kernel matching MSE^r	Kernel matching MSE	Kernel matching VAR	Kernel matching h^{opt}	Local linear matching MSE^r	Local linear matching MSE	Local linear matching VAR	Local linear matching h^{opt}	Seifert&Gasser matching MSE^r	Seifert&Gasser matching MSE	Seifert&Gasser matching VAR	Seifert&Gasser matching h^{opt}	Weighting MSE	Efficient Var
m_1	N_1-N_2	0.09	0.09	3.71	73.8	0.07	0.06	0.04	74.6	0.07	0.07	0.09	67.2	0.06	0.06	0.06	0.45	0.07
	N_1-N_3	0.19	0.19	35.05	62.7	0.12	0.12	0.05	93.5	0.18	0.18	0.22	65.3	0.13	0.12	0.01	2.89	0.13
	N_2-N_1	0.07	0.07	2.46	71.8	0.05	0.05	0.05	77.9	0.06	0.06	0.06	60.6	0.04	0.04	0.07	0.28	0.06
	N_2-N_3	0.08	0.08	0.43	76.1	0.06	0.06	0.10	80.5	0.06	0.06	0.37	66.2	0.05	0.05	0.12	0.37	0.06
	N_3-N_1	0.18	0.18	5.14	76.8	0.14	0.12	0.06	104.9	0.19	0.19	0.38	88.2	0.16	0.12	0.23	2.58	0.13
	N_3-N_2	0.09	0.09	0.11	79.7	0.07	0.07	0.11	77.8	0.07	0.07	0.11	61.2	0.05	0.05	0.20	0.21	0.07
m_2	N_1-N_2	0.05	0.05	1.90	60.8	0.03	0.03	0.06	82.5	0.04	0.04	0.04	62.4	0.03	0.03	0.08	0.34	0.03
	N_1-N_3	0.17	0.16	22.73	52.5	0.09	0.09	0.04	95.9	0.16	0.15	0.17	34.5	0.06	0.06	0.20	2.34	0.10
	N_2-N_1	0.05	0.05	1.49	72.0	0.04	0.04	0.03	67.2	0.04	0.04	0.04	59.6	0.03	0.03	0.11	0.23	0.03
	N_2-N_3	0.05	0.05	0.77	48.1	0.02	0.02	0.07	63.8	0.03	0.03	0.17	56.4	0.03	0.03	0.15	0.22	0.03
	N_3-N_1	0.18	0.17	11.45	97.0	0.17	0.13	0.06	85.6	0.15	0.15	0.35	78.6	0.14	0.09	0.07	2.11	0.11
	N_3-N_2	0.05	0.05	0.48	46.5	0.02	0.02	0.31	72.8	0.04	0.03	0.11	49.2	0.02	0.02	0.16	0.43	0.03
m_3	N_1-N_2	0.06	0.06	0.41	53.4	0.03	0.03	0.04	78.0	0.04	0.04	0.14	61.8	0.04	0.03	0.12	0.09	0.04
	N_1-N_3	0.16	0.16	3.51	65.1	0.11	0.10	0.07	75.3	0.12	0.12	0.01	55.4	0.09	0.09	0.20	0.65	0.10
	N_2-N_1	0.04	0.04	0.27	55.2	0.02	0.02	0.04	62.3	0.03	0.03	0.07	52.4	0.02	0.02	0.03	0.28	0.03
	N_2-N_3	0.05	0.05	0.05	58.3	0.03	0.03	0.03	77.1	0.04	0.04	0.05	62.0	0.03	0.03	0.09	0.06	0.03
	N_3-N_1	0.16	0.16	0.32	60.8	0.10	0.09	0.01	69.7	0.11	0.11	0.36	45.2	0.07	0.07	0.01	2.53	0.10
	N_3-N_2	0.05	0.05	0.04	62.0	0.03	0.03	0.03	75.0	0.04	0.04	0.15	66.4	0.04	0.04	0.19	0.36	0.04
m_4	N_1-N_2	0.05	0.05	0.24	46.3	0.02	0.02	0.14	71.8	0.03	0.03	0.14	46.4	0.02	0.02	0.14	0.27	0.03
	N_1-N_3	0.15	0.15	1.70	15.7	0.02	0.02	0.38	82.4	0.12	0.12	0.34	50.0	0.07	0.07	0.01	2.18	0.09
	N_2-N_1	0.05	0.05	0.12	57.7	0.03	0.03	0.04	51.8	0.03	0.03	0.11	66.9	0.03	0.03	0.11	0.32	0.02
	N_2-N_3	0.04	0.04	0.03	55.0	0.02	0.02	0.38	50.5	0.02	0.02	0.14	41.5	0.02	0.02	0.15	0.22	0.02
	N_3-N_1	0.17	0.17	0.37	73.3	0.12	0.12	0.05	144.7	0.25	0.25	0.31	71.6	0.12	0.12	0.05	3.08	0.10
	N_3-N_2	0.05	0.05	0.04	42.3	0.02	0.02	0.38	65.9	0.03	0.03	0.07	59.1	0.03	0.03	0.07	0.31	0.03
m_5	N_1-N_2	0.05	0.05	0.66	57.9	0.03	0.03	0.13	81.9	0.04	0.03	0.10	58.6	0.03	0.03	0.08	0.65	0.03
	N_1-N_3	0.14	0.14	8.66	20.8	0.03	0.03	0.32	52.4	0.08	0.07	0.38	59.7	0.09	0.09	0.20	4.75	0.09
	N_2-N_1	0.05	0.05	0.55	67.6	0.04	0.04	0.03	74.6	0.04	0.04	0.06	70.3	0.04	0.04	0.16	0.23	0.03
	N_2-N_3	0.04	0.04	0.44	53.5	0.02	0.02	0.06	42.9	0.02	0.02	0.05	50.3	0.02	0.02	0.07	0.48	0.02
	N_3-N_1	0.18	0.17	6.84	113.3	0.20	0.14	0.06	65.5	0.12	0.12	0.37	71.8	0.13	0.10	0.07	2.36	0.10
	N_3-N_2	0.05	0.05	0.41	54.7	0.03	0.02	0.06	65.3	0.03	0.03	0.06	63.9	0.03	0.03	0.17	0.41	0.03
m_6	N_1-N_2	0.08	0.08	0.10	75.8	0.06	0.06	0.04	82.8	0.07	0.06	0.18	72.2	0.06	0.06	0.06	0.04	0.06
	N_1-N_3	0.16	0.16	1.81	78.3	0.13	0.11	0.05	88.7	0.14	0.13	0.18	77.3	0.13	0.11	0.07	0.28	0.11
	N_2-N_1	0.08	0.08	0.19	80.1	0.07	0.06	0.01	88.3	0.07	0.07	0.32	78.3	0.06	0.06	0.33	0.57	0.06
	N_2-N_3	0.06	0.06	0.47	77.5	0.04	0.04	0.05	68.8	0.04	0.04	0.07	70.0	0.04	0.04	0.04	0.03	0.04
	N_3-N_1	0.19	0.19	5.83	99.5	0.19	0.15	0.05	84.1	0.16	0.16	0.25	64.7	0.12	0.12	0.33	4.73	0.13
	N_3-N_2	0.09	0.09	0.54	93.0	0.08	0.07	0.05	76.2	0.07	0.06	0.14	77.1	0.07	0.07	0.15	0.57	0.06
m_7	N_1-N_2	0.06	0.06	0.04	61.0	0.04	0.03	0.04	73.0	0.04	0.04	0.23	73.1	0.04	0.04	0.06	0.53	0.04
	N_1-N_3	0.16	0.16	0.06	97.5	0.16	0.13	0.07	76.0	0.12	0.12	0.38	90.1	0.14	0.10	0.08	4.68	0.11
	N_2-N_1	0.05	0.05	0.03	71.4	0.04	0.04	0.04	55.0	0.03	0.03	0.04	56.6	0.03	0.03	0.01	0.05	0.04
	N_2-N_3	0.05	0.05	0.03	73.5	0.04	0.04	0.04	70.4	0.04	0.04	0.14	73.6	0.04	0.04	0.04	0.52	0.04
	N_3-N_1	0.16	0.16	0.06	86.6	0.14	0.11	0.05	62.3	0.10	0.10	0.38	89.1	0.14	0.12	0.08	0.57	0.11
	N_3-N_2	0.06	0.06	0.04	78.0	0.05	0.04	0.05	63.6	0.04	0.04	0.22	75.6	0.04	0.04	0.07	0.09	0.04
m_8	N_1-N_2	0.06	0.06	1.61	102.8	0.07	0.06	0.05	88.0	0.06	0.06	0.09	69.7	0.04	0.04	0.14	0.32	0.05
	N_1-N_3	0.21	0.21	24.52	177.9	0.38	0.24	0.06	70.8	0.15	0.14	0.38	143.2	0.31	0.18	0.07	3.87	0.14
	N_2-N_1	0.05	0.05	1.57	57.1	0.03	0.03	0.05	64.0	0.03	0.03	0.02	61.1	0.03	0.03	0.08	0.06	0.03
	N_2-N_3	0.09	0.09	1.57	80.0	0.07	0.07	0.02	88.1	0.08	0.08	0.05	61.8	0.05	0.05	0.16	0.45	0.07
	N_3-N_1	0.16	0.15	24.58	31.1	0.05	0.05	0.27	68.8	0.11	0.10	0.38	51.4	0.08	0.08	0.22	0.50	0.10
	N_3-N_2	0.07	0.07	1.66	58.6	0.04	0.04	0.09	71.2	0.05	0.05	0.04	72.9	0.05	0.05	0.07	0.04	0.05
	Mean	0.10	0.10	3.65	69.0	0.07	0.06	0.09	75.1	0.08	0.07	0.18	65.8	0.07	0.06	0.11	1.03	0.06
	Median	0.07	0.07	0.51	66.3	0.05	0.04	0.05	74.6	0.06	0.06	0.14	64.3	0.05	0.05	0.08	0.42	0.05

Note: The first two columns indicate regression curve and density combination. The following columns provide the simulation results for the pair-matching, least squares, kernel, local linear and Seifert&Gasser matching estimator at the simulated optimal bandwidth value h^{opt}. The columns labelled MSE and Var provide the absolute values of the mean squared error and the variance of the estimator at its optimal bandwidth h^{opt} (multiplied by 1000). The columns labelled MSE^r give the mean squared error relative to the mean squared error of pair-matching. The second-last column contains the simulated MSE of the re-weighting estimator. The last column provides the approximation according to the asymptotic variance bound. Results based on 10^4 replications for pair-matching, least squares and re-weighting and 200 replications otherwise. Bandwidth grid 0.0075, 0.0150,..., 0.3750.

Table C.6. Mean squared error at optimal bandwidth value (sample size $n_s = 200$, $n_r = 40$)

Densities		Pair-matching		OLS	Kernel matching				Local linear matching				Seifert&Gasser matching				Weighting	Efficient
		MSE	Var	MSE	MSE^r	MSE	VAR	h^{opt}	MSE^r	MSE	VAR	h^{opt}	MSE^r	MSE	VAR	h^{opt}	MSE	Var
m_1	N_1-N_2	1.66	1.66	4.44	67.8	1.12	1.00	0.14	64.3	1.07	1.00	0.17	54.8	0.91	0.84	0.20	2.22	1.33
	N_1-N_3	1.96	1.92	36.97	69.4	1.36	1.25	0.14	84.1	1.65	1.56	0.28	49.9	0.98	0.97	0.26	14.38	1.47
	N_2-N_1	1.35	1.35	3.23	64.1	0.86	0.76	0.13	66.7	0.90	0.81	0.14	45.0	0.61	0.55	0.22	1.42	1.05
	N_2-N_3	1.41	1.41	0.88	56.9	0.80	0.74	0.20	39.5	0.56	0.55	0.35	38.0	0.54	0.53	0.35	1.83	1.11
	N_3-N_1	1.96	1.84	6.48	31.8	0.62	0.62	0.44	80.8	1.59	1.54	0.35	78.7	1.55	1.06	0.18	12.85	1.41
	N_3-N_2	1.65	1.64	0.87	54.2	0.89	0.82	0.22	47.2	0.78	0.77	0.30	47.3	0.78	0.72	0.26	1.03	1.33
m_2	N_1-N_2	0.66	0.66	2.37	50.2	0.33	0.28	0.16	78.1	0.52	0.50	0.09	45.4	0.30	0.29	0.20	1.69	0.36
	N_1-N_3	1.14	1.13	23.74	66.7	0.76	0.64	0.13	64.1	0.73	0.68	0.50	49.5	0.56	0.48	0.36	11.83	0.72
	N_2-N_1	0.80	0.80	1.79	61.8	0.49	0.43	0.10	64.1	0.51	0.33	0.50	41.9	0.34	0.33	0.24	1.17	0.51
	N_2-N_3	0.65	0.65	0.93	53.2	0.35	0.32	0.14	53.8	0.35	0.35	0.19	43.9	0.28	0.28	0.25	1.05	0.36
	N_3-N_1	1.58	1.35	12.26	79.8	1.26	0.15	0.50	67.2	1.06	1.04	0.36	84.6	1.33	0.78	0.15	10.47	0.87
	N_3-N_2	0.65	0.63	0.87	26.7	0.17	0.17	0.35	56.6	0.37	0.36	0.46	39.6	0.26	0.26	0.29	2.11	0.36
m_3	N_1-N_2	0.79	0.79	0.66	65.4	0.52	0.47	0.12	74.7	0.59	0.58	0.15	47.7	0.38	0.37	0.31	0.44	0.51
	N_1-N_3	1.27	1.26	3.95	67.5	0.85	0.76	0.12	86.8	1.10	1.10	0.06	49.2	0.62	0.59	0.45	3.30	0.81
	N_2-N_1	0.59	0.59	0.64	39.3	0.23	0.21	0.25	56.7	0.34	0.32	0.15	47.2	0.28	0.27	0.15	1.41	0.30
	N_2-N_3	0.76	0.76	0.41	58.1	0.44	0.42	0.14	54.8	0.42	0.41	0.30	51.6	0.39	0.38	0.34	0.29	0.46
	N_3-N_1	1.08	1.08	0.81	53.0	0.57	0.50	0.17	78.2	0.85	0.84	0.36	46.7	0.50	0.49	0.31	12.95	0.65
	N_3-N_2	0.79	0.79	0.46	65.5	0.52	0.49	0.12	59.3	0.47	0.47	0.30	50.0	0.40	0.40	0.32	1.80	0.51
m_4	N_1-N_2	0.59	0.59	0.40	19.4	0.11	0.11	0.50	43.1	0.26	0.20	0.47	28.7	0.17	0.17	0.21	1.32	0.31
	N_1-N_3	0.94	0.94	2.03	13.7	0.13	0.13	0.50	63.2	0.59	0.55	0.50	40.0	0.38	0.37	0.50	11.05	0.55
	N_2-N_1	0.78	0.78	0.29	39.7	0.31	0.12	0.50	43.3	0.34	0.34	0.41	33.0	0.26	0.26	0.21	1.61	0.46
	N_2-N_3	0.50	0.50	0.12	17.5	0.09	0.09	0.50	28.4	0.14	0.14	0.39	23.4	0.12	0.12	0.23	1.10	0.20
	N_3-N_1	1.65	1.58	0.70	17.9	0.30	0.15	0.50	122.1	2.02	1.92	0.14	67.2	1.11	0.95	0.12	15.21	0.81
	N_3-N_2	0.64	0.63	0.18	14.4	0.09	0.09	0.50	51.7	0.33	0.31	0.50	37.1	0.24	0.21	0.19	1.55	0.31
m_5	N_1-N_2	0.57	0.57	1.17	37.7	0.21	0.20	0.23	70.7	0.40	0.31	0.50	46.7	0.27	0.26	0.14	3.35	0.27
	N_1-N_3	0.89	0.88	9.37	19.8	0.18	0.17	0.34	57.4	0.51	0.49	0.46	37.4	0.33	0.33	0.33	23.80	0.49
	N_2-N_1	0.76	0.76	0.76	63.1	0.48	0.44	0.09	53.6	0.41	0.36	0.50	43.8	0.33	0.33	0.50	1.16	0.49
	N_2-N_3	0.43	0.43	0.62	16.3	0.07	0.07	0.50	40.8	0.18	0.16	0.16	29.2	0.13	0.13	0.18	2.47	0.14
	N_3-N_1	1.44	1.26	7.25	93.6	1.35	0.84	0.11	59.2	0.85	0.79	0.42	86.8	1.25	0.73	0.15	11.80	0.84
	N_3-N_2	0.54	0.53	0.54	53.3	0.29	0.22	0.13	45.0	0.24	0.22	0.50	33.5	0.18	0.18	0.36	2.04	0.27
m_6	N_1-N_2	1.52	1.52	1.33	79.9	1.22	1.13	0.11	70.2	1.07	1.06	0.33	68.9	1.05	0.96	0.33	0.21	1.21
	N_1-N_3	1.40	1.37	3.11	83.2	1.16	0.95	0.11	75.4	1.06	1.06	0.43	61.2	0.86	0.84	0.49	1.42	0.98
	N_2-N_1	1.49	1.49	1.06	75.7	1.13	1.10	0.10	70.3	1.05	1.05	0.28	64.9	0.97	0.96	0.34	2.83	1.21
	N_2-N_3	0.92	0.92	1.42	62.9	0.58	0.54	0.14	71.6	0.66	0.65	0.17	67.2	0.62	0.60	0.12	0.14	0.63
	N_3-N_1	1.96	1.96	6.75	100.7	1.98	1.56	0.10	108.2	2.12	2.11	0.24	85.4	1.68	1.30	0.18	23.50	1.57
	N_3-N_2	1.52	1.52	1.20	81.4	1.24	1.13	0.10	80.4	1.22	1.22	0.18	61.5	0.94	0.94	0.35	2.83	1.21
m_7	N_1-N_2	0.91	0.90	0.60	71.7	0.65	0.57	0.11	68.4	0.62	0.62	0.50	65.4	0.59	0.54	0.50	2.62	0.62
	N_1-N_3	1.28	1.25	0.65	92.1	1.18	0.89	0.10	63.1	0.81	0.81	0.50	79.7	1.02	0.60	0.50	23.75	0.88
	N_2-N_1	0.82	0.82	0.53	64.5	0.53	0.51	0.10	65.8	0.54	0.54	0.50	62.7	0.52	0.50	0.50	0.26	0.53
	N_2-N_3	0.82	0.82	0.51	63.0	0.52	0.49	0.10	66.5	0.55	0.55	0.50	62.2	0.51	0.48	0.16	2.50	0.53
	N_3-N_1	1.31	1.27	0.64	92.9	1.22	0.90	0.10	61.1	0.80	0.80	0.50	79.6	1.04	0.60	0.50	2.78	0.88
	N_3-N_2	0.89	0.89	0.61	73.2	0.65	0.59	0.10	71.2	0.63	0.63	0.50	68.6	0.61	0.56	0.50	0.48	0.62
m_8	N_1-N_2	0.99	0.96	1.94	79.9	0.79	0.61	0.11	72.6	0.71	0.55	0.50	47.2	0.46	0.46	0.35	1.64	0.75
	N_1-N_3	2.44	2.14	25.81	134.5	3.28	1.95	0.10	62.7	1.53	1.50	0.42	115.5	2.81	1.63	0.14	19.96	1.70
	N_2-N_1	0.59	0.59	2.10	21.0	0.12	0.12	0.47	58.2	0.34	0.34	0.07	44.9	0.27	0.26	0.18	0.28	0.30
	N_2-N_3	1.63	1.63	2.10	79.2	1.29	1.22	0.08	73.8	1.21	0.98	0.50	57.5	0.94	0.90	0.50	2.31	1.35
	N_3-N_1	1.13	1.07	26.75	30.9	0.35	0.34	0.29	71.7	0.81	0.81	0.39	46.6	0.53	0.51	0.29	2.50	0.65
	N_3-N_2	1.06	1.06	3.17	61.2	0.65	0.61	0.19	77.5	0.82	0.82	0.10	69.8	0.74	0.73	0.15	0.20	0.75
Mean		1.11	1.08	4.28	58.0	0.71	0.58	0.22	65.5	0.76	0.73	0.35	54.7	0.66	0.56	0.29	5.18	0.74
Median		0.96	0.95	1.11	63.0	0.58	0.50	0.14	65.1	0.64	0.63	0.38	49.4	0.53	0.50	0.28	2.07	0.64

Note: The first two columns indicate regression curve and density combination. The following columns provide the simulation results for the pair-matching, least squares, kernel, local linear and Seifert&Gasser matching estimator at the simulated optimal bandwidth value h^{opt}. The columns labelled MSE and Var provide the absolute values of the mean squared error and the variance of the estimator at its optimal bandwidth h^{opt} (multiplied by 1000). The columns labelled MSE^r give the mean squared error relative to the mean squared error of pair-matching. The second-last column contains the simulated MSE of the re-weighting estimator. The last column provides the approximation according to the asymptotic variance bound. Results based on 10^4 replications. Bandwidth grid = 0.01, 0.02, ..., 0.50.

Table C.7. Mean squared error at optimal bandwidth value (sample size $n_s = 40, n_r = 200$)

Densities	Pair-matching MSE	Pair-matching Var	OLS MSE	Kernel matching MSE^r	Kernel matching MSE	Kernel matching VAR	Kernel matching h^{opt}	Local linear matching MSE^r	Local linear matching MSE	Local linear matching VAR	Local linear matching h^{opt}	Seifert&Gasser matching MSE^r	Seifert&Gasser matching MSE	Seifert&Gasser matching VAR	Seifert&Gasser matching h^{opt}	Weighting MSE	Efficient Var
N_1-N_2	1.33	1.33	8.78	108.8	1.45	1.15	0.10	117.4	1.56	1.54	0.20	101.5	1.35	1.21	0.16	11.19	0.73
N_1-N_3	3.56	3.40	49.69	87.2	3.10	2.59	0.12	187.2	6.66	5.68	0.24	83.1	2.96	2.62	0.16	71.82	2.41
m_1 N_2-N_1	1.03	1.00	6.00	96.7	1.00	0.86	0.10	101.1	1.05	1.05	0.18	86.3	0.89	0.79	0.18	7.02	0.63
N_2-N_3	0.97	0.96	2.06	79.6	0.78	0.77	0.06	109.4	1.07	1.02	0.26	79.4	0.77	0.77	0.08	9.31	0.65
N_3-N_1	7.23	4.44	11.07	26.4	1.91	1.91	0.44	117.6	8.50	4.89	0.22	52.6	3.80	1.98	0.02	64.10	2.40
N_3-N_2	1.50	1.25	2.43	57.1	0.86	0.83	0.08	97.5	1.47	0.98	0.16	57.1	0.86	0.83	0.08	5.35	0.73
N_1-N_2	0.91	0.86	4.01	57.9	0.53	0.52	0.72	127.9	1.16	1.14	0.60	65.8	0.60	0.59	0.30	8.54	0.54
N_1-N_3	3.02	2.74	29.40	89.4	2.70	0.56	1.00	90.2	2.73	2.72	0.52	93.1	2.81	1.82	0.24	58.23	2.26
m_2 N_2-N_1	1.02	0.92	3.15	94.6	0.96	0.73	0.12	95.3	0.97	0.70	0.16	90.0	0.92	0.69	0.16	5.73	0.53
N_2-N_3	0.79	0.79	1.68	74.3	0.59	0.55	0.14	85.8	0.68	0.68	0.78	68.6	0.54	0.51	0.24	5.39	0.50
N_3-N_1	5.05	3.07	15.45	9.9	0.50	0.50	0.74	61.2	3.10	2.63	0.24	78.0	3.94	1.05	0.02	52.95	2.29
N_3-N_2	1.01	0.86	1.66	47.8	0.48	0.48	0.34	90.2	0.91	0.76	0.26	57.2	0.58	0.55	0.02	10.71	0.54
N_1-N_2	0.89	0.87	1.29	106.5	0.94	0.67	0.14	72.9	0.65	0.63	0.14	85.8	0.76	0.61	0.30	2.24	0.57
N_1-N_3	2.58	2.53	5.76	106.4	2.75	1.88	0.14	63.5	1.64	1.50	0.12	97.5	2.52	1.73	0.22	16.39	2.28
m_3 N_2-N_1	0.76	0.76	1.07	60.3	0.46	0.45	0.24	111.8	0.85	0.85	0.52	65.3	0.50	0.48	0.22	7.02	0.48
N_2-N_3	0.80	0.79	0.63	70.1	0.56	0.54	0.14	77.0	0.61	0.61	1.00	67.6	0.54	0.51	0.20	1.44	0.51
N_3-N_1	2.35	2.30	1.85	60.3	1.41	1.31	0.16	107.1	2.51	1.60	1.00	50.7	1.19	1.18	0.62	63.69	2.25
N_3-N_2	0.84	0.84	0.67	78.5	0.66	0.55	0.14	83.9	0.70	0.69	1.00	73.0	0.61	0.54	0.26	9.04	0.57
N_1-N_2	0.83	0.82	1.08	63.8	0.53	0.53	0.06	89.3	0.74	0.74	0.84	63.3	0.53	0.52	0.04	6.56	0.53
N_1-N_3	2.57	2.45	3.61	21.6	0.56	0.55	0.74	67.0	1.72	1.72	0.84	38.1	0.98	0.98	0.02	54.74	2.23
m_4 N_2-N_1	1.04	1.02	1.17	61.6	0.64	0.48	1.00	121.6	1.26	1.17	1.00	77.0	0.80	0.75	0.08	8.02	0.52
N_2-N_3	0.74	0.74	0.58	56.8	0.42	0.42	0.62	74.3	0.55	0.55	1.00	68.2	0.50	0.50	0.18	5.56	0.46
N_3-N_1	5.53	4.05	2.34	10.4	0.58	0.39	1.00	42.9	2.37	2.21	1.00	29.5	1.63	1.35	0.02	76.13	2.28
N_3-N_2	1.12	1.03	0.88	32.9	0.37	0.37	1.00	82.0	0.92	0.91	1.00	50.7	0.57	0.56	0.02	7.65	0.53
N_1-N_2	0.78	0.77	1.68	56.4	0.44	0.42	0.24	99.2	0.78	0.77	0.60	61.6	0.48	0.48	0.18	16.29	0.52
N_1-N_3	2.26	2.18	11.65	27.5	0.62	0.56	0.40	117.2	2.65	2.33	0.54	35.9	0.81	0.81	0.02	120.1	2.22
m_5 N_2-N_1	0.94	0.87	1.38	92.0	0.87	0.66	0.12	79.7	0.75	0.75	0.60	89.7	0.85	0.65	0.14	5.76	0.52
N_2-N_3	0.72	0.72	1.13	43.2	0.31	0.31	0.54	79.8	0.58	0.58	0.66	59.0	0.43	0.43	0.30	12.15	0.45
N_3-N_1	4.23	2.81	9.26	99.7	4.22	1.94	0.16	76.9	3.25	3.20	0.40	97.7	4.13	1.89	0.20	58.54	2.29
N_3-N_2	0.94	0.82	1.24	82.7	0.78	0.54	0.16	83.4	0.78	0.78	0.58	71.8	0.67	0.54	0.38	10.14	0.52
N_1-N_2	0.98	0.96	1.03	117.8	1.15	0.77	0.12	82.1	0.80	0.78	0.14	95.1	0.93	0.90	0.92	1.01	0.71
N_1-N_3	2.54	2.32	4.02	110.4	2.81	1.65	0.14	51.6	1.31	1.31	0.10	56.6	1.44	1.42	0.70	7.07	2.32
m_6 N_2-N_1	0.93	0.93	1.00	88.9	0.83	0.71	0.12	91.8	0.86	0.85	0.92	89.1	0.83	0.70	0.16	14.17	0.67
N_2-N_3	0.84	0.83	1.45	77.0	0.64	0.58	0.14	73.4	0.61	0.61	0.12	76.6	0.64	0.58	0.14	0.72	0.55
N_3-N_1	3.94	3.46	9.08	181.5	7.15	3.57	0.14	77.5	3.05	3.05	0.60	168.6	6.64	3.38	0.18	118.1	2.43
N_3-N_2	1.22	1.13	1.74	156.0	1.90	1.06	0.14	100.4	1.22	1.22	0.62	143.0	1.74	1.05	0.20	14.17	0.71
N_1-N_2	0.94	0.88	0.56	110.2	1.04	0.66	0.14	59.9	0.56	0.56	1.00	64.4	0.60	0.51	1.00	13.22	0.59
N_1-N_3	3.20	2.59	1.12	123.9	3.97	2.03	0.14	35.9	1.15	1.15	1.00	49.6	1.59	1.02	1.00	118.1	2.30
m_7 N_2-N_1	0.82	0.80	0.51	83.9	0.69	0.59	0.12	63.7	0.52	0.52	1.00	67.2	0.55	0.49	1.00	1.28	0.53
N_2-N_3	0.82	0.81	0.51	82.4	0.68	0.59	0.12	61.6	0.51	0.51	1.00	65.3	0.54	0.49	1.00	12.93	0.53
N_3-N_1	3.22	2.61	1.13	120.3	3.87	1.97	0.14	34.4	1.11	1.11	1.00	50.4	1.62	1.02	1.00	13.94	2.30
N_3-N_2	0.94	0.87	0.56	109.7	1.03	0.66	0.14	60.3	0.57	0.57	1.00	67.1	0.63	0.53	1.00	2.38	0.59
N_1-N_2	1.41	1.05	3.49	121.6	1.72	0.85	0.14	80.0	1.13	1.13	0.28	96.7	1.37	0.90	0.38	7.95	0.61
N_1-N_3	8.13	4.30	30.87	136.5	11.10	4.00	0.14	59.8	4.86	4.12	0.46	132.2	10.75	3.87	0.18	97.76	2.46
m_8 N_2-N_1	0.81	0.78	3.05	53.7	0.43	0.43	0.46	82.3	0.66	0.65	0.16	62.3	0.50	0.50	0.26	1.38	0.48
N_2-N_3	1.27	1.13	3.07	126.4	1.61	1.06	0.12	84.8	1.08	1.07	0.60	113.6	1.44	0.97	0.14	11.28	0.69
N_3-N_1	2.72	2.34	31.05	34.4	0.94	0.89	0.32	71.1	1.93	0.99	0.12	37.4	1.02	1.01	0.02	12.75	2.25
N_3-N_2	0.91	0.89	3.73	65.4	0.59	0.57	0.10	66.7	0.61	0.58	0.10	67.5	0.61	0.59	0.16	1.01	0.61
Mean	1.94	1.60	5.85	80.4	1.54	0.97	0.29	84.3	1.58	1.38	0.56	74.9	1.50	1.00	0.30	25.85	1.15
Median	1.03	0.98	1.79	81.0	0.84	0.66	0.14	82.1	1.06	0.98	0.59	67.9	0.84	0.76	0.18	10.43	0.62

Note: The first two columns indicate regression curve and density combination. The following columns provide the simulation results for the pair-matching, least squares, kernel, local linear and Seifert&Gasser matching estimator at the simulated optimal bandwidth value h^{opt}. The columns labelled MSE and Var provide the absolute values of the mean squared error and the variance of the estimator at its optimal bandwidth h^{opt} (multiplied by 1000). The columns labelled MSE^r give the mean squared error relative to the mean squared error of pair-matching. The second-last column contains the simulated MSE of the re-weighting estimator. The last column provides the approximation according to the asymptotic variance bound. Results based on 10^4 replications. Bandwidth grid = 0.02, 0.04,...,1.00.

Table C.8. Penalized cross-validation bandwidth selection (sample size $n_s = n_r = 40$)

	Densities	Kernel matching					Local linear matching					Seifert&Gasser matching				
		MSE^r	%Var	MSE^o	h	std(h)	MSE^r	%Var	MSE^o	h	std(h)	MSE^r	%Var	MSE^o	h	std(h)
m_1	N_1-N_2	96.5	85	107.6	0.11	0.03	117.7	73	127.3	0.16	0.05	89.3	91	118.9	0.14	0.06
	N_1-N_3	90.6	86	103.7	0.11	0.03	265.6	38	164.5	0.16	0.05	86.9	86	114.2	0.14	0.05
	N_2-N_1	89.3	89	121.0	0.09	0.02	133.1	75	169.3	0.13	0.03	82.0	91	130.5	0.11	0.03
	N_2-N_3	79.1	100	108.2	0.09	0.02	133.5	68	185.8	0.13	0.03	72.5	100	121.3	0.11	0.04
	N_3-N_1	69.7	58	258.2	0.09	0.03	154.0	27	132.8	0.14	0.05	68.7	59	96.6	0.12	0.06
	N_3-N_2	71.9	99	109.4	0.09	0.03	97.6	70	113.7	0.14	0.05	68.2	98	104.8	0.12	0.05
m_2	N_1-N_2	71.0	83	168.8	0.15	0.04	138.4	67	139.3	0.24	0.06	67.9	90	126.0	0.21	0.10
	N_1-N_3	93.7	66	115.5	0.15	0.04	171.0	67	190.2	0.24	0.06	95.7	70	115.7	0.21	0.10
	N_2-N_1	91.1	69	126.4	0.17	0.06	99.9	87	112.9	0.25	0.09	80.1	80	119.6	0.23	0.12
	N_2-N_3	69.6	90	108.4	0.17	0.06	121.4	84	187.8	0.25	0.09	59.2	98	111.3	0.23	0.12
	N_3-N_1	75.1	48	792.1	0.18	0.05	146.9	99	203.1	0.39	0.29	123.0	48	83.9	0.45	0.31
	N_3-N_2	55.6	94	132.7	0.18	0.05	122.6	99	141.2	0.39	0.29	80.3	88	150.6	0.46	0.32
m_3	N_1-N_2	109.7	66	125.0	0.22	0.14	101.3	92	146.6	0.33	0.20	78.5	83	116.2	0.37	0.25
	N_1-N_3	141.2	63	137.4	0.22	0.15	133.4	91	183.3	0.33	0.20	112.6	62	120.5	0.37	0.25
	N_2-N_1	57.0	99	110.8	0.18	0.05	117.1	91	127.1	0.36	0.23	71.4	99	121.9	0.42	0.28
	N_2-N_3	69.6	92	104.5	0.18	0.05	92.9	98	130.7	0.36	0.23	62.4	97	103.4	0.42	0.28
	N_3-N_1	64.9	90	106.3	0.19	0.05	197.4	94	179.5	0.39	0.27	58.2	98	113.4	0.47	0.30
	N_3-N_2	80.2	83	108.2	0.19	0.05	104.9	99	139.2	0.39	0.27	66.9	96	104.0	0.48	0.31
m_4	N_1-N_2	59.7	100	129.1	0.11	0.05	130.3	67	205.4	0.15	0.06	58.5	100	110.9	0.14	0.08
	N_1-N_3	53.8	98	266.3	0.11	0.05	270.2	35	418.2	0.15	0.06	52.7	99	115.4	0.14	0.08
	N_2-N_1	72.3	95	167.1	0.15	0.18	126.5	81	149.0	0.17	0.12	75.1	96	105.4	0.17	0.19
	N_2-N_3	58.3	100	143.1	0.15	0.18	130.0	76	234.0	0.17	0.13	58.0	100	110.1	0.18	0.20
	N_3-N_1	47.4	81	475.7	0.39	0.39	173.3	55	426.4	0.36	0.33	54.2	83	158.3	0.44	0.39
	N_3-N_2	50.8	98	194.9	0.39	0.39	126.3	79	201.0	0.36	0.33	60.8	99	109.0	0.44	0.39
m_5	N_1-N_2	56.3	99	115.0	0.17	0.05	140.9	87	165.3	0.39	0.20	75.0	99	136.8	0.52	0.28
	N_1-N_3	50.4	98	184.7	0.17	0.05	262.7	93	231.5	0.39	0.20	100.5	88	254.6	0.52	0.28
	N_2-N_1	118.2	58	143.4	0.25	0.18	87.0	98	134.9	0.43	0.21	77.5	77	105.8	0.47	0.27
	N_2-N_3	49.7	97	149.1	0.25	0.18	92.2	94	141.2	0.43	0.21	58.5	100	121.0	0.47	0.27
	N_3-N_1	136.0	29	141.1	0.59	0.38	121.0	89	155.9	0.59	0.28	125.1	37	135.4	0.64	0.29
	N_3-N_2	78.7	52	109.8	0.59	0.38	96.0	100	141.0	0.60	0.28	74.6	76	126.4	0.64	0.29
m_6	N_1-N_2	101.0	78	101.7	0.15	0.03	88.0	100	99.8	0.23	0.15	89.8	86	104.9	0.31	0.28
	N_1-N_3	107.3	62	100.4	0.15	0.03	94.3	100	128.3	0.23	0.16	96.6	77	152.3	0.30	0.28
	N_2-N_1	91.6	88	104.6	0.15	0.04	122.6	90	145.6	0.22	0.10	83.3	90	102.5	0.23	0.19
	N_2-N_3	74.8	93	106.8	0.15	0.03	87.1	99	112.4	0.21	0.09	78.8	90	107.0	0.23	0.19
	N_3-N_1	176.1	51	108.6	0.16	0.06	194.4	67	238.5	0.32	0.21	170.5	50	114.0	0.37	0.33
	N_3-N_2	128.9	64	108.3	0.16	0.06	105.1	93	121.9	0.32	0.21	110.7	69	105.7	0.37	0.33
m_7	N_1-N_2	102.0	62	109.9	0.20	0.04	71.4	100	108.8	0.91	0.20	65.5	88	102.5	0.97	0.13
	N_1-N_3	126.0	46	108.0	0.20	0.04	57.6	100	134.6	0.91	0.20	55.0	68	108.7	0.97	0.14
	N_2-N_1	89.4	75	115.4	0.19	0.05	71.2	100	105.0	0.88	0.23	66.0	93	101.0	0.95	0.16
	N_2-N_3	84.7	74	110.5	0.19	0.04	70.5	100	107.5	0.88	0.23	63.9	93	100.6	0.95	0.16
	N_3-N_1	125.7	45	111.4	0.20	0.04	48.7	100	122.5	0.91	0.21	53.1	68	109.1	0.97	0.13
	N_3-N_2	102.0	61	108.2	0.20	0.04	70.2	100	106.7	0.90	0.21	66.0	89	103.3	0.97	0.13
m_8	N_1-N_2	114.0	50	106.3	0.23	0.19	83.5	98	104.6	0.30	0.12	91.0	63	117.7	0.29	0.15
	N_1-N_3	147.6	34	111.0	0.23	0.19	111.0	61	177.9	0.30	0.12	141.0	34	112.5	0.29	0.16
	N_2-N_1	60.2	93	150.7	0.16	0.04	91.7	93	118.2	0.26	0.08	61.0	98	117.2	0.22	0.12
	N_2-N_3	117.8	66	112.9	0.16	0.04	90.1	99	126.8	0.26	0.07	100.8	70	119.2	0.22	0.12
	N_3-N_1	54.3	94	155.1	0.14	0.03	155.3	88	202.1	0.30	0.12	120.2	87	289.5	0.36	0.26
	N_3-N_2	69.5	98	106.5	0.14	0.03	105.3	98	135.0	0.30	0.12	93.4	99	139.6	0.37	0.27
Mean		87.1	77	150.0	0.19	0.09	123.4	85	162.0	0.37	0.16	81.3	83	123.9	0.40	0.20
Median		79.7	83	112.1	0.17	0.05	117.4	92	141.1	0.31	0.18	75.1	89	114.8	0.37	0.19

Note: The first two columns indicate regression curve and density combination. The following columns provide the simulation results for the kernel, local linear and Seifert&Gasser matching estimator at bandwidth values chosen by Akaike penalized cross-validation, where h gives the mean of the chosen bandwidths and std(h) their standard deviation. The column %Var indicates which fraction (in %) of the mean squared error of the estimator is due to variance. Results are based on 10^4 replications with bandwidth search grid = 0.02,0.04,...,1.00. The column MSE^r gives the mean squared error relative to the mean squared error of pair-matching. MSE^o gives the mean squared error relative to the mean squared error at the optimal bandwidth value h^{opt} (see Table C.3).

Table C.9. Penalized cross-validation bandwidth selection (sample size $n_s = n_r = 200$)

	Densities	Kernel matching					Local linear matching					Seifert&Gasser matching				
		MSE^r	%Var	MSE^o	h	std(h)	MSE^r	%Var	MSE^o	h	std(h)	MSE^r	%Var	MSE^o	h	std(h)
m_1	N_1-N_2	84.3	94	103.1	0.06	0.01	96.1	98	118.1	0.10	0.04	78.7	99	109.3	0.08	0.03
	N_1-N_3	71.3	97	106.1	0.06	0.01	154.1	69	124.2	0.10	0.04	64.6	99	107.3	0.08	0.03
	N_2-N_1	80.8	98	103.3	0.05	0.01	91.2	100	112.5	0.07	0.02	78.0	99	131.2	0.06	0.01
	N_2-N_3	75.4	100	103.8	0.05	0.01	86.3	94	121.9	0.07	0.02	77.1	100	122.8	0.06	0.01
	N_3-N_1	132.1	61	333.6	0.05	0.01	238.5	53	234.9	0.09	0.04	120.6	61	118.2	0.08	0.03
	N_3-N_2	82.9	96	115.7	0.05	0.01	93.6	88	124.1	0.09	0.04	82.4	95	114.1	0.08	0.03
m_2	N_1-N_2	66.1	92	100.6	0.09	0.02	110.8	72	126.6	0.15	0.05	60.7	99	103.7	0.12	0.03
	N_1-N_3	76.0	86	101.6	0.09	0.02	145.4	88	198.0	0.15	0.05	70.9	90	111.1	0.12	0.03
	N_2-N_1	87.6	71	120.2	0.10	0.02	96.7	80	121.7	0.13	0.04	67.5	90	110.6	0.12	0.03
	N_2-N_3	63.3	97	102.2	0.10	0.02	78.3	100	114.0	0.13	0.04	60.0	100	105.0	0.12	0.03
	N_3-N_1	103.4	58	105.3	0.10	0.02	75.1	99	107.4	0.14	0.05	98.0	55	102.7	0.13	0.03
	N_3-N_2	62.4	90	160.0	0.10	0.02	74.3	95	104.7	0.13	0.04	63.6	90	114.0	0.13	0.03
m_3	N_1-N_2	78.0	81	104.4	0.11	0.02	75.2	99	97.4	0.13	0.05	63.2	96	110.6	0.14	0.04
	N_1-N_3	73.2	84	99.8	0.11	0.02	102.9	99	140.7	0.13	0.04	64.4	93	122.3	0.14	0.04
	N_2-N_1	54.4	99	103.5	0.12	0.02	77.3	93	103.0	0.14	0.04	63.7	91	106.6	0.15	0.04
	N_2-N_3	63.7	96	100.7	0.12	0.02	74.8	95	103.6	0.14	0.04	62.9	99	100.9	0.15	0.04
	N_3-N_1	57.9	95	105.9	0.12	0.02	167.3	80	169.3	0.16	0.06	56.1	98	111.2	0.15	0.03
	N_3-N_2	75.4	87	107.4	0.12	0.02	86.2	94	113.9	0.16	0.06	62.1	98	103.2	0.15	0.03
m_4	N_1-N_2	56.4	100	126.2	0.07	0.01	80.6	90	106.6	0.10	0.04	56.9	100	113.6	0.08	0.03
	N_1-N_3	56.8	99	311.7	0.07	0.01	154.1	69	186.1	0.10	0.04	57.5	99	130.8	0.08	0.03
	N_2-N_1	64.0	100	104.0	0.07	0.01	75.4	99	113.6	0.08	0.02	63.4	100	105.4	0.08	0.01
	N_2-N_3	55.3	100	138.6	0.07	0.01	68.6	98	116.6	0.08	0.02	52.7	100	110.3	0.08	0.01
	N_3-N_1	74.6	84	297.1	0.09	0.01	147.5	73	102.2	0.12	0.04	78.7	83	102.3	0.10	0.03
	N_3-N_2	61.7	96	183.8	0.09	0.01	90.0	87	106.6	0.12	0.05	62.3	96	103.2	0.10	0.02
m_5	N_1-N_2	56.2	100	112.8	0.10	0.02	111.7	75	102.4	0.17	0.06	63.4	92	111.8	0.18	0.07
	N_1-N_3	56.2	98	257.6	0.10	0.02	173.8	84	256.9	0.17	0.06	50.9	98	121.4	0.18	0.07
	N_2-N_1	111.1	59	152.3	0.13	0.03	88.1	83	113.2	0.18	0.06	67.8	88	107.6	0.18	0.07
	N_2-N_3	51.2	95	159.2	0.13	0.03	77.2	84	115.9	0.18	0.06	51.5	98	103.7	0.19	0.07
	N_3-N_1	152.9	38	132.9	0.17	0.04	90.1	100	136.0	0.23	0.08	130.1	40	121.4	0.26	0.08
	N_3-N_2	99.5	55	132.5	0.17	0.04	88.3	86	117.2	0.23	0.08	57.3	92	101.2	0.26	0.08
m_6	N_1-N_2	92.8	84	103.1	0.10	0.02	83.3	97	102.1	0.11	0.03	80.6	91	101.3	0.12	0.02
	N_1-N_3	93.6	73	97.9	0.10	0.02	97.3	94	139.2	0.11	0.03	85.7	77	160.2	0.12	0.02
	N_2-N_1	84.0	91	105.8	0.10	0.02	89.1	98	115.0	0.11	0.03	75.6	96	105.3	0.11	0.02
	N_2-N_3	69.6	95	100.1	0.10	0.02	81.4	99	107.8	0.11	0.03	73.6	92	103.9	0.12	0.02
	N_3-N_1	135.0	62	104.1	0.10	0.02	247.0	72	169.4	0.14	0.05	105.5	70	100.3	0.13	0.03
	N_3-N_2	110.3	72	108.0	0.10	0.02	105.3	96	117.0	0.14	0.05	87.0	86	117.6	0.13	0.03
m_7	N_1-N_2	98.1	66	112.8	0.13	0.02	78.1	100	110.1	0.40	0.13	82.6	77	102.2	0.49	0.06
	N_1-N_3	123.5	54	113.3	0.13	0.02	93.7	98	163.8	0.41	0.13	96.7	47	100.0	0.49	0.06
	N_2-N_1	91.9	71	129.3	0.13	0.02	73.6	100	107.2	0.40	0.14	72.8	90	104.6	0.49	0.06
	N_2-N_3	89.1	72	128.5	0.13	0.02	69.1	100	100.6	0.41	0.14	68.4	91	99.4	0.49	0.06
	N_3-N_1	117.0	53	107.4	0.13	0.02	75.8	100	134.6	0.40	0.14	98.0	46	102.0	0.49	0.06
	N_3-N_2	100.0	67	117.9	0.13	0.02	75.6	100	109.3	0.40	0.14	80.0	79	102.4	0.49	0.06
m_8	N_1-N_2	122.5	58	107.6	0.11	0.02	105.6	99	115.7	0.17	0.05	86.5	75	137.2	0.15	0.03
	N_1-N_3	180.1	42	103.8	0.11	0.02	163.1	85	305.9	0.17	0.05	162.2	41	107.3	0.15	0.03
	N_2-N_1	60.6	93	154.9	0.10	0.02	90.0	80	122.2	0.15	0.04	56.9	99	103.5	0.12	0.03
	N_2-N_3	104.1	68	122.4	0.10	0.02	106.8	92	106.8	0.15	0.04	87.4	82	124.6	0.12	0.03
	N_3-N_1	60.5	90	221.0	0.09	0.01	115.2	100	138.5	0.16	0.05	58.7	90	117.9	0.14	0.05
	N_3-N_2	66.9	100	106.2	0.09	0.01	98.1	88	126.6	0.15	0.05	66.3	96	101.7	0.14	0.04
	Mean	85.1	82	134.0	0.10	0.02	104.2	90	131.3	0.17	0.06	75.2	87	111.0	0.17	0.04
	Median	77.0	88	107.8	0.10	0.02	90.1	94	116.3	0.14	0.05	68.1	92	107.3	0.13	0.03

Note: The first two columns indicate regression curve and density combination. The following columns provide the simulation results for the kernel, local linear and Seifert&Gasser matching estimator at bandwidth values chosen by Akaike penalized cross-validation, where h gives the mean of the chosen bandwidths and std(h) their standard deviation. The column %Var indicates which fraction (in %) of the mean squared error of the estimator is due to variance. Results are based on 5000 replications with bandwidth search grid = 0.01,0.02,...,0.50. The column MSE^r gives the mean squared error relative to the mean squared error of pair-matching. MSE^o gives the mean squared error relative to the mean squared error at the optimal bandwidth value h^{opt} (see Table C.4).

Table C.10. Penalized cross-validation bandwidth selection (sample size $n_s = n_r = 1000$)

	Densities	Kernel matching					Local linear matching					Seifert&Gasser matching				
		MSE^r	%Var	MSE^o	h	std(h)	MSE^r	%Var	MSE^o	h	std(h)	MSE^r	%Var	MSE^o	h	std(h)
m_1	N$_1$–N$_2$	82.5	96	111.7	0.04	0.01	58.2	101	78.0	0.05	0.01	60.4	100	89.9	0.05	0.02
	N$_1$–N$_3$	70.9	100	113.1	0.04	0.01	118.5	97	126.7	0.05	0.01	82.5	99	126.3	0.05	0.01
	N$_2$–N$_1$	77.2	100	107.6	0.04	0.00	72.2	100	92.6	0.04	0.00	72.9	100	120.3	0.04	0.00
	N$_2$–N$_3$	76.3	100	100.3	0.04	0.00	63.8	100	79.3	0.04	0.00	83.0	98	125.5	0.04	0.00
	N$_3$–N$_1$	108.5	86	141.3	0.04	0.00	228.3	59	217.7	0.05	0.01	111.6	94	126.5	0.05	0.02
	N$_3$–N$_2$	79.3	99	99.5	0.04	0.00	110.7	95	142.3	0.05	0.02	81.6	100	133.3	0.04	0.02
m_2	N$_1$–N$_2$	64.9	93	106.8	0.06	0.01	75.9	94	92.0	0.10	0.01	66.6	91	104.8	0.09	0.02
	N$_1$–N$_3$	63.5	97	121.0	0.06	0.01	147.6	97	154.0	0.10	0.01	58.6	100	169.8	0.08	0.02
	N$_2$–N$_1$	82.0	64	114.0	0.07	0.01	92.5	69	137.7	0.10	0.01	65.0	100	109.1	0.08	0.02
	N$_2$–N$_3$	57.1	97	118.8	0.07	0.01	57.6	94	90.2	0.09	0.01	52.0	100	92.4	0.08	0.01
	N$_3$–N$_1$	97.8	74	100.9	0.06	0.01	128.6	92	150.3	0.08	0.01	120.2	77	123.9	0.07	0.02
	N$_3$–N$_2$	61.6	98	132.5	0.06	0.01	78.9	100	108.3	0.08	0.01	65.1	83	132.3	0.07	0.01
m_3	N$_1$–N$_2$	70.1	92	131.3	0.06	0.01	73.2	99	93.9	0.08	0.01	62.0	100	100.4	0.07	0.02
	N$_1$–N$_3$	52.2	97	80.3	0.06	0.01	156.9	100	208.3	0.08	0.01	58.5	100	105.6	0.07	0.02
	N$_2$–N$_1$	55.6	95	100.6	0.07	0.01	55.0	92	88.2	0.10	0.02	64.6	87	123.3	0.09	0.02
	N$_2$–N$_3$	65.6	99	112.5	0.08	0.01	60.4	76	78.3	0.10	0.02	48.6	100	78.5	0.09	0.02
	N$_3$–N$_1$	59.9	99	98.5	0.08	0.01	137.6	97	197.3	0.10	0.01	51.4	97	113.7	0.10	0.02
	N$_3$–N$_2$	60.9	83	98.2	0.08	0.01	77.9	100	103.9	0.10	0.01	77.2	98	116.2	0.10	0.02
m_4	N$_1$–N$_2$	65.4	100	141.3	0.04	0.01	97.7	97	136.0	0.05	0.01	61.4	100	132.4	0.05	0.02
	N$_1$–N$_3$	57.8	100	367.0	0.04	0.01	110.5	92	134.1	0.06	0.02	69.8	100	139.6	0.05	0.01
	N$_2$–N$_1$	65.5	100	113.5	0.05	0.01	58.9	100	113.7	0.06	0.01	61.4	100	91.8	0.05	0.01
	N$_2$–N$_3$	63.8	100	116.0	0.05	0.01	42.3	100	83.8	0.06	0.01	47.3	100	114.0	0.05	0.01
	N$_3$–N$_1$	68.0	99	92.8	0.06	0.01	275.0	94	190.1	0.07	0.01	74.4	96	104.0	0.07	0.01
	N$_3$–N$_2$	66.5	100	157.0	0.06	0.01	85.8	100	130.3	0.07	0.01	55.9	99	94.6	0.06	0.01
m_5	N$_1$–N$_2$	54.2	100	93.6	0.06	0.01	70.0	87	85.5	0.11	0.02	52.8	94	90.2	0.10	0.04
	N$_1$–N$_3$	62.4	100	300.3	0.06	0.01	152.5	100	290.9	0.11	0.02	54.2	100	90.8	0.11	0.03
	N$_2$–N$_1$	114.0	48	168.6	0.08	0.01	134.2	67	179.8	0.14	0.02	69.3	88	98.5	0.11	0.03
	N$_2$–N$_3$	64.6	96	120.8	0.08	0.01	102.2	76	238.3	0.14	0.02	49.3	99	97.9	0.11	0.03
	N$_3$–N$_1$	160.7	43	141.8	0.10	0.02	125.3	96	191.2	0.17	0.03	126.6	44	176.2	0.14	0.03
	N$_3$–N$_2$	119.3	52	218.0	0.11	0.02	116.7	57	178.5	0.17	0.03	57.3	99	89.8	0.15	0.03
m_6	N$_1$–N$_2$	87.4	94	115.3	0.07	0.01	83.6	100	101.0	0.08	0.01	95.4	95	132.1	0.08	0.01
	N$_1$–N$_3$	94.9	89	121.2	0.07	0.01	158.0	100	178.2	0.08	0.01	75.0	88	97.0	0.08	0.01
	N$_2$–N$_1$	86.5	87	107.9	0.07	0.01	90.7	100	102.7	0.08	0.01	66.8	99	85.2	0.08	0.01
	N$_2$–N$_3$	55.1	99	71.1	0.07	0.01	68.7	94	99.8	0.08	0.01	59.5	94	85.0	0.08	0.01
	N$_3$–N$_1$	105.6	72	106.1	0.07	0.01	116.2	100	138.1	0.09	0.01	95.7	86	148.1	0.09	0.01
	N$_3$–N$_2$	90.4	85	97.2	0.07	0.01	72.1	100	94.7	0.09	0.01	75.5	100	98.0	0.09	0.01
m_7	N$_1$–N$_2$	113.0	81	185.2	0.09	0.01	57.4	100	78.7	0.34	0.06	96.9	81	132.5	0.36	0.05
	N$_1$–N$_3$	108.5	63	111.2	0.09	0.01	75.4	100	99.3	0.35	0.05	106.3	63	118.0	0.37	0.03
	N$_2$–N$_1$	89.0	62	124.7	0.09	0.01	73.8	97	134.1	0.34	0.07	76.0	78	134.3	0.37	0.00
	N$_2$–N$_3$	88.1	66	119.8	0.09	0.01	76.2	100	108.2	0.34	0.07	56.4	98	76.7	0.37	0.04
	N$_3$–N$_1$	90.4	60	104.4	0.09	0.01	53.5	100	85.9	0.35	0.05	108.4	49	121.7	0.37	0.04
	N$_3$–N$_2$	120.4	63	154.5	0.09	0.01	59.2	100	93.0	0.35	0.06	85.4	94	113.0	0.36	0.05
m_8	N$_1$–N$_2$	125.4	64	122.0	0.07	0.01	116.5	78	132.3	0.12	0.01	67.7	96	97.1	0.10	0.02
	N$_1$–N$_3$	156.8	48	88.1	0.08	0.01	138.3	100	195.3	0.12	0.01	140.4	44	98.0	0.10	0.02
	N$_2$–N$_1$	56.5	91	98.9	0.07	0.01	111.5	57	174.4	0.11	0.02	51.4	100	84.1	0.09	0.02
	N$_2$–N$_3$	114.8	78	143.6	0.07	0.01	118.6	89	134.6	0.11	0.02	91.8	94	148.6	0.09	0.02
	N$_3$–N$_1$	71.1	93	228.8	0.06	0.01	115.7	95	168.2	0.12	0.01	68.9	92	134.2	0.10	0.03
	N$_3$–N$_2$	78.0	100	133.0	0.06	0.01	120.3	72	169.0	0.11	0.02	61.6	87	84.5	0.10	0.03
Mean		83.0	86	130.3	0.07	0.01	101.5	92	135.0	0.12	0.02	73.7	91	113.1	0.12	0.02
Median		76.8	94	114.6	0.07	0.01	91.6	97	131.3	0.10	0.01	67.2	97	111.0	0.09	0.02

Note: The first two columns indicate regression curve and density combination. The following columns provide the simulation results for the kernel, local linear and Seifert&Gasser matching estimator at bandwidth values chosen by Akaike penalized cross-validation, where h gives the mean of the chosen bandwidths and std(h) their standard deviation. The column %Var indicates which fraction (in %) of the mean squared error of the estimator is due to variance. Results are based on 100 replications with bandwidth search grid = 0.0075, 0.0150, 0.0225,..., 0.3750. The column MSE^r gives the mean squared error relative to the mean squared error of pair-matching. MSE^o gives the mean squared error relative to the mean squared error at the optimal bandwidth value h^{opt} (see Table C.5).

Table C.11. Penalized cross-validation bandwidth selection (sample $n_s = 200, n_r = 40$)

	Densities	Kernel matching					Local linear matching					Seifert&Gasser matching				
		MSE^r	%Var	MSE^o	h	std(h)	MSE^r	%Var	MSE^o	h	std(h)	MSE^r	%Var	MSE^o	h	std(h)
m_1	N_1-N_2	80.5	99	118.8	0.06	0.01	76.9	97	119.6	0.09	0.03	73.0	100	133.3	0.08	0.03
	N_1-N_3	79.8	99	114.9	0.06	0.01	131.4	75	156.3	0.09	0.03	73.3	100	146.7	0.08	0.03
	N_2-N_1	76.0	100	118.6	0.05	0.01	82.0	98	122.9	0.06	0.01	76.0	100	169.0	0.06	0.01
	N_2-N_3	76.1	100	133.7	0.05	0.01	78.8	99	199.6	0.06	0.01	75.6	100	198.8	0.06	0.01
	N_3-N_1	111.2	75	349.7	0.05	0.01	191.7	51	237.2	0.08	0.03	105.4	77	133.9	0.08	0.03
	N_3-N_2	80.5	99	148.6	0.05	0.01	82.8	94	175.4	0.08	0.03	78.3	98	165.6	0.08	0.03
m_2	N_1-N_2	55.6	95	110.6	0.09	0.01	83.5	86	107.0	0.15	0.02	50.7	100	111.7	0.12	0.03
	N_1-N_3	67.0	91	100.5	0.09	0.02	157.2	88	245.1	0.15	0.02	62.3	92	125.9	0.12	0.03
	N_2-N_1	60.6	85	98.2	0.10	0.02	77.1	88	120.3	0.14	0.03	49.7	96	118.4	0.12	0.03
	N_2-N_3	54.7	99	102.9	0.10	0.02	54.2	100	100.6	0.14	0.03	54.6	100	124.4	0.12	0.03
	N_3-N_1	89.3	65	112.0	0.10	0.02	94.8	99	141.0	0.14	0.03	87.5	63	103.5	0.13	0.04
	N_3-N_2	54.2	96	202.7	0.10	0.02	66.8	98	118.1	0.14	0.03	52.9	93	133.4	0.13	0.03
m_3	N_1-N_2	68.5	92	104.7	0.11	0.02	73.1	99	97.8	0.14	0.03	57.9	99	121.5	0.14	0.04
	N_1-N_3	67.1	90	99.5	0.11	0.03	105.7	98	121.9	0.14	0.03	60.8	97	123.4	0.14	0.04
	N_2-N_1	46.4	99	118.0	0.12	0.02	55.5	95	97.9	0.15	0.03	46.4	97	98.4	0.15	0.04
	N_2-N_3	58.2	98	100.1	0.12	0.02	61.5	98	112.3	0.15	0.03	61.5	100	119.1	0.15	0.04
	N_3-N_1	57.1	96	107.7	0.12	0.02	154.8	86	197.9	0.16	0.03	54.5	100	116.9	0.15	0.03
	N_3-N_2	66.7	94	101.7	0.12	0.02	70.6	98	119.1	0.16	0.03	60.8	99	121.7	0.15	0.03
m_4	N_1-N_2	50.7	100	261.9	0.07	0.01	66.5	93	154.4	0.09	0.03	47.7	100	166.1	0.09	0.03
	N_1-N_3	53.6	99	392.2	0.07	0.01	150.5	65	238.1	0.09	0.03	53.7	97	134.3	0.08	0.03
	N_2-N_1	52.8	100	133.1	0.07	0.01	54.6	100	126.1	0.08	0.01	57.5	100	174.1	0.08	0.01
	N_2-N_3	38.3	100	219.6	0.07	0.01	48.5	99	170.5	0.08	0.01	36.6	100	156.2	0.08	0.01
	N_3-N_1	65.3	88	363.6	0.09	0.01	136.6	66	111.8	0.10	0.02	64.6	85	96.2	0.10	0.02
	N_3-N_2	45.9	97	318.7	0.09	0.01	64.2	85	124.1	0.10	0.03	46.0	98	123.8	0.10	0.03
m_5	N_1-N_2	46.6	100	123.5	0.10	0.02	81.9	84	115.8	0.18	0.04	48.8	96	104.5	0.19	0.07
	N_1-N_3	48.7	97	246.2	0.10	0.02	196.1	91	341.5	0.18	0.04	44.1	97	117.9	0.18	0.07
	N_2-N_1	68.1	77	108.0	0.13	0.03	72.4	90	135.1	0.21	0.05	52.0	96	118.7	0.18	0.07
	N_2-N_3	30.8	97	189.2	0.13	0.03	44.2	84	108.5	0.21	0.05	31.6	100	108.2	0.19	0.07
	N_3-N_1	116.1	43	124.1	0.17	0.04	92.6	100	156.5	0.27	0.07	101.2	42	116.6	0.26	0.09
	N_3-N_2	58.6	64	110.0	0.17	0.04	62.1	87	138.1	0.27	0.07	37.7	96	112.5	0.25	0.08
m_6	N_1-N_2	80.8	95	101.2	0.10	0.02	79.6	99	113.3	0.12	0.02	82.0	96	119.0	0.12	0.02
	N_1-N_3	84.0	83	101.0	0.10	0.02	97.7	96	129.4	0.12	0.02	80.9	85	132.3	0.12	0.02
	N_2-N_1	80.7	96	106.5	0.10	0.02	81.7	100	116.1	0.12	0.02	78.8	98	121.5	0.12	0.02
	N_2-N_3	63.5	98	100.9	0.10	0.02	72.6	100	101.5	0.12	0.02	73.2	98	108.9	0.11	0.02
	N_3-N_1	107.2	78	106.4	0.10	0.02	156.5	80	144.6	0.14	0.03	96.5	81	112.9	0.13	0.03
	N_3-N_2	83.6	90	102.8	0.10	0.02	86.4	99	107.6	0.13	0.03	76.2	96	123.9	0.13	0.03
m_7	N_1-N_2	73.6	86	102.7	0.13	0.02	69.0	100	100.9	0.46	0.08	66.3	92	101.3	0.49	0.06
	N_1-N_3	98.2	64	106.6	0.13	0.02	67.5	100	107.0	0.46	0.08	79.8	60	100.1	0.48	0.07
	N_2-N_1	66.2	87	102.7	0.13	0.02	65.3	100	99.2	0.46	0.09	63.1	95	100.6	0.49	0.06
	N_2-N_3	69.4	86	110.1	0.13	0.02	67.9	100	102.0	0.45	0.09	63.1	95	101.5	0.48	0.07
	N_3-N_1	100.7	64	108.4	0.13	0.02	71.8	100	117.6	0.46	0.08	76.8	58	96.5	0.46	0.06
	N_3-N_2	75.7	84	103.4	0.13	0.02	74.5	100	104.7	0.46	0.09	63.0	94	91.9	0.48	0.07
m_8	N_1-N_2	81.8	77	102.4	0.11	0.02	83.4	97	114.9	0.17	0.03	66.9	89	141.8	0.15	0.03
	N_1-N_3	137.8	55	102.5	0.11	0.02	119.3	94	190.3	0.17	0.03	120.3	54	104.1	0.15	0.03
	N_2-N_1	47.6	96	227.0	0.10	0.02	65.8	84	113.2	0.16	0.03	46.7	100	104.0	0.12	0.03
	N_2-N_3	81.5	90	103.0	0.10	0.02	87.4	95	118.4	0.16	0.03	73.5	95	127.8	0.12	0.03
	N_3-N_1	59.3	92	192.2	0.09	0.01	112.6	100	157.1	0.17	0.03	55.5	94	119.0	0.14	0.05
	N_3-N_2	69.4	100	113.4	0.09	0.01	84.9	93	109.6	0.17	0.03	69.8	99	100.0	0.14	0.04
Mean		70.6	89	146.4	0.10	0.02	89.9	92	138.7	0.18	0.04	65.3	92	123.0	0.17	0.04
Median		67.6	94	110.1	0.10	0.02	79.2	97	119.3	0.14	0.03	63.0	97	119.0	0.13	0.03

Note: The first two columns indicate regression curve and density combination. The following columns provide the simulation results for the kernel, local linear and Seifert&Gasser matching estimator at bandwidth values chosen by Akaike penalized cross-validation, where h gives the mean of the chosen bandwidths and std(h) their standard deviation. The column %Var indicates which fraction (in %) of the mean squared error of the estimator is due to variance. Results are based on 5000 replications with bandwidth search grid = 0.01,0.02,...,0.50. The column MSE^r gives the mean squared error relative to the mean squared error of pair-matching. MSE^o gives the mean squared error relative to the mean squared error at the optimal bandwidth value h^{opt} (see Table C.6).

Table C.12. Penalized cross-validation bandwidth selection (sample $n_s = 40, n_r = 200$)

	Den-sities	Kernel matching					Local linear matching					Seifert&Gasser matching				
		MSE^r	%Var	MSE^o	h	std(h)	MSE^r	%Var	MSE^o	h	std(h)	MSE^r	%Var	MSE^o	h	std(h)
m_1	N_1-N_2	111.8	79	102.8	0.11	0.03	166.0	65	141.4	0.16	0.05	112.1	84	110.5	0.14	0.06
	N_1-N_3	91.5	80	105.0	0.11	0.03	318.8	31	170.3	0.16	0.05	90.5	83	109.0	0.14	0.06
	N_2-N_1	107.7	82	111.4	0.09	0.02	198.6	66	196.5	0.13	0.03	93.5	86	108.3	0.11	0.04
	N_2-N_3	83.3	100	104.7	0.09	0.02	199.3	55	182.2	0.13	0.03	78.7	100	99.1	0.11	0.04
	N_3-N_1	66.0	52	250.2	0.09	0.03	157.8	21	134.2	0.13	0.05	66.6	51	126.6	0.12	0.05
	N_3-N_2	61.8	98	108.1	0.09	0.03	108.3	54	111.1	0.14	0.05	61.0	97	106.8	0.12	0.05
m_2	N_1-N_2	81.0	77	139.8	0.15	0.04	149.6	60	116.9	0.24	0.06	77.4	88	117.6	0.21	0.10
	N_1-N_3	100.2	64	112.0	0.15	0.04	158.5	61	175.6	0.24	0.06	98.7	66	106.0	0.21	0.10
	N_2-N_1	107.6	64	113.8	0.17	0.05	107.9	82	113.2	0.25	0.09	94.7	76	105.2	0.23	0.11
	N_2-N_3	83.7	88	112.6	0.17	0.06	144.0	82	167.9	0.25	0.09	72.0	96	105.0	0.23	0.12
	N_3-N_1	74.2	47	751.2	0.19	0.05	146.1	99	238.5	0.39	0.29	127.9	48	164.0	0.45	0.32
	N_3-N_2	55.2	92	115.5	0.19	0.05	129.3	99	143.3	0.38	0.28	90.4	86	158.0	0.45	0.32
m_3	N_1-N_2	137.2	60	128.8	0.22	0.15	111.5	89	153.0	0.33	0.20	96.0	79	111.8	0.37	0.25
	N_1-N_3	139.8	60	131.4	0.21	0.14	132.2	91	208.1	0.32	0.19	123.7	61	126.9	0.38	0.26
	N_2-N_1	63.7	99	105.6	0.18	0.05	147.9	91	132.3	0.36	0.24	83.7	99	128.1	0.42	0.28
	N_2-N_3	77.5	87	110.5	0.18	0.05	108.0	98	140.4	0.35	0.23	69.5	97	102.8	0.42	0.28
	N_3-N_1	61.9	89	102.6	0.19	0.05	202.9	94	189.5	0.40	0.27	57.7	99	113.7	0.47	0.30
	N_3-N_2	89.8	77	114.3	0.19	0.05	119.4	99	142.4	0.39	0.27	72.1	93	98.8	0.48	0.31
m_4	N_1-N_2	64.6	100	101.3	0.11	0.04	154.6	60	173.2	0.15	0.07	67.4	100	106.5	0.14	0.07
	N_1-N_3	50.1	98	231.7	0.11	0.05	260.2	29	388.3	0.15	0.06	53.7	99	141.1	0.14	0.07
	N_2-N_1	84.6	95	137.4	0.15	0.18	159.6	78	131.3	0.17	0.13	92.1	95	119.5	0.18	0.20
	N_2-N_3	65.5	100	115.3	0.15	0.18	157.1	72	211.5	0.17	0.12	71.7	99	105.2	0.17	0.19
	N_3-N_1	48.4	81	464.7	0.38	0.39	178.5	51	415.7	0.36	0.34	54.0	84	183.1	0.44	0.39
	N_3-N_2	57.2	99	173.5	0.40	0.40	150.4	76	183.4	0.36	0.33	73.9	99	145.7	0.45	0.39
m_5	N_1-N_2	60.4	99	107.1	0.17	0.05	165.0	83	166.3	0.39	0.20	87.8	100	142.4	0.52	0.28
	N_1-N_3	51.0	98	185.4	0.17	0.05	272.7	93	232.7	0.40	0.21	100.9	87	281.4	0.52	0.28
	N_2-N_1	153.1	53	166.4	0.25	0.17	95.4	97	119.7	0.43	0.21	95.6	72	106.6	0.47	0.27
	N_2-N_3	59.4	97	137.5	0.25	0.18	113.1	93	141.7	0.42	0.21	68.7	100	116.5	0.47	0.27
	N_3-N_1	148.5	28	149.0	0.59	0.38	124.1	86	161.5	0.60	0.27	131.9	37	135.1	0.63	0.29
	N_3-N_2	93.8	49	113.3	0.59	0.38	103.6	100	124.2	0.59	0.28	87.9	77	122.4	0.63	0.29
m_6	N_1-N_2	122.7	62	104.2	0.15	0.03	90.0	100	109.7	0.24	0.16	101.5	76	106.7	0.31	0.28
	N_1-N_3	111.6	54	101.1	0.15	0.03	87.1	100	169.0	0.24	0.16	100.3	72	177.2	0.30	0.27
	N_2-N_1	103.0	78	115.9	0.14	0.04	156.7	85	170.7	0.21	0.10	94.0	83	105.5	0.23	0.19
	N_2-N_3	78.9	89	102.5	0.14	0.03	91.0	98	124.1	0.22	0.10	90.3	86	117.9	0.23	0.19
	N_3-N_1	195.7	46	107.8	0.16	0.05	214.3	63	276.6	0.33	0.22	196.2	47	116.4	0.37	0.32
	N_3-N_2	185.6	51	118.9	0.17	0.06	123.4	91	122.9	0.32	0.21	153.8	58	107.5	0.36	0.32
m_7	N_1-N_2	134.2	52	121.8	0.20	0.04	65.6	100	109.5	0.91	0.20	65.0	83	100.9	0.97	0.13
	N_1-N_3	137.1	41	110.6	0.20	0.04	53.4	100	149.0	0.91	0.21	52.8	65	106.9	0.97	0.13
	N_2-N_1	110.5	67	131.7	0.19	0.05	69.1	100	108.5	0.88	0.23	67.9	90	101.1	0.95	0.16
	N_2-N_3	105.1	64	127.6	0.19	0.04	69.3	100	112.5	0.89	0.23	68.0	89	104.2	0.95	0.16
	N_3-N_1	131.0	43	108.9	0.20	0.04	46.1	100	133.9	0.91	0.21	52.7	63	104.6	0.97	0.14
	N_3-N_2	127.5	53	116.3	0.20	0.04	66.1	100	109.7	0.91	0.21	65.7	82	98.0	0.97	0.14
m_8	N_1-N_2	138.2	44	113.6	0.23	0.19	83.8	97	104.8	0.30	0.12	106.9	57	110.5	0.29	0.16
	N_1-N_3	156.8	31	114.9	0.23	0.19	113.7	57	190.1	0.30	0.12	148.7	33	112.5	0.29	0.16
	N_2-N_1	68.5	90	127.6	0.16	0.04	110.1	92	133.8	0.26	0.08	66.2	97	106.3	0.22	0.12
	N_2-N_3	149.1	52	118.0	0.16	0.04	94.8	98	111.8	0.26	0.08	128.5	61	111.3	0.23	0.13
	N_3-N_1	50.4	95	146.5	0.14	0.03	157.3	87	221.3	0.30	0.12	131.4	86	351.4	0.37	0.26
	N_3-N_2	68.4	96	104.5	0.14	0.03	124.5	97	186.6	0.30	0.12	106.6	99	157.9	0.37	0.26
Mean		98.0	73	145.8	0.19	0.09	136.6	82	165.6	0.37	0.16	90.6	81	127.1	0.40	0.20
Median		90.7	78	115.1	0.17	0.05	126.9	91	146.1	0.31	0.18	89.1	85	111.1	0.37	0.19

Note: The first two columns indicate regression curve and density combination. The following columns provide the simulation results for the kernel, local linear and Seifert&Gasser matching estimator at bandwidth values chosen by Akaike penalized cross-validation, where h gives the mean of the chosen bandwidths and std(h) their standard deviation. The column %Var indicates which fraction (in %) of the mean squared error of the estimator is due to variance. Results are based on 10^4 replications with bandwidth search grid = 0.02,0.04,...,1.00. The column MSE^r gives the mean squared error relative to the mean squared error of pair-matching. MSE^o gives the mean squared error relative to the mean squared error at the optimal bandwidth value h^{opt} (see Table C.7).

Table C.13. Selection rules

Model	Selection equation	X_{3i}	Error ε_i	Participation ratio
1	$D_i = 1\,(X_{1i} + X_{2i} + X_{3i} - 0.5 < \varepsilon_i)$	$N(0,1)$	$N(0,4)$	52 %
2	$D_i = 1\,(X_{1i} - X_{2i} + 2.5X_{3i} - 0.5 < \varepsilon_i)$	D	$U(0,12)$	48 %
3	$D_i = 1\,(X_{1i} - X_{2i} + X_{3i} - 0.5 < \varepsilon_i)$	$N(0,1)$	$N(0,4)$	52 %
4	$D_i = 1\,(X_{1i} + X_{2i} - X_{3i} - 0.5 < \varepsilon_i)$	$N(0,1)$	$N(0,4)$	52 %
5	$D_i = 1\,(-X_{1i} - X_{2i} + 2.5X_{3i} < \varepsilon_i)$	D	$U(0,12)$	45 %
6	$D_i = 1\,(2X_{1i} - X_{2i} + 2.5X_{3i} - 1.5 < \varepsilon_i)$	D	$U(0,\frac{49}{3})$	51 %

Note: Error $N(0,\sigma^2)$ stands for normal mean-zero random errors with variance σ^2, error $U(0,\sigma^2)$ denotes a uniform random error term with mean zero and variance σ^2. Variable X_1 is $\chi^2_{(1)}$ divided by $\sqrt{2}$, variable X_2 is uniform $U(0,1)$. Variable X_3 is normal in models 1, 3 and 4 and a dummy variable in the other models. The participation ratio gives the fraction of draws for which D_i equals one.

Table C.14. Outcome equations

Model	Outcome equation with normal error
1	$Y_i = X_{1i}X_{2i} + X_{3i}^2 + \sqrt{X_{1i}} + u_i$
2	$Y_i = -X_{1i} + X_{2i} + u_i$
3	$Y_i = X_{1i} \cdot 1\,(X_{3i} > X_{2i}) + u_i$
4	$Y_i = X_{1i}X_{3i} + X_{2i}^2 + \sqrt{X_{1i}} + u_i$
5	$Y_i = -X_{2i} + X_{3i} + u_i$
6	$Y_i = X_{1i} + X_{3i} \cdot 1\,(X_{1i} > X_{2i}) + X_{2i} + u_i$

Note: The outcome variable Y_i is observed only for the non-participants, i.e. the observations with $D_i = 0$. The error term u_i is standard normal.

Table C.15. Cross-validation for estimated propensity score (sample size $n_s + n_r = 200$)

D_i	Y_i	Pair-matching		Kernel matching			Local linear matching			Seifert&Gasser matching			Re-weighting no trimming		Re-weighting trimming at 10	
		MSE	%Var	MSE^r	%Var	h	MSE^r	%Var	h	MSE^r	%Var	h	MSE^r	%Var	MSE^r	%Var
1	1	0.34	87	92.6	52	0.32	108.4	92	0.34	70.9	63	0.42	406.6	97	107.9	50
	2	0.24	89	30.9	86	0.44	77.2	84	0.63	51.7	65	0.68	174.4	96	45.1	61
	3	0.14	95	45.0	59	0.66	75.0	95	0.66	45.6	82	0.71	129.3	97	48.5	74
	4	0.25	89	106.3	41	0.48	93.3	90	0.55	68.5	63	0.60	334.8	96	111.6	48
	5	0.19	100	21.9	100	0.67	63.5	99	0.67	42.3	98	0.71	78.9	100	32.5	100
	6	0.15	77	102.4	45	0.16	93.6	76	0.46	91.4	43	0.57	1118	98	142.2	37
2	1	0.08	100	58.7	92	0.28	58.7	100	0.38	51.1	100	0.45	52.8	100	52.7	100
	2	0.06	100	67.0	91	0.10	71.6	99	0.15	67.3	92	0.15	71.0	98	70.6	98
	3	0.04	100	63.8	90	0.28	61.1	99	0.30	50.7	99	0.41	54.4	100	54.3	100
	4	0.07	100	57.2	99	0.12	76.1	92	0.14	55.8	100	0.18	72.6	99	72.1	99
	5	0.06	100	88.9	76	0.16	63.5	99	0.34	61.5	89	0.41	73.1	97	72.6	98
	6	0.09	100	66.9	84	0.16	64.3	88	0.18	54.4	99	0.22	59.9	98	59.5	99
3	1	0.40	100	37.0	100	0.40	99.2	100	0.41	42.1	100	0.52	774.2	100	48.1	83
	2	0.16	83	116.8	36	0.26	64.9	77	0.70	66.4	51	0.74	311.5	93	116.6	40
	3	0.13	88	102.7	37	0.53	83.3	85	0.63	63.0	60	0.68	298.6	97	70.5	57
	4	0.25	89	104.8	39	0.48	87.7	88	0.55	68.7	62	0.60	494.1	98	110.6	48
	5	0.14	100	60.1	85	0.17	85.0	100	0.53	47.3	93	0.64	171.7	99	58.7	78
	6	0.26	88	60.4	42	0.51	84.5	86	0.59	63.0	60	0.63	164.4	94	63.4	52
4	1	0.34	87	91.1	53	0.31	102.8	93	0.34	71.6	63	0.42	567.3	98	107.5	50
	2	0.24	89	31.0	84	0.44	79.6	84	0.64	51.5	65	0.68	151.0	95	45.6	61
	3	0.13	99	24.1	99	0.68	77.4	99	0.67	41.7	98	0.71	103.8	98	36.3	92
	4	0.27	100	29.7	98	0.56	77.5	99	0.60	41.3	99	0.65	202.7	99	45.4	87
	5	0.14	100	61.2	84	0.17	89.1	100	0.53	47.6	94	0.65	180.8	99	59.9	79
	6	0.24	91	103.4	38	0.45	74.4	91	0.58	54.1	68	0.64	232.8	96	73.6	52
5	1	0.10	99	66.1	99	0.12	96.2	100	0.18	62.3	100	0.19	76.8	100	68.9	94
	2	0.13	97	68.4	83	0.17	84.7	100	0.18	62.5	90	0.19	59.4	97	52.6	92
	3	0.08	100	38.7	96	0.58	66.4	100	0.56	52.2	99	0.63	52.6	99	46.0	99
	4	0.18	96	64.6	88	0.21	103.4	96	0.21	57.1	97	0.26	63.7	96	56.6	89
	5	0.10	97	98.0	67	0.15	83.2	100	0.36	78.2	74	0.44	101.1	97	83.9	87
	6	0.11	100	65.8	99	0.10	85.5	99	0.16	66.8	98	0.16	58.8	99	55.5	98
6	1	0.07	100	76.1	75	0.32	57.3	100	0.52	51.2	100	0.59	51.5	100	51.4	100
	2	0.06	100	67.4	84	0.12	68.0	97	0.18	62.7	87	0.20	64.5	100	64.1	100
	3	0.04	100	53.9	98	0.19	62.6	99	0.29	53.1	97	0.35	55.1	100	54.9	100
	4	0.07	100	57.1	99	0.14	69.6	96	0.22	56.1	100	0.26	68.2	100	67.8	100
	5	0.07	100	107.9	61	0.21	60.9	100	0.44	59.3	89	0.54	70.2	99	69.7	99
	6	0.09	100	62.8	87	0.14	71.2	89	0.20	55.9	99	0.23	59.9	100	59.7	100
Mean		0.15	95	68.1	76	0.31	78.4	94	0.42	58.0	84	0.47	196.1	98	67.7	81
Median		0.13	100	65.2	84	0.27	77.3	98	0.43	56.0	93	0.53	90.0	98	59.8	91

Note: The first two columns indicate the selection rule D_i and the outcome equation Y_i. The following columns provide the simulation results for the pair-matching, kernel, local linear and Seifert&Gasser matching estimator at bandwidth values chosen by Akaike penalized cross-validation. The last four columns provide the results for the re-weighting estimator with and without trimming. Simulated mean squared error (multiplied by 1000) is given for the pair-matching estimator. For the other estimators MSE^r represents the mean squared error relative to the mean squared error of pair-matching (column 3). The columns labelled %Var indicate which fraction (in %) of the MSE is due to the variance of the estimator. The columns labelled h provide the mean of the chosen bandwidth values. Results are based on about 19.000 replications for the pair-matching estimator, 13.000 replications for the kernel, 6.000 for the local linear and 19.000 for the Seifert&Gasser estimator, with bandwidth search grid = 0.01,0.02,..,0.80. Results for the re-weighting estimator are based on about 12.000 replications. Trimming at 10 means that a ceiling for the propensity score ratio is set at 10.

Table C.16. Cross-validation for estimated propensity score (sample size $n_s + n_r = 500$)

D_i	Y_i	Pair-matching		Kernel matching			Local linear matching			Seifert&Gasser matching			Re-weighting no trimming		Re-weighting trimming at 20	
		MSE	%Var	MSE^r	%Var	h	MSE^r	%Var	h	MSE^r	%Var	h	MSE^r	%Var	MSE^r	%Var
1	1	0.17	89	79.4	65	0.13	128.5	99	0.17	73.2	62	0.22	1439	100	122.3	65
	2	0.13	89	38.0	62	0.29	86.1	79	0.57	60.4	52	0.62	246.3	98	53.3	64
	3	0.07	97	55.1	47	0.59	75.5	92	0.64	43.4	76	0.68	548.5	100	55.2	79
	4	0.14	90	114.4	37	0.30	90.7	93	0.41	67.3	62	0.45	1023	99	121.4	62
	5	0.09	100	21.8	100	0.62	64.3	100	0.59	40.9	96	0.63	98.2	100	38.0	100
	6	0.08	77	106.1	42	0.11	89.6	75	0.28	123.4	32	0.36	3319	100	163.7	50
2	1	0.03	100	55.4	91	0.19	60.9	100	0.24	52.7	100	0.27	49.7	99	49.7	99
	2	0.03	100	63.9	96	0.06	74.2	100	0.09	62.7	96	0.07	70.7	96	70.7	96
	3	0.02	100	53.9	100	0.09	60.8	92	0.13	50.7	99	0.15	52.5	100	52.5	100
	4	0.03	100	55.3	98	0.05	66.0	80	0.08	53.3	99	0.06	70.7	97	70.7	97
	5	0.02	100	75.9	78	0.09	63.7	95	0.17	61.9	89	0.18	75.6	93	75.6	93
	6	0.03	100	64.3	92	0.08	63.9	95	0.10	56.1	100	0.10	58.3	97	58.3	97
3	1	0.22	100	42.8	100	0.19	129.7	100	0.22	42.6	100	0.29	389.5	100	52.5	94
	2	0.07	83	135.0	29	0.19	67.0	61	0.69	75.5	41	0.72	1707	99	135.8	51
	3	0.07	87	131.9	33	0.37	100.7	83	0.57	68.8	51	0.59	717.5	99	83.8	62
	4	0.13	90	116.9	39	0.30	78.6	92	0.40	67.7	60	0.45	3838	100	121.0	62
	5	0.07	100	52.4	89	0.12	89.6	100	0.39	45.2	92	0.49	538.1	100	69.5	88
	6	0.12	90	89.2	34	0.31	78.5	90	0.44	66.5	57	0.48	330.2	98	74.4	58
4	1	0.17	92	83.2	63	0.12	128.4	99	0.17	72.0	65	0.22	1149	99	125.4	65
	2	0.12	88	38.2	63	0.30	92.5	76	0.59	63.1	53	0.62	307.9	98	53.0	64
	3	0.07	99	22.1	97	0.66	85.4	100	0.63	37.2	96	0.67	140.5	99	41.9	94
	4	0.15	99	29.4	94	0.40	87.5	96	0.50	38.9	94	0.54	259.4	100	45.9	96
	5	0.07	100	52.9	91	0.12	79.0	100	0.39	44.4	92	0.49	259.5	100	68.2	89
	6	0.11	92	120.0	36	0.28	73.0	92	0.43	53.9	65	0.47	638.0	99	83.9	60
5	1	0.04	99	59.7	98	0.08	78.9	100	0.10	60.4	100	0.11	64.7	99	64.4	99
	2	0.05	98	72.0	81	0.08	76.6	98	0.11	64.7	88	0.10	58.9	94	58.6	94
	3	0.03	99	43.1	94	0.47	68.7	100	0.42	48.9	99	0.50	48.5	99	48.4	99
	4	0.07	95	65.6	82	0.09	88.8	100	0.10	59.1	87	0.10	57.4	93	57.1	92
	5	0.04	98	96.2	63	0.11	75.9	100	0.19	88.6	67	0.20	98.2	93	97.5	92
	6	0.05	99	65.6	100	0.07	74.6	100	0.09	62.9	100	0.08	56.6	99	56.5	99
6	1	0.03	100	71.2	73	0.25	57.2	100	0.42	51.8	100	0.51	51.0	100	51.0	100
	2	0.02	100	65.2	89	0.08	64.2	93	0.12	60.2	92	0.11	62.7	99	62.7	99
	3	0.02	100	51.2	100	0.10	59.0	98	0.16	51.2	98	0.18	52.5	100	52.5	100
	4	0.03	100	55.7	93	0.09	69.6	87	0.12	55.9	100	0.13	65.5	99	65.5	99
	5	0.03	100	100.4	59	0.12	67.9	94	0.22	61.3	88	0.24	66.9	99	66.9	99
	6	0.04	100	63.3	86	0.09	65.5	79	0.12	54.1	98	0.12	56.7	100	56.7	100
Mean		0.07	96	69.6	75	0.21	79.5	93	0.31	59.5	82	0.34	501.9	98	72.9	85
Median		0.07	99	64.1	84	0.12	75.7	96	0.23	59.7	92	0.28	98.2	99	63.6	94

Note: The first two columns indicate the selection rule D_i and the outcome equation Y_i. The following columns provide the simulation results for the pair-matching, kernel, local linear and Seifert&Gasser matching estimator at bandwidth values chosen by Akaike penalized cross-validation. The last four columns provide the results for the re-weighting estimator with and without trimming. Simulated mean squared error (multiplied by 1000) is given for the pair-matching estimator. For the other estimators MSE^r represents the mean squared error relative to the mean squared error of pair-matching (column 3). The columns labelled %Var indicate which fraction (in %) of the MSE is due to the variance of the estimator. The columns labelled h provide the mean of the chosen bandwidth values. Results are based on about 17.000 replications for the pair-matching estimator, 3.000 replications for the kernel, 500 for the local linear and 6.000 for the Seifert&Gasser estimator, with bandwidth search grid = 0.01,0.02,..,0.80. Results for the re-weighting estimator are based on about 17.000 replications. Trimming at 20 means that a ceiling for the propensity score ratio is set at 20.

Table C.17. Cross-validation for estimated propensity score (sample size $n_s + n_r = 2000$)

D_i	Y_i	Pair-matching		Kernel matching			Local linear matching			Seifert&Gasser matching			Re-weighting no trimming		Re-weighting trimming at 50	
		MSE	%Var	MSE^r	%Var	h	MSE^r	%Var	h	MSE^r	%Var	h	MSE^r	%Var	MSE^r	%Var
	1	0.07	95	77.6	74	0.05	142.8	100	0.09	75.6	71	0.08	3610	100	149.1	75
	2	0.04	86	67.6	42	0.17	91.2	80	0.41	80.5	42	0.44	500.8	99	71.9	67
1	3	0.03	96	79.5	42	0.38	73.6	91	0.54	49.5	61	0.58	8818	100	66.3	82
	4	0.05	91	114.3	34	0.14	83.3	100	0.22	66.0	55	0.24	1909	100	145.9	71
	5	0.03	100	20.2	97	0.39	52.2	100	0.33	40.2	98	0.37	188.2	100	43.2	100
	6	0.03	74	123.7	36	0.07	76.7	81	0.15	177.3	22	0.19	5278	100	227.6	59
	1	0.01	100	45.6	89	0.10	47.9	100	0.10	61.5	99	0.12	51.7	96	51.7	96
	2	0.01	100	50.2	100	0.04	73.4	100	0.05	61.1	100	0.04	75.2	86	75.2	86
2	3	0.00	100	47.8	100	0.04	46.3	100	0.06	43.9	100	0.04	52.5	99	52.5	99
	4	0.01	100	48.8	99	0.03	90.2	74	0.05	49.9	100	0.04	79.2	86	79.2	86
	5	0.01	100	74.1	78	0.07	61.6	96	0.10	61.0	97	0.10	89.5	76	89.5	76
	6	0.01	100	57.0	99	0.04	48.4	97	0.05	50.6	100	0.04	66.8	87	66.8	87
	1	0.09	100	52.1	100	0.06	188.2	100	0.09	48.3	96	0.09	335.9	100	55.7	98
	2	0.02	82	177.0	20	0.13	90.0	48	0.57	117.2	23	0.65	3817	100	183.5	61
3	3	0.02	87	177.2	28	0.18	76.2	83	0.34	85.3	49	0.37	1971	100	111.5	70
	4	0.05	92	106.5	34	0.14	78.4	99	0.23	77.3	53	0.25	992.0	100	146.4	73
	5	0.02	100	51.2	93	0.08	94.2	100	0.18	43.6	90	0.22	232.9	100	79.0	93
	6	0.04	88	122.6	29	0.15	55.2	91	0.25	49.8	50	0.26	571.2	99	100.0	64
	1	0.06	94	69.1	66	0.05	177.1	99	0.08	76.9	70	0.08	2673	100	153.2	77
	2	0.04	89	85.9	35	0.18	83.2	72	0.38	82.1	48	0.43	655.0	100	72.2	69
4	3	0.03	100	18.6	85	0.53	54.5	99	0.55	32.0	88	0.58	252.2	100	46.3	95
	4	0.07	98	32.4	91	0.18	80.7	96	0.28	39.6	84	0.31	399.2	100	47.2	99
	5	0.02	100	50.7	96	0.08	88.3	100	0.19	45.2	89	0.23	568.2	100	77.7	91
	6	0.04	91	122.7	30	0.15	74.1	99	0.22	67.3	49	0.24	1345	100	111.1	67
	1	0.01	98	56.0	96	0.04	72.1	100	0.06	75.1	99	0.05	64.4	95	64.4	95
	2	0.01	97	71.4	71	0.05	68.8	100	0.07	66.5	76	0.06	64.9	83	64.9	83
5	3	0.01	97	43.3	96	0.14	63.1	98	0.17	48.5	99	0.20	47.0	98	47.0	98
	4	0.02	92	84.7	73	0.05	52.1	100	0.07	69.1	80	0.06	65.4	78	65.4	78
	5	0.01	98	113.0	55	0.07	74.1	97	0.10	96.9	64	0.10	116.3	77	116.2	77
	6	0.01	97	57.6	97	0.04	70.9	98	0.05	69.6	99	0.04	53.9	97	53.9	97
	1	0.01	100	90.2	60	0.19	61.6	97	0.21	57.2	96	0.27	49.5	100	49.5	100
	2	0.01	98	65.4	93	0.05	64.5	87	0.07	62.8	98	0.06	60.5	97	60.5	97
6	3	0.00	100	49.1	100	0.06	60.3	94	0.09	56.3	97	0.09	51.8	100	51.8	100
	4	0.01	100	60.8	91	0.05	85.3	74	0.07	47.5	100	0.06	67.1	94	67.1	94
	5	0.01	99	113.1	49	0.08	69.5	91	0.10	61.5	91	0.10	65.8	95	65.8	95
	6	0.01	100	64.8	85	0.05	61.1	95	0.07	59.8	97	0.06	55.0	100	55.0	100
Mean		0.03	95	76.2	71	0.12	78.7	93	0.18	65.3	79	0.20	980.4	96	85.1	85
Median		0.02	98	66.5	82	0.08	73.5	98	0.10	61.2	89	0.11	152.3	100	66.9	87

Note: The first two columns indicate the selection rule D_i and the outcome equation Y_i. The following columns provide the simulation results for the pair-matching, kernel, local linear and Seifert&Gasser matching estimator at bandwidth values chosen by Akaike penalized cross-validation. The last four columns provide the results for the re-weighting estimator with and without trimming. Simulated mean squared error (multiplied by 1000) is given for the pair-matching estimator. For the other estimators MSE^r represents the mean squared error relative to the mean squared error of pair-matching (column 3). The columns labelled $\%Var$ indicate which fraction (in %) of the MSE is due to the variance of the estimator. The columns labelled h provide the mean of the chosen bandwidth values. Results are based on about 5.000 replications for the pair-matching estimator, 300 replications for the kernel, 200 for the local linear and 200 for the Seifert&Gasser estimator, with bandwidth search grid $= 0.01, 0.02, .., 0.80$. Results for the re-weighting estimator are based on about 5.000 replications. Trimming at 50 means that a ceiling for the propensity score ratio is set at 50.

D Appendix

The following figures provide the simulated and the approximated mean squared error for all regression curves. Sections D.1 to D.3 present the simulated MSE for the sample sizes 40, 200 and 1000, analogously to Figure 3.4. Sections D.4 to D.7 show the MSE approximations for kernel matching and local linear matching (for the sample sizes 200 and 1000), analogously to Figure 3.5.

D.1 Simulated Mean Squared Error for Sample Size 40

Fig. D.1 Simulated MSE for regression curve m_1 (sample size $n_0 = n_1 = 40$)

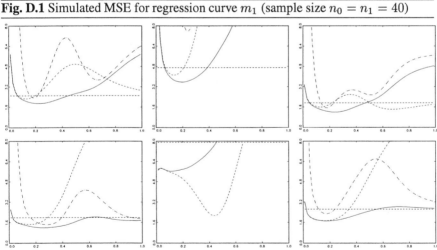

Abscissa: Bandwidth h from 0.02 to 1.00, Ordinate: MSE*1000; Matching (horizontal line), Kernel (short-dashed), local linear (long-dashed) and Seifert&Gasser (solid). Density combinations $N_1 - N_2$, $N_1 - N_3$, $N_2 - N_1$ from top left to top right picture, density combinations $N_2 - N_3$, $N_3 - N_1$, $N_3 - N_2$ from bottom left to bottom right picture.

Fig. D.2 Simulated MSE for regression curve m_2 (sample size $n_0 = n_1 = 40$)

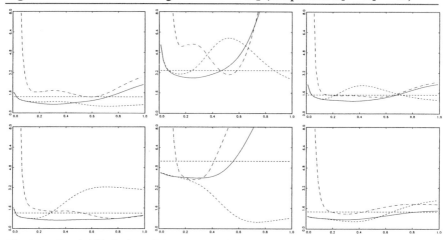

Abscissa: Bandwidth h from 0.02 to 1.00, Ordinate: MSE*1000; Matching (horizontal line), Kernel (short-dashed), local linear (long-dashed) and Seifert&Gasser (solid). Density combinations $N_1 - N_2$, $N_1 - N_3$, $N_2 - N_1$ from top left to top right picture, density combinations $N_2 - N_3$, $N_3 - N_1$, $N_3 - N_2$ from bottom left to bottom right picture.

Fig. D.3 Simulated MSE for regression curve m_3 (sample size $n_0 = n_1 = 40$)

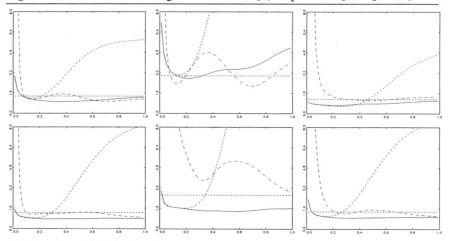

Abscissa: Bandwidth h from 0.02 to 1.00, Ordinate: MSE*1000; Matching (horizontal line), Kernel (short-dashed), local linear (long-dashed) and Seifert&Gasser (solid). Density combinations $N_1 - N_2$, $N_1 - N_3$, $N_2 - N_1$ from top left to top right picture, density combinations $N_2 - N_3$, $N_3 - N_1$, $N_3 - N_2$ from bottom left to bottom right picture.

Fig. D.4 Simulated MSE for regression curve m_4 (sample size $n_0 = n_1 = 40$)

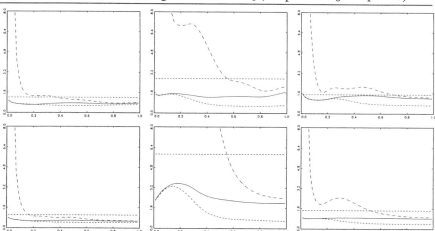

Abscissa: Bandwidth h from 0.02 to 1.00, Ordinate: MSE*1000; Matching (horizontal line), Kernel (short-dashed), local linear (long-dashed) and Seifert&Gasser (solid). Density combinations $N_1 - N_2$, $N_1 - N_3$, $N_2 - N_1$ from top left to top right picture, density combinations $N_2 - N_3$, $N_3 - N_1$, $N_3 - N_2$ from bottom left to bottom right picture.

Fig. D.5 Simulated MSE for regression curve m_5 (sample size $n_0 = n_1 = 40$)

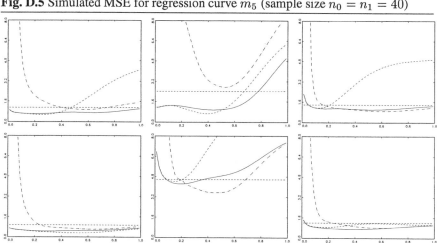

Abscissa: Bandwidth h from 0.02 to 1.00, Ordinate: MSE*1000; Matching (horizontal line), Kernel (short-dashed), local linear (long-dashed) and Seifert&Gasser (solid). Density combinations $N_1 - N_2$, $N_1 - N_3$, $N_2 - N_1$ from top left to top right picture, density combinations $N_2 - N_3$, $N_3 - N_1$, $N_3 - N_2$ from bottom left to bottom right picture.

Fig. D.6 Simulated MSE for regression curve m_6 (sample size $n_0 = n_1 = 40$)

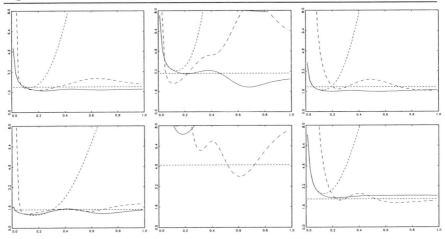

Abscissa: Bandwidth h from 0.02 to 1.00, Ordinate: MSE*1000; Matching (horizontal line), Kernel (short-dashed), local linear (long-dashed) and Seifert&Gasser (solid). Density combinations $N_1 - N_2$, $N_1 - N_3$, $N_2 - N_1$ from top left to top right picture, density combinations $N_2 - N_3$, $N_3 - N_1$, $N_3 - N_2$ from bottom left to bottom right picture.

Fig. D.7 Simulated MSE for regression curve m_7 (sample size $n_0 = n_1 = 40$)

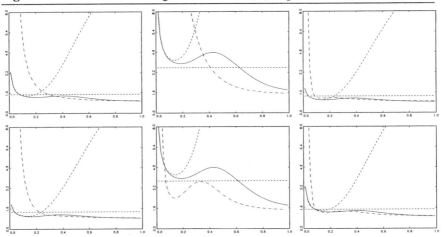

Abscissa: Bandwidth h from 0.02 to 1.00, Ordinate: MSE*1000; Matching (horizontal line), Kernel (short-dashed), local linear (long-dashed) and Seifert&Gasser (solid). Density combinations $N_1 - N_2$, $N_1 - N_3$, $N_2 - N_1$ from top left to top right picture, density combinations $N_2 - N_3$, $N_3 - N_1$, $N_3 - N_2$ from bottom left to bottom right picture.

Fig. D.8 Simulated MSE for regression curve m_8 (sample size $n_0 = n_1 = 40$)

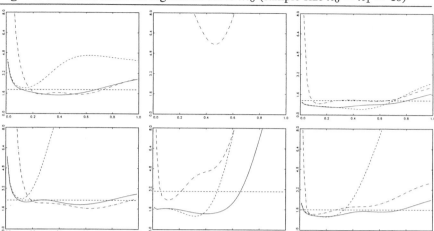

Abscissa: Bandwidth h from 0.02 to 1.00, Ordinate: MSE*1000; Matching (horizontal line), Kernel (short-dashed), local linear (long-dashed) and Seifert&Gasser (solid). Density combinations $N_1 - N_2$, $N_1 - N_3$, $N_2 - N_1$ from top left to top right picture, density combinations $N_2 - N_3$, $N_3 - N_1$, $N_3 - N_2$ from bottom left to bottom right picture.

D.2 Simulated Mean Squared Error for Sample Size 200

Fig. D.9 Simulated MSE for regression curve m_1 (sample size $n_0 = n_1 = 200$)

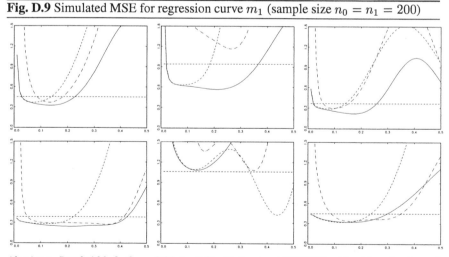

Abscissa: Bandwidth h from 0.01 to 0.50, Ordinate: MSE*1000; Matching (horizontal line), Kernel (short-dashed), local linear (long-dashed) and Seifert&Gasser (solid). Density combinations $N_1 - N_2$, $N_1 - N_3$, $N_2 - N_1$ from top left to top right picture, density combinations $N_2 - N_3$, $N_3 - N_1$, $N_3 - N_2$ from bottom left to bottom right picture.

Fig. D.10 Simulated MSE for regression curve m_2 (sample size $n_0 = n_1 = 200$)

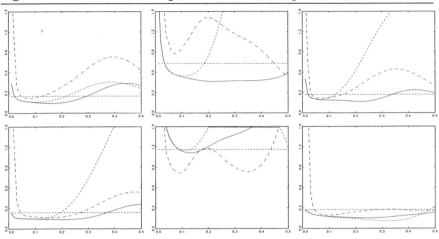

Abscissa: Bandwidth h from 0.01 to 0.50, Ordinate: MSE*1000; Matching (horizontal line), Kernel (short-dashed), local linear (long-dashed) and Seifert&Gasser (solid). Density combinations $N_1 - N_2$, $N_1 - N_3$, $N_2 - N_1$ from top left to top right picture, density combinations $N_2 - N_3$, $N_3 - N_1$, $N_3 - N_2$ from bottom left to bottom right picture.

Fig. D.11 Simulated MSE for regression curve m_3 (sample size $n_0 = n_1 = 200$)

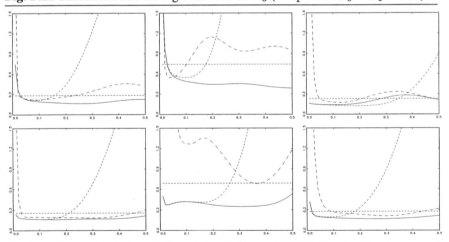

Abscissa: Bandwidth h from 0.01 to 0.50, Ordinate: MSE*1000; Matching (horizontal line), Kernel (short-dashed), local linear (long-dashed) and Seifert&Gasser (solid). Density combinations $N_1 - N_2$, $N_1 - N_3$, $N_2 - N_1$ from top left to top right picture, density combinations $N_2 - N_3$, $N_3 - N_1$, $N_3 - N_2$ from bottom left to bottom right picture.

Fig. D.12 Simulated MSE for regression curve m_4 (sample size $n_0 = n_1 = 200$)

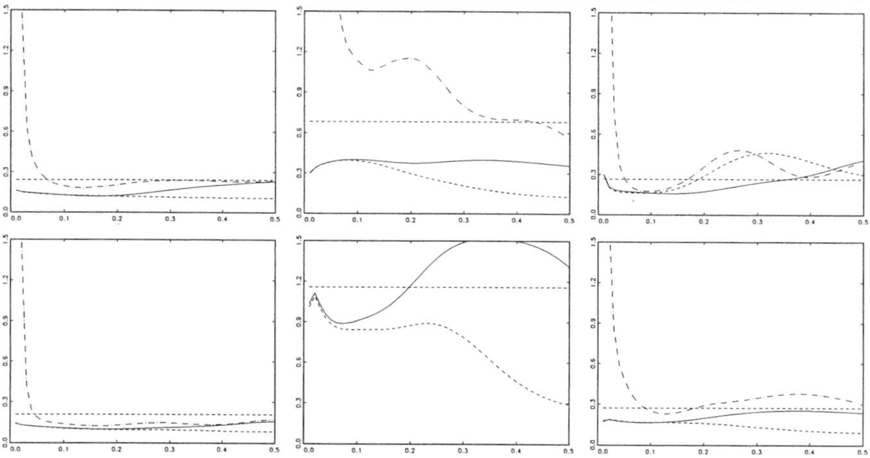

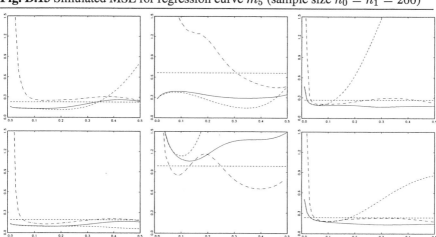

Abscissa: Bandwidth h from 0.01 to 0.50, Ordinate: MSE*1000; Matching (horizontal line), Kernel (short-dashed), local linear (long-dashed) and Seifert&Gasser (solid). Density combinations $N_1 - N_2$, $N_1 - N_3$, $N_2 - N_1$ from top left to top right picture, density combinations $N_2 - N_3$, $N_3 - N_1$, $N_3 - N_2$ from bottom left to bottom right picture.

Fig. D.13 Simulated MSE for regression curve m_5 (sample size $n_0 = n_1 = 200$)

Abscissa: Bandwidth h from 0.01 to 0.50, Ordinate: MSE*1000; Matching (horizontal line), Kernel (short-dashed), local linear (long-dashed) and Seifert&Gasser (solid). Density combinations $N_1 - N_2$, $N_1 - N_3$, $N_2 - N_1$ from top left to top right picture, density combinations $N_2 - N_3$, $N_3 - N_1$, $N_3 - N_2$ from bottom left to bottom right picture.

Fig. D.14 Simulated MSE for regression curve m_6 (sample size $n_0 = n_1 = 200$)

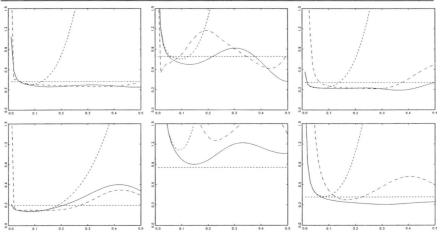

Abscissa: Bandwidth h from 0.01 to 0.50, Ordinate: MSE*1000; Matching (horizontal line), Kernel (short-dashed), local linear (long-dashed) and Seifert&Gasser (solid). Density combinations $N_1 - N_2$, $N_1 - N_3$, $N_2 - N_1$ from top left to top right picture, density combinations $N_2 - N_3$, $N_3 - N_1$, $N_3 - N_2$ from bottom left to bottom right picture.

Fig. D.15 Simulated MSE for regression curve m_7 (sample size $n_0 = n_1 = 200$)

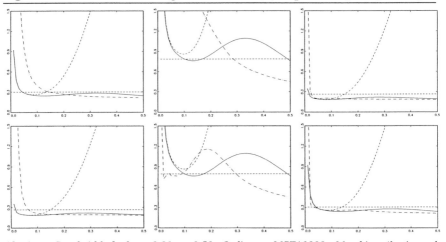

Abscissa: Bandwidth h from 0.01 to 0.50, Ordinate: MSE*1000; Matching (horizontal line), Kernel (short-dashed), local linear (long-dashed) and Seifert&Gasser (solid). Density combinations $N_1 - N_2$, $N_1 - N_3$, $N_2 - N_1$ from top left to top right picture, density combinations $N_2 - N_3$, $N_3 - N_1$, $N_3 - N_2$ from bottom left to bottom right picture.

Fig. D.16 Simulated MSE for regression curve m_8 (sample size $n_0 = n_1 = 200$)

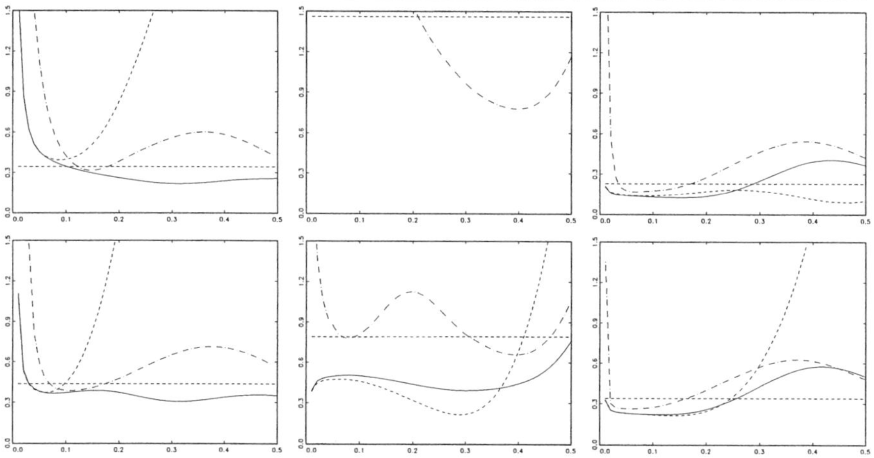

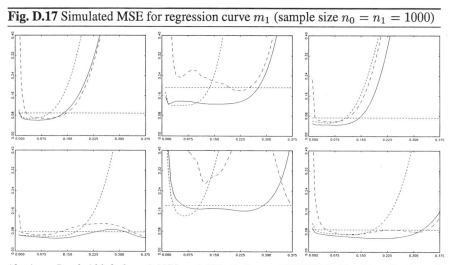

Abscissa: Bandwidth h from 0.01 to 0.50, Ordinate: MSE*1000; Matching (horizontal line), Kernel (short-dashed), local linear (long-dashed) and Seifert&Gasser (solid). Density combinations $N_1 - N_2$, $N_1 - N_3$, $N_2 - N_1$ from top left to top right picture, density combinations $N_2 - N_3$, $N_3 - N_1$, $N_3 - N_2$ from bottom left to bottom right picture.

D.3 Simulated Mean Squared Error for Sample Size 1000

Fig. D.17 Simulated MSE for regression curve m_1 (sample size $n_0 = n_1 = 1000$)

Abscissa: Bandwidth h from 0.0075 to 0.375, Ordinate: MSE*1000; Matching (horizontal line), Kernel (short-dashed), local linear (long-dashed) and Seifert&Gasser (solid). Density combinations $N_1 - N_2$, $N_1 - N_3$, $N_2 - N_1$ from top left to top right picture, density combinations $N_2 - N_3$, $N_3 - N_1$, $N_3 - N_2$ from bottom left to bottom right picture.

Fig. D.18 Simulated MSE for regression curve m_2 (sample size $n_0 = n_1 = 1000$)

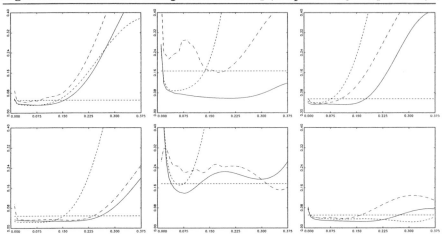

Abscissa: Bandwidth h from 0.0075 to 0.375, Ordinate: MSE*1000; Matching (horizontal line), Kernel (short-dashed), local linear (long-dashed) and Seifert&Gasser (solid). Density combinations $N_1 - N_2$, $N_1 - N_3$, $N_2 - N_1$ from top left to top right picture, density combinations $N_2 - N_3$, $N_3 - N_1$, $N_3 - N_2$ from bottom left to bottom right picture.

Fig. D.19 Simulated MSE for regression curve m_3 (sample size $n_0 = n_1 = 1000$)

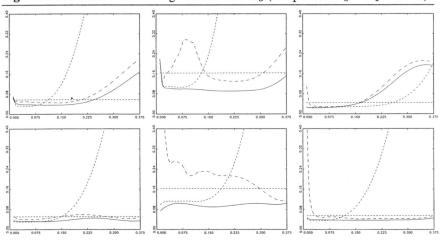

Abscissa: Bandwidth h from 0.0075 to 0.375, Ordinate: MSE*1000; Matching (horizontal line), Kernel (short-dashed), local linear (long-dashed) and Seifert&Gasser (solid). Density combinations $N_1 - N_2$, $N_1 - N_3$, $N_2 - N_1$ from top left to top right picture, density combinations $N_2 - N_3$, $N_3 - N_1$, $N_3 - N_2$ from bottom left to bottom right picture.

Fig. D.20 Simulated MSE for regression curve m_4 (sample size $n_0 = n_1 = 1000$)

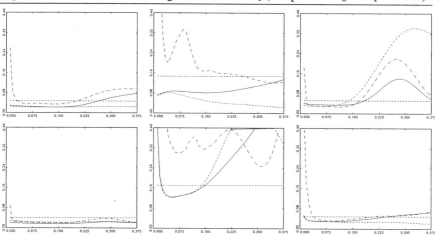

Abscissa: Bandwidth h from 0.0075 to 0.375, Ordinate: MSE*1000; Matching (horizontal line), Kernel (short-dashed), local linear (long-dashed) and Seifert&Gasser (solid). Density combinations $N_1 - N_2$, $N_1 - N_3$, $N_2 - N_1$ from top left to top right picture, density combinations $N_2 - N_3$, $N_3 - N_1$, $N_3 - N_2$ from bottom left to bottom right picture.

Fig. D.21 Simulated MSE for regression curve m_5 (sample size $n_0 = n_1 = 1000$)

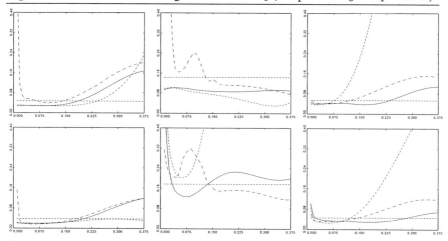

Abscissa: Bandwidth h from 0.0075 to 0.375, Ordinate: MSE*1000; Matching (horizontal line), Kernel (short-dashed), local linear (long-dashed) and Seifert&Gasser (solid). Density combinations $N_1 - N_2$, $N_1 - N_3$, $N_2 - N_1$ from top left to top right picture, density combinations $N_2 - N_3$, $N_3 - N_1$, $N_3 - N_2$ from bottom left to bottom right picture.

Fig. D.22 Simulated MSE for regression curve m_6 (sample size $n_0 = n_1 = 1000$)

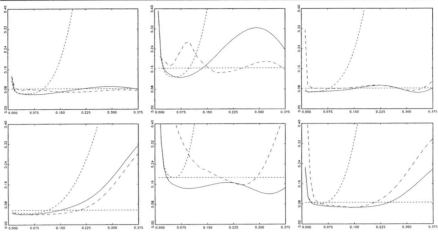

Abscissa: Bandwidth h from 0.0075 to 0.375, Ordinate: MSE*1000; Matching (horizontal line), Kernel (short-dashed), local linear (long-dashed) and Seifert&Gasser (solid). Density combinations $N_1 - N_2$, $N_1 - N_3$, $N_2 - N_1$ from top left to top right picture, density combinations $N_2 - N_3$, $N_3 - N_1$, $N_3 - N_2$ from bottom left to bottom right picture.

Fig. D.23 Simulated MSE for regression curve m_7 (sample size $n_0 = n_1 = 1000$)

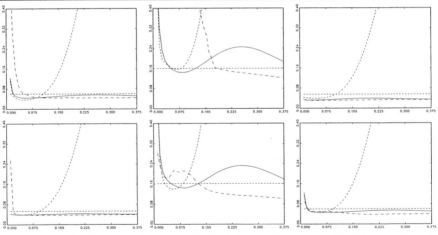

Abscissa: Bandwidth h from 0.0075 to 0.375, Ordinate: MSE*1000; Matching (horizontal line), Kernel (short-dashed), local linear (long-dashed) and Seifert&Gasser (solid). Density combinations $N_1 - N_2$, $N_1 - N_3$, $N_2 - N_1$ from top left to top right picture, density combinations $N_2 - N_3$, $N_3 - N_1$, $N_3 - N_2$ from bottom left to bottom right picture.

Fig. D.24 Simulated MSE for regression curve m_8 (sample size $n_0 = n_1 = 1000$)

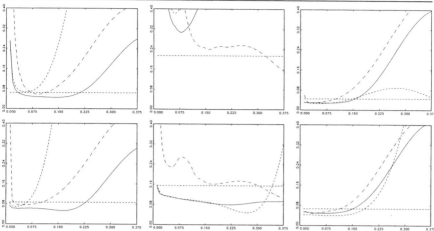

Abscissa: Bandwidth h from 0.0075 to 0.375, Ordinate: MSE*1000; Matching (horizontal line), Kernel (short-dashed), local linear (long-dashed) and Seifert&Gasser (solid). Density combinations $N_1 - N_2$, $N_1 - N_3$, $N_2 - N_1$ from top left to top right picture, density combinations $N_2 - N_3$, $N_3 - N_1$, $N_3 - N_2$ from bottom left to bottom right picture.

D.4 MSE Approximation: Kernel Matching, Sample Size 200

Fig. D.25 MSE approximations for Kernel matching (curve m_1, $n_0 = n_1 = 200$)

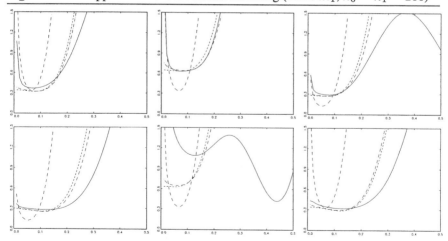

Abscissa: Bandwidth h, Ordinate: MSE*1000, MISE*100. Simulated MSE (solid), two-terms approximation to MSE (dotted-dashed), first-term approximation to MSE (short-dashed) and approximation to MISE (long-dashed). Density combinations $N_1 - N_2$, $N_1 - N_3$, $N_2 - N_1$ (top row) and combinations $N_2 - N_3$, $N_3 - N_1$, $N_3 - N_2$ (bottom row).

Fig. D.26 MSE approximations for Kernel matching (curve m_2, $n_0 = n_1 = 200$)

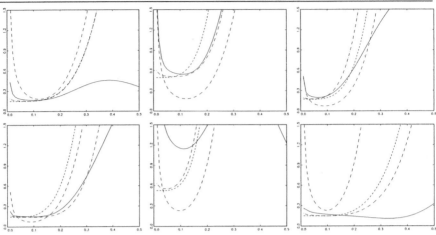

Abscissa: Bandwidth h, Ordinate: MSE*1000, MISE*100. Simulated MSE (solid), two-terms approximation to MSE (dotted-dashed), first-term approximation to MSE (short-dashed) and approximation to MISE (long-dashed). Density combinations $N_1 - N_2$, $N_1 - N_3$, $N_2 - N_1$ (top row) and combinations $N_2 - N_3$, $N_3 - N_1$, $N_3 - N_2$ (bottom row).

Fig. D.27 MSE approximations for Kernel matching (curve m_3, $n_0 = n_1 = 200$)

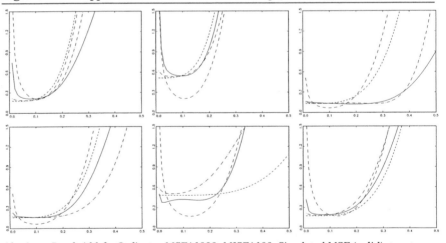

Abscissa: Bandwidth h, Ordinate: MSE*1000, MISE*100. Simulated MSE (solid), two-terms approximation to MSE (dotted-dashed), first-term approximation to MSE (short-dashed) and approximation to MISE (long-dashed). Density combinations $N_1 - N_2$, $N_1 - N_3$, $N_2 - N_1$ (top row) and combinations $N_2 - N_3$, $N_3 - N_1$, $N_3 - N_2$ (bottom row).

Fig. D.28 MSE approximations for Kernel matching (curve m_4, $n_0 = n_1 = 200$)

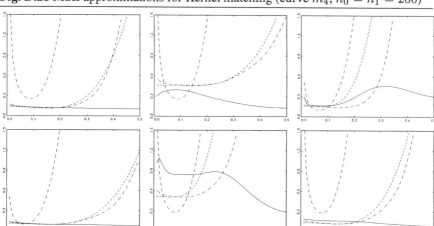

Abscissa: Bandwidth h, Ordinate: MSE*1000, MISE*100. Simulated MSE (solid), two-terms approximation to MSE (dotted-dashed), first-term approximation to MSE (short-dashed) and approximation to MISE (long-dashed). Density combinations $N_1 - N_2$, $N_1 - N_3$, $N_2 - N_1$ (top row) and combinations $N_2 - N_3$, $N_3 - N_1$, $N_3 - N_2$ (bottom row).

The approximations for regression curve m_5 were unstable and are not plotted.

Fig. D.29 MSE approximations for Kernel matching (curve m_6, $n_0 = n_1 = 200$)

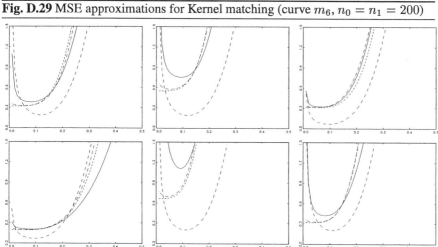

Abscissa: Bandwidth h, Ordinate: MSE*1000, MISE*100. Simulated MSE (solid), two-terms approximation to MSE (dotted-dashed), first-term approximation to MSE (short-dashed) and approximation to MISE (long-dashed). Density combinations $N_1 - N_2$, $N_1 - N_3$, $N_2 - N_1$ (top row) and combinations $N_2 - N_3$, $N_3 - N_1$, $N_3 - N_2$ (bottom row).

Fig. D.30 MSE approximations for Kernel matching (curve m_7, $n_0 = n_1 = 200$)

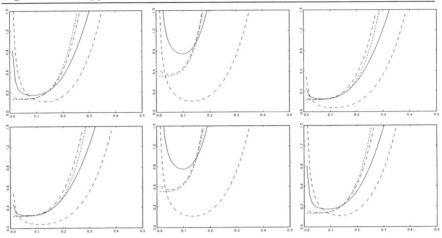

Abscissa: Bandwidth h, Ordinate: MSE*1000, MISE*100. Simulated MSE (solid), two-terms approximation to MSE (dotted-dashed), first-term approximation to MSE (short-dashed) and approximation to MISE (long-dashed). Density combinations $N_1 - N_2$, $N_1 - N_3$, $N_2 - N_1$ (top row) and combinations $N_2 - N_3$, $N_3 - N_1$, $N_3 - N_2$ (bottom row).

Fig. D.31 MSE approximations for Kernel matching (curve m_8, $n_0 = n_1 = 200$)

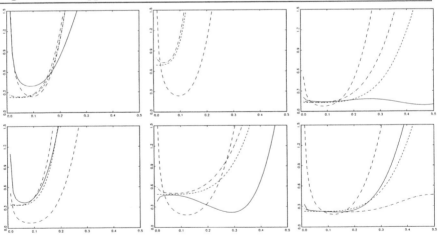

Abscissa: Bandwidth h, Ordinate: MSE*1000, MISE*100. Simulated MSE (solid), two-terms approximation to MSE (dotted-dashed), first-term approximation to MSE (short-dashed) and approximation to MISE (long-dashed). Density combinations $N_1 - N_2$, $N_1 - N_3$, $N_2 - N_1$ (top row) and combinations $N_2 - N_3$, $N_3 - N_1$, $N_3 - N_2$ (bottom row).

D.5 MSE Approximation: Kernel Matching, Sample Size 1000

Fig. D.32 MSE approximations for Kernel matching (curve m_1, $n_0 = n_1 = 1000$)

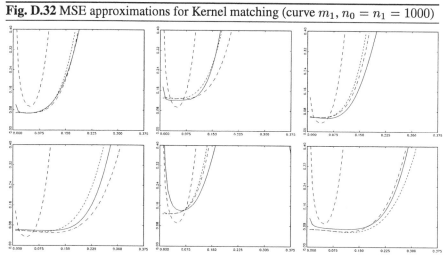

Abscissa: Bandwidth h, Ordinate: MSE*1000, MISE*100. Simulated MSE (solid), two-terms approximation to MSE (dotted-dashed), first-term approximation to MSE (short-dashed) and approximation to MISE (long-dashed). Density combinations $N_1 - N_2$, $N_1 - N_3$, $N_2 - N_1$ (top row) and combinations $N_2 - N_3$, $N_3 - N_1$, $N_3 - N_2$ (bottom row).

Fig. D.33 MSE approximations for Kernel matching (curve m_2, $n_0 = n_1 = 1000$)

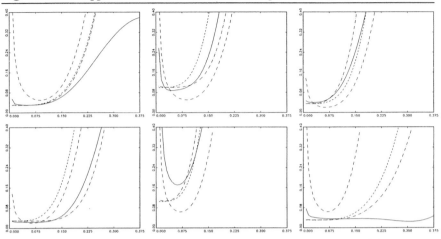

*Abscissa: Bandwidth h, Ordinate: MSE*1000, MISE*100. Simulated MSE (solid), two-terms approximation to MSE (dotted-dashed), first-term approximation to MSE (short-dashed) and approximation to MISE (long-dashed). Density combinations $N_1 - N_2$, $N_1 - N_3$, $N_2 - N_1$ (top row) and combinations $N_2 - N_3$, $N_3 - N_1$, $N_3 - N_2$ (bottom row).*

Fig. D.34 MSE approximations for Kernel matching (curve m_3, $n_0 = n_1 = 1000$)

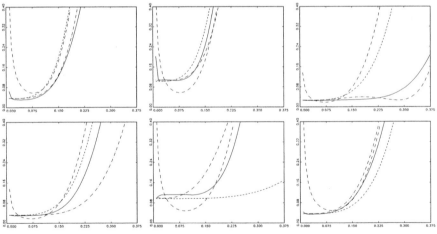

*Abscissa: Bandwidth h, Ordinate: MSE*1000, MISE*100. Simulated MSE (solid), two-terms approximation to MSE (dotted-dashed), first-term approximation to MSE (short-dashed) and approximation to MISE (long-dashed). Density combinations $N_1 - N_2$, $N_1 - N_3$, $N_2 - N_1$ (top row) and combinations $N_2 - N_3$, $N_3 - N_1$, $N_3 - N_2$ (bottom row).*

Fig. D.35 MSE approximations for Kernel matching (curve m_4, $n_0 = n_1 = 1000$)

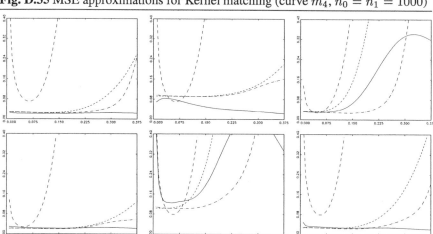

Abscissa: Bandwidth h, Ordinate: MSE*1000, MISE*100. Simulated MSE (solid), two-terms approximation to MSE (dotted-dashed), first-term approximation to MSE (short-dashed) and approximation to MISE (long-dashed). Density combinations $N_1 - N_2$, $N_1 - N_3$, $N_2 - N_1$ (top row) and combinations $N_2 - N_3$, $N_3 - N_1$, $N_3 - N_2$ (bottom row).

The approximations for regression curve m_5 were unstable and are not plotted.

Fig. D.36 MSE approximations for Kernel matching (curve m_6, $n_0 = n_1 = 1000$)

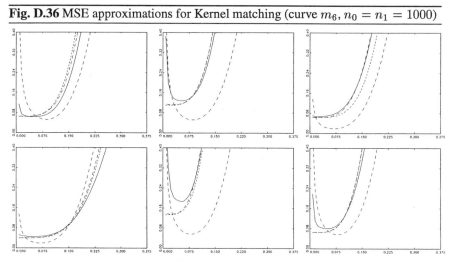

Abscissa: Bandwidth h, Ordinate: MSE*1000, MISE*100. Simulated MSE (solid), two-terms approximation to MSE (dotted-dashed), first-term approximation to MSE (short-dashed) and approximation to MISE (long-dashed). Density combinations $N_1 - N_2$, $N_1 - N_3$, $N_2 - N_1$ (top row) and combinations $N_2 - N_3$, $N_3 - N_1$, $N_3 - N_2$ (bottom row).

Fig. D.37 MSE approximations for Kernel matching (curve m_7, $n_0 = n_1 = 1000$)

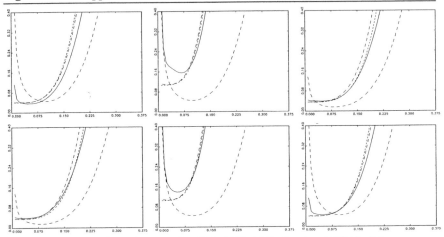

Abscissa: Bandwidth h, Ordinate: MSE*1000, MISE*100. Simulated MSE (solid), two-terms approximation to MSE (dotted-dashed), first-term approximation to MSE (short-dashed) and approximation to MISE (long-dashed). Density combinations $N_1 - N_2$, $N_1 - N_3$, $N_2 - N_1$ (top row) and combinations $N_2 - N_3$, $N_3 - N_1$, $N_3 - N_2$ (bottom row).

Fig. D.38 MSE approximations for Kernel matching (curve m_8, $n_0 = n_1 = 1000$)

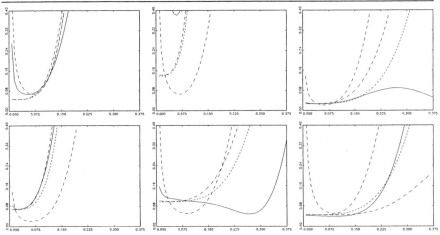

Abscissa: Bandwidth h, Ordinate: MSE*1000, MISE*100. Simulated MSE (solid), two-terms approximation to MSE (dotted-dashed), first-term approximation to MSE (short-dashed) and approximation to MISE (long-dashed). Density combinations $N_1 - N_2$, $N_1 - N_3$, $N_2 - N_1$ (top row) and combinations $N_2 - N_3$, $N_3 - N_1$, $N_3 - N_2$ (bottom row).

D.6 MSE Approximation: Local Linear, Sample Size 200

Fig. D.39 Approximations for local linear matching (curve m_1, $n_0 = n_1 = 200$)

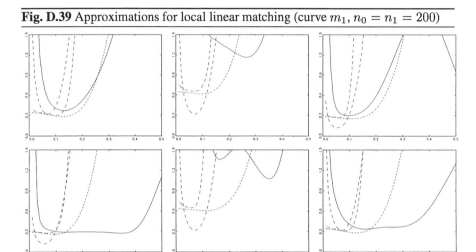

Abscissa: Bandwidth h, Ordinate: MSE*1000, MISE*100. Simulated MSE (solid), two-terms approximation to MSE (dotted-dashed), first-term approximation to MSE (short-dashed) and approximation to MISE (long-dashed). Density combinations $N_1 - N_2$, $N_1 - N_3$, $N_2 - N_1$ (top row) and combinations $N_2 - N_3$, $N_3 - N_1$, $N_3 - N_2$ (bottom row).

Fig. D.40 Approximations for local linear matching (curve m_2, $n_0 = n_1 = 200$)

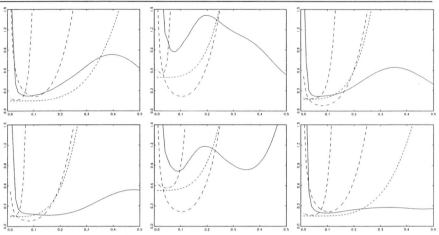

Abscissa: Bandwidth h, Ordinate: MSE*1000, MISE*100. Simulated MSE (solid), two-terms approximation to MSE (dotted-dashed), first-term approximation to MSE (short-dashed) and approximation to MISE (long-dashed). Density combinations $N_1 - N_2$, $N_1 - N_3$, $N_2 - N_1$ (top row) and combinations $N_2 - N_3$, $N_3 - N_1$, $N_3 - N_2$ (bottom row).

Fig. D.41 Approximations for local linear matching (curve m_3, $n_0 = n_1 = 200$)

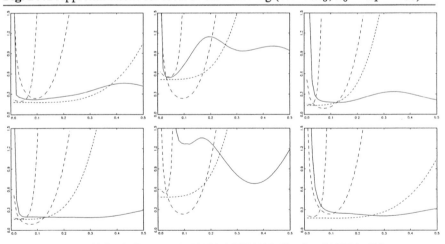

Abscissa: Bandwidth h, Ordinate: MSE*1000, MISE*100. Simulated MSE (solid), two-terms approximation to MSE (dotted-dashed), first-term approximation to MSE (short-dashed) and approximation to MISE (long-dashed). Density combinations $N_1 - N_2$, $N_1 - N_3$, $N_2 - N_1$ (top row) and combinations $N_2 - N_3$, $N_3 - N_1$, $N_3 - N_2$ (bottom row).

Fig. D.42 Approximations for local linear matching (curve m_4, $n_0 = n_1 = 200$)

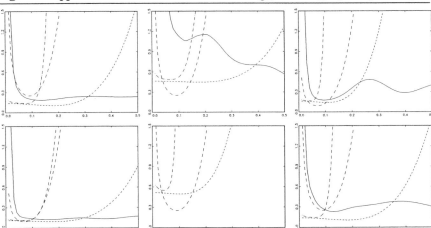

Abscissa: Bandwidth h, Ordinate: MSE*1000, MISE*100. Simulated MSE (solid), two-terms approximation to MSE (dotted-dashed), first-term approximation to MSE (short-dashed) and approximation to MISE (long-dashed). Density combinations $N_1 - N_2$, $N_1 - N_3$, $N_2 - N_1$ (top row) and combinations $N_2 - N_3$, $N_3 - N_1$, $N_3 - N_2$ (bottom row).

The approximations for regression curve m_5 were unstable and are not plotted.

Fig. D.43 Approximations for local linear matching (curve m_6, $n_0 = n_1 = 200$)

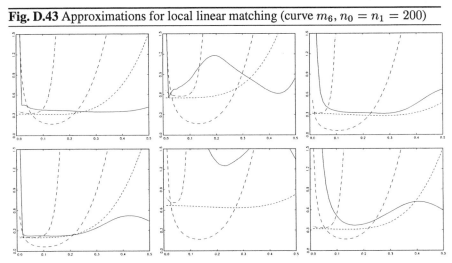

Abscissa: Bandwidth h, Ordinate: MSE*1000, MISE*100. Simulated MSE (solid), two-terms approximation to MSE (dotted-dashed), first-term approximation to MSE (short-dashed) and approximation to MISE (long-dashed). Density combinations $N_1 - N_2$, $N_1 - N_3$, $N_2 - N_1$ (top row) and combinations $N_2 - N_3$, $N_3 - N_1$, $N_3 - N_2$ (bottom row).

Fig. D.44 Approximations for local linear matching (curve m_7, $n_0 = n_1 = 200$)

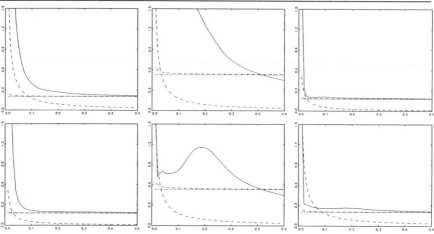

Abscissa: Bandwidth h, Ordinate: MSE*1000, MISE*100. Simulated MSE (solid), two-terms approximation to MSE (dotted-dashed), first-term approximation to MSE (short-dashed) and approximation to MISE (long-dashed). Density combinations $N_1 - N_2$, $N_1 - N_3$, $N_2 - N_1$ (top row) and combinations $N_2 - N_3$, $N_3 - N_1$, $N_3 - N_2$ (bottom row).

Fig. D.45 Approximations for local linear matching (curve m_8, $n_0 = n_1 = 200$)

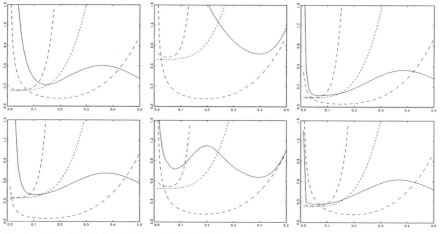

Abscissa: Bandwidth h, Ordinate: MSE*1000, MISE*100. Simulated MSE (solid), two-terms approximation to MSE (dotted-dashed), first-term approximation to MSE (short-dashed) and approximation to MISE (long-dashed). Density combinations $N_1 - N_2$, $N_1 - N_3$, $N_2 - N_1$ (top row) and combinations $N_2 - N_3$, $N_3 - N_1$, $N_3 - N_2$ (bottom row).

D.7 MSE Approximation: Local Linear, Sample Size 1000

Fig. D.46 Approximations for local linear matching (curve m_1, $n_0 = n_1 = 1000$)

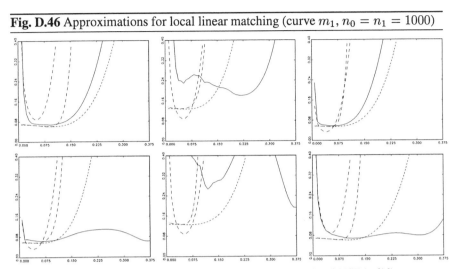

Abscissa: Bandwidth h, Ordinate: MSE*1000, MISE*100. Simulated MSE (solid), two-terms approximation to MSE (dotted-dashed), first-term approximation to MSE (short-dashed) and approximation to MISE (long-dashed). Density combinations $N_1 - N_2$, $N_1 - N_3$, $N_2 - N_1$ (top row) and combinations $N_2 - N_3$, $N_3 - N_1$, $N_3 - N_2$ (bottom row).

Fig. D.47 Approximations for local linear matching (curve m_2, $n_0 = n_1 = 1000$)

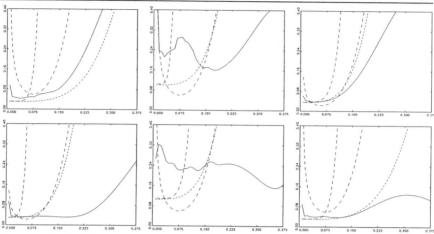

Abscissa: Bandwidth h, Ordinate: MSE*1000, MISE*100. Simulated MSE (solid), two-terms approximation to MSE (dotted-dashed), first-term approximation to MSE (short-dashed) and approximation to MISE (long-dashed). Density combinations $N_1 - N_2$, $N_1 - N_3$, $N_2 - N_1$ (top row) and combinations $N_2 - N_3$, $N_3 - N_1$, $N_3 - N_2$ (bottom row).

Fig. D.48 Approximations for local linear matching (curve m_3, $n_0 = n_1 = 1000$)

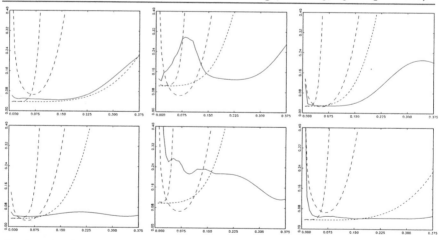

Abscissa: Bandwidth h, Ordinate: MSE*1000, MISE*100. Simulated MSE (solid), two-terms approximation to MSE (dotted-dashed), first-term approximation to MSE (short-dashed) and approximation to MISE (long-dashed). Density combinations $N_1 - N_2$, $N_1 - N_3$, $N_2 - N_1$ (top row) and combinations $N_2 - N_3$, $N_3 - N_1$, $N_3 - N_2$ (bottom row).

Fig. D.49 Approximations for local linear matching (curve m_4, $n_0 = n_1 = 1000$)

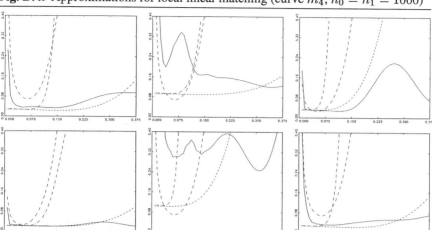

Abscissa: Bandwidth h, Ordinate: MSE*1000, MISE*100. Simulated MSE (solid), two-terms approximation to MSE (dotted-dashed), first-term approximation to MSE (short-dashed) and approximation to MISE (long-dashed). Density combinations $N_1 - N_2$, $N_1 - N_3$, $N_2 - N_1$ (top row) and combinations $N_2 - N_3$, $N_3 - N_1$, $N_3 - N_2$ (bottom row).

The approximations for regression curve m_5 were unstable and are not plotted.

Fig. D.50 Approximations for local linear matching (curve m_6, $n_0 = n_1 = 1000$)

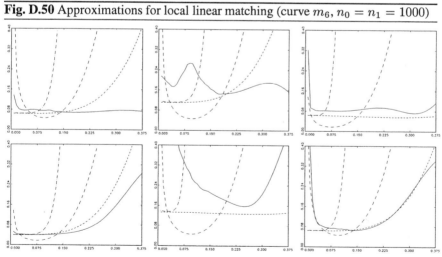

Abscissa: Bandwidth h, Ordinate: MSE*1000, MISE*100. Simulated MSE (solid), two-terms approximation to MSE (dotted-dashed), first-term approximation to MSE (short-dashed) and approximation to MISE (long-dashed). Density combinations $N_1 - N_2$, $N_1 - N_3$, $N_2 - N_1$ (top row) and combinations $N_2 - N_3$, $N_3 - N_1$, $N_3 - N_2$ (bottom row).

Fig. D.51 Approximations for local linear matching (curve m_7, $n_0 = n_1 = 1000$)

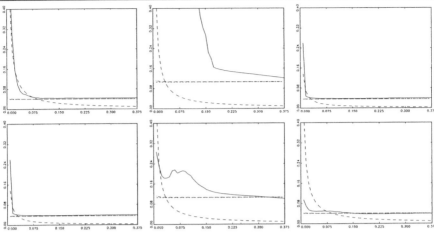

Abscissa: Bandwidth h, Ordinate: MSE*1000, MISE*100. Simulated MSE (solid), two-terms approximation to MSE (dotted-dashed), first-term approximation to MSE (short-dashed) and approximation to MISE (long-dashed). Density combinations $N_1 - N_2$, $N_1 - N_3$, $N_2 - N_1$ (top row) and combinations $N_2 - N_3$, $N_3 - N_1$, $N_3 - N_2$ (bottom row).

Fig. D.52 Approximations for local linear matching (curve m_8, $n_0 = n_1 = 1000$)

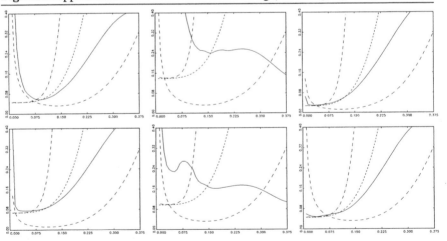

Abscissa: Bandwidth h, Ordinate: MSE*1000, MISE*100. Simulated MSE (solid), two-terms approximation to MSE (dotted-dashed), first-term approximation to MSE (short-dashed) and approximation to MISE (long-dashed). Density combinations $N_1 - N_2$, $N_1 - N_3$, $N_2 - N_1$ (top row) and combinations $N_2 - N_3$, $N_3 - N_1$, $N_3 - N_2$ (bottom row).

E Appendix

E.1 Asymptotic Properties of the GMM Estimator

In this appendix consistency and asymptotic normality of the proposed GMM estimator under correct parametric specification are derived, and explicit expressions for the influence functions are given. The derivation of the asymptotic properties draws on the results of Newey and McFadden (1994), Heckman, Ichimura, and Todd (1998), Hoeffding (1948) and Serfling (1980). Recall the moment vector (4.9) of length $k + VL$

$$
\begin{aligned}
& g_n^r(\theta^r, \hat{\mathbf{m}}_{VL}^r, \hat{p}^r) \\
& = \frac{1}{n} \sum_i \binom{A^r(X_i) \cdot (Y_i - \varphi^r(X_i, \theta^r)) \cdot 1(D_i = r)}{(\Lambda(X_i) \otimes \varphi^r(X_i, \theta^r) - \hat{\mathbf{m}}_{VL}^r(\hat{p}^r(X_i))) \cdot 1(D_i \neq r) 1(X_i \in \hat{S}^r)},
\end{aligned}
$$

(E.1)

where $\hat{S}^r = \{x : \hat{p}^r(x) > 0\} = \{x : \hat{f}_{X|D=r}(x) > 0\}$ is an estimate of the support S^r of X among the participants in programme r, and

$$
\begin{aligned}
& \hat{\mathbf{m}}_{VL}^r(\hat{p}^r(X_i)) = \\
& (\hat{m}_1^{r\prime}(\hat{p}^r(X_i)) \cdot \Lambda_1(X_i), .., \hat{m}_l^{r\prime}(\hat{p}^r(X_i)) \cdot \Lambda_l(X_i), .., \hat{m}_L^{r\prime}(\hat{p}^r(X_i)) \cdot \Lambda_L(X_i))',
\end{aligned}
$$

is the vector of nonparametric estimates for all subpopulations $l = 1, .., L$ multiplied by the population indicator function Λ. $\hat{m}_l^r(\cdot) = (\hat{m}_{1l}^r(\cdot), .., \hat{m}_{vl}^r(\cdot), .., \hat{m}_{Vl}^r(\cdot))'$ is the *vector-valued* estimator of the conditional expected outcome vector $E[Y^r | p^r(X) = \rho, \Lambda_l(X) = 1, X \in S^r]$ in subpopulation l, and $\hat{m}_{vl}^r(\rho)$ is the estimator of the *v-th component* of the conditional expectation of the outcome vector $E[Y_v^r | p^r(X) = \rho, \Lambda_l(X) = 1, X \in S^r]$.

Theorem 1 (Consistency). *If*
(i) the parametric function $\varphi^r(x, \theta^r)$ is continuous in θ^r,
(ii) has a unique solution $\theta_0^r \in \Theta^r$, with Θ^r compact, such that $\varphi^r(x, \theta^r) = E[Y^r | X = x] \, \forall x$ iff $\theta^r = \theta_0^r$,
(iii) the moments $E \sup_{\theta^r \in \Theta^r} \|A^r(X) \cdot (Y^r - \varphi^r(X, \theta^r))\|$ and

$$E \sup_{\theta^r \in \Theta^r} \| \varphi^r(X, \theta^r) \cdot \Lambda(X) 1(D \neq r) 1(X \in \hat{S}^r)$$

$$- E[Y^r \cdot \Lambda(X) 1(D \neq r) 1(X \in S^r)] \|$$

are finite, in all subpopulations defined by $\Lambda(x)$,
(iv) the number of subpopulations L is finite,
(v) $\hat{m}^r_{vl}(\hat{p}^r(x))$ is a consistent estimator of $E[Y^r_v | p^r(X) = p^r(x), \Lambda_l(X) = 1, X \in S^r]$,
(vi) the weighting matrix $\hat{W}^r$ converges in probability to a positive definite matrix,
then the GMM estimator $\hat{\theta}^r_n = \arg\min_{\theta^r} g^r_n(\theta^r, \hat{m}^r_{VL}, \hat{p}^r)' \hat{W}^r g^r_n(\theta^r, \hat{m}^r_{VL}, \hat{p}^r)$ with
moment vector (4.9) is consistent.

   Assumptions (iii) and (iv) could be relaxed to the form given in Corollary 6 (f). If the parametric specification φ^r is bounded, condition (iii) is automatically satisfied.
   The proof proceeds in three steps, similar to Newey and McFadden (1994). In Corollary 5 sufficient conditions for the consistency of an extremum estimator $\hat{\theta}(\hat{\alpha}) = \arg\min \hat{Q}_n(\theta, \hat{\alpha})$ are given. In Corollary 6 these conditions are specified more precisely for a generic GMM estimator. Finally, it is shown that the specific GMM estimator with moment function (4.9) satisfies these conditions. (In the first two corollaries the superscripts r are suppressed to ease notation.)

   Consider a generic extremum estimator of the form

$$\hat{\theta}(\hat{\alpha}) = \arg\min_{\theta} \hat{Q}_n(\theta, \hat{\alpha}),$$

where $\hat{\alpha}$ is a nonparametric estimate of α_0 and $\hat{Q}_n$ is a stochastic objective function. Let Q_0 denote the nonstochastic limit function of $\hat{Q}_n$ and let θ_0 (the true value) be the minimizer of Q_0. Suppose that the estimator $\hat{\alpha}$ converges in probability to α_0. Define $B(\alpha_0)$ as an arbitrarily small neighbourhood around α_0. Consistency of $\hat{\alpha}$ means that w.p.a.1 (with probability approaching one) $\hat{\alpha}$ lies in the neighbourhood $B(\alpha_0)$:

$$\lim_{n \to \infty} P(\hat{\alpha} \in B(\alpha_0)) = 1. \tag{E.2}$$

Corollary 5. *If*
(i) $Q_0(\theta, \alpha)$ is uniquely minimized at (θ_0, α_0),
(ii) $\theta_0 \in \Theta$, with Θ a compact parameter space,
(iii) $Q_0(\theta, \alpha)$ is continuous,
(iv) $\hat{Q}_n(\theta, \alpha)$ converges uniformly in Θ to $Q_0(\theta, \alpha)$ for all $\alpha \in B(\alpha_0)$:

$$\lim_{n \to \infty} P\left(\sup_{\theta \in \Theta} \left| \hat{Q}_n(\theta, \alpha) - Q_0(\theta, \alpha) \right| < \varepsilon_1 \right) = 1 \qquad \forall \alpha \in B(\alpha_0) \qquad with \; \varepsilon_1 > 0, \tag{E.3}$$

(v) plim $\hat{\alpha} = \alpha_0$,
then the estimator $\hat{\theta}(\hat{\alpha}) = \arg\min_{\theta \in \Theta} \hat{Q}_n(\theta, \hat{\alpha})$ converges in probability to θ_0.

Proof. With $\hat{\alpha}$ consistent it follows by the Slutzky theorem that also the nonstochastic function $Q_0(\theta_0, \hat{\alpha})$ is convergent:

$$\lim_{n\to\infty} P\left(|Q_0(\theta_0, \hat{\alpha}) - Q_0(\theta_0, \alpha_0)| < \varepsilon_2\right) = 1 \qquad \text{with } \varepsilon_2 > 0 \qquad (E.4)$$

First it is shown that $Q_0(\hat{\theta}, \hat{\alpha})$ converges to $Q_0(\theta_0, \alpha_0)$ from above. Notice that

$$Q_0(\hat{\theta}, \hat{\alpha}) - Q_0(\theta_0, \alpha_0) = \left(Q_0(\hat{\theta}, \hat{\alpha}) - \hat{Q}_n(\hat{\theta}, \hat{\alpha})\right) + \left(\hat{Q}_n(\hat{\theta}, \hat{\alpha}) - \hat{Q}_n(\theta_0, \hat{\alpha})\right)$$
$$+ \left(\hat{Q}_n(\theta_0, \hat{\alpha}) - Q_0(\theta_0, \hat{\alpha})\right) + (Q_0(\theta_0, \hat{\alpha}) - Q_0(\theta_0, \alpha_0)).$$

From the uniform convergence assumption (E.3) together with (E.2) it follows that w.p.a.1 $\left|\hat{Q}_n(\hat{\theta}, \hat{\alpha}) - Q_0(\hat{\theta}, \hat{\alpha})\right| < \varepsilon_1$ and w.p.a.1 $\left|\hat{Q}_n(\theta_0, \hat{\alpha}) - Q_0(\theta_0, \hat{\alpha})\right| < \varepsilon_1$. From (E.4) it follows that w.p.a.1 $|Q_0(\theta_0, \hat{\alpha}) - Q_0(\theta_0, \alpha_0)| < \varepsilon_2$. The term $\hat{Q}_n(\hat{\theta}, \hat{\alpha}) - \hat{Q}_n(\theta_0, \hat{\alpha})$ is negative by the definition of the estimator with $\hat{Q}_n(\hat{\theta}, \hat{\alpha}) = \min_{\theta \in \Theta} \hat{Q}_n(\theta, \hat{\alpha})$. Thus the first, third and fourth terms are w.p.a.1 smaller than an arbitrarily small number and the second term is smaller than zero. Accordingly it follows with $\varepsilon \equiv \max(\varepsilon_1, \varepsilon_2)$

$$Q_0(\hat{\theta}, \hat{\alpha}) < Q_0(\theta_0, \alpha_0) + 3\varepsilon \qquad \text{w.p.a.1.} \qquad (E.5)$$

The following reasoning is similar in spirit to that of Theorem 2.1 in Newey and McFadden (1994). Let $\mathcal{N}$ be any open subset of Θ with $\theta_0 \in \mathcal{N}$ and let $\mathcal{N}^c = \Theta \setminus \mathcal{N}$ be its complement. From $\mathcal{N}^c$ compact and $Q_0(\theta, \alpha)$ continuous it follows that $\inf_{\theta \in \mathcal{N}^c} Q_0(\theta, \alpha_0) > Q_0(\theta_0, \alpha_0)$, since θ_0 uniquely minimizes Q_0. Choosing $3\varepsilon = \inf_{\theta \in \mathcal{N}^c} Q_0(\theta, \alpha_0) - Q_0(\theta_0, \alpha_0)$ it follows w.p.a.1 that $Q_0(\hat{\theta}, \hat{\alpha}) < \inf_{\theta \in \mathcal{N}^c} Q_0(\theta, \alpha_0)$. This means that w.p.a.1 $\hat{\theta}$ cannot be element of $\mathcal{N}^c$ and thus $\hat{\theta} \in \mathcal{N}$ must hold. Hence for sufficiently small ε all open subsets of Θ which contain θ_0 also w.p.a.1 contain $\hat{\theta}$, and all subsets of Θ which do not contain θ_0 also w.p.a.1 do not contain $\hat{\theta}$. Thus $\hat{\theta}$ converges in probability to θ_0.

Now the sufficient conditions of Corollary 5 are specified for a generic GMM estimator.

Corollary 6. *Suppose*
(a) $\hat{\alpha}$ is a consistent estimator of α_0 and $B(\alpha_0)$ a ball around α_0, such that $\lim_{n\to\infty} P(\hat{\alpha} \in B(\alpha_0)) = 1$,
(b) the data Z_i are iid, $\hat{W} \xrightarrow{p} W$, where W a positive semidefinite matrix,
(c) $W E\left[g(Z, \theta, \alpha)\right] = 0$ if and only if $\theta = \theta_0$ and $\alpha = \alpha_0$,
(d) $\theta_0 \in \Theta$, with Θ compact,

(e) $g(Z, \theta, \alpha)$ is continuous in θ and α

(f) $E \left(\sup\limits_{\alpha \in B(\alpha_0)} \sup\limits_{\theta \in \Theta} \|g(Z, \theta, \alpha)\| \right) < \infty,$

then the GMM estimator of $\hat{Q}_n(\theta, \hat{\alpha}) = \left(\frac{1}{n} \sum g(Z_i, \theta, \hat{\alpha}) \right)' \hat{W} \left(\frac{1}{n} \sum g(Z_i, \theta, \hat{\alpha}) \right)$ with limit function $Q_0(\theta, \alpha) = (Eg(Z, \theta, \alpha))' W (Eg(Z, \theta, \alpha))$ satisfies the conditions of Corollary 5 and the GMM estimator is consistent.

Proof. Showing that the conditions of Corollary 5 are satisfied follows with only minor modifications Lemma 2.4 and Theorem 2.6 of Newey and McFadden (1994) and is omitted.

Proof (of Theorem 1). It must be shown that the conditions (a) to (f) of Corollary 6 are satisfied by the assumptions (i) to (vi) of Theorem 1. Define

$$\hat{\alpha}^r(\hat{\mathbf{m}}^r_{VL}, \hat{p}^r) = n^{-1} \sum_i \hat{\mathbf{m}}^r_{VL}(\hat{p}^r(X_i)) \cdot 1(D_i \neq r) \cdot 1(X_i \in \hat{S}^r),$$

as the column vector of length VL. Each element $\hat{\alpha}^r_{vl}(\hat{\mathbf{m}}^r_{VL}, \hat{p}^r)$ converges under assumption (v) in probability to

$$\plim_{n \to \infty} \hat{\alpha}^r_{vl}(\hat{\mathbf{m}}^r_{VL}, \hat{p}^r) = E\left[Y^r_v \cdot \Lambda_l(X) \cdot 1(D \neq r) \cdot 1(X \in S^r) \right] \equiv \alpha^r_{vl,0}.$$

Hence condition (a) is satisfied. Denote $\alpha^r_0 = \plim \hat{\alpha}^r(\hat{\mathbf{m}}^r_{VL}, \hat{p}^r)$. The moment function can be written as

$$g^r_n = n^{-1} \sum_i \begin{pmatrix} A^r(X_i) \cdot (Y_i - \varphi^r(X_i, \theta^r)) \cdot 1(D_i = r) \\ \Lambda(X_i) \otimes \varphi^r(X_i, \theta^r) 1(D_i \neq r) 1(X_i \in \hat{S}^r) \end{pmatrix} - \begin{pmatrix} 0_k \\ \hat{\alpha}^r(\hat{\mathbf{m}}^r_{VL}, \hat{p}^r) \end{pmatrix},$$

and continuity of g^r_n depends only on the specification φ^r. Thus condition (e) is satisfied by assumption (i). Furthermore, conditions (b) and (d) are satisfied by assumptions (vi) and (ii).

The identification condition (c) is implied by assumption (ii): Since the upper part of the moment vector is independent of α it can only have expectation zero if it represents the true mean function. By assumption (ii) this can only be the case if $\theta = \theta_0$. Yet in this case the lower part of the moment vector can only be zero if $\alpha = \alpha_0$.

Condition (f) is implied by assumptions (iii) and (iv):

$$E \sup_{\alpha^r \in B(\alpha_0^r)} \sup_{\theta^r \in \Theta^r} \|g(Z, \theta^r, \alpha^r)\|$$

$$= E \sup_{\alpha^r \in B(\alpha_0^r)} \sup_{\theta^r \in \Theta^r} \left\| \begin{pmatrix} \frac{1}{n}\sum_i \begin{pmatrix} A^r(X) \cdot (Y - \varphi^r(X,\theta^r)) \cdot 1(D=r) \\ \Lambda(X) \otimes \varphi^r(X,\theta^r) 1(D\neq r) 1(X \in \hat{S}^r) - \alpha_0^r \end{pmatrix} \\ + \begin{pmatrix} 0_k \\ \alpha_0^r - \alpha^r \end{pmatrix} \end{pmatrix} \right\|$$

$$\leq E \sup_{\alpha^r \in B(\alpha_0^r)} \sup_{\theta^r \in \Theta^r} \left\| \begin{pmatrix} A^r(X) \cdot (Y - \varphi^r(X,\theta^r)) \cdot 1(D=r) \\ \Lambda(X) \otimes \varphi^r(X,\theta^r) 1(D \neq r) 1(X \in \hat{S}^r) - \alpha_0^r \end{pmatrix} \right\|$$

$$+ E \sup_{\alpha^r \in B(\alpha_0^r)} \sup_{\theta^r \in \Theta^r} \left\| \begin{pmatrix} 0_k \\ \alpha_0^r - \alpha^r \end{pmatrix} \right\|$$

$$= E \sup_{\theta^r \in \Theta^r} \left\| \begin{pmatrix} A^r(X) \cdot (Y - \varphi^r(X,\theta^r)) \cdot 1(D=r) \\ \Lambda(X) \otimes \varphi^r(X,\theta^r) 1(D \neq r) 1(X \in \hat{S}^r) - \alpha_0^r \end{pmatrix} \right\|$$

$$+ E \sup_{\alpha^r \in B(\alpha_0^r)} \|\alpha_0^r - \alpha^r\|$$

$$\leq E \sup_{\theta^r \in \Theta^r} \left(\begin{array}{c} \|A^r(X) \cdot (Y - \varphi^r(X,\theta^r)) \cdot 1(D=r)\| \\ + \sum_l^L |\Lambda_l(X)\varphi^r(X,\theta^r) 1(D \neq r) 1(X \in \hat{S}^r) - \alpha_{l,0}^r| \end{array} \right)$$

$$+ E \sup_{\alpha^r \in B(\alpha_0^r)} \|\alpha_0^r - \alpha^r\|$$

$$\leq E \sup_{\theta^r \in \Theta^r} (\|A^r(X) \cdot (Y - \varphi^r(X,\theta^r))\|)$$

$$+ L \cdot E\max_l \sup_{\theta^r \in \Theta^r} |\Lambda_l(X) \cdot \varphi^r(X,\theta^r) \cdot 1(D \neq r) 1(X \in \hat{S}^r) - \alpha_{l,0}^r|$$

$$+ E \sup_{\alpha^r \in B(\alpha_0^r)} \|\alpha_0^r - \alpha^r\|$$

if all these terms have finite expectations. The last term is finite, as the size of the ball $B(\alpha_0)$ around α_0 becomes arbitrarily small. Since the expectations in the first two terms are bounded in each subpopulation by assumption (iii) and since the number of subpopulations L is finite by (iv), the whole expression is finite and condition (f) is satisfied.

To establish asymptotic normality I draw on the results of Heckman, Ichimura, and Todd (1998) for asymptotically linear estimators with trimming (as introduced in Section 2.3). The estimator $\hat{m}_{vl}^r(\hat{p}^r(x))$ is asymptotically linear with trimming if it can be written as

$$[\hat{m}_{vl}^r(\hat{p}^r(x)) - m_{vl}^r(p^r(x))] \cdot \Lambda_l(x) 1(x \in \hat{S}^r) =$$

$$n_{l,r}^{-1} \sum_j \Psi_{vl,m}^r(Y_j^r, D_j, X_j; x) + n^{-1} \sum_j \Psi_{vl,p}^r(Y_j^r, D_j, X_j; x) + \hat{b}_{vl}^r(x) + \hat{R}_{vl}^r(x),$$

with $E[\Psi_{vl,p}^r(Y_j^r, D_j, X_j; X)|X = x] = 0$ and $E[\Psi_{vl,m}^r(Y_j^r, D_j, X_j; X)|X = x] = 0$. Furthermore $plim \; n_{l,r}^{-1/2} \sum \hat{b}_{vl}^r(X_j) = b_{vl}^r < \infty$ and $n_{l,r}^{-1/2} \sum \hat{R}_{vl}^r(X_j) =$

$o_p(1)$, where $n_{l,r}$ is the number of participants in treatment r who belong to the l-th subpopulation. $\Psi^r_{vl,p}$ and $\Psi^r_{vl,m}$ are the mean-zero influence functions stemming from the estimation of the participation probability $p^r(\cdot)$ and the regression curve $m^r_{vl}(\cdot)$, respectively. These local influence functions may depend on the sample size, e.g. through bandwidth parameters that converge to zero with increasing sample size. Corollaries 2 and 3 give conditions on the estimators $\hat{p}^r$ and $\hat{m}^r_{vl}$.

Theorem 2 (Asymptotic Normality). *If the conditions of Theorem 1 hold and*
(i) the estimator $\hat{m}^r_{vl}(\hat{p}^r(x))$ is asymptotically linear with trimming in all subpopulations l and with respect to all outcome variables v,
(ii) $VL \cdot Var\left(\Psi^r_{vl,m}(Y^r_j, D_j, X_j; X_i)\right)$ and $VL \cdot Var\left(\Psi^r_{vl,p}(Y^r_j, D_j, X_j; X_i)\right)$
are of order $o(n)$ for each outcome variable v and each subpopulation l,
(iii) $\varphi^r(x, \theta^r)$ is continuously differentiable with bounded derivative in a neighbourhood of θ^r_0,
$E\left[\|A^r(X)(Y - \varphi^r(X, \theta^r)\|^2\right] < \infty$, *and $G^{r\prime}W^rG^r$ nonsingular, where G^r is the expected gradient of the moment vector,*
(iv) $\lim\limits_{n\to\infty} \frac{n_{l,r}}{n} = \lambda_{l,r}$ with $0 < \lambda_{l,r} < \infty$, for each subpopulation $l = 1, .., L$,
then the GMM estimator $\hat{\theta}^r = \arg\min\limits_{\theta^r} g^r_n(\theta^r, \hat{\mathbf{m}}^r_{VL}, \hat{p}^r)'\hat{W}^r g^r_n(\theta^r, \hat{\mathbf{m}}^r_{VL}, \hat{p}^r)$ with moment vector (4.9) is asymptotically normal distributed

$$n^{\frac{1}{2}}(\hat{\theta}^r - \theta^r_0) \xrightarrow{d} N\left(\mathcal{B}, (G^{r\prime}W^rG^r)^{-1}G^{r\prime}W^r \cdot E[J^r J^{r\prime}] \cdot W^rG^r(G^{r\prime}W^rG^r)^{-1}\right)$$
$$(\text{E.6})$$

where

$$\mathcal{B} = -(G^{r\prime}W^rG^r)^{-1}G^{r\prime}W^r\mathbf{b}^r_{VL}$$

and

$$J^r = g^r(Y, D, X, \theta^r_0, \mathbf{m}^r_{VL}) - \begin{pmatrix} \mathbf{0}_k \\ E[\Psi^r_{11,p}(Y, D, X; X_2)1(D_2 \neq r)|Y, D, X] \\ \vdots \\ E[\Psi^r_{VL,p}(Y, D, X; X_2)1(D_2 \neq r)|Y, D, X] \end{pmatrix}$$
$$- \begin{pmatrix} \mathbf{0}_k \\ \lambda^{-1}_{1,r} \cdot E[\Psi^r_{11,m}(Y, D, X; X_2)1(D_2 \neq r)|Y, D, X] \\ \vdots \\ \lambda^{-1}_{L,r} \cdot E[\Psi^r_{VL,m}(Y, D, X; X_2)1(D_2 \neq r)|Y, D, X] \end{pmatrix},$$

where the expectation operator is with respect to X_2 and D_2, and $\mathbf{0}_k$ is a column vector of zeros of length k.

Remark 1. The asymptotic bias $\mathcal{B}$ could be eliminated by undersmoothing, see Heckman, Ichimura, and Todd (1998).

The matrix $E[J^r J^{r\prime}]$ can be estimated by the sample average $n^{-1} \sum J_i^r J_i^{r\prime}$. Its inverse $\Omega^r = [E J^r J^{r\prime}]^{-1}$ can be used as the weighting matrix in a second step GMM estimator. The computation of J_i^r requires the conditional expected values of the influence functions $\Psi_{vl,p}$ and $\Psi_{vl,m}$, which again can be estimated by sample averages, using the appropriate expressions for $\Psi_{vl,p}$ and $\Psi_{vl,m}$ according to the specific estimators of p^r and m_{vl}^r used.

Proof (of Theorem 2). The estimator $\hat{\theta}_n^r = \arg\min_{\theta^r} g_n^{r\prime} \hat{W}^r g_n^r$ with moment vector (4.9) can be expressed by its first order condition (with superscripts r suppressed to improve readability) as

$$G_n(\hat{\theta}, \hat{p})' \hat{W} \cdot g_n(\theta, \hat{\mathbf{m}}_{VL}, \hat{p}) = 0. \qquad (E.7)$$

$G_n = \frac{\partial g_n(\cdot)}{\partial \theta'}$ is the gradient of g_n with respect to θ and does not depend on $\hat{\mathbf{m}}_{VL}$. Applying the mean value theorem to $g_n(\theta, \hat{\mathbf{m}}_{VL}, \hat{p})$ about the true coefficient vector θ_0 yields, with $\bar{\theta}$ on the line between $\hat{\theta}$ and θ_0,

$$G_n'(\hat{\theta}, \hat{p}) \hat{W} \cdot \left[g_n(\theta_0, \hat{\mathbf{m}}_{VL}, \hat{p}) + G_n(\bar{\theta}, \hat{p}) \cdot (\hat{\theta} - \theta_0) \right] = 0. \qquad (E.8)$$

Solving for $\hat{\theta} - \theta_0$ gives

$$n^{\frac{1}{2}}(\hat{\theta} - \theta_0) = - \left(G_n(\hat{\theta}, \hat{p})' \hat{W} G_n(\bar{\theta}, \hat{p}) \right)^{-1} G_n(\hat{\theta}, \hat{p})' \hat{W} \cdot n^{\frac{1}{2}} g_n(\theta_0, \hat{\mathbf{m}}_{VL}, \hat{p}). \qquad (E.9)$$

Turning first to the term $n^{\frac{1}{2}} g_n(\theta_0, \hat{\mathbf{m}}_{VL}, \hat{p})$. Inserting (4.9) gives

$$n g_n(\theta_0, \hat{\mathbf{m}}_{VL}, \hat{p}) \qquad (E.10)$$

$$= \sum g(Z_i, \theta_0, \mathbf{m}_{VL}, p) +$$

$$\sum \left(\overset{0_k}{(\Lambda(X_i) \otimes \varphi(X_i, \theta_0) - \mathbf{m}_{VL}(p(X_i)))} 1(D_i \neq r)(1(X_i \in \hat{S}) - 1(X_i \in S)) \right)$$

$$- \sum \left(\overset{0_k}{(\hat{\mathbf{m}}_{VL}(\hat{p}(X_i)) - \mathbf{m}_{VL}(p(X_i)))} \cdot 1(D_i \neq r) \cdot 1(X_i \in \hat{S}) \right),$$

where $Z_i = (Y_i, D_i, X_i)$, and $\mathbf{m}_{VL}$, p and S denote the (true) nonstochastic limit functions of $\hat{\mathbf{m}}_{VL}$, $\hat{p}$ and $\hat{S}$. If $\mathbf{m}_{VL}$ and the participation probability p were known, only the first term would remain and the usual GMM properties would apply, see e.g. Newey and McFadden (1994). With $\mathbf{m}_{VL}$ and p estimated, the second term accounts for the estimation of the support and the third term takes account for the estimation of $\mathbf{m}_{VL}$. The second term is $o_p(1)$ as shown in Heckman, Ichimura, and Todd (1998, p. 291). Inserting the definition (4.8) of $\hat{\mathbf{m}}_{VL}$, expression (E.10) can be written as

$$n^{\frac{1}{2}} g_n(\theta_0, \hat{\mathbf{m}}_{VL}, \hat{p})$$

$$= n^{-\frac{1}{2}} \sum g(Z_i, \theta_0, \mathbf{m}_{VL}, p) + o_p(1)$$

$$- n^{-\frac{1}{2}} \sum_i \begin{pmatrix} \mathbf{0}_k \\ (\hat{m}_{11}(\hat{p}(X_i)) - m_{11}(p(X_i))) \cdot \Lambda_1(X_i) \mathbf{1}(D_i \neq r) \mathbf{1}(X_i \in \hat{S}) \\ \vdots \\ (\hat{m}_{VL}(\hat{p}(X_i)) - m_{VL}(p(X_i))) \cdot \Lambda_L(X_i) \mathbf{1}(D_i \neq r) \mathbf{1}(X_i \in \hat{S}) \end{pmatrix},$$

and with $\hat{m}_{vl}^r(\hat{p}^r(\cdot))$ asymptotically linear with trimming this equals

$$= n^{-\frac{1}{2}} \sum g(Z_i, \theta_0, \mathbf{m}_{VL}, p) + o_p(1) \tag{E.11}$$

$$-n^{-\frac{1}{2}} \sum_i \begin{pmatrix} \mathbf{0}_k \\ \left[n^{-1} \sum_j \Psi_{11,p}(Y_j, D_j, X_j; X_i) + \hat{b}_{11}(X_i) + \hat{R}_{11}(X_i) \right] \\ \vdots \\ \left[n^{-1} \sum_j \Psi_{VL,p}(Y_j, D_j, X_j; X_i) + \hat{b}_{VL}(X_i) + \hat{R}_{VL}(X_i) \right] \end{pmatrix}$$
$$\cdot \mathbf{1}(D_i \neq r)$$

$$-n^{-\frac{1}{2}} \sum_i \begin{pmatrix} \mathbf{0}_k \\ \left[n_{1,r}^{-1} \sum_j \Psi_{11,m}(Y_j, D_j, X_j; X_i) \right] \cdot \mathbf{1}(D_i \neq r) \\ \vdots \\ \left[n_{L,r}^{-1} \sum_j \Psi_{VL,m}(Y_j, D_j, X_j; X_i) \right] \cdot \mathbf{1}(D_i \neq r) \end{pmatrix}.$$

Examine the vl-th element in the last two terms of (E.11) in more detail:

$$n^{-\frac{1}{2}} \sum_i \left[n^{-1} \sum_j \Psi_{vl,p}(Y_j, D_j, X_j; X_i) + \hat{b}_{vl}(X_i) + \hat{R}_{vl}(X_i) \right] \cdot \mathbf{1}(D_i \neq r)$$

$$+ n^{-\frac{1}{2}} \sum_i \left[n_{l,r}^{-1} \sum_j \Psi_{vl,m}(Y_j, D_j, X_j; X_i) \right] \cdot \mathbf{1}(D_i \neq r), \quad \text{(E.12)}$$

which can be reformulated as

$$= \frac{n^{\frac{3}{2}}}{2n_{l,r}} \left\{ n^{-2} \sum_i \sum_j \left(\Psi_{vl,m}^{j,i} D_i^{\neq r} + \Psi_{vl,m}^{i,j} D_j^{\neq r} \right) \right\}$$

$$+ \frac{n^{\frac{1}{2}}}{2} \left\{ n^{-2} \sum_i \sum_j \left(\Psi_{vl,p}^{j,i} D_i^{\neq r} + \Psi_{vl,p}^{i,j} D_j^{\neq r} \right) \right\}$$

$$+ n^{-\frac{1}{2}} \sum_i \hat{b}_{vl}(X_i) D_i^{\neq r} + n^{-\frac{1}{2}} \sum_i \hat{R}_{vl}(X_i) D_i^{\neq r},$$

where $\Psi_{vl,m}(Y_j, D_j, X_j; X_i)$ and $\Psi_{vl,p}(Y_j, D_j, X_j; X_i)$ are abbreviated by $\Psi_{vl,m}^{j,i}$ and $\Psi_{vl,p}^{j,i}$, respectively, and $D_i^{\neq r}$ stands for $1(D_i \neq r)$. The last term converges to zero and the third term to a nonstochastic bias term. Hence the asymptotic distribution is driven by the first two terms. These terms are von Mises statistics (e.g. see Serfling 1980) and according to Corollary 4 are asymptotically equivalent to the projections of their corresponding U-statistics if

$$E \left\| \Psi_{vl,m}^{j,i} D_i^{\neq r} + \Psi_{vl,m}^{i,j} D_j^{\neq r} + \Psi_{vl,p}^{j,i} D_i^{\neq r} + \Psi_{vl,p}^{i,j} D_j^{\neq r} \right\|^2 = o(n) \qquad (E.13)$$

holds. Since all influence functions are mean-zero, the left-hand side of (E.13) equals

$$= Var \left(\Psi_{vl,m}^{j,i} D_i^{\neq r} + \Psi_{vl,m}^{i,j} D_j^{\neq r} + \Psi_{vl,p}^{j,i} D_i^{\neq r} + \Psi_{vl,p}^{i,j} D_j^{\neq r} \right)$$

$$\leq 16 \cdot \max \left(Var \left(\Psi_{vl,m}^{j,i} D_i^{\neq r} \right), Var \left(\Psi_{vl,p}^{j,i} D_i^{\neq r} \right) \right)$$

$$\leq 16 \cdot \max \left(Var \left(\Psi_{vl,m}^{j,i} \right), Var \left(\Psi_{vl,p}^{j,i} \right) \right) = o(n),$$

as implied by assumption (ii). Thus the U-statistics projection theorem (Corollary 4) can be applied and the term (E.12) is equivalent to

$$= \frac{n^{\frac{1}{2}}}{n_{l,r}} \sum_i E \left[\Psi_{vl,m}(Y_i, D_i, X_i; X_j) 1(D_j \neq r) | Y_i, D_i, X_i \right]$$

$$+ n^{-\frac{1}{2}} \sum_i E \left[\Psi_{vl,p}(Y_i, D_i, X_i; X_j) 1(D_j \neq r) | Y_i, D_i, X_i \right]$$

$$+ n^{-\frac{1}{2}} \sum_i \hat{b}_{vl}(X_i) D_j^{\neq r} + n^{-\frac{1}{2}} \sum_i \hat{R}_{vl}(X_i) D_j^{\neq r} + o_p \left(\frac{n}{n_{l,r}} \right) + o_p(1),$$

where $n_{l,r}/n$ converges to $\lambda_{l,r}$ by assumption (iv). The asymptotic distribution of this expression depends on the first three terms. The first two terms determine the asymptotic variance and the third term converges in probability to the asymptotic bias.

Applying the U-statistic projection theorem simultaneously to all outcome variables v and all subpopulations l in expression (E.11) requires that the full influence function vector with respect to all outcome variables and all subpopulations has expected squared norm of order $o(n)$. In other words, (E.13) must hold for the *vectors* Ψ_m and Ψ_p. This is satisfied by assumption (i) since the squared norm of a vector is smaller or equal than the sum of the squared norms of all vector elements, which are $o(n)$ as shown in (E.13).

Having replaced the double sums by single sums a central limit theorem can be applied to (E.11). Define J_i as

$$J_i = g(Z_i, \theta_0, \mathbf{m}_{VL}, p) - \begin{pmatrix} \mathbf{0}_k \\ E[\Psi_{11,p}(Y_i, D_i, X_i; X_j)1(D_j \neq r)|Y_i, D_i, X_i] \\ \vdots \\ E[\Psi_{VL,p}(Y_i, D_i, X_i; X_j)1(D_j \neq r)|Y_i, D_i, X_i] \end{pmatrix}$$

$$- \begin{pmatrix} \mathbf{0}_k \\ \lambda_{1,r}^{-1} \cdot E[\Psi_{11,m}(Y_i, D_i, X_i; X_j)1(D_j \neq r)|Y_i, D_i, X_i] \\ \vdots \\ \lambda_{L,r}^{-1} \cdot E[\Psi_{VL,m}(Y_i, D_i, X_i; X_j)1(D_j \neq r)|Y_i, D_i, X_i] \end{pmatrix}.$$

Imposing the regularity conditions that $E[J_i J_i'] < \infty \; \forall i$, that all mixed third moments of the multivariate distribution are finite, that $E[JJ'] = \lim n^{-1} \sum E[J_i J_i']$ is a finite and positive definite matrix, and that $\lim_{n \to \infty} \left(\sum_{i=1}^{n} E[J_i J_i'] \right)^{-1} E[J_i J_i'] = 0 \; \forall i$, it follows by the multivariate Lindeberg-Feller central limit theorem (Greene 1997, Theorem 4.14) that the moment function (4.9) is asymptotically normal distributed:

$$n^{\frac{1}{2}} g_n(\theta_0, \hat{\mathbf{m}}_{VL}, \hat{p}) \xrightarrow{d} N(\mathbf{b}_{VL}, E[JJ']), \tag{E.14}$$

where $\mathbf{b}_{VL}$ is a vector of asymptotic bias terms.

It remains to show that G_n converges in probability to the nonstochastic expected gradient G. The gradient of the moment vector (4.9) is

$$G_n(\hat{\theta}, \hat{p}) = \frac{1}{n} \sum_i \begin{pmatrix} -A(X_i) \cdot \frac{\partial \varphi(X_i, \theta)}{\partial \theta'} \cdot 1(D_i = r) \\ A(X_i) \otimes \frac{\partial \varphi(X_i, \theta)}{\partial \theta'} \cdot 1(D_i \neq r) \cdot 1(X_i \in \hat{S}) \end{pmatrix}$$

$$= \frac{1}{n} \sum_i \begin{pmatrix} -A(X_i) \cdot \frac{\partial \varphi(X_i, \theta)}{\partial \theta'} \cdot 1(D_i = r) \\ A(X_i) \otimes \frac{\partial \varphi(X_i, \theta)}{\partial \theta'} 1(D_i \neq r) \cdot 1(X_i \in S) \end{pmatrix}$$

$$+ \frac{1}{n} \sum_i \begin{pmatrix} \mathbf{0}_k \\ A(X_i) \otimes \frac{\partial \varphi(X_i, \theta)}{\partial \theta'} 1(D_i \neq r) \cdot (1(X_i \in \hat{S}) - 1(X_i \in S)) \end{pmatrix}$$

The latter term converges to zero since the first derivative of φ is bounded by assumption (iii) and $1(X_i \in \hat{S})$ converges to $1(X_i \in S)$. The first term converges to the expected gradient G by a law of large numbers. Hence the GMM estimator $\hat{\theta}$ is asymptotically normal with

$$n^{\frac{1}{2}}(\hat{\theta} - \theta_0) \xrightarrow{d}$$
$$N\left(-(G'WG)^{-1}G'W\mathbf{b}_{VL}, (G'WG)^{-1}G'WE[JJ']WG(G'WG)^{-1} \right).$$

Influence Functions for Particular Estimators

For estimating $E[JJ']$ the influence functions need to be known. These are derived below for Maximum Likelihood estimation of the participation probabilities p^r and for kernel or local linear estimation of m^r. Maximum Likelihood estimators of the coefficients β of a parametric regression model $\mu(x, \beta)$ with likelihood function $l(Y, X; \beta)$ can be written in asymptotically linear form as

$$n^{\frac{1}{2}}(\hat{\beta} - \beta_0) = n^{-\frac{1}{2}} \sum_{j=1}^{n} \left[-E \frac{\partial^2 \ln l(Y, X; \beta_0)}{\partial \beta \partial \beta'} \right]^{-1} \frac{\partial \ln l(Y_j, X_j; \beta_0)}{\partial \beta} + o_p(1),$$

(E.15)

see Newey and McFadden (1994, p. 2141 ff). This expression represents the 'global' influence function for the coefficients β. It is global in the sense that it affects the estimated conditional mean function $\mu(x, \hat{\beta})$ at all points x. To obtain an expression for the estimated conditional mean $\mu(x, \hat{\beta})$ at a particular point, $\mu(\cdot)$ is expanded about β_0 to obtain the local asymptotically linear representation

$$n^{-\frac{1}{2}} \left(\mu(x, \hat{\beta}) - \mu(x, \beta_0) \right)$$

$$= -n^{-\frac{1}{2}} \frac{\partial \mu(x, \beta_0)}{\partial \beta'} [EH]^{-1} \sum_{j=1}^{n} \frac{\partial \ln l(Y_j, X_j; \beta_0)}{\partial \beta} + o_p(1), \quad \text{(E.16)}$$

where $EH = E \frac{\partial^2 \ln l(Y, X; \beta_0)}{\partial \beta \partial \beta'}$ is the expected Hessian at β_0, as in (E.15). Hence the parametric Maximum Likelihood estimate is asymptotically linear with zero local bias.

The local influence function for *kernel* and *local linear regression* at interior points in the one-dimensional regression setting is (Heckman, Ichimura, and Todd 1998)

$$\psi_m(Y_j^r, p^r(X_j); p^r(x))$$

$$= \left(Y_j^r - E[Y_j^r | p^r(X_j), D_j = r] \right) \frac{K \left(\frac{p^r(X_j) - p^r}{h_{n_r}} \right)}{\underset{X_j|D=r}{E} K \left(\frac{p^r(X_j) - p^r}{h_{n_r}} \right)} 1(D_j = r) 1(p^r(x) > 0)$$

$$= \left(Y_j^r - m^r(p^r(X_j)) \right) \frac{1}{h_{n_r}} \frac{K \left(\frac{p^r(X_j) - p^r}{h_{n_r}} \right)}{\underset{X_j|D=r}{E} \hat{f}_{p^r|D=r}(p^r(x))} 1(D_j = r) 1(p^r(x) > 0),$$

where $\hat{f}_{p^r|D=r}(\rho) = \frac{1}{n_r h_{n_r}} \sum_l K((p^r(x_l) - \rho)/h_{n_r}) 1(D_l = r)$ is a kernel

density estimate of $f_{p^r|D=r}$. Noting that by continuity of the density function $\int h^{-1} K \left(\frac{p^r(u) - p^r(x)}{h} \right) \cdot f_{p|D=r}(p^r(u)) du$ converges to $f_{p|D=r}(p^r(x)) \cdot \int K(u) du$

(Pagan and Ullah (1999), p. 362, 364 or Parzen (1962)) and since the kernel function is supposed to integrate to one, the influence function converges to

$$\psi_m(Y_j^r, p^r(X_j); p^r(x)) \rightarrow$$

$$(Y_j^r - m^r(p^r(X_j))) \frac{1}{h_{n_r}} \frac{K\left(\frac{p^r(X_j)-p^r}{h_{n_r}}\right)}{f_{p^r|D=r}(p^r(x))} 1(D_j = r)1(p^r(x) > 0). \quad \text{(E.17)}$$

Combination of Both Estimators

If the participation probability is estimated by Maximum Likelihood and the regression function $m_{vl}^r(\hat{p}^r)$ is estimated by kernel or local linear regression, the combined influence function in the asymptotically linear representation with trimming is

$$[\hat{m}_{vl}^r(\hat{p}^r(x)) - m_{vl}^r(p^r(x))] \cdot \Lambda_l(x)1(x \in \hat{S}^r) =$$

$$n_{l,r}^{-1} \sum_j \Psi_{vl,m}^r(Y_j^r, D_j, X_j; x) + n^{-1} \sum_j \Psi_{vl,p}^r(Y_j^r, D_j, X_j; x) + \hat{b}_{vl}^r(x) + \hat{R}_{vl}^r(x),$$

for the outcome variable v and the subpopulation l defined as $\{x|\Lambda_l(x) = 1\}$, where

$$\Psi_{vl,p}^r(Y_j^r, D_j, X_j; x)$$
$$= -\frac{\partial m_{vl}^r(p^r(x))}{\partial p^r} \frac{\partial p^r(x, \beta_0)}{\partial \beta'} [EH]^{-1} \frac{\partial \ln l(D_j, X_j; \beta_0)}{\partial \beta} \Lambda_l(x)1(x \in S^r),$$

with $p^r(x)$ parametrically specified as $p^r(x, \beta_0)$ and EH the expected Hessian at β_0. Further

$$\Psi_{vl,m}^r(Y_j^r, D_j, X_j; x) = \frac{\Lambda_l(X_j)1(D_j = r)}{h_{n_{l,r}}} (Y_{v,j}^r - m_{vl}^r(p^r(X_j)))$$

$$\cdot K\left(\frac{p^r(X_j) - p^r(x)}{h_{n_{l,r}}}\right) \cdot \frac{\Lambda_l(x)1(x \in S^r)}{f_{p^r|D=r,\Lambda_l=1}(p^r(x))}.$$

$f_{p^r|D=r,\Lambda_l=1}(p^r)$ is the density of the participation probability p^r among the participants in treatment r belonging to subpopulation l.

If the participation probability is, for example, estimated by Probit, i.e. $p^r(x, \beta_0) = \Phi(x'\beta_0)$, the influence function $\Psi_{vl,p}^r$ is

$$\Psi_{vl,p}^r(Y_j^r, D_j, X_j; x)$$
$$= \frac{\partial m_{vl}^r(p^r(x))}{\partial p^r} \phi(x'\beta_0)x' \left(E\left[\frac{\phi^2(X'\beta_0)XX'}{\Phi(X_j'\beta_0)\left(1 - \Phi(X_j'\beta_0)\right)}\right]\right)^{-1}$$

$$\cdot [1(D_j = r) - \Phi(X_j'\beta_0)] \frac{\phi(X_j'\beta_0)X_j}{\Phi(X_j'\beta_0)\left(1 - \Phi(X_j'\beta_0)\right)} \Lambda_l(x)1(x \in S^r).$$

Table E.1. Power of J-tests when parametric specification is incorrect, Ymodel 1

Y-model 1		n=500						n=2000					
		φ_0		φ_2		φ_3		φ_0		φ_2		φ_3	
Tests		10%	5%	10%	5%	10%	5%	10%	5%	10%	5%	10%	5%
L=1	J_1	100.0	100.0	97.8	96.3	100.0	100.0	100.0	100.0	100.0	100.0	100.0	100.0
	LM_1	100.0	100.0	96.7	91.5	100.0	100.0	100.0	100.0	100.0	100.0	100.0	100.0
	J_2	99.8	98.8	94.8	88.5	99.8	99.2	99.9	99.9	99.9	99.9	100.0	100.0
	LM_2	93.6	81.4	71.1	45.2	98.8	95.0	99.9	99.9	99.2	97.4	100.0	100.0
L=4	J_1	100.0	100.0	100.0	100.0	100.0	100.0	100.0	100.0	100.0	100.0	100.0	100.0
	LM_1	100.0	99.8	92.1	86.5	100.0	100.0	100.0	100.0	98.0	96.3	100.0	100.0
	J_2	99.3	98.6	99.1	98.4	99.3	98.1	100.0	100.0	100.0	99.9	100.0	100.0
	LM_2	72.4	55.6	70.4	56.3	68.7	48.6	99.7	99.0	99.4	99.1	99.9	99.6
L=7	J_1	100.0	100.0	100.0	100.0	100.0	100.0	100.0	100.0	100.0	100.0	100.0	100.0
	LM_1	99.7	99.4	93.7	85.9	100.0	99.7	100.0	100.0	100.0	100.0	100.0	100.0
	J_2	99.8	99.3	99.7	99.5	99.1	98.1	100.0	100.0	100.0	100.0	100.0	100.0
	LM_2	59.3	44.1	62.8	47.9	39.6	24.1	99.5	99.0	99.9	99.7	99.4	98.1
L=10	J_1	100.0	100.0	100.0	100.0	100.0	100.0	100.0	100.0	100.0	100.0	100.0	100.0
	LM_1	98.9	97.2	86.3	76.7	99.8	99.3	100.0	100.0	100.0	100.0	100.0	100.0
	J_2	100.0	100.0	100.0	100.0	99.8	99.8	100.0	100.0	100.0	100.0	100.0	100.0
	LM_2	60.2	39.7	75.7	62.8	55.0	38.4	99.9	99.9	100.0	100.0	99.6	99.3
L=14	J_1	100.0	100.0	100.0	100.0	100.0	100.0	100.0	100.0	100.0	100.0	100.0	100.0
	LM_1	97.5	92.9	77.0	69.2	99.6	98.5	100.0	100.0	100.0	100.0	100.0	100.0
	J_2	100.0	100.0	100.0	100.0	100.0	99.9	100.0	100.0	100.0	100.0	100.0	100.0
	LM_2	37.0	24.0	62.9	48.2	53.6	37.5	100.0	99.9	100.0	100.0	100.0	99.6

Note: Rejection frequencies of the J and the LM tests at nominal size 10% (left column) and 5% (right column) for different numbers of nonparametric moments ($L=1,4,7,10,14$). True data generating process corresponds to Y-model 1, and the specifications φ_0, φ_2 and φ_3 are all incorrect. J_1 and LM_1 are the J and the LM tests based on the estimates of the first GMM estimator, $J_1 = J(\hat{\theta}_1)$, $LM_1 = LM(\hat{\theta}_1)$, whereas J_2 and LM_2 are the J and the LM tests based on the estimates of the second GMM estimator, $J_2 = J(\hat{\theta}_2)$, $LM_2 = LM(\hat{\theta}_2)$. 1000 replications.

E.2 Power of the J-tests - Additional Monte Carlo Results

The power of the J-tests in rejecting incorrect parametric specifications is analyzed in the following tables. Tables E.1 to E.3 present the rejection frequencies, where Table E.1 contains the results for Y-model 1, Table E.2 the results for Y-model 2 and E.3 the results for Y-model 3. These tables are structured like the lower part of Table 4.4, but contain the results in the case of misspecification (analogous to Tables 4.1 to 4.3). Generally it is seen that the rejection frequencies are in almost all cases higher than the frequencies obtained under the correct specification (cf. Table 4.4) and, furthermore, are often quite large, particularly at larger sample sizes and when there are only few overidentifying moments L. For $L=1$ and n=2000 the rejection frequencies at the 10% level are in most cases close to 100%, with the exception of specification φ_0 in Y-model 2 where the LM_2 test rejects only with a probability of 43%.

Table E.2. Power of J-tests when parametric specification is incorrect, Ymodel 2

Y-model 2		\multicolumn{6}{c}{n=500}						\multicolumn{6}{c}{n=2000}					
		φ_0		φ_1		φ_3		φ_0		φ_1		φ_3	
Tests		10%	5%	10%	5%	10%	5%	10%	5%	10%	5%	10%	5%
L=1	J_1	37.7	28.9	89.7	87.1	45.5	36.7	62.5	54.7	100.0	99.9	83.7	79.2
	LM_1	51.7	41.5	93.5	91.6	53.3	41.5	71.2	64.6	100.0	100.0	88.9	85.4
	J_2	29.1	19.6	84.7	79.4	33.6	22.0	45.8	36.2	99.4	98.7	71.2	62.9
	LM_2	38.1	27.8	85.0	79.6	43.5	31.1	42.9	35.1	97.3	95.2	76.0	66.5
L=4	J_1	60.4	48.6	93.3	91.6	73.0	63.6	79.3	72.5	100.0	100.0	95.2	92.5
	LM_1	47.5	35.2	90.3	88.0	37.2	22.1	71.9	65.5	100.0	99.9	94.0	89.8
	J_2	47.1	35.1	90.3	85.4	42.8	33.1	70.1	62.0	100.0	99.8	84.0	77.4
	LM_2	30.4	21.6	75.8	69.2	25.2	15.6	52.2	47.1	95.0	91.4	73.9	68.5
L=7	J_1	56.8	47.6	92.1	88.7	80.0	72.5	80.5	74.5	100.0	100.0	96.7	95.1
	LM_1	27.0	16.1	84.7	78.9	18.5	10.1	66.4	59.6	99.9	99.5	82.5	72.3
	J_2	39.0	29.0	85.7	78.6	39.4	29.9	66.2	57.6	99.9	99.8	79.2	72.0
	LM_2	17.3	11.3	63.3	55.4	14.4	9.2	42.4	36.8	89.5	84.8	63.1	55.5
L=10	J_1	75.4	67.6	96.3	94.8	90.6	85.6	94.4	92.1	100.0	100.0	99.7	99.2
	LM_1	21.8	13.0	79.8	71.8	14.5	9.4	73.4	63.2	99.7	99.4	61.7	48.8
	J_2	59.7	49.1	93.0	88.9	59.0	49.0	87.7	82.2	100.0	100.0	92.3	89.6
	LM_2	15.7	11.2	55.6	46.4	13.3	8.8	38.4	32.9	86.0	81.6	57.0	48.3
L=14	J_1	82.1	75.5	98.7	97.9	93.9	89.9	96.3	94.0	100.0	100.0	99.7	99.5
	LM_1	20.6	12.4	81.5	74.2	22.5	15.1	65.5	53.2	99.9	99.7	60.7	49.1
	J_2	69.3	60.6	96.0	93.6	67.5	56.4	90.8	86.8	100.0	100.0	94.6	92.1
	LM_2	16.3	10.4	54.1	44.2	11.2	8.0	34.4	28.3	81.7	75.7	45.9	36.9

Note: See note below Table E.1. True data generating process corresponds to Y-model 2, and the specifications φ_0, φ_1 and φ_3 are all incorrect.

E.3 Additional Tables to Swedish Rehabilitation Programmes

The tables E.4 to E.13 provide subgroup estimates of average counterfactual outcomes, a comparison of the observed and the optimal allocation and a sensitivity analysis for the semiparametric GMM estimator regarding variable choice and the number of subpopulations included.

In Table E.4 the observed treatment outcomes and the nonparametrically estimated counterfactual outcomes for the non-participants are displayed for the 11 populations used in the main specification in Section 4.2. For example, the entry 48.3 (second row/third column) indicates that among the participants in *No rehabilitation* an average re-employment rate of 48.3% was observed. In the fourth column, the expected potential outcome for the *No rehabilitation* treatment for those who had not participated in *No rehabilitation* is given for the different subpopulations. For example, the mean counterfactual employment rate for *No rehabilitation* is 41.5% for the 46-55 years old who participated in any treatment except *No rehabilitation*. These mean counterfactual outcomes are estimated separately for each population by SG matching, with the bandwidth value chosen by least-squares cross-validation from the bandwidth grid $\{0.02, 0.04, ..., 1\}$.

Table E.3. Power of J-tests when parametric specification is incorrect, Ymodel 3

Y-model 3		\multicolumn{6}{c}{n=500}						\multicolumn{6}{c}{n=2000}					
		φ_0		φ_1		φ_2		φ_0		φ_1		φ_2	
Tests		10%	5%	10%	5%	10%	5%	10%	5%	10%	5%	10%	5%
L=1	J_1	100.0	100.0	88.4	84.4	100.0	100.0	100.0	100.0	100.0	100.0	100.0	100.0
	LM_1	100.0	99.9	88.7	84.8	100.0	100.0	100.0	100.0	100.0	100.0	100.0	100.0
	J_2	99.5	98.7	74.5	63.3	100.0	100.0	100.0	100.0	99.8	98.6	100.0	100.0
	LM_2	72.5	52.7	34.6	16.2	96.4	91.1	93.7	87.7	92.5	77.5	100.0	100.0
L=4	J_1	100.0	100.0	90.0	87.1	100.0	100.0	100.0	100.0	100.0	100.0	100.0	100.0
	LM_1	98.1	95.1	75.0	66.9	100.0	99.8	100.0	100.0	99.9	99.7	100.0	100.0
	J_2	99.0	98.1	67.0	52.4	100.0	99.8	100.0	100.0	97.5	94.5	100.0	100.0
	LM_2	59.0	42.2	3.9	1.8	92.3	85.4	76.6	66.4	21.4	6.4	99.8	99.5
L=7	J_1	100.0	100.0	90.4	86.2	100.0	100.0	100.0	100.0	100.0	100.0	100.0	100.0
	LM_1	95.6	90.1	63.2	52.1	99.8	99.3	100.0	100.0	99.7	99.4	100.0	100.0
	J_2	99.2	98.5	62.8	50.7	100.0	99.9	100.0	100.0	99.6	98.8	100.0	100.0
	LM_2	54.2	39.6	2.4	1.2	90.6	81.0	97.4	96.1	9.3	3.4	100.0	100.0
L=10	J_1	100.0	100.0	93.6	90.6	100.0	100.0	100.0	100.0	100.0	100.0	100.0	100.0
	LM_1	92.1	84.4	56.7	45.3	97.3	93.1	100.0	100.0	99.3	99.2	100.0	100.0
	J_2	99.7	98.5	75.4	64.4	100.0	100.0	100.0	100.0	99.6	99.1	100.0	100.0
	LM_2	49.6	36.3	3.6	2.4	78.2	60.1	97.4	95.4	5.6	2.6	100.0	100.0
L=14	J_1	100.0	100.0	93.5	91.3	100.0	100.0	100.0	100.0	100.0	100.0	100.0	100.0
	LM_1	76.9	60.1	45.8	33.3	86.9	74.1	100.0	100.0	99.6	99.4	100.0	100.0
	J_2	99.2	97.9	74.0	62.8	100.0	100.0	100.0	100.0	100.0	100.0	100.0	100.0
	LM_2	29.6	16.9	3.5	1.9	41.4	24.2	96.9	94.3	41.0	29.4	100.0	100.0

Note: See note below Table E.1. True data generating process corresponds to Y-model 3, and the specifications φ_0, φ_1 and φ_2 are all incorrect.

These estimates provide some indications of heterogeneity among individuals: Whereas the re-employment rate for *No rehabilitation* is as high as 52.6% among those participants who had previously been sick for less than 15 days, it is estimated to be only 32.5% among those occupied in agriculture who did not participate in *No rehabilitation*. Regarding *educational* rehabilitation, only 20.2% of the participants with psychiatric problems became immediately re-employed, whereas a counterfactual re-employment rate of above 38% is predicted for the non-participants who had previously been sick for less than 15 days or who live in the Älvsborg. Generally, the participants in *No* and in *workplace* rehabilitation seem to enjoy better re-employment chances than the participants in *educational* or *medical* rehabilitation irrespective of the treatment received, since their observed outcomes are in all subpopulations higher than the corresponding mean counterfactual outcome for the non-participants. For *medical* rehabilitation, on the other hand, this relationship is often reversed. Despite these indications of heterogeneity, *educational* rehabilitation appears nevertheless almost always as the worst programme.

Table E.5 complements the comparison of actual and optimal allocation of Table 4.10. It contains all 38 X characteristics used in the main specification in Section

Table E.4. Observed outcomes and estimated counterfactual outcomes for the 11 populations

(Sub)Population	obs	EY^N D=N	$\hat{E}Y^N$ D≠N	EY^W D=W	$\hat{E}Y^W$ D≠W	EY^E D=E	$\hat{E}Y^E$ D≠E	EY^M D=M	$\hat{E}Y^M$ D≠M
All	6287	48.3	43.6	52.4	44.2	28.9	33.1	40.5	41.2
Age 46-55 years	2354	49.8	41.5	56.0	50.8	21.7	20.9	38.6	39.3
Occupation in agriculture	1921	38.5	32.5	50.5	42.7	26.4	33.0	30.9	29.5
Previous sickness < 15 days	3725	52.6	47.0	57.4	47.2	34.7	38.3	47.1	47.3
Previous sickness > 60 days	1374	36.3	35.9	44.6	39.6	23.8	27.8	27.0	26.1
No prior VR participation	5611	49.7	45.3	53.3	44.8	29.6	32.3	42.7	42.9
Living in Älvsborg	1829	47.2	39.7	56.5	49.5	32.8	38.6	31.8	35.7
Living in Värmland	1470	46.1	44.7	49.5	41.5	28.3	28.2	39.8	43.9
Sickness in year 1992/93	2203	48.6	42.6	54.6	47.7	30.8	28.8	41.1	40.5
Diagnosis: psychiatric	1102	41.6	36.1	47.6	38.7	20.2	21.3	30.6	33.5
Sickness registered by health care centre or hospital	5041	50.5	46.3	54.6	47.1	29.4	35.0	42.6	42.0

Note: obs = Number of observations in each subpopulation; $E[Y^{No}|D = No]$, $E[Y^{Work}|D = Work]$, $E[Y^{Edu}|D = Edu]$, $E[Y^{Med}|D = Med]$ are the average observed employment rates among the respective participants; $\hat{E}[Y^{No}|D \neq No]$, $\hat{E}[Y^{Work}|D \neq Work]$, $\hat{E}[Y^{Edu}|D \neq Edu]$, $\hat{E}[Y^{Med}|D \neq Med]$ are the counterfactual employment rates among the respective non-participants, estimated by SG propensity score matching. 'No prior VR participation' means no participation in vocational rehabilitation (= workplace or educational rehabilitation) in the 12 months before the current sickness spell. The bandwidth values selected by cross-validation for the estimation of the Y^{No} potential outcome for the various subpopulations are: 0.16, 0.20, 0.16, 0.10, 0.58, 0.60, 0.16, 0.16, 0.38, 0.14, 1.00, respectively. For the estimation of Y^{Work} the bandwidths are: 0.06, 1.00, 1.00, 0.14, 1.00, 0.64, 0.06, 0.06, 1.00, 0.06, 1.00; for Y^{Edu}: 1.00, 0.14, 0.22, 0.14, 1.00, 1.00, 0.80, 0.50, 0.12, 1.00, 0.44; and for Y^{Med}: 0.62, 0.50, 0.06, 0.10, 0.74, 0.04, 1.00, 0.58, 0.78, 0.46, 0.66.

4.2, except Age 18-35 years, Age 46-55 years and gender (which are found in Table 4.10).

Sensitivity Analysis

In the following tables, the sensitivity of the estimated optimal allocation to the number of subpopulations included in the GMM estimator and to the choice of explanatory variables is analyzed. The results show that the estimated optimal allocation is quite robust to changes in the specification. The Tables E.6 to E.10 indicate how the optimal allocation changes if different numbers of subpopulations (L=0, 1, 6, 16, 21) are included (maintaining the same set of 38 explanatory regressors). The Tables E.11 to E.13 investigate changes in the specification where the number of subpopulations is kept at L=11, but the number of explanatory regressors is reduced.

Table E.6 compares the optimal allocation, estimated with L=11 subpopulations (=main specification), to the allocation that is obtained if no subpopulation

Table E.5. Average characteristics according to optimal and actual allocation

Variable		$r_i^* =$				All	$D_i =$			
		N	W	E	M		N	W	E	M
Citizenship:	Swedish born	85	88	83	87	86	86	88	90	83
Employment status:	unemployed	2	27	47	2	19	20	9	32	21
Income	(in SEK/1000)	1.4	1.2	1.4	1.1	1.3	1.3	1.3	1.3	1.3
Labour market position:	blue collar, low educated	36	57	37	50	45	42	52	47	47
	blue collar, high educated	43	9	19	17	20	20	23	23	20
	white collar	18	23	24	26	23	26	20	16	21
Occupation in:	health care	5	7	20	8	10	9	11	10	11
	various sciences	27	30	12	38	28	30	25	25	25
	manufacturing	51	23	23	38	32	30	38	32	32
Previous sickness days	31-60 days	15	11	0	7	10	9	9	10	11
(in last 6 months):	> 60 days	19	32	25	5	22	20	24	35	22
Prior participation in	vocational rehabilitation	4	15	21	0	11	7	15	23	14
County:	Bohuslän	32	21	27	19	25	27	17	24	30
	Älvsborgslän	26	38	42	8	29	32	42	32	10
	Värmlandslän	21	17	22	41	23	23	29	29	18
Community type:	urban / suburban region	37	23	23	13	26	31	17	21	21
	major / middle large city	13	15	12	10	14	13	11	11	21
	industrial city	9	18	14	5	12	10	14	11	16
Unemployment rate	(in %)	6.4	7.0	6.2	6.4	6.5	6.5	6.6	6.7	6.6
Sickness registration by	psych./social medicine centre	9	5	5	14	8	7	6	14	10
	private or other	6	9	15	21	12	11	13	13	11
Sickness degree:	100% sick leave	94	92	88	62	86	84	92	91	86
Medical diagnosis:	psychiatric	20	21	11	15	18	18	13	28	18
	musculoskeletal	40	46	45	48	44	39	51	44	51
	injuries	28	6	18	7	14	15	15	11	12
	other	4	22	19	16	15	18	13	10	12
Case assessed by:	the employer	28	30	15	13	23	17	40	25	25
	insurance office	14	23	23	4	16	13	16	33	22
	IO on behalf of employer	11	9	6	23	11	8	14	13	17
	not needed	21	13	28	49	26	36	10	9	16
Medical	wait and see	79	64	19	53	55	61	40	37	56
recommendation	VR needed and defined	10	27	42	32	26	14	47	55	34
Case worker recomm.:	VR needed and defined	11	51	39	35	32	17	63	62	38
Medical reasons	prevented VR	35	20	27	15	25	23	22	23	32
Med. & case worker rec.	VR needed and defined	10	15	29	25	19	9	35	44	25

See note below Table 4.10. VR stands for vocation rehabilitation, rec. means recommendation, IO is insurance office.

moments are included (L=0). Hence it compares the semiparametric estimator with overidentifying restrictions to the fully parametric estimator. The columns (r_i^*) refer to the allocation according to the main specification (L=11), whereas the rows (r_i^{**}) reflect the allocation according to the alternative specification (L=0). For example, the entry 3 in the cell $(r_i^*, r_i^{**}) = (M, N)$ indicates that of all the individuals whose optimal programme is medical rehabilitation (as estimated under the main specification) three would be advised to participate in No rehabilitation under the alternative specification (at level 1-α=0.7). Generally both specifications lead to rather similar predictions, since the number of individuals in the off-diagonals is small (apart from indefinite cases). Leaving aside the undefined cases, the fraction of misclassification Δ measures the mismatch between both estimated allocations by the sum of the off-diagonal elements, divided by the number of cases with defined optimal treatment (under both specifications). At the 0.7 probability level, only 1% of optimal programme predictions differ between the two specifications. At the 0.6 level this increases to 4% and to 14% at the 0.5 probability level.

The simulation of the attainable re-employment rate under optimal allocation leads to similar results for both specifications. When all individuals, for whom an optimal programme is defined (at 1-α=0.5), are assigned to their optimal programme, and all other individuals are assigned randomly to No or workplace rehabilitation, the predicted optimal employment rate is 55.7% under the main specification (and it is 54.9% if educational rehabilitation is completely eliminated). Under the alternative specification these figures are 56.9% and 55.2%, respectively. (Results not shown in the tables.)

Table E.7 repeats the above analysis for an alternative specification with L=1 populations. Table E.8 contains the results for a specification with L=6, Table E.9 for L=16 and Table E.10 for L=21 populations. Generally, the estimated optimal treatment choices are very similar to those obtained with the main specification. The mismatch is at most 0.1% at the 0.7 probability level, at most 2.4% at the 0.6 level and at most 11% at the 0.5 level. In addition, the maximum attainable re-employment rate is estimated in all specifications to be about 55-56% (with educational rehabilitation) and about 54-55% (after elimination of educational rehabilitation). This shows that the optimal programme predictions are robust to the number of moments included.

In the Tables E.11 to E.13 the optimal allocations according to different sets of explanatory regressors are examined. In Table E.11 the allocation according to a specification with 30 variables (Specification A) is compared to the main specification. Table E.12 contains this analysis for a specification with 28 variables (Specification B) and Table E.13 corresponds to Specification C with 24 variables. In all specifications the same L=11 subpopulations are used. Specification A differs from the main specification by leaving out the eight variables: *Citizenship; white collar; occupation in various sciences; previous sick-leave 31-60 days; medical diagnosis: other; medical rehabilitation rehabilitation: wait&see; medical reasons prevented vocational rehabilitation;* and *medical and case worker*

Table E.6. Comparison of estimated optimal allocations: L=0 versus L=11

	r_i^* at 1-α =70%					r_i^* at 1-α =60%					r_i^* at 1-α =50%				
	N	W	E	M	i	N	W	E	M	i	N	W	E	M	i
r_i^{**}=N	516	5	0	3	334	764	17	1	8	330	1062	82	5	31	255
r_i^{**}=W	0	368	0	0	405	0	630	15	10	513	22	1034	86	58	454
r_i^{**}=E	0	0	228	0	290	1	13	429	2	314	11	84	687	22	246
r_i^{**}=M	5	0	0	96	228	17	1	2	195	325	58	28	26	355	329
r_i^{**}=i	97	167	66	81	3398	138	232	105	137	2088	149	158	101	140	804
Δ(%)			1.1					4.1					14.1		

Note: Number of individuals with estimated optimal programme r_i^* ∈ {No,Work,Edu,Med,indefinite} under the main specification and estimated optimal programme r_i^{**} ∈ {No,Work,Edu,Med,indefinite} under the alternative specification (L=0), at the level 1-α=0.7 (left), 0.6 (middle) and 0.5 (right). The columns/rows labelled i stand for indefinite optimal programme. Δ gives the fraction of misclassification in %, i.e. the number of individuals for whom the optimal programme under the main specification (r_i^*) and under the alternative specification (r_i^{**}) do not coincide (off-diagonal elements) to the total number of individuals with defined optimal programme (under both specifications), leaving aside the undefined cases. The optimal choices r_i^{**} are simulated by 817 bootstrap replications.

Table E.7. Comparison of estimated optimal allocations: L=1 versus L=11

	r_i^* at 1-α =70%					r_i^* at 1-α =60%					r_i^* at 1-α =50%				
	N	W	E	M	i	N	W	E	M	i	N	W	E	M	i
r_i^{**}=N	589	0	0	0	455	870	10	0	7	448	1212	72	4	43	339
r_i^{**}=W	0	394	0	1	349	0	660	8	7	454	10	1039	59	49	406
r_i^{**}=E	0	0	251	0	351	1	15	470	4	371	12	96	754	23	301
r_i^{**}=M	0	0	0	107	154	1	1	0	203	201	20	20	10	351	235
r_i^{**}=i	29	146	43	72	3346	48	207	74	131	2096	48	159	78	140	807
Δ(%)			0.1					2.4					11.1		

Note: See note below Table E.6. Optimal choices r_i^{**} under the alternative specification (L=1 population moments) are simulated by 413 bootstrap replications.

Table E.8. Comparison of estimated optimal allocations: L=6 versus L=11

	r_i^* at 1-α =70%					r_i^* at 1-α =60%					r_i^* at 1-α =50%				
	N	W	E	M	i	N	W	E	M	i	N	W	E	M	i
r_i^{**}=N	601	0	0	0	365	886	0	0	3	374	1240	27	6	20	322
r_i^{**}=W	0	462	0	0	333	0	742	0	6	391	12	1150	31	42	351
r_i^{**}=E	0	0	260	0	271	0	2	473	3	300	3	43	778	18	273
r_i^{**}=M	0	0	0	117	158	1	0	0	216	212	16	24	8	372	234
r_i^{**}=i	17	78	34	63	3528	33	149	79	124	2293	31	142	82	154	908
Δ(%)			0.0					0.6					6.6		

Note: See note below Table E.6. Optimal choices r_i^{**} under the alternative specification (L=6 population moments).

Table E.9. Comparison of estimated optimal allocations: L=16 versus L=11

	r_i^* at 1-α =70%					r_i^* at 1-α =60%					r_i^* at 1-α =50%				
	N	W	E	M	i	N	W	E	M	i	N	W	E	M	i
r_i^{**}=N	465	0	0	1	221	724	1	0	2	308	1074	36	18	23	291
r_i^{**}=W	0	364	0	0	140	0	655	0	4	220	18	1083	28	24	235
r_i^{**}=E	0	0	125	0	39	0	0	301	0	84	9	18	605	9	98
r_i^{**}=M	0	0	0	74	44	1	1	0	177	111	19	20	11	328	153
r_i^{**}=i	153	176	169	105	4211	195	236	251	169	2847	182	229	243	222	1311
Δ(%)	0.1					0.5					7.0				

Note: See note below Table E.6. Optimal choices r_i^{**} under the alternative specification (L=16 population moments).

Table E.10. Comparison of estimated optimal allocations: L=21 versus L=11

	r_i^* at 1-α =70%					r_i^* at 1-α =60%					r_i^* at 1-α =50%				
	N	W	E	M	i	N	W	E	M	i	N	W	E	M	i
r_i^{**}=N	456	0	0	1	279	724	5	2	6	368	1041	44	18	39	276
r_i^{**}=W	0	320	0	0	202	3	608	1	2	323	34	994	45	36	295
r_i^{**}=E	0	0	130	0	96	0	8	317	8	216	2	41	589	32	211
r_i^{**}=M	0	0	0	51	37	4	5	0	150	92	16	32	6	277	155
r_i^{**}=i	162	220	164	128	4041	189	267	232	186	2571	209	275	247	222	1151
Δ(%)	0.1					2.4					10.6				

Note: See note below Table E.6. Optimal choices r_i^{**} under the alternative specification (L=21 population moments).

Table E.11. Comparison of estimated allocations: Main specification vs. specification A

	r_i^* at 1-α =70%					r_i^* at 1-α =60%					r_i^* at 1-α =50%				
	N	W	E	M	i	N	W	E	M	i	N	W	E	M	i
r_i^{**}=N	346	1	0	0	157	569	14	12	0	209	854	53	40	11	197
r_i^{**}=W	1	339	2	0	394	18	595	34	1	528	115	981	129	13	470
r_i^{**}=E	0	1	112	0	147	2	6	248	0	215	27	65	473	21	230
r_i^{**}=M	0	0	1	119	123	0	4	5	235	180	10	18	29	418	187
r_i^{**}=i	271	199	179	61	3834	331	274	253	116	2438	296	269	234	143	1004
Δ(%)	0.7					5.5					16.3				

Note: See note below Table E.6. Optimal choices r_i^{**} under the alternative specification A (with 30 variables).

Table E.12. Comparison of estimated allocations: Main specification vs. specification B

	r_i^* at 1-α =70%					r_i^* at 1-α =60%					r_i^* at 1-α =50%				
	N	W	E	M	i	N	W	E	M	i	N	W	E	M	i
r_i^{**}=N	437	0	0	0	298	688	17	9	0	392	1011	78	32	9	340
r_i^{**}=W	1	378	4	0	403	16	649	25	3	519	70	1037	118	30	449
r_i^{**}=E	0	0	122	0	86	1	1	263	0	124	14	31	511	5	145
r_i^{**}=M	0	0	0	131	93	2	2	4	261	135	21	14	21	439	170
r_i^{**}=i	180	162	168	49	3775	213	224	251	88	2400	186	226	223	123	984
Δ(%)			0.5					4.1					12.9		

Note: See note below Table E.6. Optimal choices r_i^{**} under the alternative specification B (with 28 variables).

Table E.13. Comparison of estimated allocations: Main specification vs. specification C

	r_i^* at 1-α =70%					r_i^* at 1-α =60%					r_i^* at 1-α =50%				
	N	W	E	M	i	N	W	E	M	i	N	W	E	M	i
r_i^{**}=N	270	6	7	14	329	450	21	20	36	382	658	67	61	89	299
r_i^{**}=W	2	263	10	1	347	27	451	52	9	504	92	787	181	38	433
r_i^{**}=E	4	1	66	3	167	14	13	169	19	267	56	86	369	74	272
r_i^{**}=M	23	25	22	28	465	75	83	46	89	547	186	203	111	199	459
r_i^{**}=i	319	245	189	134	3347	354	325	265	199	1870	310	243	183	206	625
Δ(%)			15.8					26.4					38.2		

Note: See note below Table E.6. Optimal choices r_i^{**} under the alternative specification C (with 24 variables).

recommendation: vocational rehabilitation needed. Specification B differs from the main specification by dropping the ten variables: *Gender; low educated blue-collar; educated blue-collar; white collar; occupation in health care,* or in *various sciences; sickness registration by private or other; medical diagnosis: psychiatric,* or *other; medical reasons prevented vocational rehabilitation.*[1] Hence in both specifications some socioeconomic characteristics as well as some supplementary information about the rehabilitation examination (in Specification A) or about sickness registration (in Specification B) are neglected. In addition the indicator *medical reasons prevented vocational rehabilitation* is left out in both specifications (as this information is often only ex-post available). Nevertheless the most relevant indicators about the rehabilitation examination are kept. The resulting estimated allocations are still quite similar to the main allocation and differ in about 0.5% of the defined cases at the 0.7 level, and about 5% and 14.5% at the 0.6 and 0.5 level, respectively.

However, neglecting even more variables changes the estimated optimal allocation markedly. Table E.13 compares the allocation according to the main specification and according to Specification C. Specification C leaves out the same

---

[1] This specification resembles more closely the variable selection of Frölich, Heshmati, and Lechner (2000b).

variables as Specification A, but drops further the variables: *Income, occupation in health care, rehabilitation examination not needed* and all *county* indicators. With this sparse specification, the misclassification rates Δ are 15.8% and 26.4% at the 0.7 and 0.6 level, respectively, and increase to almost 40% at the 0.5 level.

References

ABADIE, A., AND G. IMBENS (2001): "Simple and Bias-Corrected Matching Estimators for Average Treatment Effects," mimeo, Harvard University.

AKAIKE, H. (1970): "Statistical Predictor Information," *Annals of the Institute of Statistical Mathematics*, 22, 203–217.

ALTONJI, J., AND L. SEGAL (1996): "Small Sample Bias in GMM Estimation of Covariance Structures," *Journal of Business and Economic Statistics*, 14, 353–366.

ANGRIST, J. (1990): "Lifetime Earnings and the Vietnam Era Draft Lottery: Evidence From Social Security Administrative Records," *American Economic Review*, 80, 313–336.

——— (1998): "Estimating Labour Market Impact of Voluntary Military Service using Social Security Data," *Econometrica*, 66, 249–288.

ANGRIST, J., G. IMBENS, AND D. RUBIN (1996): "Identification of Causal Effects using Instrumental Variables," *Journal of American Statistical Association*, 91, 444–472 (with discussion).

ANGRIST, J., AND A. KRUEGER (1991): "Does Compulsory School Attendance Affect Schooling and Earnings?," *Quarterly Journal of Economics*, 106, 979–1014.

——— (1999): "Empirical Strategies in Labor Economics," in *The Handbook of Labor Economics*, ed. by O. Ashenfelter, and D. Card, pp. 1277–1366. North-Holland, New York.

ANGRIST, J., AND V. LAVY (1999): "Using Maimonides Rule to Estimate the Effect of Class Size on Scholastic Achievement," *Quarterly Journal of Economics*, 114, 533–575.

ASHENFELTER, O. (1978): "Estimating the Effect of Training Programms on Earnings," *Review of Economics and Statistics*, 6, 47–57.

BACK, K., AND D. BROWN (1993): "Implied Probabilities in GMM Estimators," *Econometrica*, 61, 971–976.

BARNOW, B., G. CAIN, AND A. GOLDBERGER (1981): "Selection on Observables," *Evaluation Studies Review Annual*, 5, 43–59.

BERGEMANN, A., B. FITZENBERGER, B. SCHULTZ, AND S. SPECKESSER (2000): "Multiple Active Labor Market Policy Participation in East Germany: An Assessment of Outcomes," *Konjunkturpolitik*, 51, 195–244.

BERGEMANN, A., B. FITZENBERGER, AND S. SPECKESSER (2001): "Evaluating the Employment Effects of Public Sector Sponsored Training in East Germany: Conditional Difference-in-Differences and Ashenfelter's Dip," mimeo, University of Mannheim.

BERGER, M., D. BLACK, AND J. SMITH (2001): "Evaluating Profiling as a Means of Allocating Government Services," in *Econometric Evaluation of Labour Market Policies*, ed. by M. Lechner, and F. Pfeiffer, pp. 59–84. Physica/Springer, Heidelberg.

BERK, R., AND D. RAUMA (1983): "Capitalizing on Nonrandom Assignment to Treatments: A Regression-Discontinuity Evaluation of a Crime-Control Program," *Journal of American Statistical Association*, 78, 21–27.

BLACK, D., J. SMITH, M. BERGER, AND B. NOEL (1999): "Is the Threat of Training more Effective than Training itself?," *University of Western Ontario, Department of Economics Working Papers*, 9913.

BLACK, S. (1999): "Do 'Better' Schools Matter? Parental Valuation of Elementary Education," *Quarterly Journal of Economics*, 114, 577–599.

BLANCHARD, O., AND P. DIAMOND (1989): "The Beveridge Curve," *Brookings Papers on Economic Activity*, 1, 1–60.

——— (1990): "The Aggregate Matching Function," in *Growth, Productivity, Unemployment, Essays to Celebrate Bob Solow's Birthday*, ed. by P. Diamond, pp. 159–201. MIT Press, Cambridge.

BLOOM, H., L. ORR, S. BELL, G. CAVE, F. DOOLITTLE, W. LIN, AND J. BOS (1997): "The Benefits and Costs of JTPA Title II-A Programs: Key Findings from the National Job Training Partnership Act Study," *Journal of Human Resources*, 32, 549–576.

BRODATY, T., B. CREPON, AND D. FOUGERE (2001): "Using matching estimators to evaluate alternative youth employment programmes: Evidence from France, 1986-1988," in *Econometric Evaluation of Labour Market Policies*, ed. by M. Lechner, and F. Pfeiffer, pp. 85–124. Physica/Springer, Heidelberg.

BROWN, B., AND W. NEWEY (2002): "GMM, Efficient Bootstrapping, and Improved Inference," *forthcoming in Journal of Business and Economic Statistics*.

BROWN, B., W. NEWEY, AND S. MAY (2001): "Bootstrapping with Moment Restrictions," mimeo, Rice University and MIT.

BURNSIDE, C., AND M. EICHENBAUM (1996): "Small Sample Properties of Generalized Method of Moments based Wald Tests," *Journal of Business and Economic Statistics*, 14, 294–308.

CARD, D. (1995): "Using Geographic Variation in College Proximity to Estimate the Return to Schooling," in *Aspects of Labor Market Behaviour: Essays in Honour of John Vanderkamp*, ed. by L. Christofides, E. Grant, and R. Swidinsky, pp. 201–222. University of Toronto Press, Toronto.

COCHRAN, W., AND D. RUBIN (1973): "Controlling Bias in Observational Studies," *Sankyha*, 35, 417–446.

COLPITTS, T. (1999): "Targeting Reemployment Services in Canada: The Service and Outcome Measurement System (SOMS) Experience," Department of Human Resources Development, Ottawa.

COX, D. (1958): *Planning of Experiments*. Wiley, New York.

DAWID, A. (1979): "Conditional Independence in Statistical Theory," *Journal of the Royal Statistical Society, Series B*, 41, 1–31.

DE KONING, J. (1999): "The chance-meter: Measuring the Individual Chance of Long-term Unemployment," Netherlands Economic Institute, Rotterdam.

DEHEJIA, R. (2002): "Program Evaluation as a Decision Problem," *forthcoming in Journal of Econometrics*.

DEHEJIA, R., AND S. WAHBA (1999): "Causal Effects in Non-experimental Studies: Reevaluating the Evaluation of Training Programmes," *Journal of American Statistical Association*, 94, 1053–1062.

DOL (1999): *Evaluation of Worker Profiling and Reemployment Services Policy Workgroup: Final Report and Recommendations*. U.S. Department of Labor, Employment and Training Administration, Washington D.C.

EBERTS, R. (2002): "The Use of Profiling to Target Services in State Welfare-to-Work Programs: An Example of Process and Implementation," .

EBERTS, R., AND C. O'LEARY (1999): "A Frontline Decision Support System for One-Stop Career Centers," mimeo, W.E. Upjohn Institute for Employment Reserach.

EICHLER, M., AND M. LECHNER (2002): "An Evaluation of Public Employment Programmes in the East German State of Sachsen-Anhalt," *Labour Economics*, 9, 143–186.

EUBANK, R. (1988): *Spline Smoothing and Nonparametric Regression*. Marcel Dekker, New York.

FAN, J. (1992): "Design-adaptive Nonparametric Regression," *Journal of American Statistical Association*, 87, 998–1004.

———— (1993): "Local Linear Regression Smoothers and their Minimax Efficiency," *Annals of Statistics*, 21, 196–216.

FAN, J., T. GASSER, I. GIJBELS, M. BROCKMANN, AND J. ENGEL (1997): "Local Polynomial Regression: Optimal Kernels and Asymptotic Minimax Efficiency," *Annals of the Institute of Mathematical Statistics*, 49, 79–99.

FAN, J., AND I. GIJBELS (1995): "Data-driven Bandwidth Selection in Local Polynomial Fitting: Variable Bandwidth and Spatial Adaptation," *Journal of the Royal Statistical Society, Series B*, 57, 371–394.

———— (1996): *Local Polynomial Modeling and its Applications*. Chapman and Hall, London.

FAN, J., P. HALL, M. MARTIN, AND P. PATIL (1996): "On Local Smoothing of Nonparametric Curve Estimators," *Journal of American Statistical Association*, 91, 258–266.

FAY, R. (1996): "Enhancing the Effectiveness of Active Labour Market Policies: Evidence from Programme Evaluations in OECD Countries," *Labour Market and Social Policy Occasional Papers, OECD*, 18.

FISHER, R. (1935): *Design of Experiments*. Oliver and Boyd, Edinburgh.

FRASER, N. (1999): "How Strong is the Case for Targeting Active Labour Market Policies? A Review of Efficiency and Equity Arguments," *International Journal of Manpower*, 20, 151–164.

FRIEDLANDER, D., D. GREENBERG, AND P. ROBINS (1997): "Evaluating Government Training Programs for the Economically Disadvantaged," *Journal of Economic Literature*, 35, 1809–1855.

FRÖLICH, M. (2001a): "Applied higher-dimensional nonparametric regression," *University of St. Gallen Economics Discussion Paper Series*, 2001-12.

———— (2001b): "Nonparametric IV estimation of local average treatment effects with covariates," *IZA Discussion Paper*, 588.

FRÖLICH, M., A. HESHMATI, AND M. LECHNER (2000a): "A Microeconometric Evaluation of Rehabilitation of Long-term Sickness in Sweden," *University of St. Gallen Economics Discussion Paper Series*, 2000-04.

———— (2000b): "Mikrokonometrische Evaluierung berufsbezogener Rehabilitation in Schweden," *Schweizerische Zeitschrift fr Volkswirtschaft und Statistik*, 136, 433–461.

GERFIN, M., AND M. LECHNER (2002): "Microeconometric Evaluation of the Active Labour Market Policy in Switzerland," *forthcoming in Economic Journal*.

GREENE, W. (1997): *Econometric Analysis*. Prentice Hall, New Jersey, 3 edn.

GU, X., AND P. ROSENBAUM (1993): "Comparison of Multivariate Matching Methods: Structures, Distance, and Algorithms," *Journal of Computational and Graphical Statistics*, 2, 405–420.

HAHN, J. (1998): "On the Role of the Propensity Score in Efficient Semiparametric Estimation of Average Treatment Effects," *Econometrica*, 66, 315–331.

HAHN, J., P. TODD, AND W. VAN DER KLAAUW (1999): "Evaluating the Effect of an Antidiscrimination Law Using a Regression-Discontinuity Design," *NBER working paper*, 7131.

———— (2001): "Identification and Estimation of Treatment Effects with a Regression-Discontinuity Design," *Econometrica*, 69, 201–209.

HALL, P., AND J. HOROWITZ (1996): "Bootstrap Critical Values for Tests based on Generalized-Method-of-Moments Estimators," *Econometrica*, 64, 891–916.

HALL, P., B. PARK, AND B. TURLACH (1998): "A Note on Design Transformation and Binning in Nonparametric Curve Estimation," *Biometrika*, 85, 469–476.

HALL, P., AND B. TURLACH (1997): "Interpolation Methods for Adapting to Sparse Design in Nonparametric Regression," *Journal of American Statistical Association*, 92, 466–476.

HANSEN, L. (1982): "Large Sample Properties of Generalized Method of Moment Estimators," *Econometrica*, 50, 1029–1054.

HÄRDLE, W. (1991): *Applied Nonparametric Regression*. Cambridge University Press, Cambridge.

HÄRDLE, W., AND S. MARRON (1987): "Optimal Bandwidth Selection in Nonparametric Regression Function Estimation," *Annals of Statistics*, 13, 1465–1481.

HEARST, N., T. NEWMAN, AND S. HULLEY (1986): "Delayed Effects of the Military Draft on Mortality: A Randomized Natural Experiment," *New England Journal of Medicine*, 314, 620–624.

HECKMAN, J., H. ICHIMURA, J. SMITH, AND P. TODD (1998): "Characterizing Selection Bias Using Experimental Data," *Econometrica*, 66, 1017–1098.

HECKMAN, J., H. ICHIMURA, AND P. TODD (1997): "Matching as an Econometric Evaluation Estimator: Evidence from Evaluating a Job Training Programme," *Review of Economic Studies*, 64, 605–654.

——— (1998): "Matching as an Econometric Evaluation Estimator," *Review of Economic Studies*, 65, 261–294.

HECKMAN, J., R. LALONDE, AND J. SMITH (1999): "The Economics and Econometrics of Active Labour Market Programs," in *The Handbook of Labor Economics*, ed. by O. Ashenfelter, and D. Card, pp. 1865–2097. North-Holland, New York.

HECKMAN, J., AND R. ROBB (1985): "Alternative Methods for Evaluating the Impact of Interventions," in *Longitudinal Analysis of Labour Market Data*, ed. by J. Heckman, and B. Singer. Cambridge University Press, Cambridge.

HECKMAN, J., AND J. SMITH (1995): "Assessing the Case for Social Experiments," *Journal of Economic Perspectives*, 9, 85–110.

HECKMAN, J., J. SMITH, AND N. CLEMENTS (1997): "Making the Most out of Programme Evaluations and Social Experiments: Accounting for Heterogeneity in Programme Impacts," *Review of Economic Studies*, 64, 487–535.

HECKMAN, J., AND E. VYTLACIL (1999): "Local Instrumental Variables and Latent Variable Models for Identifying and Bounding Treatment Effects," *Proceedings National Academic Sciences USA, Economic Sciences*, 96, 4730–4734.

HIRANO, K., G. IMBENS, AND G. RIDDER (2000): "Efficient Estimation of Average Treatment Effects Using the Estimated Propensity Score," *NBER, Technical Working Paper*, 251.

HOEFFDING, W. (1948): "A Class of Statistics with Asymptotically Normal Distribution," *Annals of Mathematical Statistics*, 19, 293–325.

HOLLAND, P. (1986): "Statistics and Causal Inference," *Journal of American Statistical Association*, 81, 945–970.

HORRACE, W., AND P. SCHMIDT (2000): "Multiple Comparisons with the Best, with Economic Applications," *Journal of Applied Econometrics*, 15, 1–26.

HORVITZ, D., AND D. THOMPSON (1952): "A Generalization of Sampling without Replacement from a Finite Population," *Journal of American Statistical Association*, 47, 663–685.

HSU, J. (1996): *Multiple Comparisons: Theory and Methods*, vol. 1. Chapman and Hall, London.

ICHIMURA, H., AND O. LINTON (2001): "Asymptotic Expansions for Some Semiparametric Program Evaluation Estimators," mimeo, University College London.

IMBENS, G. (2000): "The Role of the Propensity Score in Estimating Dose-Response Functions," *Biometrika*, 87, 706–710.

———— (2001): "Some remarks on instrumental variables," in *Econometric Evaluation of Labour Market Policies*, ed. by M. Lechner, and F. Pfeiffer, pp. 17–42. Physica/Springer, Heidelberg.

IMBENS, G., AND J. ANGRIST (1994): "Identification and Estimation of Local Average Treatment Effects," *Econometrica*, 62, 467–475.

IMBENS, G., R. SPADY, AND P. JOHNSON (1998): "Information theoretic approaches to inference in moment condition models," *Econometrica*, 66, 333–357.

IMBENS, G., AND W. VAN DER KLAAUW (1995): "Evaluating the Cost of Conscription in the Netherlands," *Journal of Business and Economic Statistics*, 13, 207–215.

INKMANN, J. (2001): *Conditional Moment Estimation of Nonlinear Equation Systems.* Springer Verlag, Berlin.

JALAN, J., AND M. RAVALLION (2002): "Estimating the Benefit Incidence of an Antipoverty Program by Propensity Score Matching," *Journal of Business and Economic Statistics*, forthcoming.

LARSSON, L. (2000): "Evaluation of Swedish Youth Labour Market Programmes," *Scandinavian Working Papers in Economics*, 2000:1.

LECHNER, M. (1999): "Earnings and Employment Effects of Continuous Off-the-Job Training in East Germany after Unification," *Journal of Business and Economic Statistics*, 17, 74–90.

———— (2000): "An Evaluation of Public Sector Sponsored Continuous Vocational Training Programs in East Germany," *Journal of Human Resources*, 35, 347–375.

———— (2001a): "Identification and Estimation of Causal Effects of Multiple Treatments under the Conditional Independence Assumption," in *Econometric Evaluation of Labour Market Policies*, ed. by M. Lechner, and F. Pfeiffer, pp. 43–58. Physica/Springer, Heidelberg.

———— (2001b): "A Note on the Common Support Problem in Applied Evaluation Studies," *University of St. Gallen Economics Discussion Paper Series*, 2001-01.

———— (2002a): "Program Heterogeneity and Propensity Score Matching: An Application to the Evaluation of Active Labor Market Policies," *Review of Economics and Statistics*, 84, 205–220.

———— (2002b): "Some Practical Issues in the Evaluation of Heterogeneous Labour Market Programmes by Matching Methods," *Journal of the Royal Statistical Society, Series A*, 165, 59–82.

LECHNER, M., AND R. MIQUEL (2002): "Identification of Effects of Dynamic Treatments by Sequential Conditional Independence Assumptions," *University of St. Gallen Economics Discussion Paper Series*, 2001-07.

LOADER, C. (1999): "Bandwidth Selection: Classical or Plug-In?," *Annals of Statistics*, 27, 415–438.

MANSKI, C. (1989): "Anatomy of the Selection Problem," *Journal of Human Resources*, 24, 343–360.

———— (1990): "Nonparametric Bounds on Treatment Effects," *American Economic Review, Papers and Proceedings*, 80, 319–323.

———— (1993): "The Selection Problem in Econometrics and Statistics," in *Handbook of Statistics*, ed. by G. Maddala, C. Rao, and H. Vinod. Elsevier Science Publishers.

———— (1997): "Monotone Treatment Response," *Econometrica*, 65, 1311–1334.

———— (2000a): "Identification Problems and Decisions under Ambiguity: Empirical Analysis of Treatment Response and Normative Analysis of Treatment Choice," *Journal of Econometrics*, 95, 415–442.

———— (2000b): "Using Studies of Treatment Response to Inform Treatment Choice in Heterogeneous Populations," *NBER, Technical Working Paper*, 263.

———— (2001): "Designing Programs for Heterogeneous Populations: The Value of Covariate Information," *American Economic Review, Papers and Proceedings*, 91, 103–106.

MANSKI, C., AND J. PEPPER (2000): "Monotone Instrumental variables: With an Application to the Returns to Schooling," *Econometrica*, 68, 997–1010.

MEYER, B. (1995): "Natural and Quasi-Experiments in Economics," *Journal of Business and Economic Statistics*, 13, 151–161.

NADARAYA, E. (1965): "On Nonparametric Estimates of Density Functions and Regression Curves," *Theory of Applied Probability*, 10, 186–190.

NEWEY, W., AND D. MCFADDEN (1994): "Large Sample Estimation and Hypothesis Testing," in *Handbook of Econometrics*, ed. by R. Engle, and D. McFadden. Elsevier, Amsterdam.

NEYMAN, J. (1923): "On the Application of Probability Theory to Agricultural Experiments. Essay on Principles.," *Statistical Science*, Reprint, 5, 463–480.

OECD (1998): "The Early Identification of Jobseekers who are at Greatest Risk of Long-term Unemployment in Australia," in *Early Identification of Jobseekers at Risk of Long-term Unemployment: The Role of Profiling*, pp. 31–61. OECD Proceedings, Paris.

O'LEARY, C., P. DECKER, AND S. WANDNER (1998): "Reemployment Bonuses and Profiling," *W.E. Upjohn Institute for Employment Reserach Working Paper*, 98-51.

OWEN, A. (1988): "Empirical Likelihood Ratio Confidence Intervals for a Single Functional," *Biometrika*, 75, 237–249.

PAGAN, A., AND A. ULLAH (1999): *Nonparametric Econometrics*. Cambridge University Press, Cambridge.

PARZEN, E. (1962): "On Estimation of a Probability Density and Mode," *Annals of Mathematical Statistics*, 33, 1065–1076.

PEARL, J. (2000): *Causality: Models, Reasoning, and Inference*. Cambridge University Press, Cambridge.

POWELL, J., J. STOCK, AND T. STOKER (1989): "Semiparametric Estimation of Index Coefficients," *Econometrica*, 57, 1403–1430.

PUHANI, P. (1999): *Evaluating Active Labour Market Policies: Empirical Evidence for Poland during Transition*. Physica, Heidelberg.

QIN, J., AND J. LAWLESS (1994): "Empirical Likelihood and General Estimating Equations," *Annals of Statistics*, 22, 300–325.

RICE, J. (1984): "Bandwidth Choice for Nonparametric Regression," *Annals of Statistics*, 12, 1215–1230.

ROSENBAUM, P., AND D. RUBIN (1983): "The Central Role of the Propensity Score in Observational Studies for Causal Effects," *Biometrika*, 70, 41–55.

ROY, A. (1951): "Some Thoughts on the Distribution of Earnings," *Oxford Economic Papers*, 3, 135–146.

RUBIN, D. (1974): "Estimating Causal Effects of Treatments in Randomized and Nonrandomized Studies," *Journal of Educational Psychology*, 66, 688–701.

———— (1977): "Assignment to Treatment Group on the Basis of a Covariate," *Journal of Educational Statistics*, 2, 1–26.

———— (1980): "Comment on 'Randomization Analysis of Experimental Data: The Fisher Randomization Test' by D. Basu," *Journal of American Statistical Association*, 75, 591–593.

RUPPERT, D. (1997): "Empirical-Bias Bandwidths for Local Polynomial Nonparametric Regression and Density Estimation," *Journal of American Statistical Association*, 92, 1049–1062.

RUPPERT, D., S. SHEATHER, AND M. WAND (1995): "An Effective Bandwidth Selector for Local Least Squares Regression," *Journal of American Statistical Association*, 90, 1257–1270.

RUPPERT, D., AND M. WAND (1994): "Multivariate Locally Weighted Least Squares Regression," *Annals of Statistics*, 22, 1346–1370.

SCHUCANY, W. (1995): "Adaptive Bandwidth Choice for Kernel Regression," *Journal of American Statistical Association*, 90, 535–540.

SEIFERT, B., AND T. GASSER (1996): "Finite-Sample Variance of Local Polynomials: Analysis and Solutions," *Journal of American Statistical Association*, 91, 267–275.

———— (2000): "Data Adaptive Ridging in Local Polynomial Regression," *Journal of Computational and Graphical Statistics*, 9.

SERFLING, R. (1980): *Approximation Theorems of Mathematical Statistics*. Wiley, New York.

SHIBATA, R. (1981): "An Optimal Selection of Regression Variables," *Biometrika*, 68, 45–54.

SMITH, J., AND P. TODD (2002): "Does Matching Overcome LaLonde's Critique of Nonexperimental Estimators?," *forthcoming in Journal of Econometrics*.

STONE, C. (1974): "Cross-validatory Choice and Assessment of Statistical Predictions," *Journal of Royal Statistical Society, Series B*, 36, 111–147, (with discussion).

———— (1980): "Optimal rates of convergence of nonparametric estimators," *Annals of Statistics*, 8, 1348–1360.

———— (1982): "Optimal Global Rates of Convergence for Nonparametric Regression," *Annals of Statistics*, 10, 1040–1053.

THISTLETHWAITE, D., AND D. CAMPBELL (1960): "Regression-discontinuity analysis: An alternative to the ex post facto experiment," *Journal of Educational Psychology*, 51, 309–317.

TODD, P. (1999): "Matching and Local Linear Approaches to Program Evaluation using a Semiparametric Propensity Score," mimeo, University of Pennsylvania.

TROCHIM, W. (1984): *Research Design for Program Evaluation: The Regression-Discontinuity Approach*. Sage Publications, Beverly Hills.

VAN DER KLAAUW, W. (2002): "Estimating the Effect of Financial Aid Offers on College Enrollment: A Regression-Discontinuity Approach," *forthcoming in International Economic Review*.

WALD, A. (1950): *Statistical Decision Functions*. Wiley, New York.

WATSON, G. (1964): "Smooth regression analysis," *Sankhya*, 26:15, 175–184.

.

Druck und Bindung: Strauss Offsetdruck GmbH

Lecture Notes in Economics and Mathematical Systems

For information about Vols. 1–429
please contact your bookseller or Springer-Verlag

Vol. 430: J. R. Daduna, I. Branco, J. M. Pinto Paixão (Eds.), Computer-Aided Transit Scheduling. XIV, 374 pages. 1995.

Vol. 431: A. Aulin, Causal and Stochastic Elements in Business Cycles. XI, 116 pages. 1996.

Vol. 432: M. Tamiz (Ed.), Multi-Objective Programming and Goal Programming. VI, 359 pages. 1996.

Vol. 433: J. Menon, Exchange Rates and Prices. XIV, 313 pages. 1996.

Vol. 434: M. W. J. Blok, Dynamic Models of the Firm. VII, 193 pages. 1996.

Vol. 435: L. Chen, Interest Rate Dynamics, Derivatives Pricing, and Risk Management. XII, 149 pages. 1996.

Vol. 436: M. Klemisch-Ahlert, Bargaining in Economic and Ethical Environments. IX, 155 pages. 1996.

Vol. 437: C. Jordan, Batching and Scheduling. IX, 178 pages. 1996.

Vol. 438: A. Villar, General Equilibrium with Increasing Returns. XIII, 164 pages. 1996.

Vol. 439: M. Zenner, Learning to Become Rational. VII, 201 pages. 1996.

Vol. 440: W. Ryll, Litigation and Settlement in a Game with Incomplete Information. VIII, 174 pages. 1996.

Vol. 441: H. Dawid, Adaptive Learning by Genetic Algorithms. IX, 166 pages.1996.

Vol. 442: L. Corchón, Theories of Imperfectly Competitive Markets. XIII, 163 pages. 1996.

Vol. 443: G. Lang, On Overlapping Generations Models with Productive Capital. X, 98 pages. 1996.

Vol. 444: S. Jørgensen, G. Zaccour (Eds.), Dynamic Competitive Analysis in Marketing. X, 285 pages. 1996.

Vol. 445: A. H. Christer, S. Osaki, L. C. Thomas (Eds.), Stochastic Modelling in Innovative Manufactoring. X, 361 pages. 1997.

Vol. 446: G. Dhaene, Encompassing. X, 160 pages. 1997.

Vol. 447: A. Artale, Rings in Auctions. X, 172 pages. 1997.

Vol. 448: G. Fandel, T. Gal (Eds.), Multiple Criteria Decision Making. XII, 678 pages. 1997.

Vol. 449: F. Fang, M. Sanglier (Eds.), Complexity and Self-Organization in Social and Economic Systems. IX, 317 pages, 1997.

Vol. 450: P. M. Pardalos, D. W. Hearn, W. W. Hager, (Eds.), Network Optimization. VIII, 485 pages, 1997.

Vol. 451: M. Salge, Rational Bubbles. Theoretical Basis, Economic Relevance, and Empirical Evidence with a Special Emphasis on the German Stock Market.IX, 265 pages. 1997.

Vol. 452: P. Gritzmann, R. Horst, E. Sachs, R. Tichatschke (Eds.), Recent Advances in Optimization. VIII, 379 pages. 1997.

Vol. 453: A. S. Tangian, J. Gruber (Eds.), Constructing Scalar-Valued Objective Functions. VIII, 298 pages. 1997.

Vol. 454: H.-M. Krolzig, Markov-Switching Vector Autoregressions. XIV, 358 pages. 1997.

Vol. 455: R. Caballero, F. Ruiz, R. E. Steuer (Eds.), Advances in Multiple Objective and Goal Programming. VIII, 391 pages. 1997.

Vol. 456: R. Conte, R. Hegselmann, P. Terna (Eds.), Simulating Social Phenomena. VIII, 536 pages. 1997.

Vol. 457: C. Hsu, Volume and the Nonlinear Dynamics of Stock Returns. VIII, 133 pages. 1998.

Vol. 458: K. Marti, P. Kall (Eds.), Stochastic Programming Methods and Technical Applications. X, 437 pages. 1998.

Vol. 459: H. K. Ryu, D. J. Slottje, Measuring Trends in U.S. Income Inequality. XI, 195 pages. 1998.

Vol. 460: B. Fleischmann, J. A. E. E. van Nunen, M. G. Speranza, P. Stähly, Advances in Distribution Logistic. XI, 535 pages. 1998.

Vol. 461: U. Schmidt, Axiomatic Utility Theory under Risk. XV, 201 pages. 1998.

Vol. 462: L. von Auer, Dynamic Preferences, Choice Mechanisms, and Welfare. XII, 226 pages. 1998.

Vol. 463: G. Abraham-Frois (Ed.), Non-Linear Dynamics and Endogenous Cycles. VI, 204 pages. 1998.

Vol. 464: A. Aulin, The Impact of Science on Economic Growth and its Cycles. IX, 204 pages. 1998.

Vol. 465: T. J. Stewart, R. C. van den Honert (Eds.), Trends in Multicriteria Decision Making. X, 448 pages. 1998.

Vol. 466: A. Sadrieh, The Alternating Double Auction Market. VII, 350 pages. 1998.

Vol. 467: H. Hennig-Schmidt, Bargaining in a Video Experiment. Determinants of Boundedly Rational Behavior. XII, 221 pages. 1999.

Vol. 468: A. Ziegler, A Game Theory Analysis of Options. XIV, 145 pages. 1999.

Vol. 469: M. P. Vogel, Environmental Kuznets Curves. XIII, 197 pages. 1999.

Vol. 470: M. Ammann, Pricing Derivative Credit Risk. XII, 228 pages. 1999.

Vol. 471: N. H. M. Wilson (Ed.), Computer-Aided Transit Scheduling. XI, 444 pages. 1999.

Vol. 472: J.-R. Tyran, Money Illusion and Strategic Complementarity as Causes of Monetary Non-Neutrality. X, 228 pages. 1999.

Vol. 473: S. Helber, Performance Analysis of Flow Lines with Non-Linear Flow of Material. IX, 280 pages. 1999.

Vol. 474: U. Schwalbe, The Core of Economies with Asymmetric Information. IX, 141 pages. 1999.

Vol. 475: L. Kaas, Dynamic Macroeconomics with Imperfect Competition. XI. 155 pages. 1999.

Vol. 476: R. Demel, Fiscal Policy, Public Debt and the Term Structure of Interest Rates. X, 279 pages. 1999.

Vol. 477: M. Théra, R. Tichatschke (Eds.), Ill-posed Variational Problems and Regularization Techniques. VIII, 274 pages. 1999.

Vol. 478: S. Hartmann, Project Scheduling under Limited Resources. XII, 221 pages. 1999.

Vol. 479: L. v. Thadden, Money, Inflation, and Capital Formation. IX, 192 pages. 1999.

Vol. 480: M. Grazia Speranza, P. Stähly (Eds.), New Trends in Distribution Logistics. X, 336 pages. 1999.

Vol. 481: V. H. Nguyen, J. J. Strodiot, P. Tossings (Eds.). Optimation. IX, 498 pages. 2000.

Vol. 482: W. B. Zhang, A Theory of International Trade. XI, 192 pages. 2000.

Vol. 483: M. Königstein, Equity, Efficiency and Evolutionary Stability in Bargaining Games with Joint Production. XII, 197 pages. 2000.

Vol. 484: D. D. Gatti, M. Gallegati, A. Kirman, Interaction and Market Structure. VI, 298 pages. 2000.

Vol. 485: A. Garnaev, Search Games and Other Applications of Game Theory. VIII, 145 pages. 2000.

Vol. 486: M. Neugart, Nonlinear Labor Market Dynamics. X, 175 pages. 2000.

Vol. 487: Y. Y. Haimes, R. E. Steuer (Eds.), Research and Practice in Multiple Criteria Decision Making. XVII, 553 pages. 2000.

Vol. 488: B. Schmolck, Ommitted Variable Tests and Dynamic Specification. X, 144 pages. 2000.

Vol. 489: T. Steger, Transitional Dynamics and Economic Growth in Developing Countries. VIII, 151 pages. 2000.

Vol. 490: S. Minner, Strategic Safety Stocks in Supply Chains. XI, 214 pages. 2000.

Vol. 491: M. Ehrgott, Multicriteria Optimization. VIII, 242 pages. 2000.

Vol. 492: T. Phan Huy, Constraint Propagation in Flexible Manufacturing. IX, 258 pages. 2000.

Vol. 493: J. Zhu, Modular Pricing of Options. X, 170 pages. 2000.

Vol. 494: D. Franzen, Design of Master Agreements for OTC Derivatives. VIII, 175 pages. 2001.

Vol. 495: I Konnov, Combined Relaxation Methods for Variational Inequalities. XI, 181 pages. 2001.

Vol. 496: P. Weiß, Unemployment in Open Economies. XII, 226 pages. 2001.

Vol. 497: J. Inkmann, Conditional Moment Estimation of Nonlinear Equation Systems. VIII, 214 pages. 2001.

Vol. 498: M. Reutter, A Macroeconomic Model of West German Unemployment. X, 125 pages. 2001.

Vol. 499: A. Casajus, Focal Points in Framed Games. XI, 131 pages. 2001.

Vol. 500: F. Nardini, Technical Progress and Economic Growth. XVII, 191 pages. 2001.

Vol. 501: M. Fleischmann, Quantitative Models for Reverse Logistics. XI, 181 pages. 2001.

Vol. 502: N. Hadjisavvas, J. E. Martínez-Legaz, J.-P. Penot (Eds.), Generalized Convexity and Generalized Monotonicity. IX, 410 pages. 2001.

Vol. 503: A. Kirman, J.-B. Zimmermann (Eds.), Economics with Heterogenous Interacting Agents. VII, 343 pages. 2001.

Vol. 504: P.-Y. Moix (Ed.),The Measurement of Market Risk. XI, 272 pages. 2001.

Vol. 505: S. Voß, J. R. Daduna (Eds.), Computer-Aided Scheduling of Public Transport. XI, 466 pages. 2001.

Vol. 506: B. P. Kellerhals, Financial Pricing Models in Continuous Time and Kalman Filtering. XIV. 247 pages. 2001.

Vol. 507: M. Koksalan, S. Zionts, Multiple Criteria Decision Making in the New Millenium. XII, 481 pages. 2001.

Vol. 508: K. Neumann, C. Schwindt, J. Zimmermann, Project Scheduling with Time Windows and Scarce Resources. XI, 335 pages. 2002.

Vol. 509: D. Hornung, Investment, R&D, and Long-Run Growth. XVI, 194 pages. 2002.

Vol. 510: A. S. Tangian, Constructing and Applying Objective Functions. XII, 582 pages. 2002.

Vol. 511: M. Külpmann, Stock Market Overreaction and Fundamental Valuation. IX, 198 pages. 2002.

Vol. 512: W.-B. Zhang, An Economic Theory of Cities.XI, 220 pages. 2002.

Vol. 513: K. Marti, Stochastic Optimization Techniques. VIII, 364 pages. 2002.

Vol. 514: S. Wang, Y. Xia, Portfolio and Asset Pricing. XII, 200 pages. 2002.

Vol. 515: G. Heisig, Planning Stability in Material Requirements Planning System. XII, 264 pages. 2002.

Vol. 516: B. Schmid, Pricing Credit Linked Financial Instruments. X, 246 pages. 2002.

Vol. 517: H. I. Meinhardt, Cooperative Decision Making in Common Pool Situations. VIII, 205 pages. 2002.

Vol. 518: S. Napel, Bilateral Bargaining. VIII, 188 pages. 2002.

Vol. 519: A. Klose, G. Speranza, L. N. Van Wassenhove (Eds.), Quantitative Approaches to Distribution Logistics and Supply Chain Management. XIII, 421 pages. 2002.

Vol. 520: B. Glaser, Efficiency versus Sustainability in Dynamic Decision Making. IX, 252 pages. 2002.

Vol. 521: R. Cowan, N. Jonard (Eds.), Heterogenous Agents, Interactions and Economic Performance. XIV, 339 pages. 2003.

Vol. 522: C. Neff, Corporate Finance, Innovation, and Strategic Competition. IX, 218 pages. 2003.

Vol. 523: W.-B. Zhang, A Theory of Interregional Dynamics. XI, 231 pages. 2003.

Vol. 524: M. Frölich, Programme Evaluation and Treatment Choise. VIII, 191 pages. 2003.